Nadia Lemp
10-2

p.55

Our World this Century

Russian Revolution

Advantages
- Leader
- Army
- Support

Causes
- Russification
- Government
- Poverty + working
- WWI :
- Rasputin

Riot - Bloody Sunday
Strike - Putilov Steel
Reform - Stolypin (changes)
Mutiny - boats
Economic Strike - War of Japan

Outcome
New Government
Treaty of Brest-Lovic
Civil war :
War communism

Consequences
USSR
NEP
Execution of Tsar
Communism

Therefore the Bolsheviks easily took over the government

Ulyanov

Our World this Century

Derek Heater

Oxford University Press

Oxford University Press, Walton Street, Oxford OX2 6DP

Oxford New York
Athens Auckland Bangkok Bombay
Calcutta Cape Town Dar es Salaam Delhi
Florence Hong Kong Istanbul Karachi
Kuala Lumpur Madras Madrid Melbourne
Mexico City Nairobi Paris Singapore
Taipei Tokyo Toronto

and associated companies in
Berlin Ibadan

Oxford is a trade mark of Oxford University Press

First published 1982
Reprinted 1982, 1983, 1984, 1985
Second Edition 1987
Reprinted 1988, 1989, 1991, 1992, 1993 (twice), 1994
ISBN 0 19 913324 7

Phototypeset by Tradespools Limited, Frome, Somerset
Printed in Great Britain by Butler & Tanner Ltd, Frome

Contents

Contents

Preface

Twentieth-century World History has been established now for many years as a particularly popular course at the 15–16 year age-level. This book seeks to fill a gap in this market. The basic principles underlying the book are as follows.

First, the text is simply written, avoiding long and complex sentences, and organised with clear sections, sub-sections, and lists where appropriate. Secondly, the amount of detail provided is limited to that necessary for examination purposes, though leavened with some anecdote and literary extracts. Thirdly, a high proportion of information is presented in pictorial form, lavish use being made of photographs, cartoons, charts, diagrams and maps. Fourthly, the subject matter has been chosen in a highly selective way in order to keep the book to a reasonable size and price and cross-references used both to prevent unnecessary repetition and to encourage young students in the art of using books. Fifthly, some important examples of historians' disagreements over interpretation have been included so that, even at this elementary level, the pupil may start to appreciate that history is not a static subject. A final word of explanation is perhaps necessary about the chronological scope of the book. Basically it covers the period 1900–1980: 1980 because that was the year in which the text was completed. There is no suggestion, of course, that the year represents anything but an historically arbitrary date. It was felt, however, that the book's usefulness would be enhanced if it was as up-to-date as possible on publication; hence, too, the Postscript to add in significant events after the chapters were completed.

Preface to the second edition

Interest in this book has been so pleasing that it has been possible to produce a new edition. The opportunity has been taken to introduce a number of changes, which, it is hoped, will enhance its usefulness. The 'stop-press' material, which has hitherto appeared in the Postscript, has been incorporated into the body of the text. In many places information in text, captions and maps has been expanded. The chronological span is now 1900–1985 and a new Postscript adds material to August 1986. Finally, extra questions and GCSE specimen questions have been added to provide practice in analysing primary sources and to reflect the objectives of the GCSE examination.

Note

In this new impression, material in the Postscript has been extended chronologically to cover the period from 1985 up to May 1993.

1/The century begins

Queen Victoria Street, London 1897. What do you notice about the clothes, transport and street lighting?

The world in 1900

To enjoy History you need a good imagination. You need to be able to imagine what life was like in the past or what it would have been like to be involved in past events. For example, what would your life have been like if you had lived at the beginning of the century? Ask your grandparents if they can remember anything their mothers or fathers told them and ask if they have an old photograph album.

From old photographs you will see that clothes, especially of children and women, were very different from today's. If you were a poor family your clothes would be old and ragged. For example, a survey undertaken in York in 1899 showed that two out of every seven people had not enough clothes to keep them warm, nor indeed enough to eat to keep them from being hungry. Most young people left school to start work at the age of fourteen. And once out to work there was little time for leisure. If you worked in a shop, for example, you could well have worked for 11–12 hours per day for six days a week. You would have walked to work through streets quite deserted compared with today's busy traffic. Transport still relied on the horse—some towns had horse-drawn buses. The motor-car had only just been invented and was a luxury that could be afforded only by the very rich. When you returned home there would, of course, be no radio or television for entertainment.

Yet Britain was one of the wealthiest countries in the world. Standards of living had risen greatly in the second half of the nineteenth century. The chances of dying young provide a useful indication of the wealth and health of a community. At the beginning of the century 145 out of every 1,000 babies died before the age of one and the average age of death was about 50. In Russia, however, the figures were 260 and 30.

The world in 1900

As you can see from the following diagram the population of the world nearly trebled in the years 1900–80.

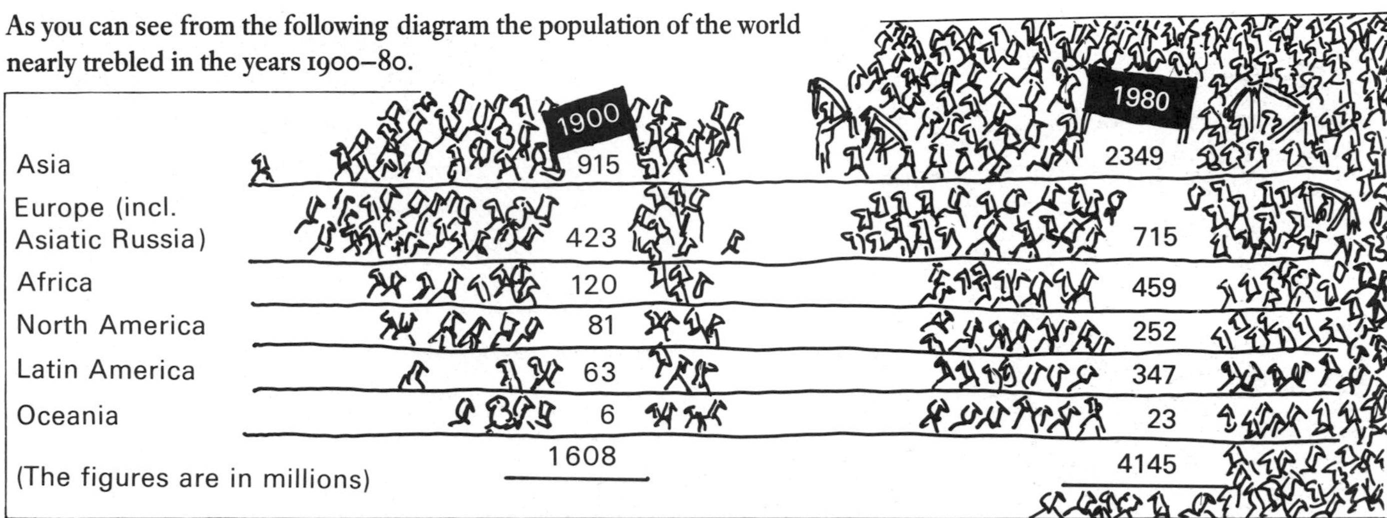

1900
1980
Asia 915 2349
Europe (incl. Asiatic Russia) 423 715
Africa 120 459
North America 81 252
Latin America 63 347
Oceania 6 23
1608
4145
(The figures are in millions)

Figure 1 The increase in the world's population between 1900 and 1980

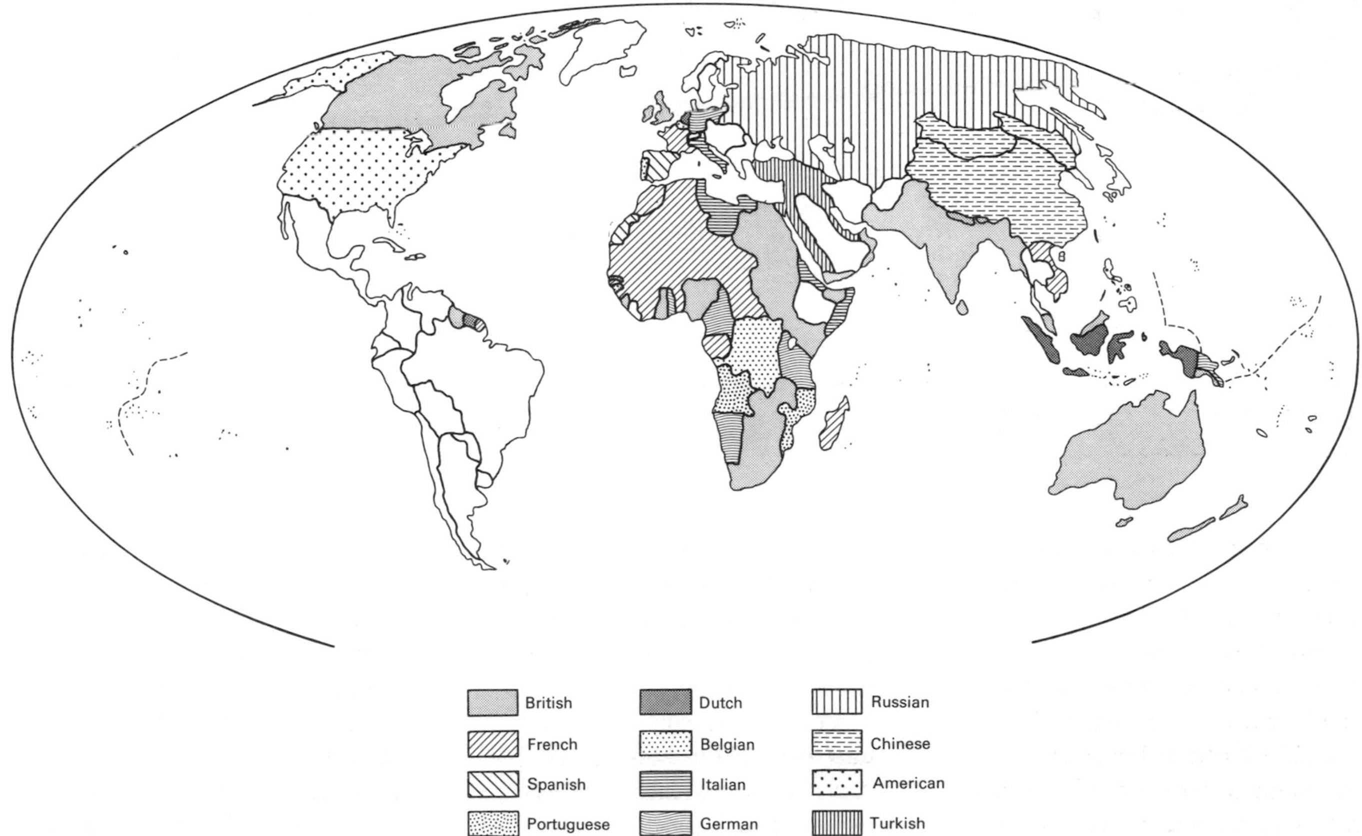

Map 1 The main empires of the world in 1900. List the present-day names of the countries that were ruled by Britain, France and Turkey in 1900

What other differences do you notice?

By 1900 most of the planet had been explored and very large areas were ruled by a small number of governments. It was an age of empires. As you can see from Map 1, just ten empires covered the great majority of the land mass of the world. Compare this with the situation in 1985 when there were about 180 independent countries. Today we believe that people of a particular nationality should govern themselves. But at the start of the century Europeans thought (some quite sincerely) that they had a duty to bring Christianity and civilisation to the peoples of Africa and Asia.

Origins of the First World War

Map 2 Europe and the Middle East in 1914

The map of Europe

In 1914 one of the most terrible wars in modern history broke out. In the next chapter we shall find out what happened. But in order to understand how it came about we need to know about the quarrels that were developing in Europe in the early years of the century.

First of all you need to know what the map of Europe looked like in 1914. There is a lot of information on Map 2 that we shall refer to later. For the moment you just need to know where the countries are. Notice particularly—

1 There was a large empire in the middle of the continent called Austria-Hungary.
2 To the south of that empire there was a small country called Serbia.
3 The Turkish empire stretched over much of the Middle East.

Germany v. France

For centuries clashes between the French and German peoples had taken place. But after 1871 the rivalry became especially deadly for the following reasons:

1 In 1870–71 Germany easily defeated France in a war.
2 At the end of the war Germany took from France the areas of Alsace and Lorraine marked on the map.
3 Many important people in France were afterwards determined to get their revenge on Germany.

Yet France had good reasons for fearing Germany, which was a very much stronger country. The strength of a country to fight a war can be roughly estimated from the size of its population and its coal and steel production. Armies need men as soldiers; coal and steel are needed to make their weapons. The power of Germany in 1914 can be seen from the next diagram:

Figure 2 A comparison between French and German coal and steel production in 1913

Austria-Hungary and the Balkans

Look at Map 3—this is a simplified map of the Austro-Hungarian empire in 1914. You can see that there were eleven different main nationalities. The Germans tended to control the empire, though the Hungarians had had some independence since 1867. The other peoples were unhappy about this and wanted independence too. The country was described as a 'ramshackle empire'.

The people who were most discontented were the Slavs. And you can see from the map that there were some Slav people living outside Austria-Hungary. The Serbs were the most important. By the early twentieth century the Austro-Hungarian government was worried that the Slav peoples in the southern part of the empire would join up with Serbia to form a separate country. They thought that this would lead to the complete break-up of the empire as other peoples gained independence. (We shall see that this was what happened in 1918–19.)

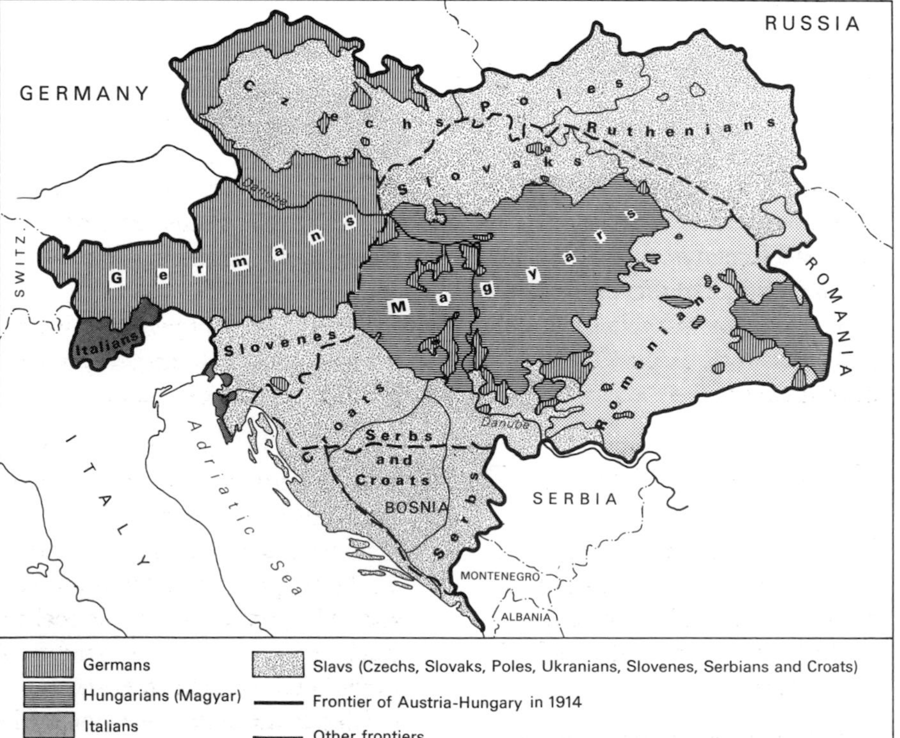

Map 3 The peoples of Austria-Hungary

Nationalism

When a group of people feels that it is a single and separate nation and wishes to be independent it is called nationalism. In Europe this feeling of belonging together and wishing to be free of control from foreigners is often connected with language. So, for example, most people who speak French feel they should belong to France. Nationalism has been a very powerful force in the nineteenth and twentieth centuries and we shall be referring to it several times in this book.

Origins of the First World War

Britain v. Germany

By the early twentieth century Britain, as you can see from Map 1, had the largest empire in the world. It was described as 'the empire on which the sun never sets'. Why do you think it was given this description?

Britain also had the largest navy. This huge navy was necessary for four reasons:

1 To protect the empire.
2 To protect food supplies coming across the oceans. Britain could not grow enough food to feed her crowded population.
3 To protect her trade routes. Britain's wealth depended on selling her manufactured goods.
4 To protect her against invasion from the mainland of Europe.

In contrast, Germany's strength lay in her army. The great nineteenth-century German statesman, Bismarck, believed that Germany and Britain should be friends. He said, 'A land rat has no quarrel with a water rat.' But in 1890 the young Kaiser (that is, Emperor of Germany), William II, dismissed Bismarck. The Kaiser was an unpleasant, arrogant man and he hated the idea of Britain being so much stronger on the oceans than Germany. He therefore ordered a massive increase in the Germany navy.

There then started a great race to build more and better warships. In 1906 Britain launched the first of a new kind of super-battleship, called H.M.S. *Dreadnought*. All ships of this kind became known as 'Dreadnoughts'. Many people in Britain became worried about the German naval threat. They were concerned that Germany would build more Dreadnoughts than Britain. One of the earliest spy stories, *The Thirty-Nine Steps*, was based on these fears. In this story the hero uncovers a German plot to capture British naval secrets. And the belief that Britain should start building eight Dreadnoughts in 1909 was chanted out by audiences in the music-halls: 'We want eight and we won't wait!'

Why did Britain choose France as an ally when she had been a traditional enemy for centuries?

Alliances

When a country thinks it might be involved in a war and is weaker than its enemy or enemies, it looks around for friends. One government will then sign a treaty with another to say that they will help each other if a war does break out. These friendships are call 'alliances'.

As early as 1879 Germany and Austria-Hungary had become allies. Three years later they were joined by Italy. These three countries came to be called the 'Triple Alliance' or the 'Central Powers'. Then, in 1892, France became an ally of Russia. Finally, in 1904 and 1907 Britain entered into 'ententes' with France, then Russia. An entente is a general understanding rather than a firm alliance. These three countries came to be called the 'Entente Powers' or the 'Allies'. By 1914, therefore, as you can see from Map 2, the six most powerful countries in Europe were lined up against each other, three a side.

Kaiser William II

Origins of the First World War

Crises

From the early years of the century a series of events took place, each of which might have sparked off a war. The countries of Europe were becoming more and more jittery. Their need for stronger armed forces and for allies increased. Here is a list of the most serious of these crises. You can find the places marked on Map 2.

1 Morocco, 1905. France felt that the area surrounding the western Mediterranean Sea should be under her influence. She already controlled Tunisia and Algeria on the African coast and wanted Morocco. In 1905 the Kaiser visited Tangier and said that Germany would protect Morocco. The French were worried and annoyed.

2 Bosnia, 1908. Germany became very interested in increasing its influence and power in Turkey and the Middle East. A railway to connect Berlin and Baghdad was started. Then in 1908 Austria-Hungary took control of the Turkish province of Bosnia. The Serbians also wanted Bosnia, and were backed up by the Russians. But the Kaiser declared that if Russia attacked Austria-Hungary, Germany would fight Russia.

3 Morocco, 1911. The French increased their control over Morocco. Germany sent a warship, the *Panther*, to the Moroccan port of Agadir in protest. The Germans were persuaded to withdraw, but only after France had given them some of its West African territory in exchange.

4 The Balkan Wars, 1912 and 1913. The big powers had interests in the Balkans and the Balkan countries themselves had their own quarrels. People began to fear that the troubles in this corner of Europe would flare up into general war. These people were to be proved right. Serbia, Romania, Bulgaria and Greece attacked Turkey in 1912 and took large areas of land from her. Then the next year they fought each other over the share-out of the spoils. But Serbia emerged much strengthened, in fact about twice the size the country had been in 1912. This increased the worries of the Austro-Hungarian government. These fears caused the final crisis that really did lead to a general European war—a war so many people had predicted but no one was able to prevent.

Archduke Franz Ferdinand arriving at Sarajevo. Later that day he was assassinated

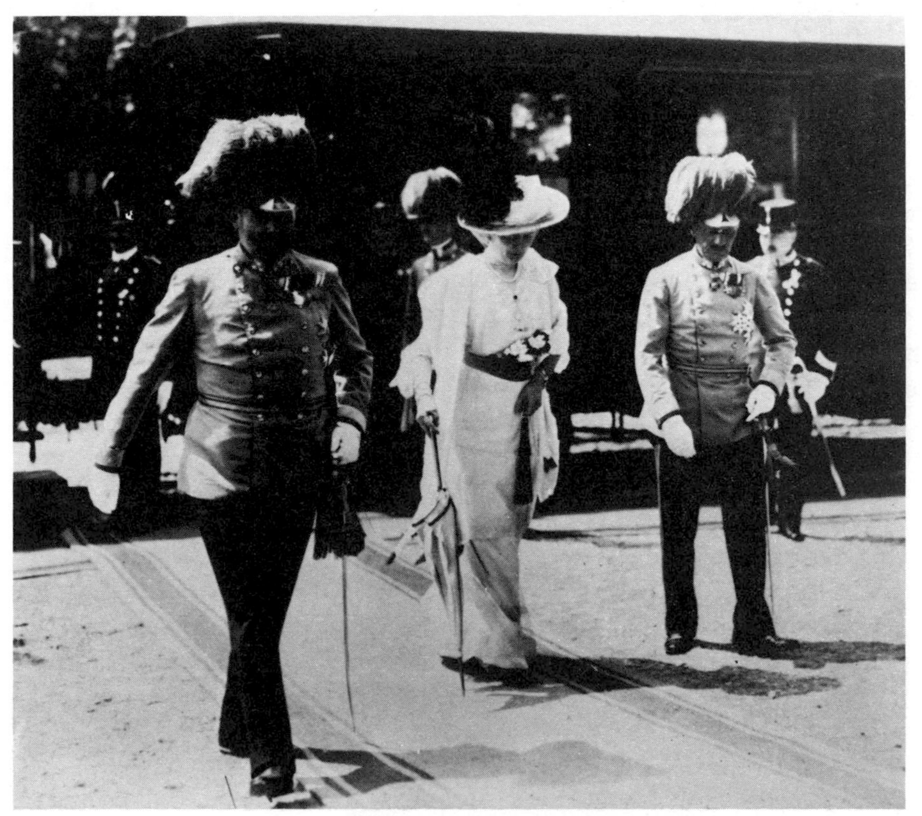

The Sarajevo Murder

On 28 June 1914 the Archduke Franz Ferdinand of Austria and his wife were driving through the streets of Sarajevo. They were on a state visit to this city, the capital of Bosnia. By 1914 Bosnia was a province of Austria. Serbia had laid claim to it in 1908 but that crisis had passed. Many Serbs thought, however, that Bosnia belonged to them and were prepared to fight the Austrians to get it. Suddenly, the car stopped and reversed. The driver had missed a turning. Then, a young man stepped from the crowd and shot the Archduke and his wife at point-blank range. Both died within a few minutes. The murderer was a student named Gavrilo Princip. He was supported by a Serbian secret society, the 'Black Hand'.

Time chart

The century begins

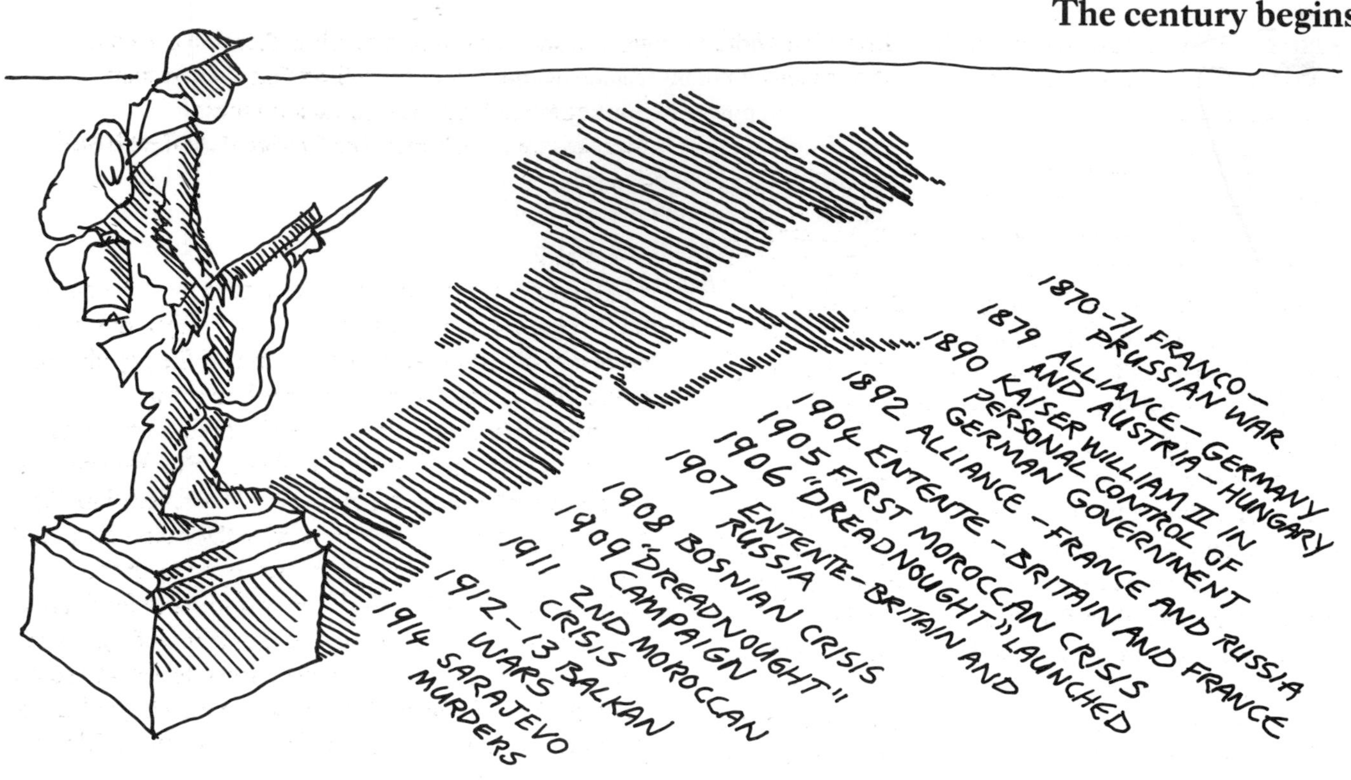

1870–71 FRANCO–PRUSSIAN WAR
1879 ALLIANCE – GERMANY AND AUSTRIA–HUNGARY
1890 KAISER WILLIAM II IN PERSONAL CONTROL OF GERMAN GOVERNMENT
1892 ALLIANCE – FRANCE AND RUSSIA
1904 ENTENTE – BRITAIN AND FRANCE
1905 FIRST MOROCCAN CRISIS
1906 "DREADNOUGHT" LAUNCHED
1907 ENTENTE – BRITAIN AND RUSSIA
1908 BOSNIAN CRISIS
1909 "DREADNOUGHT" CAMPAIGN
1911 2ND MOROCCAN CRISIS
1912–13 BALKAN WARS
1914 SARAJEVO MURDERS

Questions

1 Read the following quotations which refer to crises occurring before the First World War. In each case give details of the event and explain why it led to increased tension between the powers or to their eventual participation in the war.

- a 'We, Francis Joseph, Emperor of Austria ... remembering the ties that existed of yore between our glorious ancestors on the Hungarian throne, we extend our suzerainty over these lands. ...' *Francis Joseph, 7th October, 1908.*
- b 'Suddenly and unexpectedly, on the morning of July 1st, 1911 it was announced that His Imperial Majesty ... had sent his gunboat, the *Panther*, to maintain and protect German interests. ...' *Sir W. Churchill 'The World Crisis'.*
- c Austrian Heir Shot. Double Assassination. Bombs and Bullets. *'The Times', Monday 29th June, 1914.*
- d 'Without consulting the cabinet Grey sent off an ultimatum to Germany, demanding by midnight a promise to respect the neutrality. ... At 7 p.m. Bethmann Hollweg refused to make such a promise. He complained that Great Britain would not go to war over "A Scrap of Paper" ...' *A. J. P. Taylor.*

2 By 1900, Europe was divided into two rival alliance systems and involved in a race in armaments. Britain considered her own safety depended on the maintenance of her naval supremacy, so she joined in the armaments race. The question was, should Britain also take part in the rival alliances?

- a Name the members of the Triple Alliance and explain how and why it was formed.
- b Which TWO powers formed the opposing alliance that existed in 1900? Give TWO reasons why this alliance had been made.
- c Which alliance system did Britain eventually join? Describe how and explain why Britain joined this alliance.

3 Describe in a paragraph (10–20 lines) the part played by the Balkans in European history 1900–1914.

4 Explain why the First World War broke out in 1914. You may find it useful to include in your answer:

- a the Alliance between Germany and Austria,
- b the forming of the Triple Entente,
- c Germany's quarrels with Britain and France,
- d growing tension in South-East Europe,
- e the assassination of Archduke Franz Ferdinand.

Questions

5 Read the following extract and decide with which of the statements below it you can agree. Give the reasons for your decisions.

'After a long interval devoted to more controversial but less important subjects, the House of Commons today resumes the discussion of the Navy Estimates, and it is believed that Mr McKenna will announce the decision of the Government immediately to lay down the four additional Dreadnoughts. This decision will be welcomed throughout the Empire. We should all of us be glad if it were possible to dispense with the proposed increase in the Navy, and still more glad if it were possible to reduce the present vast expenditure. But nations, like individuals, have to take facts as they find them; and the dominating fact of the existing situation is the unconcealed desire of Germany to challenge our naval supremacy. That desire is quite intelligible. The Germans are a great people, and they wish to be second to none either on sea or on land. We, however, are compelled to look at the problem from our point of view, and not from theirs. To us sea supremacy is a necessary of national life; to Germany it is a luxury of Imperial ambition. If we lost the command of the sea our commerce could be destroyed and our industries brought to a standstill, and the overwhelming German army could effect a landing where it listed. Germany runs no such risk. The utmost injury we could inflict upon her would be to blockade Hamburg and Bremen, and force her to send overland that portion of her foreign commerce which now passes through these ports. Her ordinary industrial life would continue almost unaffected. The stakes are, therefore, not even. She is playing for pride, we are playing for life – and we mean to win.'
(*Daily Graphic*, 26 July 1909.)

a The writer believed that other countries as well as Britain would benefit from the extra Dreadnoughts.
b It was not necessary for Germany to have a large navy.
c Because this extract comes from a British newspaper it is bound to be a fair summary of the matter.

6 Read the following extracts from three historians and answer the questions below.

Source A
'The great armaments helped to keep the peace – so long as they were not used. But as soon as one power, in order to reinforce its diplomacy, began to mobilize, its action made military men everywhere jittery, for no general staff was willing to allow a rival to get a start. "Once the dice were set rolling," as the German chancellor said, nothing could stop them.'
(Bernadotte E. Schmitt, *The Origins of the First World War*, 1958.)

Source B
'The public interest and involvement in the arms race, the curiosity about new weapons, ever bigger and more fantastic, accustomed large segments of the population to the idea of war and created a wish to see its instruments in action. It may well be that, for reasons which the historian can only dimly perceive, Europe was deeply ready for war. It is not just that a generation "had been taught how to howl". It may be that some profound boredom with the long years of peace and with the tedium of industrial life led men to volunteer for France and to find in that Hell a final confirmation of manhood. The sentiment I am trying to describe was well stated on 4 August by a German General, von Falkenhayn: "Even if we end in ruin, it was beautiful." It was "Vain Glory" but it was glory.'
(Zara S. Steiner, *Britain and the Origins of the First World War*, 1977.)

Source C
'It is often said that the relations between the Great European Powers were especially tense and strained in the early months of 1914 as a preliminary to the outbreak of war in August. This is totally inaccurate. The truth is the exact reverse: relations between the Great Powers had never been better. . . .

'It is difficult, in fact, to discover any cause of hostility between the European Great Powers in the early summer of 1914. But there was one cause of estrangement. This was the system of alliances which distanced the Great Powers unnecessarily. These Alliances dragged Powers into wars which did not concern them. They were supposed to make for peace, they made for war. They were supposed to make Powers secure, they dragged them into danger.'
(A. J. P. Taylor, 'The entente that ended in slaughter' in *The Guardian*, 4 August 1984.)

a Explain briefly in your own words how each of these historians explain the causes of the First World War.
b How far do they agree with each other and how far do they differ?
c What do these extracts tell you about the way historians explain the causes of important events?

2/The war to end all wars

Eager young British soldiers are seen off from the station by their families

The outbreak of war

As soon as the news of the murders at Sarajevo reached Vienna, the Austrian government accused the government of Serbia of being behind them. After a few weeks of arguing, the Austrian army invaded Serbia. Within days—

1 Germany entered the war to help Austria;

2 Russia then went to help Serbia;

3 France helped Russia.

Sir Edward Grey, the British foreign minister, tried hard to stop war from breaking out. And certainly it seemed possible at first that Britain would be able to avoid being involved. But the German scheme, called the Schlieffen Plan, was to attack France quickly through Belgium (see Map 1). Now Britain had signed a treaty promising to protect Belgium. So, when the German army invaded Belgium, the British government said it would declare war if the German soldiers advanced any further. The German Chancellor was angry that Britain should go to war, as he put it, over 'a scrap of paper'. Grey sadly said, 'The lamps are going out all over Europe; we shall not see them lit again in our lifetime.' By midnight on 4 August Britain was at war.

Who was to blame?

Just as many people feared, the problems of the little Balkan countries (see p. 7) got out of control and led to a war that affected almost the whole continent. It was to be one of the most terrible wars that Europe has known.

The war caused the deaths and suffering of many millions of people. Who do you think was to blame for starting it? At first, historians blamed Germany. After all, it was Germany that built up most quickly a strong army, frightening the French and a strong navy, frightening the British. If Germany had not supported Austria against Serbia, the war could perhaps have been kept to the Balkans. It was Germany that invaded innocent Belgium and brought Britain into the war. But that was only one side of the picture. Germany was frightened of being attacked on two sides at once—by France and Russia. Also, Germany was lagging behind the other Great Powers in gaining colonies and overseas trade. Do you think perhaps that the war was caused by jealousy and fear between several nations?

Campaigns

The Western Front

The Schlieffen Plan

In August and September the Germans tried to gain a quick victory against France. The British were also involved because they sent the small British Expeditionary Force (B.E.F.). This was described by the Kaiser as 'a contemptible little force'. You can follow the events of the early fighting on Map 1.

1 The German Schlieffen Plan for attacking France was very clever in theory. It aimed to do the following:
a) Avoid attacking the heavily defended parts of eastern France
b) Attack quickly through a defenceless Belgium
c) Encircle Paris
d) Attack the armies in eastern France from behind.
However, after advancing some way into northern France the Germans were slowed down by the British and French armies.
2 The German general gave up the idea of advancing round Paris.
3 Then the French counter-attacked in the first of the big battles of the war, the Battle of the Marne, and recaptured important ground.
4 The Germans tried to take the ports of Calais and Boulogne that were so important for supplying the British army. For six weeks the most bitter fighting raged, the British stubbornly holding on to the vital town of Ypres.

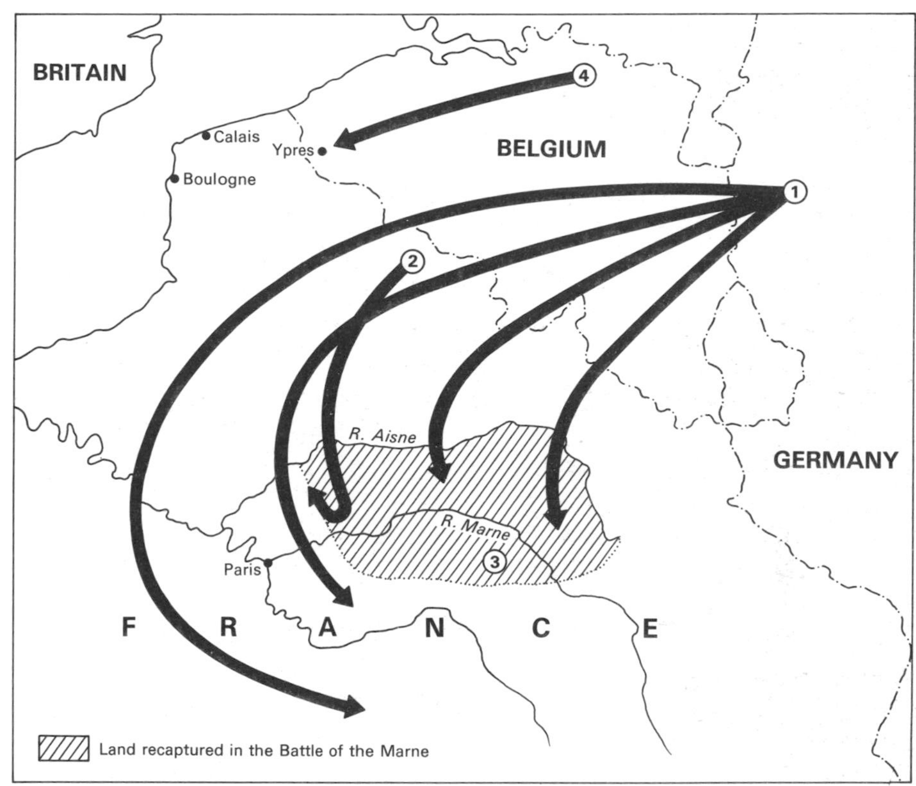

Map 1 The Schlieffen Plan

Map 2 Main battles on the Western Front, 1915–17

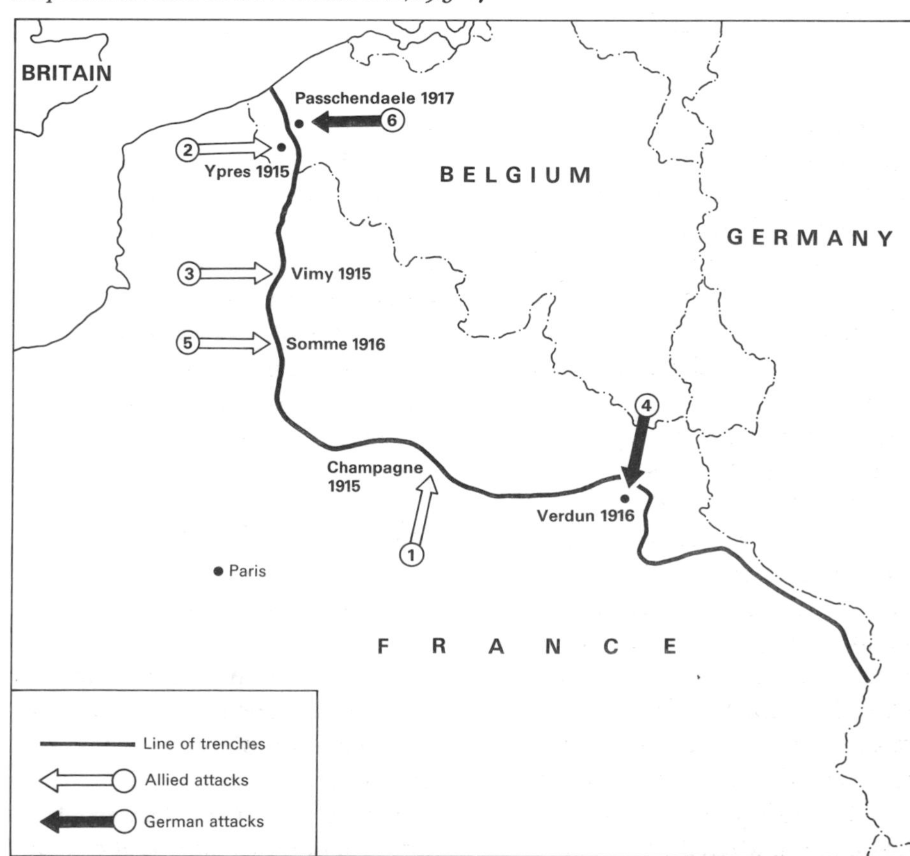

Stalemate

For four years it was stalemate. Great lines of trenches were dug (see p.15) for four years the soldiers on both sides emerged from these trenches to attack the enemy in unsuccessful and bloody attempts to break through the other's defences. The following were some of the main battles. Map 2 shows you where they took place.

1 Champagne, 1915. French advance.
2 Second battle of Ypres, 1915. German advance; first use of poison gas.
3 Vimy, 1915. French advance.
4 Verdun, 1916. The battle raged for six months as the French sent more and more soldiers to 'the mincing machine' to fill the gaps caused by the casualties. 'They shall not pass!' declared General Pétain. The Germans did not take Verdun; but 360,000 Frenchman died.
5 Somme, 1916. British (mainly) and French advance; first use of tanks. One million soldiers died.
6 Passchendaele (or third Battle of Ypres), 1917. British advance.

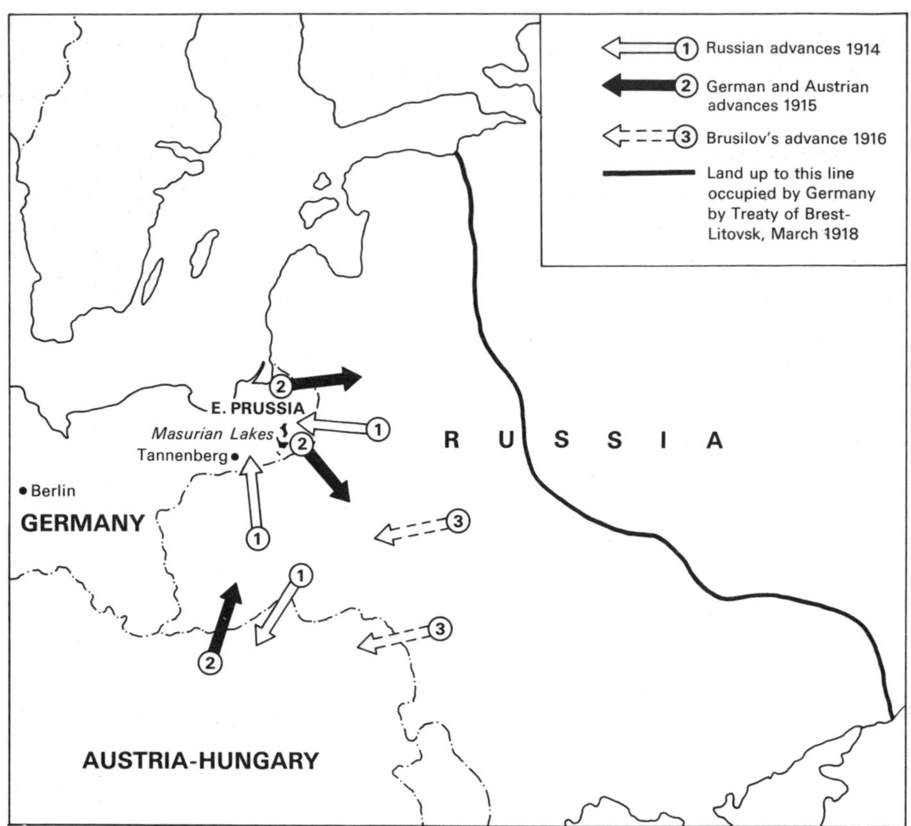

Map 3 The Eastern Front

Final efforts

The lack of any real success combined with the huge casualties led to mutinies in the French Army in 1917. By 1918 the dreadful slaughter was beginning to weaken both sides very severely. But the Allies were strengthened by the arrival of fresh American troops under the command of General Pershing. In March the German commander, Ludendorff, made a great effort to break through the Allied lines. With the help of enormous artillery bombardments, the Germans advanced in several places. The Allies appointed a supreme commander, Marshal Foch. In August the French, British and Americans attacked and forced the Germans to retreat back into Belgium.

The Eastern Front

Russian attacks

In Eastern Europe Russia fought both Germany and Austria-Hungary. The fighting in the east took place without the trench systems of the western front.

Soon after the war started Russian armies invaded East Prussia (the arrows marked 1 on Map 3). By looking at the map can you see why this attack was so dangerous for Germany? The German armies there were commanded by two of the greatest generals of the war, Hindenburg and Ludendorff. The Russians were poorly equipped and supplied. They were soundly defeated at two great battles: a) Tannenberg; b) the Masurian Lakes. In these two battles alone the Russians lost over a quarter of a million men, dead and as prisoners of war.

At the same time as these battles were being fought, other Russian armies invaded Austria-Hungary and had rather more success.

German and Austrian advances

But in 1915 the Germans decided to concentrate on an attack on Russia. The idea was to make Russia ask for peace so that the Germans could then be free to move all their forces against France. The main attacks are shown by arrows marked 2 on the map. By the autumn the Germans and Austrians had occupied huge areas of Russia.

In 1916 the Russian commander, Brusilov, won back some of this land. But the next year revolutions occurred in Russia (see chapter 3). The new Communist government made peace with the Germans in 1918 and Russia surrendered the huge area shown on the map. The war in eastern Europe was over.

The Mediterranean and the Middle East

The Dardanelles

Because the war in France soon became a stalemate, plans were thought up in Britain for attacking the Central Powers in other places. One idea was to attack Turkey and capture Constantinople, the capital. As you can see from Map 4 (a) this would help Russia. In order to do this the Dardanelles had to be taken—this is the narrow strip of water between Asia Minor and Europe.

In 1915 attacks were made on the Gallipoli peninsula, a narrow tongue of land on the European side. Soldiers, including many from Australia and New Zealand, were landed. But the Turks prevented them from advancing and were able to fire on them from higher ground. The Allied soldiers dug trenches and through the summer suffered badly from the heat, flies and sickness. Early in 1916 they were evacuated. The scheme had failed. Winston Churchill was First Lord of the Admiralty at the time and although he was not the only supporter of the scheme, he was made to take the blame and was forced to resign.

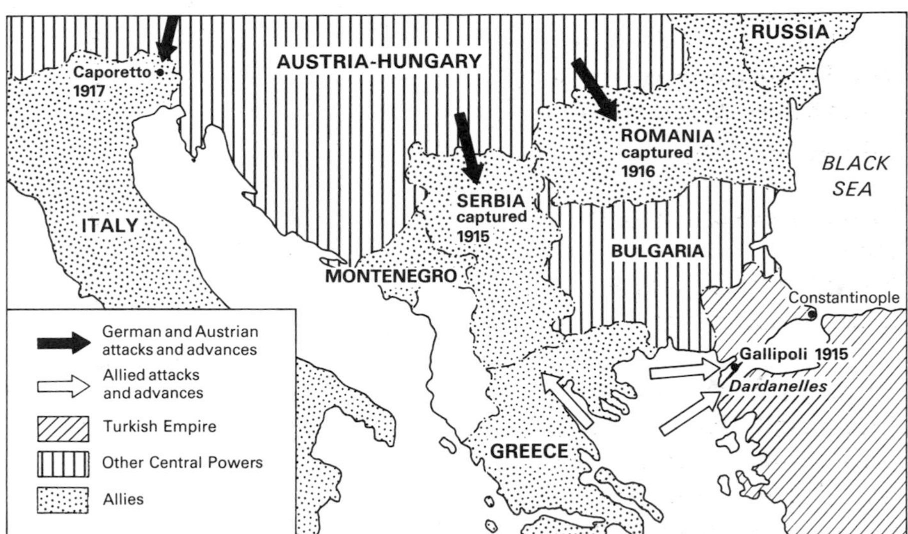

Map 4 (a) The war in the Mediterranean

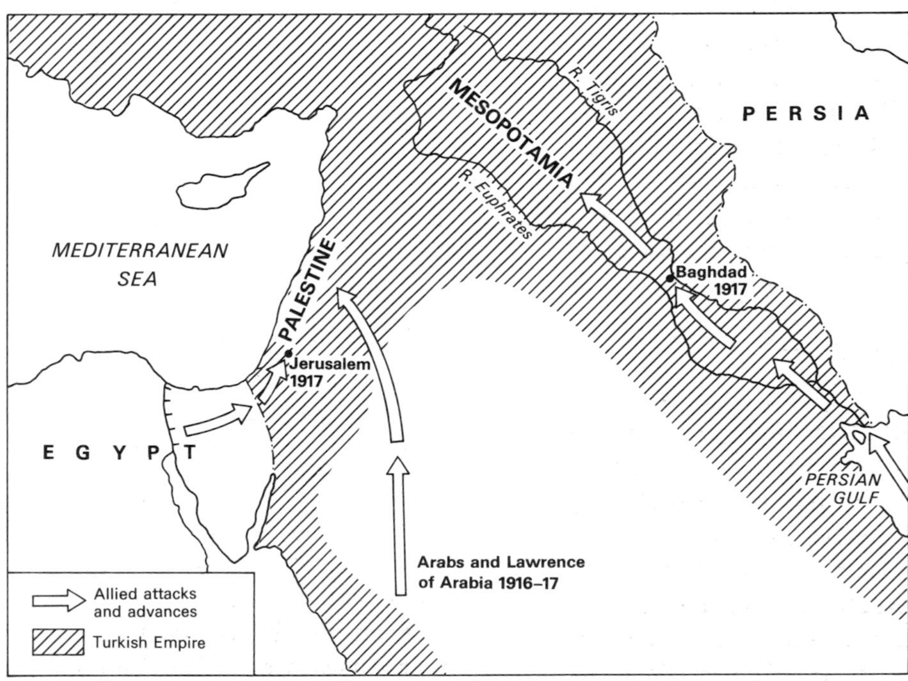

Map 4 (b) The war in the Middle East

The Balkans and Italy

Several countries in southern parts of Europe were also involved in fighting. Austrian and German armies conquered Serbia in 1915 and Romania in 1916. British and French troops were sent to Greece to try to help, but could do very little.

Although Italy was a member of the Triple Alliance (see p. 6) she joined the war on the side of the Allies in 1915. The Italians hoped to obtain some land from Austria. A number of battles were fought in the north-east corner of Italy, some high in the mountains. In 1917 the Italians were soundly defeated in the Battle of Caporetto.

The Middle East

As you can see from Map 4 (b) the Turkish Empire at the time of the First World War spread over much of the Middle East and therefore over lands inhabited by Arabs. However, the British controlled Egypt. Attacks were made by British, Indian, Australian and New Zealand soldiers from Egypt into Palestine and from the Persian Gulf into Mesopotamia (now Iraq). Also the Arabs rose up in revolt. They took over the Arabian peninsula and attacked the Turks in Palestine. They were led by an Englishman, T. E. Lawrence, who came to be known as Lawrence of Arabia.

Naval war

The nature of naval warfare

You may remember from Chapter 1 that one reason that Britain and Germany became enemies was their naval rivalry. Yet when the war started the great battleships were so precious that the admirals on each side hardly dared risk a battle with them in case too many of them were sunk! The British did, however, blockade German ports. They did this to prevent food and other important supplies from being imported. As a result of this blockade the German people were desperately short of food by 1918. In reply, Germany sent out submarines (U-boats) to sink British merchant ships. But Britain bought food from neutral countries (that is, countries not fighting in the war). So what complications do you think were likely as a result of this use of submarines?

Naval battles

In the meantime, a number of small naval battles took place in the North Sea. One, for example, took place at the Dogger Bank in 1915. Then, in 1916, the one great naval battle of the war took place, the Battle of Jutland. The British Grand Fleet under Admiral Jellicoe fought the German High Seas Fleet under Admiral Scheer off the coast of Denmark. Eleven German ships and fourteen British ships were sunk. Both sides claimed the victory. The British lost more ships and more men, but the Germans had retreated back to port.

Submarines

The Germans now increased their U-boat warfare. In April 1917 alone U-boats sank over 300 merchant ships. It looked as though Britain might be starved into defeat. Then the convoy system was introduced—warships sailing with a group of merchant ships to protect them—and the crisis for Britain was over. In 1918 a daring raid was made on Zeebrugge in Belgium to block the U-boat harbour entrance.

In order to stop as many supplies from reaching Britain as possible, German U-boat commanders were told to sink neutral ships as well. This is what you were asked to think about earlier. The most important neutral country was the U.S.A. Already in 1915 the Americans had been made very angry when a number of their people were drowned in the sinking by a U-boat of the British ocean liner *Lusitania*. So many American merchant ships were sunk in 1917 that the U.S.A. declared war on Germany. The U.S. soldiers under the command of General Pershing were very valuable in forcing the retreat of the German armies on the Western Front in 1918 (see p.12).

Direct hit—another allied ship falls victim to a U-boat

Some aspects of the fighting

Loss of life and the trenches

The horror of war

Compare these two quotations.

'God blast your neck!' (For days he'd had no sleep),
'Get up and guide me through this stinking place.'
Savage, he kicked a soft, unanswering heap,
And flashed his beam across the livid face
Terribly glaring up, whose eyes yet wore
Agony dying hard ten days before;
And fists of fingers clutched a blackening wound.

We see men living with their skulls blown open; we see soldiers run with their two feet cut off, they stagger on their splintered stumps into the next shell-hole. . . . The sun goes down, night comes, the shells whine, life is at an end.

Still the little piece of convulsed earth in which we lie is held. We have yielded no more than a few hundred yards of it as a prize to the enemy. But on every yard there lies a dead man.

The first is from the poem, 'The Rear-Guard', written in 1917 by the English poet, Sassoon. The second is from *All Quiet on the Western Front*, written in 1929 by the German novelist, Remarque. Both show the horror so many people felt both during the war and after at the enormous amount of bloodshed and suffering caused by what was called at the time the Great War. Many people hoped that it would be 'the war to end all wars'.

The arithmetic of death

Another way of showing the dreadful bloodshed is by listing the estimated numbers killed in the fighting. Compare the following chart with that in Chapter 6 on losses in the Second World War.

A French soldier meets his death during an attack at Verdun where nearly one million soldiers died over a nine-month period

One of the reasons for the horror at the number of casualties on the Western Front was that so little seemed to be achieved by so many deaths. Each side dug lines of trenches stretching from the English Channel to the frontier of Switzerland. Most battles consisted of hundreds of thousands of men trying, usually unsuccessfully, to capture and penetrate through these lines.

It is not surprising that many people then and now thought that the generals on both sides were stupid or heartless to order their men to charge against barbed-wire fences and trenches defended by machine-guns.

Figure 1 The World War dead

Some aspects of the fighting

Aerial dog-fight—by 1918 aerial fights had become very common on the Western Front

Zeppelin—the first kind of aircraft to bomb Britain

A heavy field-gun used for artillery bombardments

Big Bertha—the famous huge long-range German gun

Tank—the only way to break the stalemate produced by trenches and machine-guns

U-boat — these German submarines very nearly cut Britain off from essential supplies of food.

Some aspects of the fighting

Weapons

How weapons developed

It is often said that generals are always prepared to fight the *previous* war. In 1914 most people rather assumed that the battleships and field guns would be used to fight an 'up-dated' version of a nineteenth-century war in which large armies met on open ground and battles were won and lost in a day and wars were over within weeks or months. By 1918 the invention and development of new weapons had, however, made warfare very different indeed. Some of these are pictured on the previous page. Compare these weapons with some of those used in the Second World War and illustrated in Chapter 6.

Weapons for land and sea war

The armies used field guns and howitzers for huge artillery bombardments sometimes for several days before their infantry made an attack. Poison gas was a new weapon used in some battles, (such as Vimy, 1915) but was difficult to control. Why do you think this was so? The tank was invented during the war. It was an obvious way of breaking through the deadly machine-gun fire. The British used tanks first in 1916.

In the war at sea the most important new weapons were the submarine and torpedo. Together they enabled attacks to be made on ships when the attacker was out of sight underneath the surface of the sea.

The war in the air

But the truly new invention was the aeroplane. For the first time fighting took place in the air as well as on land and on the sea. Great advances were made during the war in the design of aeroplanes. At first they were used just to collect information for the army about the position of enemy soldiers and guns and about the accuracy of artillery bombardments. But soon machine-guns were fitted and aeroplanes fought each other. These aerial battles were known as 'dog-fights'. Some pilots became very famous 'aces'. Probably the most famous was the German, von Richthofen. Both the Germans and British used aeroplanes to bomb each others' towns. Germans also used huge airships known as Zeppelins. Over one thousand British civilians were killed in air raids. Do you think that this kind of bombing was fair?

World war and total war

Why do you think the war is called the First World War? After all, some wars in earlier ages had been fought over many parts of the planet. But never before had so many different countries from so many different parts of the world been involved. Fighting took place in Europe, Asia and Africa and on many seas. Besides the main countries involved in the war, even China and five south American countries had joined in by the end. In Europe, only Norway, Denmark, Sweden, Switzerland, Holland, Albania and Spain remained neutral.

Furthermore, as we shall see in the next section, the war was for many countries 'total'. That is, civilians as well as soldiers, sailors and airmen were involved. Civilians made bullets and shells and some civilians, as we have just described, were bombed. Also, because there were not enough volunteers to replace the huge numbers of casualties, men were 'conscripted' into the army, that is, made to become soldiers whether they wanted to or not. At first, in Britain for example, there was a great rush of men volunteering to join the army. They responded to a now famous poster of Lord Kitchener, the War Minister saying, 'Your country needs YOU'.

The Lord Kitchener recruiting poster

Making the weapons

The supplies needed

Wars can be fought only if there are weapons available. In the First World War millions of soldiers, sailors and airmen had to be provided with huge supplies of guns, bullets and shells as well as lorries, ships and aeroplanes. Just look at the diagram opposite showing the increase in some British munitions in the middle of the war.

Effects of munitions production

Other countries increased their war production in similar ways. The need to produce so many munitions had two main effects:

1 Governments had to take control of some industries to ensure that enough munitions were produced and of the right kind. The British and German governments were the most efficient in this way. For example, a new Ministry of Munitions was set up in Britain in 1915.

2 Because so many men were needed for the fighting, there were not enough men to work in the factories. Women therefore had to be used for this work. Women were, in fact, used for many jobs previously done by men, including farming. On the continent of Europe women were especially important in agriculture.

Figure 2 The increase in British munitions 1915 to 1917

Women trimming sugar beet, 1916. Sugar beet was introduced into this country during the war as an alternative source of sugar to sugar cane. What does this picture tell you about the production of food in Britain?

Hardship

Shortages of food

In a number of countries food became scarce during the war. If you refer to page 14 you will remember that Britain and Germany tried to starve each other by using their navies to prevent imports. In Britain many kinds of food like sugar, meat and butter were rationed—that is, people were allowed to buy only a limited amount each week. But conditions in Germany by 1917 were very much worse. Even bread and potatoes were in short supply.

Discontent

After three or four years of war people became very discontented and angry with their goverments—particularly in France, Germany and Russia. There were three main reasons for this:

1 The huge numbers of men being killed and injured in the fighting.

2 The shortage of food.

3 The rich people suffered much less than the majority of the people.

As a result, in Russia in 1917 and in Germany in 1918 there were revolutions which destroyed the old systems of government (see pp.22 and 30).

The peace settlement

The end of the War

Peace negotiators

By the autumn of 1918 it was obvious that the Germans had neither the strength nor the will-power to continue the war. It was eventually agreed that the fighting should stop ('armistice') at 11.00 a.m. on 11 November.

Early the next year representatives gathered in Paris to work out the details of the peace treaties. The outline had already been provided by the American President, Woodrow Wilson, in his Fourteen Points. He had been a Professor of Politics and dreamed of producing a peace settlement that would prevent war from breaking out in Europe again. He was one of the three most important men at the peace conference. The others were the French and British leaders—very different men. Clemenceau, the French Prime Minister, wanted to punish and weaken Germany as much as possible. He was known as 'The Tiger'. Lloyd George, the British prime minister, saw the dangers of being too harsh on Germany, but at the same time scoffed at President Wilson's theories. (When told of the Fourteen Points, he said, 'The good Lord needed only Ten!') Italy, not as important as the other three victors, was represented by her prime minister, Orlando.

National self-determination

The main idea of President Wilson's was national self-determination. This means the right of a people to be ruled by a government of their own people, not by foreigners. For example, Poles should be governed by Poles, not by Russians and Poland should therefore be a separate country, not part of Russia. Is this a good idea?

The three leaders at Versailles (from left to right, Clemenceau, Wilson, Lloyd George). Why do you think Lloyd George was so rude about Woodrow Wilson's Fourteen Points?

It is, in fact, impossible in many areas to draw a frontier so that all the people speaking a particular language, for example, are included in 'their' country. (See e.g. Map 3 on p.5.) There were many minorities left like this in 'wrong' countries in central and eastern Europe. Treaties were signed to try to protect them.

The changes made

Several treaties were signed with the defeated Central Powers. Together they are usually called the Versailles Settlement (because the main treaty with Germany was signed in the Palace there).

Germany

Germany was the main defeated country. Let us look first of all at the way she was treated.

1 We saw in the last chapter that the causes of the war were very complicated. But the peace treaty declared that Germany alone was guilty of causing the war. Germany was therefore required to pay reparations—that is, compensation to the Allied countries for the deaths and damage caused by the war. This was calculated at what was then the vast sum of £6,600 million.

2 Germany was forbidden to have any submarines or warplanes and only a small army of 100,000 men. The German fleet was scuttled when it surrendered in the harbour of Scapa Flow.

3 Germany also lost a lot of land. All her colonies in Africa and the Pacific were taken away (see p. 3). The land shaded on Map 5 was transferred to her neighbours as shown.

4 In several small areas the people were allowed to vote to decide whether to stay in Germany or not. This voting was called a plebiscite. The Saar was controlled by the League of Nations until 1935 when the people voted to return to being part of Germany.

5 Germany was forbidden to station any soldiers in the Rhineland—that is, the demilitarised zone shown on

The peace settlement

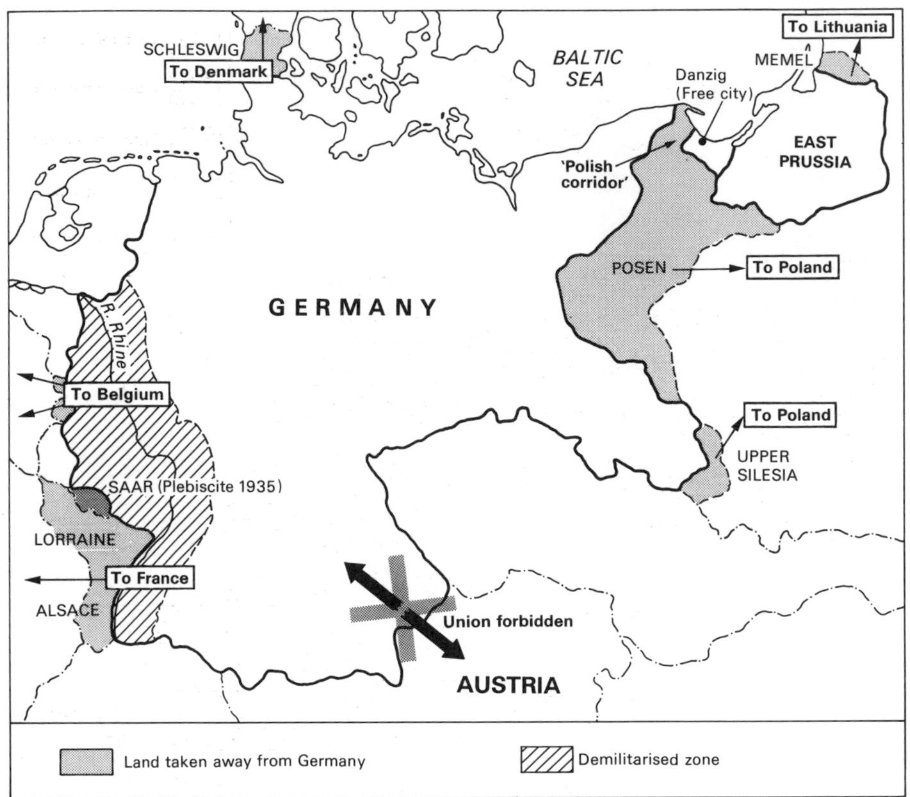

Map 5 German losses as a result of the Versailles Peace Settlement

Poland

In the eighteenth century Poland had been attacked and partitioned by Austria, Prussia and Russia. It was now recreated as an independent country from lands taken from Austria, Germany and Russia. Some of the land taken from Germany was called the 'Polish corridor'. It was given to the new Poland so that she could have a seaport (on the Baltic Sea). The Baltic port of Danzig was made a 'free city' administered by the League of Nations. It also meant, as you can see from Map 5, that East Prussia was separated from the rest of Germany.

The eastern frontier of Poland was laid down by the British foreign minister, Lord Curzon. This is shown on Map 6. But the Poles were not satisfied with this and captured the land shown on the map to the east of the Curzon Line from the Russians.

the map. This was to prevent the Germans collecting an army there to invade France again at any time in the future.

6 To prevent Germany from becoming too strong any joining together with Austria was forbidden.

Austria-Hungary

We saw in the last chapter that the Austro-Hungarian Empire was made up of many different peoples. They each wanted to be a separate country. So when the war was coming to an end they declared their independence and the Empire broke up. They were putting President Wilson's idea of national self-determination into practice. As you can see from Map 6, a number of new countries came into existence. Compare the countries with the map on p. 5.

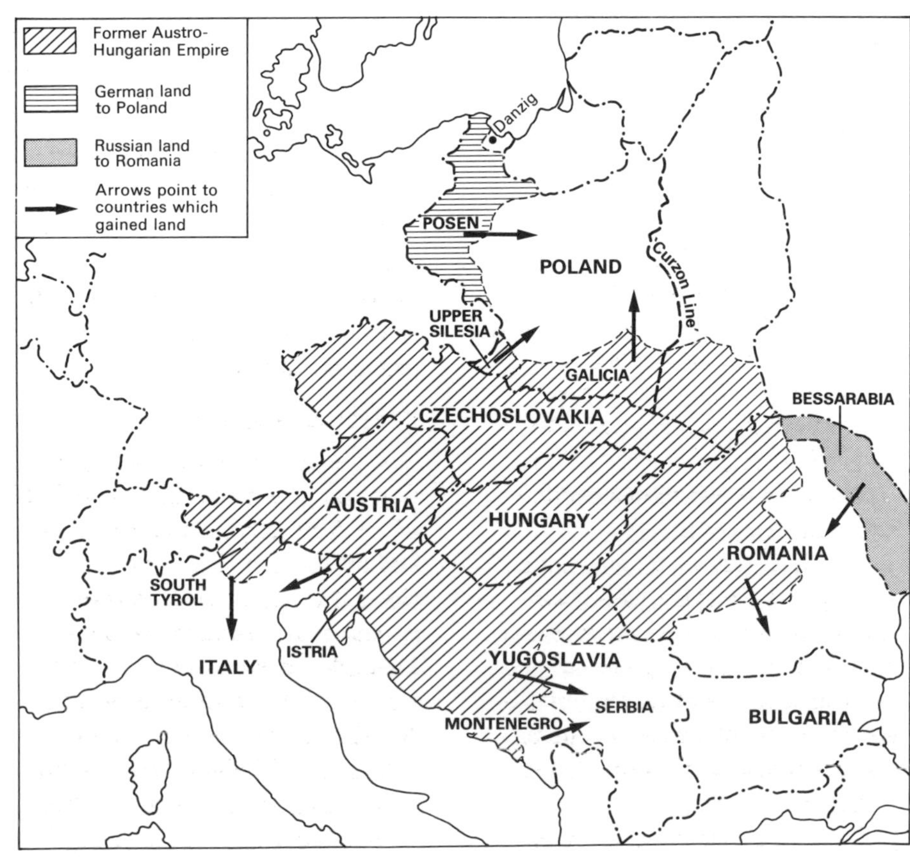

Map 6 Eastern and Central Europe after the Versailles Peace Settlement

The peace settlement

The Turkish Empire

The peace treaty of Sèvres, which ended the war with the Turkish Empire, was very harsh. The new Turkish leader, Mustapha Kemal (Kemal Ataturk) fought a war against the Greeks and forced them to give up the land they had occupied. A new Treaty of Lausanne was then signed in 1923. You can see from Map 7 that Turkey lost all her land apart from Asia Minor and Eastern Thrace.

The Arabs were disappointed and angry that Britain and France took over the rule of so many of the lands where they lived. They would rather have become independent. There was also another complication in the area. The British government made a promise in 1917 (the Balfour Declaration) that the Jewish people could have a homeland in Palestine. But no one explained how this could be done without interfering with the Arab people already living there (see Chapter 11).

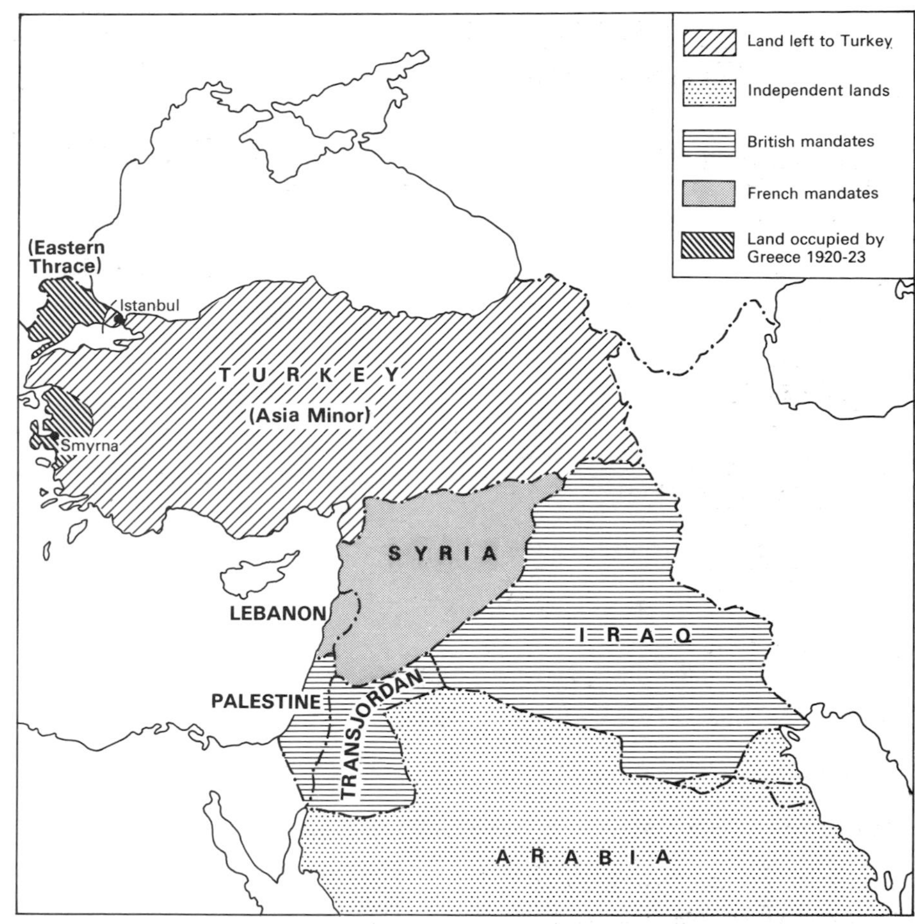

Map 7 The break-up of the Turkish empire

The League of Nations

How the League was formed

President Wilson may have been rather starry-eyed in thinking that the peace settlement could prevent future wars. But he realised that it would be necessary to set up an organisation to prevent war. This was called the League of Nations. Its work was outlined in a document called the Covenant.

The main tasks were as follows:

1 To persuade quarrelling countries to talk about their disputes and resolve them without going to war.

2 To arrange for other countries to go to the help of a member country if it was attacked. This was called 'collective security'.

3 To ensure that the lands taken from Turkey and the colonies from Germany were governed justly and were prepared eventually for independence. These lands were handed over to Allied powers such as France and Britain and were called mandates.

What the League did

The headquarters were set up in Geneva. There, meetings were held of the Assembly (all member states) and the Council (ten countries). Several agencies were also created to deal with particular problems. Examples include the Permanent Court of International Justice, the Mandates Commission and the International Labour Organisation.

The League managed to settle some minor quarrels peacefully in the 1920s. But it was very weak. The U.S.A. refused to join and Germany and Russia were not allowed to be members at first. Also, the League had no forces of its own. And member countries were unwilling to use their own forces to uphold the principle of collective security when international crises occurred in the 1930s. You can find out about the failure of the League in Manchuria on p.61 and in Abyssinia on p.63.

Conclusions

The peace settlement

Was it a good peace settlement? Compare these two comments. The first is by Harold Nicolson, a famous British diplomat; the second is by Winston Churchill, a minister during the war and prime minister during the Second World War.

The historian, with every justification, will come to the conclusion that we were very stupid men.... We arrived determined that a Peace of justice and wisdom should be negotiated: we left it conscious that the treaties imposed upon our enemies were neither just nor wise....

... a fair judgment upon the settlement, a simple explanation of how it arose, cannot leave the authors of the new map of Europe under serious reproach. To an overwhelming extent the wishes of the various populations prevailed.

The settlement certainly left two very serious problems:

1 National self-determination (one country for every nationality) could never be strictly applied. People of a particular nationality just do not live in compact areas around which neat frontiers can be drawn. The idea that you *can* draw such accurate frontiers therefore later led to quarrels. And what about the people of Austria who were forbidden to join with the other German-speaking people of Germany itself? And why were the Arab people of Syria and Palestine, for example, not allowed to be independent?

2 Germany was humiliated. Many German people wanted to undo many of the terms of the treaty which they considered quite unjust. We shall see later how Hitler won great popularity because he promised to do this.

But who do you think was nearer the truth—Nicolson or Churchill?

Social and economic effects of the War

People wanted more equality. In Britain, the importance of the work done by women was recognised by giving most the right to vote in 1918.

The pre-war systems of trade and industry had been thrown into chaos. Many countries were deeply in debt because of the money they had borrowed to pay for the war.

Most seriously, in 1918, the war brought hunger and chaos to many countries. There was particularly severe suffering in Russia and in Germany. Also when the soldiers returned to their homes they often could not find work.

Revolutions

Some people thought that a change of government would improve matters. There were Communist revolutions in some countries.

1 Russia. See p.31

2 Hungary. In 1919 a man named Bela Kun set up a Communist government. It was soon defeated.

3 Germany. Kaiser William II abdicated (that is, gave up his throne) and a new government was set up by the Socialist politician Ebert. But after this revolution many people remained discontented. There was an attempted Communist revolution in 1919 by a group called the Spartacists (named after Spartacus, leader of a slave revolt in ancient Rome). But it was defeated by the government.

Spartacists carrying the Red Flag through the streets of Berlin during the revolution of 1919

Time chart

The war to end all wars

Questions

1 The map, shows the Versailles Settlement in Central Europe, 1919.

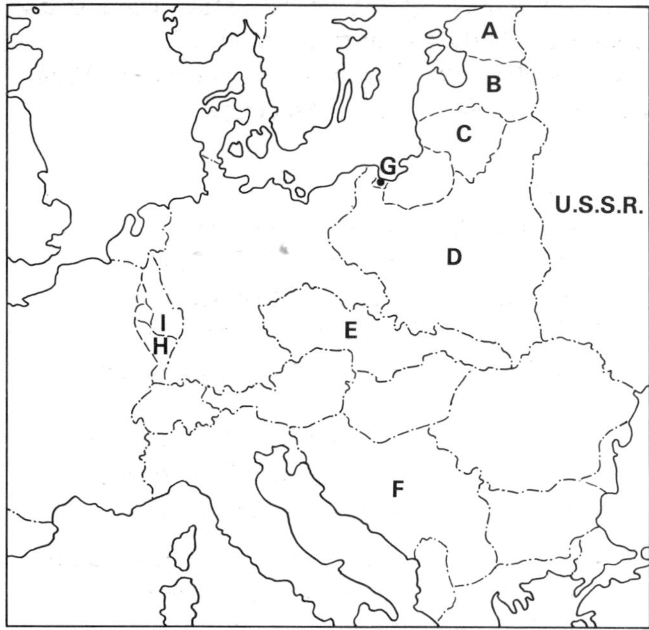

a Name the new states *A, B, C, D* and *E* created at Versailles.

b Name the **two** most important areas which were combined to form state *F*.

c Name the port at *G*. What was to be its status?

d Name the area *H*. Which country regained this area?

e Name the area *I*. Describe the conditions which the treaty laid down about its future.

f What other conditions were imposed upon Germany apart from territorial losses in Europe?

g What criticisms can be made of the Versailles Settlement?

2 Write a paragraph (10–20 lines) explaining why the Archduke Ferdinand was assassinated at Sarajevo and the immediate results of his death.

3 a Where did British troops first go into action in 1914? Where was the German advance checked in September 1914?

b Name the weapon first used by Germany at Ypres in 1915. On which side did Russia fight in the First World War?

c Which major naval action took place in May 1916? Which French soldier first became famous in 1916 at Verdun?

d Where was the first mass attack by tanks in 1917? Name the major battle fought by Italy in 1917.

e What were attacked at Zeebrugge in 1918? Who became the allied commander in chief in 1918?

4 In a paragraph (10–20 lines) describe how fighting on the Western Front was different from that of any previous European war.

5 Write a paragraph on each of any **two** of the following and show its importance in the First World War:

a the Gallipoli campaign;

b the Battle of Jutland;

c Verdun;

d the aeroplane;

e Italy's part in the war.

6 During the First World War (1914–18), what was meant by the expression 'the Western Front'? Why did armies find it necessary to resort to 'trench warfare' along this front?'
Mention some of the campaigns fought on the Western Front during the First World War and give details of the personalities involved and of the weapons used.

7 There were three main areas of fighting in the First World War—the Western Front, the Eastern Front, and at Sea.

a Name **two** battles fought during the war in each of these areas.

b Choose any **two** battles or campaigns from that war and describe them. You should include in your answer: why the battle was fought; details of the fighting; the effects on the rest of the war; any other point which you think is important.

8 a Explain why, during the First World War, there was only one major sea battle involving the main battle fleets of Britain and Germany.

b Describe this battle in as much detail as you can.

c Why were both the British and Germans able to claim it as a victory?

d What does 'unrestricted submarine warfare' mean?

e Why did the Germans declare this in 1917?

f What methods were used by the Allies to counter German submarines? How successful were these methods?

9 Write an account of the way in which the First World War affected life in Britain.

10 Answer the following questions concerning the League of Nations:

a How and why was it established?

b How was it organised?

c How successful was it?

Questions

11 Look carefully at Sources A–D and answer the questions below.

Source A

'Strategically, the battle of the Somme was an unredeemed defeat . . . The Somme set the picture by which future generations saw the First World War: brave helpless soldiers; blundering obstinate generals; nothing achieved. After the Somme men decided that the war would go on for ever.'
(From *The First World War*, by A. J. P. Taylor, 1963.)

Source B

British soldiers capturing German rifles on the Somme

Source C

'The men in the dugouts . . . waited ready, belts full of hand-grenades around them, gripping their rifles . . . It was of vital importance to lose not a second in taking up position in the open to meet the British infantry which would advance immediately behind the artillery barrage . . .

'At 7.30 a.m. the hurricane of shells ceased . . . Our men at once clambered up the steep shafts leading from the dugouts to daylight and ran . . . to the nearest craters. The machine-guns were pulled out of the dugouts and hurriedly placed in position . . . As soon as the men were in position, a series of lines were seen moving forward from the British trenches. The first line appeared without end to right and left. It was quickly followed by a second, then a third and fourth . . .

'"Get ready" was passed along our front from crater to crater . . . A few minutes later, when the leading British line was within a hundred yards, the rattle of machine-gun and rifle broke out along the whole line of shell holes.

'Whole sections seemed to fall . . . The advance rapidly crumbled under the hail of shells and bullets. All along the line men could be seen throwing up their arms and collapsing, never to move again. Badly wounded rolled about in their agony . . .'
(The first day of the Somme – a German view. From *The Somme* by A. H. Farrar-Hockley.)

Source D

i) 'If I should die, think only this of me:
That there's some corner of a foreign field
That is for ever England. There shall be
In that rich earth a richer dust concealed
A dust whom England bore, shaped, made aware,
Gave once, her flowers to love, her ways to roam,
A body of England's breathing English air,
Washed by the waves, blest by suns of home.'

ii) 'What passing-bells for those who died as cattle?
Only the monstrous anger of the guns.
Only the stuttering rifles' rapid rattle
Can patter out their hasty orisons.
No mockeries for them from prayers or bells.
Nor any voice of mourning save the choirs, –
The shrill, demented choirs of wailing shells;
And bugles calling for them from sad shires.'

(From poems written by soldiers serving in the British army.)

a What is meant by
i) 'artillery barrage' (Source C)?
ii) 'dugout' (Source C)?

b Source B shows British soldiers capturing German rifles during the battle of the Somme. This proves that the author of Source A is wrong in his judgment. Do you agree with this conclusion? Explain your answer fully.

c Sources D (i) and D (ii) were written by soldiers who served in the British army. One of these soldiers died in 1915. Using all of the Sources to help you decide, which poem would you say was most likely to have been written by the soldier who died in 1915? Explain your answer fully.

d How reliable would you regard the following sources of evidence if you were preparing a report on life in the trenches on the Western Front?
i) poems written by soldiers who were there (as in Source D).
ii) accounts given by soldiers in the front line (as in Source C).

3/Russia from Empire to Soviet Union

Map 1 Russia in 1900

Russia at the beginning of the century

The Russian land and people

Russia is a huge country. But vast areas of Siberia were not inhabited in the early years of the century. The population was 133 millions. Eighty per cent of these were peasants. The peasants were becoming very discontented because they did not own the land on which they worked.

During the early years of the twentieth century Russian industry started to develop quite rapidly. Railways were built and the number of factories increased. Many peasants left their villages to work in the industrial towns. Living conditions for many were dreadful.

The two most important towns in Russia at the beginning of the century were Moscow and St. Petersburg. St. Petersburg was the capital. When the First World War started it was renamed Petrograd and then, after the revolution, Leningrad, its present-day name.

The Government

Russia was ruled by the Tsar (the Russian word for Emperor) of the Romanov royal family. He was an 'autocrat', that is he had complete control of the government. He could appoint and dismiss ministers as he pleased. The Tsar's power was strengthened by the belief that he was God's chosen ruler on earth.

In 1894 Nicholas II became Tsar. He was a weak rather than an evil man, too weak to manage the enormous problems from which Russia suffered during his reign.

In 1905 there was a revolution. This was partly caused because the incompetence of the government had led to Russia being defeated in a war with Japan (1904–5). The revolution was actually sparked off by the killing of hundreds of peaceful demonstrators in St. Petersburg. This was called, 'Bloody Sunday'. A revolution is a violent uprising of people to force a change of government. However, the revolution of 1905 did not bring many changes to

Russia. The Tsar had to agree to hold elections for a Duma (a parliament), but it was never allowed to have any real power.

By 1916 Nicholas and his wife Alexandra (the Tsarina) were becoming very unpopular. They were blamed for the sufferings of the country which we shall describe later. The Tsarina was especially unpopular because she was a foreigner, a German. At this time a strange holy-man named Rasputin had great influence over the Tsarina. This was another reason for her unpopularity. Rasputin had a very bad reputation and tried to become more powerful through her. He even arranged for the dismissal of many ministers and the appointment of quite incompetent ones. Rasputin's death was as strange as his life. Two noblemen plotted to kill him to save their country from his influence. They invited him to supper and gave him poisoned cakes and wine, yet these had no effect! More conspirators in an upstairs room kept playing and replaying a record of 'Yankee Doodle Dandy' while they were waiting. In desperation one of the nobles shot Rasputin. He appeared to be dead. But when they tried to move the body, Rasputin rose up and staggered out of the house. His body was later found in the river.

Two Russian workers at the turn of the century. Why do you think living conditions were so bad for working people?

The assassination of Alexander II in 1881

Opposition

Discontent with the Tsar's Government

Discontent with the system of government had been brewing for many years. Russia was very backward compared with west European countries like France and Britain. Different groups of people had different ideas about how to improve matters. Some decided to use violence. For example, in 1881, the Tsar Alexander II was murdered by a bomb. In 1911 the Tsar's chief minister, Stolypin, was also murdered despite the fact that he was introducing reforms.

The government reacted by using their secret police, the 'Okhrana', to track down and arrest people who were working against them. People who were arrested were sometimes sent to Siberia as a punishment.

In order to continue their work safe from arrest some people left Russia and settled in other countries. They organised political parties and printed newspapers that were smuggled into Russia.

Russia at the beginning of the century

THE THEORY OF COMMUNISM a) class conflict is the most important of all happenings throughout history

b) The final quarrel between social classes (below) is between the middle class (bourgeois-capitalists) and the working class (proletariat). This will break out as . .

A REVOLUTION – this breaks out in industrialised countries where there are a large number of working-people in the towns to rise up in revolt.

c) After the revolution, the party rules the country for a while on behalf of the working class. This government is called the dictatorship of the Proletariat.

d) When all opposition to the new government has been crushed, no government is needed because all people are treated fairly and are contented. "The State will wither away"

e) Then the Communist soceity comes into being. There are no different classes. All people are treated in the following way:

FROM EACH ACCORDING TO HIS ABILITY : TO EACH ACCORDING TO HIS NEEDS

Russia at the beginning of the century

The Communists

The most important of these groups were the people who believed that Karl Marx had shown the best way for progress. Marx was a German who lived much of his life in exile in Britain. He wrote some of his books and pamphlets in collaboration with his friend Engels. Their most famous was *The Communist Manifesto*. The last words of this are the following:

> Let the ruling classes tremble at a communist revolution. The proletarians have nothing to lose but their chains. They have a world to win.
>
> Working men of all countries, unite!

'Proletarians' are working-class people in the towns. Marx believed that these working people would become so unhappy that they would destroy the governments of their countries. Communism would then spread throughout the world.

It is not easy to explain communism in a few words. The cartoon may help. A phrase that explains part of what it stands for is 'From each according to his means, to each according to his needs'. There would be no different social classes and no great differences of wealth.

In 1903 the Russian Marxists quarrelled among themselves. The more powerful group was called the Bolsheviks. Its leader was a man who took the secret name of Lenin to escape from the Tsar's police. His real name was Vladimir Ilyich Ulyanov.

Effects of the First World War

By 1914, when the First World War started, the government was unpopular and many people were discontented with their standard of living. But as the war continued, the problems became far worse in the following ways:

1 More peasants moved into the towns as more and more weapons were made in the factories for fighting the war.

2 Prices rose very steeply. The price of food in the towns was a particular problem.

3 Millions of men and thousands of horses were drafted into the army. This had serious effects on the production of food on the farms.

4 The Russian armies suffered huge casualties. The soldiers therefore became very angry about the way the war was being managed.

5 In 1915 the Tsar took over as Commander-in-Chief of the Russian armies, so he came to be blamed personally for the defeats.

Nikita Khrushchev, prime minister of Russia in the 1960s, placing a wreath on the tomb of Karl Marx in Highgate cemetery, London

A queue for bread in Petrograd, 1917. Why do you think there was a shortage of food?

Revolution and civil war

The March Revolution

The events

By the end of 1916 to early 1917 the discontent in Russia was becoming very serious. Politicians in the Duma demanded that the Tsar introduce reforms. They wanted a new form of government. The working people of Petrograd went on strike and rioted, protesting especially about the price and scarcity of food.

The Tsar was completely incapable of dealing with these serious problems. In March 1917 discontented soldiers joined the rioters. The government had lost control. Twelve members of the Duma decided that they should take over. They forced the Tsar to abdicate. The revolution had occurred, but Russia's problems were, of course, by no means solved.

How did it happen?

Revolutions are very important events in History. Do you think it is possible for a revolution to happen without someone organising it very carefully? Historians disagree in their explanations for the revolution in Russia in March 1917. Here are three explanations:

1 The Empress and Rasputin were mainly responsible.
2 The First World War helped to bring the revolution about more quickly.
3 There was no obvious cause—the revolution was spontaneous.

Which cause do you think was most important—the royal government, the war or 'it just happened'?

Note: In 1917 Russia was still using an inaccurate calendar. By that calendar, the March Revolution occurred in February and the November Revolution in October.

Alexander Kerensky, leader of the provisional government, March-November 1917

The Provisional Government

Continuing problems

Members of the Duma organised themselves into a Provisional Government (a temporary government until a new system of government could be organised). Kerensky was the prime minister.

But they discovered that governing Russia was very difficult, for the following reasons:

1 The First World War was still being fought and was going very badly. Many soldiers were deserting.
2 Prices were still rising and food was becoming very short in the towns.
3 The peasants were becoming so discontented that they started to take over the land from the landlords.
4 In Petrograd a Council of Workers, Peasants and Soldiers was formed as an alternative government. This was known as the Petrograd Soviet. 'Soviet' is the Russian word for Council.

The arrival of Lenin

In the spring and summer of 1917 the Bolsheviks, the main Communist party, were not very strong inside Russia. Their leader, Lenin, was still in exile in Switzerland.

However, when the revolution broke out he arranged to travel back by train to Russia so that he could take control. In April he arrived at the Finland Station in Petrograd. A welcoming committee met him in the special room that had originally been set aside for the Tsar. An eyewitness wrote this description of the occasion:

'Lenin walked, or rather ran, into the "Tsar's Room" in a round hat, his faced chilled, and a luxurious bouquet in his arms.' A representative then gave a little speech of welcome. Lenin replied: 'Dear comrades, soldiers, sailors and workers, I am happy to greet in you the victorious Russian revolution. . . . The Russian revolution achieved by you has opened a new epoch. Long live the worldwide socialist revolution!' Then Lenin was carried on top of an armoured car away from the station in a triumphal procession.

Compare Lenin's speech with the last words of *Communist Manifesto* on page 29. They both show the belief that the Communist (or socialist) revolution would be *world-wide*.

Revolution and civil war

The November Revolution

The Bolsheviks organise

Lenin immediately set about plans to take over control of the government. An attempt in July was unsuccessful and he had to escape to Finland for fear of being arrested.

By the autumn, however, the Bolsheviks were very much more powerful:

1 Their promises of reforms made them popular.

2 Another great leader of the Bolsheviks, Trotsky, was chairman of the Petrograd Soviet.

3 Thousands of workers had been given weapons to form 'Red Guards'. The Provisional Government could not rely on the loyalty of the army.

The Bolsheviks take over

Trotsky carefully organised a new revolution. On 6 November important buildings like the telephone exchange and government offices were captured. There was little violence. The warship *Aurora* fired a few shells at the Winter Palace, the government headquarters. Similar uprisings were organised in other main towns. Within ten days the Bolsheviks had taken over from the Provisional Government.

The careful organisation of the Bolshevik revolution is clear from the following eye-witness account by the American newspaper correspondent, John Reed:

> Petrograd presented a curious spectacle in those days. In the factories the committee-rooms were filled with stacks of rifles, couriers came and went, the Red Guard drilled.... In all the barracks meetings every night, and all day long interminable hot arguments. Men literally out of themselves, living prodigies of sleeplessness and work—men unshaven, filthy, with burning eyes who drove with fixed purpose full speed on engines of exultation. So much they had to do, so much!

Lenin was the head of the new Bolshevik government. He took three most important actions:

1 He issued a decree giving the land to the peasants.

2 He declared that the war would be brought to an end at once.

3 He arranged elections for a Constituent Assembly (this is a kind of parliament for drawing up a constitution for a new system of government). But the Bolsheviks did not win a majority so Lenin stopped it meeting!

A Red Guard standing in front of the throne in the Winter palace. The title of this painting is 'The inevitable'. Do you think pictures like this are important as propaganda?

Lenin addressing a crowd. The man standing to the right of the platform is Leon Trotsky. In later years, after Trotsky had quarrelled with Stalin, this photograph was shown with the figure of Trotsky blotted out. Why do you think this was done?

Revolution and civil war

Civil war

Many people disliked or were afraid of the Bolsheviks:

1 The supporters of the Tsar who wanted the return of the royal government.

2 Other politicians who wanted at least a share in the government.

3 The rich people because their land was being taken from them.

4 The Allies. The First World War was still being fought in the West. In 1918 the Bolsheviks signed the peace Treaty of Brest-Litovsk to end the war with the Central Powers (see p. 12). The Allies thought that any other government in Russia would continue the war. The Allies were also frightened that, as Lenin forecast, Communist revolutions would break out in other countries.

Civil war therefore broke out in Russia and lasted until 1920. The Bolsheviks (or Communists as we shall now call them) controlled the central block of European Russia as shown on Map 2. The Red (Communist) Army was commanded by Trotsky. The anti-Communist, White armies had no central command and were therefore very inefficient. So, despite being attacked by so many armies and navies as you can see on the map, the Red Army eventually won. But during the war the Russian people suffered in the most horrible ways. Both sides committed cruel acts, disease spread and the disorganisation of farming led to hunger, and eventually, widespread starvation. At the start of these troubles, in 1918, the royal family were taken to Ekaterinburg, beyond the Ural Mountains, and shot.

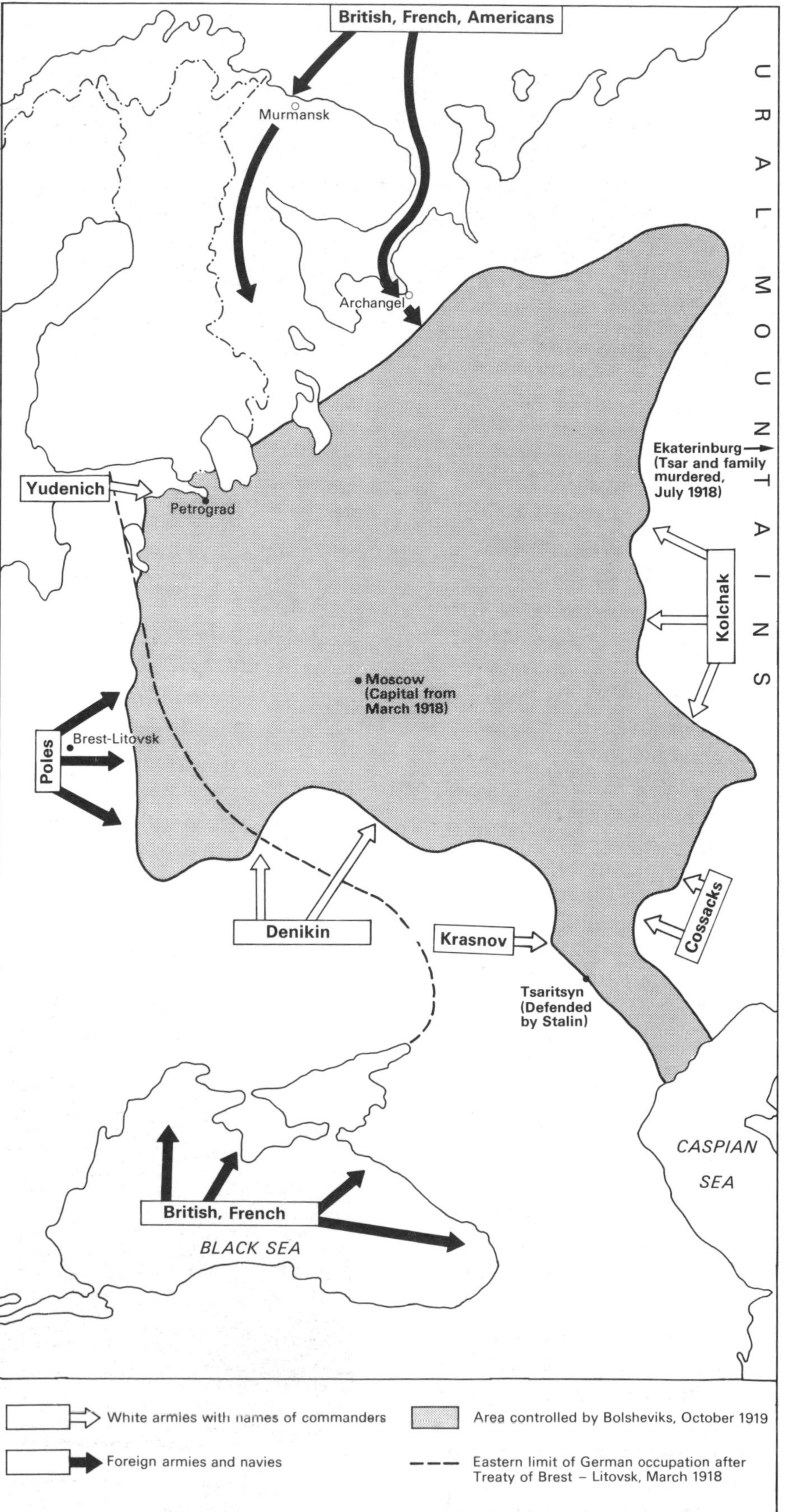

Map 2 The Russian Civil War

Trotsky (left) with Stalin (right) before Trotsky's disgrace

Lenin's government

Lenin now had to face the enormous task of governing a country devastated by war, civil war and famine. What is more, few Russian people supported the Communists, especially as they had taken over factories and confiscated food during the time of the civil war.

In order to keep the Communists in control of the country and to cope with all these huge problems, Lenin made three main changes:

1 He set up the New Economic Policy (N.E.P.). This allowed working people like peasants to make a profit by selling goods they produced themselves.

2 He turned the country into the Union of Soviet Socialist Republics (U.S.S.R.). The theory was that each of the provinces of this huge country would be semi-independent.

3 He set up a system of government as harsh as the Tsar's. A secret police force was organised, called the Cheka. By the early 1920s about one million people had become members of the Communist Party. It was these men who controlled the country.

Many people were disappointed that the Communist government had not brought a freer political system. In 1921 the sailors at the naval base of Kronstadt rose in rebellion demanding more freedom. The uprising was put down by force by Trotsky.

Some historians think that Lenin's undemocratic system was just an emergency. We do not know, however, if he intended to change this system of controlling the country because he died in 1924. But he is still very much revered in Russia today. People queue to see his embalmed body in its tomb in Red Square in Moscow.

There were two rivals for replacing Lenin as the head of the government: Trotsky, who had been so important in both the revolution and the civil war, and a man called Joseph Stalin, who was the General Secretary of the Communist Party. Stalin won because he controlled the party officials throughout the country. Trotsky was expelled from Russia in 1929.

Stakhanov. This coal-miner, with two assistants, succeeded in producing 102 tons of coal in a 5¾ hour shift and was used as a symbol of efficiency for the rest of the country

Stalin's character

Stalin was born in 1879. He ruled Russia from 1929, by which year he had defeated his rivals, until 1953, when he died. He is one of the most important men of the twentieth century. He was a dictator, that is he personally had complete control of the government.

Stalin was utterly ruthless in his governing of Russia. Many millions of people were sent to prison camps or died because of him. He worked very long hours in his rooms in the Kremlin, the headquarters of the government in Moscow. He was a secretive, lonely man, trusting no one. Although he terrified many people, he also tried to persuade the ordinary men and women of Russia that he was a kindly, all-powerful, almost god-like person. Artists and writers were encouraged to give that impression. Sympathisers outside Russia called him 'Uncle Joe'.

Industry

Compared with other main European countries Russia's industries were very backward. Also the years of war and civil war had caused much damage and disorganisation. Stalin decided that a huge effort must be made to develop the main, 'heavy' industries like steel. He was afraid that Russia might be attacked again, as she had been in the civil war, by countries who wanted to destroy Communism. Russia therefore had to be made strong and the way to be strong was to build up her industries.

Stalin decided to set targets for production in the form of Five-Year Plans. These involved vast increases. You can see from the diagram how ambitious they were.

Figure 2 Industrial production. Five Year Plans and actual figures

What other information can you gain from these figures? Were the plans generally successful? Which parts of the plan were most successful?

Try to imagine the changes that must have taken place in the industrial towns of Russia. Many more mines, factories, oil-refineries and generating stations had to be developed during the ten years 1928–38. Millions more workers were needed. In fact, during those ten years the proportion of the whole population living in towns increased from one-fifth to one-third.

Stalin

Stalin organised a great publicity campaign to persuade peasants to move to the towns and to encourage the workers to work extra hard. A man called Stakhanov devised a system for increasing coal-production. He became a hero. Other men who copied his example came to be called 'Stakhanovites'. You can see from the poster that Stalin looks very friendly. In fact, as we shall see later, millions of people suffered and died so that Russia could become a strong industrial country.

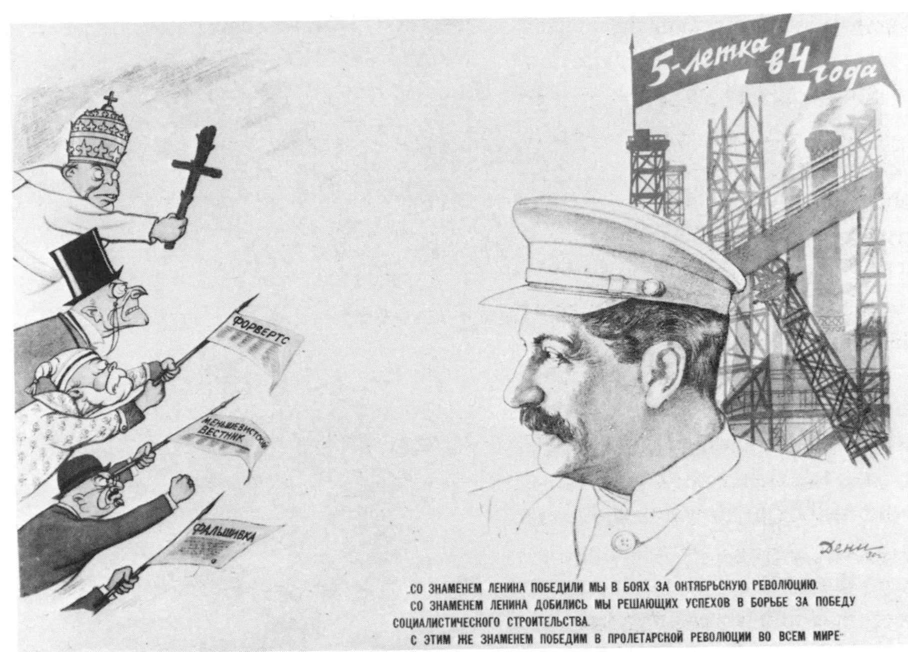

This is a poster showing that Stalin is achieving the Five-year Plan in four years in spite of foreign enemies and 'wreckers' inside the country. It was produced in 1930 and contains the following quotation from Stalin: 'With the banner of Lenin we achieved decisive successes in the struggle for the victory of socialist construction. With this same banner we shall conquer in the proletarian revolution throughout the world'

Agriculture

The problem

Russian farming was very backward indeed. Most of the peasants were extremely poor and used the most primitive methods to cultivate the land. Flails for threshing and even wooden ploughs were still widely used.

Yet Stalin urgently needed to increase the production of food. The first Five-Year Plan, as we have seen, needed a huge increase in the number of industrial workers. Food had to be available in the towns for them.

Stalin's solution

Stalin produced a scheme to solve all these problems. The small peasant plots would be joined together to form big 'collective' farms. These would have the following advantages:

1 They would be big enough to use modern methods of farming, including tractors.

2 A very large farm would need fewer peasants than the smaller plots separately. The surplus people could go to the towns to work in the factories.

The problem of the private plot. This cartoon from the Russian magazine Krokodil *shows how difficult it was to persuade the peasant to spend as much time and care on collective land as on his private plot.*

3 Communist Party officials could control the collectives through their organising committees.

The changes were introduced very quickly. The result was anger and chaos. The peasants were forced to give up their land, their animals, even their tools to the collective. And in return the government took an increasing proportion of the grain harvest! Many peasants managed to keep their own vegetable plots and worked harder on these than on the farm. Many also slaughtered their animals rather than give them up to the collective.

The following diagram shows the disastrous effect of collectivisation on Russian livestock:

Figure 4 The decrease in the numbers of Russian livestock between 1928 and 1933

However, Stalin's treatment of the majority, the poor peasants, was not nearly so harsh as the way he treated the richer peasants. These were called 'kulaks'. These farmers and their families were removed from their land—over four million people. Some were sent to labour camps, some to farm in Siberia. The majority died in the appalling conditions.

Stalin's 'Terror'

Labour camps

Lenin's secret police, the Cheka, was greatly increased in size and power by Stalin and renamed the O.G.P.U. (later N.K.V.D.). During Stalin's time hardly anyone felt safe. Individuals would disappear in the middle of the night. Whole groups of people, like the kulaks for example, would be set to build towns, factories or communications systems in the bitterly cold expanses of northern Russia and Siberia. Stalin was so determined to transform Russia into a modern industrial country and so determined to crush all opposition that no human sacrifice was too big. Many millions of people died of starvation, disease, exhaustion or exposure to the cold.

One of the most famous Russians to have survived the labour camps and to have written about them is Alexander Solzhenitsyn. The following extract from his short novel, *One Day in the Life of Ivan Denisovich*, will give you an idea of what conditions were like.

A scene from the film, One Day in the Life of Ivan Denisovich, *showing labour camp prisoners. Why do you think we could not find a real photograph of a scene from within the labour camp?*

As usual, at five o'clock that morning reveille was sounded by the blows of a hammer on a length of rail hanging near the staff quarters. The intermittent sound barely penetrated the window-panes on which the frost lay two inches thick....

[Shukhov] didn't get up. He lay there in his bunk on the top tier, his head buried in a blanket and a coat, his two feet stuffed into one sleeve, with the end tucked under, of his wadded jacket....

Shukhov remembered that this morning his fate hung in the balance: they wanted to shift the 104th from the building-shops to a new site, the 'Socialist Way of Life' settlement. It lay in open country covered with snow-drifts, and before anything else could be done there they would have to dig pits and put up posts and attach barbed wire to them. Wire themselves in, so that they couldn't run away. Only then would they start building.

There wouldn't be a warm corner for a whole month. Not a dog-kennel. And fires were out of the question. Where was the wood to come from?...

They sat in the cold mess-hall, most of them eating with their hats on, eating slowly, picking out putrid little fish from under the leaves of boiled black cabbage.

Elimination of political opponents

Stalin moved further and further away from the ideals of the revolution. He rid himself of all possible political opponents. Political leaders and ordinary party members and even generals were arrested. Many were executed, the rest were sent to the labour camps. In 1936 and 1937 great 'show trials' were held in Moscow. Leading members of the party (e.g. Zinoviev, Bukharin) confessed to the most incredible false charges of plotting against the government and Stalin. They had not been able to resist the persuasive methods of the N.K.V.D.! But Stalin's greatest enemy was still Trotsky. He was living in exile in Mexico. However, in 1940 one of Stalin's agents managed to enter his well-guarded house and smashed his skull with an ice-axe he had hidden in his coat pocket.

Foreign policy

One of the reasons that Stalin quarrelled with Trotsky was that Stalin wanted to concentrate on making Russia strong while Trotsky thought that Russia should concentrate on helping to spread Communism to other countries. An international organisation of Communist parties was set up—it was called the Comintern. Its headquarters was in Moscow. But Stalin did not help it very much.

Stalin did, however, help the Communists in Spain during the Spanish Civil War (see p.63).

By August 1939 Europe was on the brink of the Second World War. In order to protect Russia against a possible attack from Germany, a treaty was signed between the two countries (see p. 68). By this treaty it was arranged that Poland should be divided between Russia and Germany. This treaty lasted until 1941 when the Germans invaded Russia.

Map 3 Land gained by Russia, 1939–40

Russia also took control of the small Baltic countries and, after a short but fierce war, parts of Finland. As a result of acquiring these lands Russia regained much of the territory she lost after the First World War. These additions also meant that her western frontier was now further from Moscow.

Russia since 1945

The condition of Russia after the Second World War

Russia suffered more than any other country in the Second World War. Vast areas were fought over. Towns, villages, communications systems and farm animals were efficiently destroyed. Probably 20 million people were killed. Russia emerged from the war a poor, exhausted and shattered country. Also, as we shall see in Chapter 9, for many years after 1945 the Russian government devoted much of the country's resources to building up powerful armed forces. Compared with the countries of Western Europe, therefore, the standard of living remained very low.

Stalin's funeral. Beria (second from left) was chief of the secret police. He was executed not long afterwards. Malenkov, prime minister, 1953–55, is third from left; Bulganin, prime minister, 1955–58, is third from right.

Political control

Stalin's last years

Even in these dreadfully hard times, Stalin kept his terror system of secret police and labour camps. The chief of the secret police (by this time called M.V.D.) was Beria. Millions of men were sent to the labour camps—returning prisoners of war as well as those suspected of opposing Stalin. These men were used to develop the wastelands of Siberia and the Arctic.

'The Thaw'

Stalin died in 1953. The group of politicians who took over from him had Beria executed. From 1953 to 1964 the most important politician was Nikita Khrushchev. He was both prime minister and First Secretary of the Communist Party from 1958. He was a much more colourful personality than Stalin. He travelled more and tried to introduce a number of changes into Russia. At the Twentieth Congress of the Communist Party of the Soviet Union in 1956 Khrushchev made a speech attacking Stalin. As Stalin had been almost worshipped in his lifetime, this came as a great surprise. In particular Khrushchev denounced Stalin for being

Khrushchev at the United Nations. Here he is seen drawing attention to himself by pounding the desk with his fists. He seemed to be enjoying himself!

responsible for the misery and deaths caused by his police and labour camps system.
Khrushchev allowed a thaw to take off the chill of the icy terror. The number of people in camps was considerably reduced. The power of the M.V.D. was reduced. Censorship was relaxed. For example, Khrushchev allowed Solzhenitsyn's *One Day in the Life of Ivan Denisovich* (see p.36) to be published.

Continuing restrictions

Khrushchev fell from power in 1964 and was replaced as Party Secretary by Leonid Brezhnev and as prime

Leonid Brezhnev, who became both General Secretary of the Communist Party and President of the Supreme Soviet

Alexander Solzhenitsyn

minister by Alexei Kosygin. Brezhnev tried to prevent too much criticism from being published. Those who were complaining about the lack of freedom were called 'dissidents'. Some were placed in lunatic asylums on the grounds that they must be mad to criticise the Communist system! Some famous men, including the novelist, Solzhenitsyn, fled from Russia. Naturally, the newspapers (the main ones being *Pravda* and *Izvestia*) remained under government control.

People in Moscow reading Pravda, *the official Communist Party newspaper*

Changes in the Leadership in the 1980s

For several years before his death in 1982, Brezhnev suffered from ill-health. As a result, the government lacked firm leadership. And yet his two successors as General Secretary of the Party and President were both old, sick men, who quickly died in office. These were Yuri Andropov (1982–84) and Konstantin Chernenko (1984–85). But in 1985 a younger man (born in 1931) became

Mikhail Gorbachev, Soviet leader from 1985 to 1991

Party Secretary: this was Mikhail Gorbachev. His immediate policy was as follows:

1 To be more popular with and less remote from the ordinary people.
2 To replace inefficient men in important positions.
3 To reduce drunkenness, a widespread problem in Russia.
4 To seek better relations with the U.S.A. (see p.140).

The economy

Industry

By 1980 Russia was the equal of the U.S.A. in military strength. This was a remarkable achievement for

Russian industry considering the poverty and devastation of the country in 1945. But the people suffered for many years by having very few goods to buy. Factories were producing tanks rather than cars, for instance. Only in recent years have the Russian people been able to catch up with western Europe in enjoying such belongings as televisions, refrigerators, cars and good quality clothes.

Agriculture

Khrushchev tried to solve the problem of food supply by arranging for the cultivation of 'Virgin Lands' in Kazakhstan. It was a characteristically bold scheme, but it failed because the land was not suitable. In years of poor harvest Russia has had to continue to buy grain from abroad.

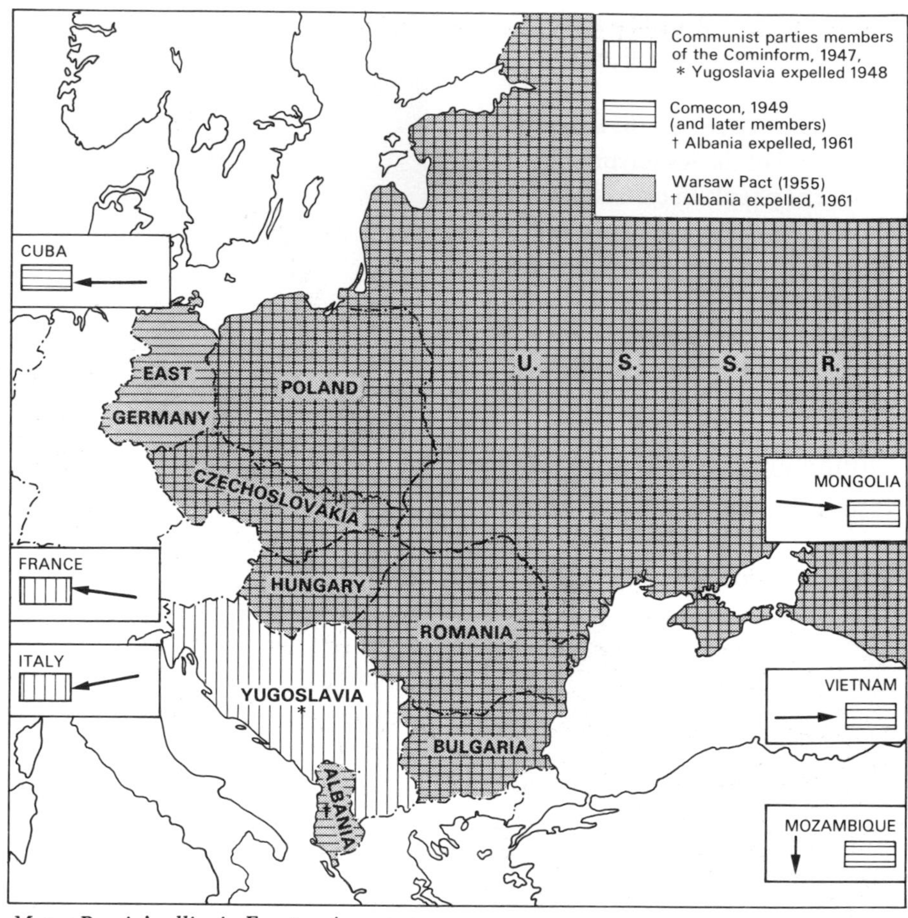

Map 4 Russia's allies in Europe, since 1945

Relations with the outside world

Eastern Europe

The countries of eastern Europe were kept closely connected with Russia in the following ways:

1 Cominform. The Communist parties of the various countries were connected through the Cominform from 1947 to 1956. Even after it was abolished, changes in the leadership of the east European countries were sometimes affected by Russia. For example, those closely associated with Stalin fell from power after Khrushchev's 'De-Stalinisation' campaign of 1956.

2 Comecon. This was set up in 1949 as a kind of Communist Common Market.

3 Warsaw Pact. Military alliance set up in 1955. Attempts by Hungary (1956) and Czechoslovakia (1968) to set up governments independent of Russia were put down by force (see p.136).

China

See Chapter 8

The Third World

Russia has given help to a number of revolutionary movements—e.g. 1950s—Egypt; 1960s—Vietnam, Cuba; 1970s—Angola, Ethiopia (see Chapters 9, 11, and 12).

U.S.A.

See Chapter 9.

Summary

Now that you have read this chapter, think about the following two questions.

1 The revolutions of 1917 aimed to free Russia from the autocracy of the Tsar. Was the tyranny of Stalin any different? You may have read George Orwell's *Animal Farm*. This 'fairy story', based on the Russian Revolution, shows how the pigs who led the farmyard revolution against the humans ended up looking exactly like humans!

2 By 1980 Russia was one of the most powerful countries of the world largely because of the changes introduced by Stalin. The standard of living of the ordinary Russian was much higher than it had ever been. By these standards the revolution had been a success. But there was little freedom as we know it in the West. Do you think the revolution was worth the cost in human lives and loss of freedom?

Time chart

Russia from Empire to Soviet Union

Questions

1 Study the statistics on Russia 1918–45 and then answer the questions below:

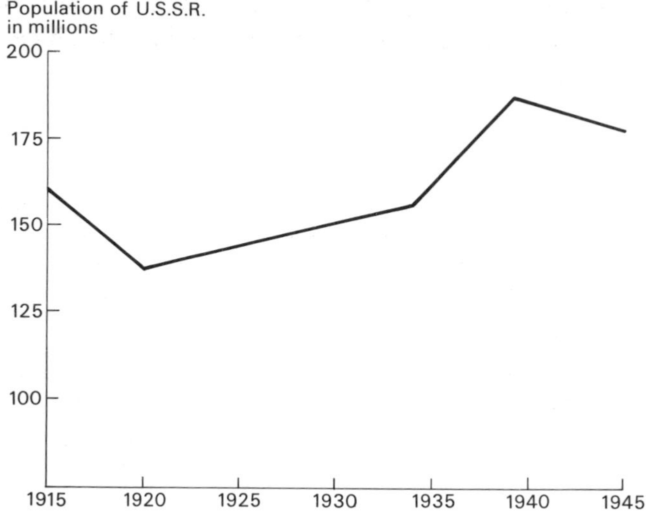

Number of farms:	
1928	24,000,000
1938	250,000

Number of animals in millions:	1928	1932	1934	1938
Horses	33	19	15	17
Cattle	70	40	33	63

Grain production in tons:

1928	74 million	1933	69 million
1938	75 million	1940	95 million

Industrial production in millions of tons:	1920	1928	1932	1938
Coal	9	35	64	132
Iron and Steel	0.3	8	12	32

a In which year between 1918 and 1945 was the population of Russia at its lowest?
b Give **one** reason why it continued to go down after 1918.
c In which year did it begin to go down again?
d Give **one** reason why.
e Explain why there was such a drastic fall in the number of farms in Russia between 1928 and 1938.
f Why was there such a great fall in the number of animals in Russia between 1928 and 1934?
g Name the Russian leader who introduced new agricultural policies between 1927 and 1932.
h When do you think these new policies began to show some improvement in Russia?
i Describe how the increase in industrial production was achieved between 1928 and 1938.

2 **Either:** Describe events in Russia between 1900 and 1917. You may find it useful to include in your answer:
a conditions in Russia in 1900,
b the war against Japan and the 1905 revolution,
c The First World War,
d the revolutions of 1917.
Or: Describe events in Russia between 1917 and 1928. You may find it useful to include in your answer:
a the revolutions of 1917,
b the Civil War,
c N.E.P. and Lenin's death,
d Stalin's struggle with Trotsky.

3 a What problems for Russia, between 1914–17, created a revolutionary situation?
b Describe the events of the year 1917 to show how the Bolsheviks gained power.
c Give reasons for the Bolsheviks' success up to the outbreak of the civil war.

4 a Who was the last Tsar of Russia? What happened at Ekaterinburg in 1918?
b Who led the procession on Bloody Sunday 1905? What name was assumed by Vladimir Ilyich Ulyanov?
c What was the name given to Tsarist Parliaments? What was the Cheka?
d Who headed the government overthrown by the Bolsheviks in October 1917? What happened to him?
e Which Tsarist adviser was murdered in 1916? How did Germany allow Lenin to return to Russia in 1917?

5 In a paragraph (10–20 lines) outline the chief reasons for the outbreak of revolution in *February* 1917.

6 Write an account of Lenin's work for Russia from the March revolution of 1917 to his death in 1924.

7 Write notes about **four** of the following:
a the Treaty of Brest-Litovsk (1917).
b the Civil War in Russia (1917–22).
c the power struggle that followed the death of Lenin.
d Stalin's introduction of collective farming.
e the Five Year Plans and the modernisation of Russian industry.
f Stalin's purges.

Questions

8 Look carefully at Sources A–C. Then answer the questions below.

Source A Reports from British refugees on conditions in Russia, October 1918.
'These people are unanimous in describing conditions as unbearable, owing to the rule of the Bolsheviks, as well as to the appalling economic conditions brought about by Lenin's regime.

'The Russian nation is groaning under the tyranny of the Bolsheviks. Workers and peasants are compelled to work under threat of death. Since only the Red Guards have weapons, a rising of the people is not possible.

'Famine is widespread. The peasants refuse to sell food but will only barter it. Unless people have about 1000 roubles (£100) a month they have to starve. It is possible to buy food from the Red Guards who are well fed. Lenin and his colleagues are living in luxury.'

Source B Instructions for Harvesting and Grain Requisitioning Detachments, August 1918.

'1 All Soviets of Workers' and Peasants' Deputies, all committees of the poor and all trade unions are to form detachments.
2 The tasks of the detachments are:
   a) Harvest winter grain in former landlord-owned estates.
   b) Harvest grain in front line areas.
   c) Harvest grain on the land of kulaks or rich people.
   d) Help in harvests everywhere.
3 Grain for the poor must be stored locally, the rest must be sent to grain collection centres.
4 Every food requisition detachment is to consist of not fewer than 75 men and two or three machine guns.'

Source C The Economy in 1913 and in 1921

Production	1913	1921
Coal (million tons)	2.9	9
Oil (million tons)	9.2	3.8
Pig Iron (million tons)	4.2	0.1
Steel (million tons)	4.3	0.2
Bricks (millions)	2.1	0.01
Agriculture (million tons of grain)	100	60

a What is meant by
   i) 'kulaks' (Source B, 2c)?
   ii) 'Soviets' (Source B,1)?

b What had happened between 1913 and 1921, apart from the Revolutions of 1917, to bring about the state of the Russian economy as revealed in Source C? Explain your answer briefly.

c i) Why was the Grain Requisitioning programme, described in Source B, issued?
   ii) In what ways does Extract B indicate that the Bolshevik Government had a number of difficulties in obtaining grain?

d What criticisms of Bolshevik rule are made in Source A? In what ways do the other sources support or contradict these criticisms?

4/Fascists and Nazis

Features of dictatorship:
The march—young 'blackshirts' parade past Mussolini

Censorship—burning banned books in Berlin

The rally—Hitler at Nuremberg

How did dictators come to power?

What is dictatorship?

We often complain about our government and our police force. But, by and large, we in Britain live in a very free and fair society. People who criticise the government do not have their books and articles censored. People are not imprisoned or tortured for demonstrating against the government. Regular, free elections are held so that the government can be changed if it is unpopular. Many countries in the world today do not enjoy these basic freedoms of democracy.

At the end of the First World War, the Allied leaders hoped very much that democracy would spread to most European countries. At first, it looked as though this would happen. But many countries had enormous difficulties. Democratically elected politicians seemed to spend more time arguing than solving the problems. Then, in each of several countries, one man with the support of a political party took complete control. We call such a man a 'dictator'. Often the people were so impatient with the other politicians, that they were quite happy that a leader was at last doing something positive. But when they later wanted to protest, it was too late: the dictator had stopped free elections, banned certain newspapers and created a powerful police force which he used like a private army.

European dictators

The most famous dictators in Europe in the 1930s and 1940s were Stalin (see Chapter 3), Mussolini and Hitler. But other countries had dictators too. For example, we shall see in Chapter 5 how General Franco became dictator of Spain. In some countries there were also unsuccessful attempts by politicians to become dictators. For example, there was a very small 'Blackshirt' party in Britain called the British Union of Fascists (B.U.F.), led by Sir Oswald Mosley.

General Franco, Dictator of Spain, 1936–75

Oswald Mosley, leader of the B.U.F., 1932–40

The popularity of dictators

In some countries the dictators were very popular. We shall see later in this chapter that many millions of people voted for Hitler. There were two main reasons for this.

Economic problems

People become badly discontented if they suddenly become poorer. This happens when prices rise more rapidly than wages, when savings drop in value or when people become unemployed.

As we shall see on p.49 savings in Germany in 1923 were made worthless by the collapse in the value of the mark. In Chapter 7 we shall see how Americans who owned stocks and shares were ruined by the 'Wall Street crash' of 1929.

In fact, the year 1929 marked the start of what became known as the Great Depression. In 1931 the largest Austrian bank announced that it would not be able to repay the money that people had invested. In America and Europe, firms very quickly went bankrupt, banks closed, international trade slowed down. And if there is no business, there are no jobs. Millions of people became unemployed. People became poor, some even starved. They therefore became angry with the governments who, they believed, had allowed all this to happen. The dictators promised to put things right.

National glory

The other reason for the popularity of men like Hitler and Mussolini was their promise to restore the pride and glory of their countries in the eyes of the world. But this led them to invade and occupy other countries. Gradually, a Second World War became more likely (see Chapter 5).

Mussolini and Fascism

Mussolini the man

The first of the European dictators was Benito Mussolini. He became dictator of Italy in 1922. Mussolini was a vain, boastful man. He once said to his mother, 'One day I shall astonish the world.' He spent his early years as a teacher, a wandering casual labourer, a soldier in the First World War and a journalist. In later years he liked to think of himself as an all-rounder—as a sportsman (he fenced, rode and swam), as a musician (he played the violin) and as a lover (he had many mistresses). He also had a certain air of authority and people came to have confidence in him.

Benito Mussolini, Dictator of Italy, 1922–43

Mussolini's seizure of power

In 1919 Mussolini formed the Fascist party. The word 'fascist' comes from the Latin word, 'fasces'. They were the bundles of rods and an axe carried in ancient Rome as symbols of authority. Mussolini used the fasces as his symbol to show that he was going to revive the glories of the ancient Roman empire.

In 1922 Mussolini and his Fascists took control of the government. This is how it happened. Italy had a series of weak governments. The latest resigned in October 1922. Thousands of Mussolini's followers were then organised for a 'March on Rome' (although Mussolini went by train!). There were also Fascist demonstrations in other towns, supported by the army. The king of Italy, Victor Emmanuel III, invited Mussolini to be prime minister. Soon, he had all the powers of a dictator.

The March on Rome of Mussolini's followers in 1922

The aims and achievements of Fascism

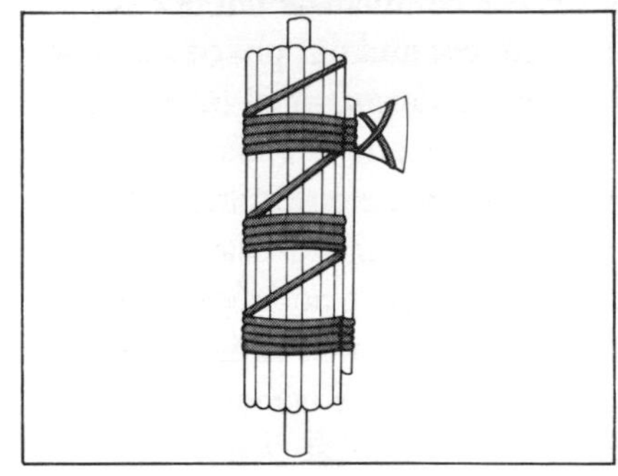

Figure 1 The fasces

Violence and discipline

Mussolini's followers wore a uniform of black shirts. Many were bullies by nature and beat up their opponents. One act of violence by the blackshirts shocked many people throughout the world. This was the murder in 1924 of Mussolini's most outspoken opponent, the Socialist politician, Matteotti. As he left his house one afternoon he was hustled into a car that drove off at high speed. Two months later his body, was found in a shallow grave some distance outside Rome. He had been stabbed to death.

Mussolini & Fascism

The corporative state

Yet much of Mussolini's popularity lay in his promise to bring discipline to Italy, a country that was in many ways in a chaotic condition. Also many people were afraid that the Communists might take over and preferred what Mussolini promised.

The basic idea of Fascism was that the government should control the whole of a person's life. Mussolini himself wrote that 'outside the state no human or spiritual values can exist'. The government took firm control over education, newspapers, trade unions, even sport. Newspapers were censored and opponents of the government were imprisoned.

Mussolini would not, of course, allow parliament or the trade unions to remain free of his control. The government came to be run by the Fascist Grand Council instead of the elected parliament. Also workers and professional people were forced to join corporations. These were controlled by the government and replaced the trade unions. This system was called 'the corporative state'.

At the head of it all was Mussolini who took the title of 'Duce' or Leader. There were slogans everywhere to persuade the people that the Fascist government benefited them. One of the most common said, 'Mussolini is always right.'

The Lateran Treaty

Many people who were unimpressed by Fascism were influenced by the Lateran Treaty, which Mussolini signed with Pope Pius XI in 1929. This recognised Roman Catholicism as the only official religion in Italy. But more importantly, Mussolini could now show that he was officially recognised by the Pope: he had become respectable!

Mussolini takes the salute at a meeting in Rome, where University students were sworn into the army. The words mean 'believe', 'obey' and 'fight'

The economy

Mussolini tried to take control of the economy just as he took control over the government. His main aim was to make Italy self-sufficient so that she would not have to rely on imports. These were some of the most important schemes:

1 Help was given to the really poor areas of Sicily and southern Italy.
2 The 'Battle for Grain' was a campaign that improved wheat production enormously.
3 The malaria-infested Pontine marshes near Rome were drained and put to good use.
4 Road and rail transport were improved. Some people sum up Mussolini's achievements by saying that he made the trains run on time!
5 The 'Battle for Births' was a campaign to increase the population of Italy by encouraging people to have more babies.

But much of what was done was for 'show' with no really solid improvement for the country.

The balance sheet of fascism

If you lived in Italy in about 1940 would you think that your country had on balance benefited or suffered from Fascism? Read through the following list and consider which you would put on the credit side and which on the debit.

1 Many countries copied the Italian Fascist movement. For example, the British Union of Fascists (see p.45), the German Nazis (see pp.52-56) and the Romanian Iron Guard.
2 Mussolini expanded the Italian empire especially in Africa (see pp. 62–3).
3 Italy was more efficiently run and more Italian people were better fed than in 1920.
4 Political freedom was crushed by police violence, imprisonment and even murdering of opponents, censorship of books and newspapers and the abolition of trade unions and parliament.

Hitler's rise to power

Adolf Hitler

Hitler's character

The most notorious of all the dictators was Adolf Hitler. Although he became dictator of Germany (from 1933 to 1945), he was, in fact, born in 1889 in Austria. He failed in his ambition to become an architect. However, he served bravely in the First World War. Then after the war, he became involved in politics with discontented demobilised soldiers.

Hitler was by no means an imposing figure to look at. He was of medium height and had a funny little black moustache. How then did he become so powerful? He had tremendous will-power, a most powerful personality, almost hypnotic eyes and a most fearful temper. Important men like generals or ministers would enter Hitler's room determined to make him change his mind; they would emerge either utterly convinced that they were wrong or frightened into quivering jellies!

Hitler had just as much power over huge crowds as over individuals. Otto Strasser bitterly disliked him. Nevertheless he recognised his brilliance as a speaker. When he spoke, so Strasser wrote:

> as the spirit moves him, he is promptly transformed into one of the greatest speakers of the century. Adolf Hitler enters a hall. He sniffs the air. For a minute he gropes, feels his way, senses the atmosphere. Suddenly he bursts forth. His words go like an arrow to their target, he touches each private wound on the raw, liberating the mass unconscious, expressing its innermost aspirations, telling it what it most wants to hear.

Crowds, sometimes of hundreds of thousands, would roar their support, rather like an excited football crowd when a particularly fine goal is scored. They would stand up and chant, 'Ein Reich, ein Volk, ein Führer!' that is, 'One state, one people, one leader!' Hitler took the title of 'Führer' or leader of his country. (Compare the title Mussolini gave himself.)

The weakness of the Weimar Republic

However, it took Hitler many years of planning and struggle before he became Führer. The system of government set up in Germany after the First World War was called the Weimar Republic. Its governments were weak and they had huge problems to cope with. The three most serious difficulties were these.

Inflation

This means the rise of prices and therefore a drop in the value of money. We have suffered from this problem in Britain in recent years—but not as disastrously as Germany in 1923. In 1921 the British pound sterling was worth 500 marks. By

Hitler's rise to power

A kite made from worthless German banknotes, 1923

the end of 1923 its value was 16,000,000,000,000 marks! There are many stories about how worthless German banknotes became. People had to take bags full of notes when they went shopping. A woman left a shopping basket heaped with money outside a shop and when she went to fetch it the basket had been stolen but the less valuable banknotes had been left behind! All this may sound amusing until you realise that people's savings were made utterly worthless in this way.

Unemployment

This was a particularly serious problem in the early 1930s. As you can see from Figure 2 the numbers shot up from 3 million in 1930 to about 6 million in 1932.

Lack of confidence in the government

The government seemed unable to cope. People tended to vote for other parties in the hope that they would make things better. One of the parties to benefit was Hitler's Nazi Party.

The success of the Nazis was due to the following:

1 The economic depression and discontent with the government of the Centre parties (see p.45).
2 Very careful organisation of the Nazi Party and tireless campaigning.
3 Fear of Communism, especially among businessmen. Many donated money to the Nazis.
4 They took advantage of the resentment felt for the terms of the Treaty of Versailles.

Look at Figure 2 again. Consider whether Hitler would have been so successful if the German people had been happier.

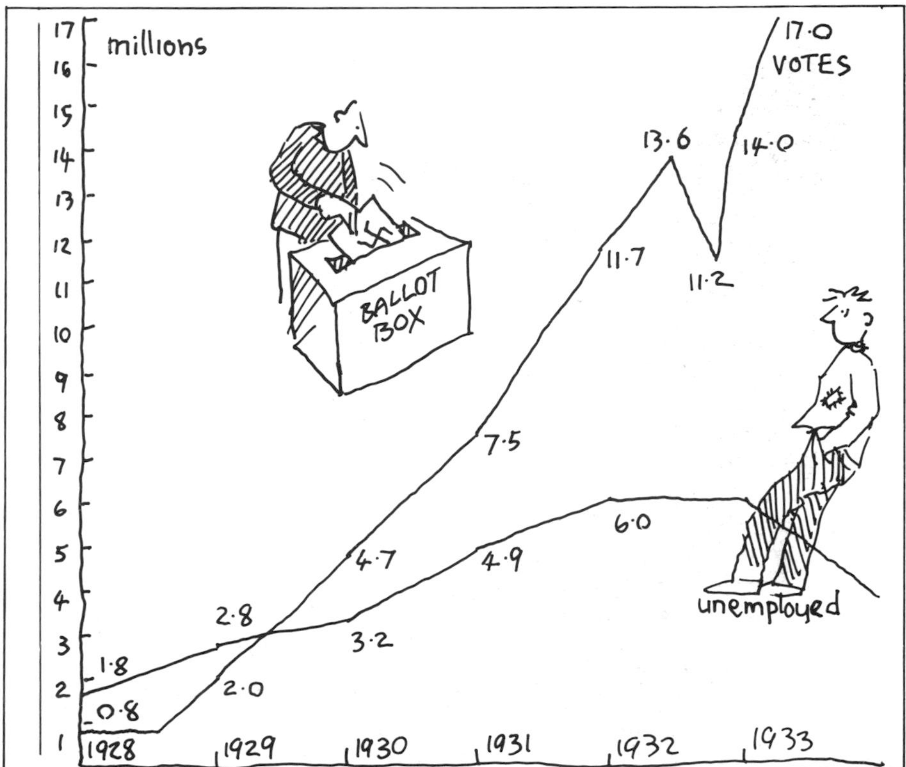

Figure 2 The relationship between unemployment and votes for the Nazis

Hitler's early struggle for power

The Munich putsch

The story of Hitler's rise to power really starts in 1923. By that year he had become a leading member of the small National Socialist German Workers Party (Nazi for short). Like the Italian Fascists they had their own private army of strong-arm men, the S.A. or 'Brownshirts'.

The main strength of the party was in Bavaria. In November 1923 Hitler and other Nazi leaders in Munich (the capital of Bavaria) organised a demonstration in an attempt to take over the government. The German word for such a violent seizing of power is 'putsch'. A rather pathetic group, carrying their new flag, marched from a beer-hall through the streets of Munich. They were quickly dispersed and the leaders, including Hitler, were arrested.

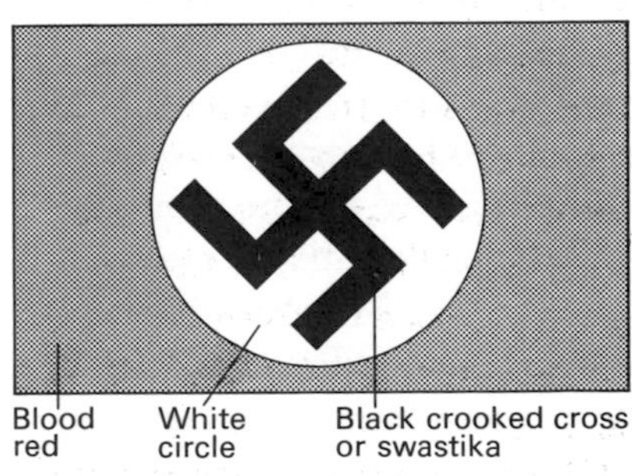

Figure 3 The Swastika flag

Hitler's rise to power

Mein Kampf

Hitler was imprisoned in Landsberg Castle. Here he wrote his book *Mein Kampf* (My Struggle). It is a long, rambling book about Germany, history, race, and is partly autobiographical. Here is a typical extract:

For myself and all other true National-Socialists there is only one doctrine: Nation and Fatherland.

What we have to fight for is security for the existence and increase of our race and our nation, nourishment of its children and purity of its blood, freedom and independence for the Fatherland, and that our nation may be able to ripen for the fulfilment of the mission appointed for them by the Creator of the Universe.

Strengthening of the party

The lesson Hitler learned from the failure of the Munich putsch was to proceed very carefully. From now on he would concentrate on the legal path to power—by strengthening the party in the country and increasing its number of seats in the Reichstag (the German parliament). You can see from Figure 2 how quickly the Nazis increased their power.

Hitler secures power, 1932–34

Hitler becomes Chancellor

As you can see from Figure 4 the Nazis were the largest single party in the Reichstag in November 1932, though they did not have a majority over all the other parties combined. Hitler demanded that he should be made Chancellor (that is, prime minister). Field Marshal von Hindenburg, the aged President, refused the suggestion with contempt. But the government of von Papen was weak with both the Communists and Nazis in opposition. A new Chancellor, von Schleicher, was appointed, but his government was no stronger. Eventually, on 30 January 1933 the President was forced to ask Hitler to be Chancellor. Cheering crowds thronged Berlin that night.

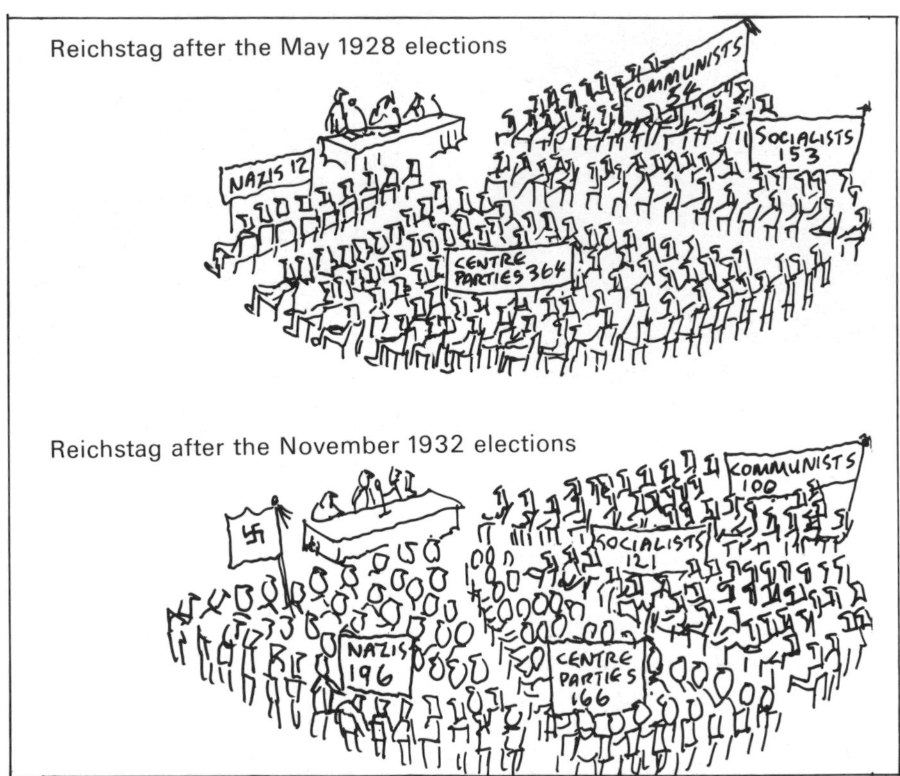

Figure 4 Nazi seats in the Reichstag

The Reichstag fire

The most serious immediate threat to Hitler was the strong Communist Party. On the night of 27 February 1933 the Reichstag building was gutted by fire. A young Dutch Communist, van der Lubbe, was arrested and found guilty of starting the blaze. The next month, elections were held and the Nazis secured a majority in the Reichstag by declaring the Communist Party illegal because of their supposed plots. But were the Communists really guilty? The fire and the arrest of van der Lubbe were so convenient to the Nazis that it has even been suggested that the Nazis set the building ablaze themselves in a scheme to discredit the Communists.

Field Marshal von Hindenburg, President of Germany, 1925–34

Hitler's rise to power

A parade of brownshirts (S.A.)

The Enabling Law

Hitler immediately made the Reichstag pass an 'Enabling Law' which gave him enormous powers. He had made a start to becoming dictator. He then used these powers to destroy the independence of the trade unions and make all other political parties, apart from the Nazis, illegal.

The Night of the Long Knives

But Hitler could not feel that he had complete control unless he had control of the army and the S.A. We saw on page 49 how the Nazi Party had organised its own private army of brownshirted 'Stormtroopers' (S.A.). By 1934 there were about two million of these men, commanded by Ernst Röhm. Hitler decided to destroy this threat to his personal power. He had already created his own black-shirted guard of S.S. (Schutz-Staffen). At 3 o'clock in the morning of 30 June members of the S.S. visited the S.A. leaders and shot them dead. Later, Hitler presented the murderers with ceremonial daggers as a reward for their bloodthirsty work on the 'night of the long knives'.

Hitler—Führer

The next month President Hindenburg died. Hitler immediately took over the powers of the president and took the title of Führer (Leader). He also required the army to take a new oath of allegiance:

> I will render unconditional obedience to the Führer, Adolf Hitler, Supreme Commander of the Armed Forces, and will be ready as a brave soldier to stake my life at any time for this oath.

Hitler was now complete dictator of Germany, now called the Third Reich (the first had been the Holy Roman Empire and the second, the Empire created by Bismarck). He boasted that, like the first, it would last for a thousand years.

Nazism in theory and practice

The theory of the Master Race

The basic ideas of Nazism were as follows:

1 Mankind is divided into different races, and some races are 'better' than others. The 'best' races are those that are 'pure' and have not inter-bred with others. In the past the best race was the 'Aryan' race and the present-day Germans are descended from the Aryans.

2 For the sake of human progress the Germans must keep themselves pure in order to become the 'Master Race'. The greatest danger to the purity of the Germans was inter-breeding with Jews.

3 The Slavs (that is, people like the Poles and Russians) are an inferior race. The Germans were too crowded in their own country. They needed extra 'living space' ('lebensraum'). This could be had by occupying countries like Russia and making the people there serve the Master Race. Compare this list with the short extract from *Mein Kampf* on p.50.

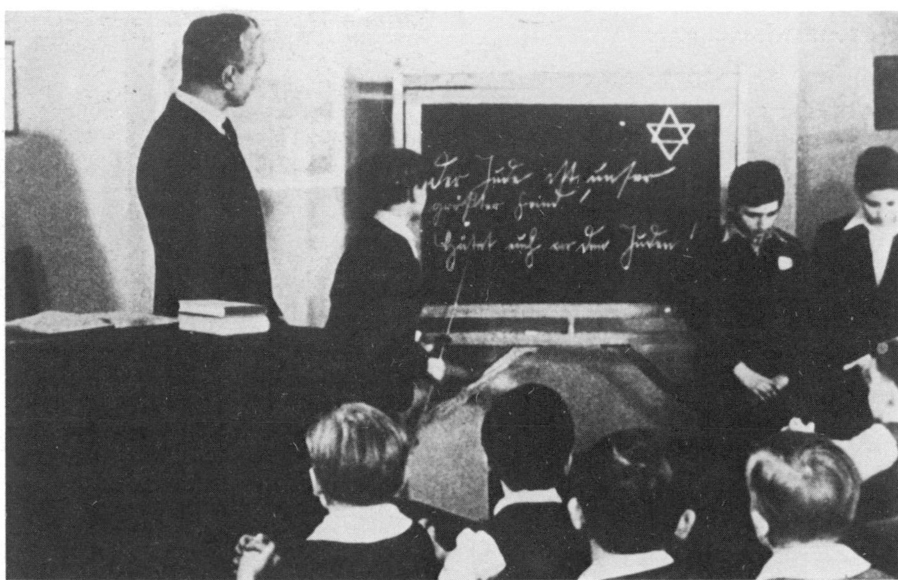

Two Jewish boys being taught that they belong to an inferior race

Jewish people being taken to a concentration camp

Anti-Semitism

There was no scientific evidence for these theories. Yet a most thorough and horrible campaign was organised against the Jews. Dislike or hatred of Jews is called anti-Semitism. Here are some of the main events in the steady build-up of the persecution of the Jews:

The two Nuremberg Laws, 1935

1 Reich Citizen Act: 'No Jew can be a Reich citizen. The right to vote on political questions is not extended to him and he may not be appointed to any office of State.'

2 Law for the Protection of German Blood and German Honour: 'Marriages between Jews and citizens of German or kindred blood are hereby forbidden.'

Many restrictions, 1933–39

For example, Jews were forbidden to practise many professions such as medicine and teaching. Their jewels and radios were confiscated.

'Kristallnacht' ('Crystal Night'), 1938

The windows of Jewish shops, homes and synagogues were smashed. There was much looting and destruction.

Concentration camps

Many Jews were sent to these camps, especially after the start of the Second World War. There most of them died from the work they were forced to do, or were murdered directly. Then, Jews were collected from all parts of German-occupied Europe and transported to the concentration camps for what was planned to be the 'Final Solution' of the Jewish problem—their total extermination. (see below for a description of these camps.)

A pile of bodies at the Belsen concentration camp

The Nazi system of control

Censorship

As early as 1933 bonfires were made of books whose authors or contents the Nazis disliked. Soon school textbooks were rewritten and newspapers were controlled.

The S.S. and Gestapo

Apart from Hitler the most feared man in Germany from 1936 to 1945 (and during the Second World War, in German-occupied Europe) was Heinrich Himmler. There were many police organisations in Germany. In 1936 Himmler was put in charge of them all with the grand title of Reichsführer S.S. and Chief of the German Police. The two most famous police organisations were the Gestapo and the S.S. The Gestapo were particularly feared as they hunted down anyone who opposed the Nazis. The S.S. had a number of duties including running the concentration camps.

Heinrich Himmler (left), with one of his senior officers in the SS, Reinhard Heydrich

The concentration camps

The most horrifying part of the history of Nazi Germany was the system of concentration camps. Any people the Nazis did not like were rounded up—beggars, gypsies, homosexuals, for example, as well as Jews. Without any trial they were imprisoned in concentration camps. By 1939 there were about 25,000 people in four camps. At first they were just harsh prisons. But by 1941 there were very many more. The most notorious concentration camps were Belsen and Dachau. Some camps were turned into extermination camps: people were sent there deliberately to be slaughtered. The camps became very efficient at this. Gas chambers and gas ovens were built for killing people and then for burning the bodies. The most notorious extermination camp was at Auschwitz in Poland, where 3 million people died. Here are descriptions of the gassing and cremation at Auschwitz:

With blows from different kinds of sticks they were forced to go in [to the gas chambers] and stay there, because when they realised they were going to their deaths they tried to come out again. Finally, they succeeded in locking the doors. One heard cries and shouts and they started to fight against each other, knocking on the walls. This went on for two minutes and then there was complete silence....
When the doors were opened a crowd of bodies fell out because they were compressed so much. They were quite contracted and it was almost impossible to separate one from the other.

Firewood was stacked between the bodies and when approximately 100 bodies were in the pit the wood was lighted with rags soaked in paraffin. When the flames had taken hold more bodies were piled on. The fat which collected in the bottom of the pits was put into the fire with buckets when it was raining to keep it alight.

But for many, death was a happy release after starvation to the point of cannibalism or torture to the point of insanity. The S.S. carefully collected the clothes, hair, gold rings and gold tooth-fillings of their victims.

Enthusiasm and support for Nazism

Hitler could not terrorise or kill everyone. He needed the support of the majority of the people. How did he achieve this?

Rallies

We have already seen (p.48) that Hitler was a very gifted speaker. He used this ability very skilfully to whip up mass enthusiasm for himself and his policies. Sometimes great rallies were held in huge open-air arenas; sometimes in large halls. The most famous arena of all was at Nuremberg. Always the events were very carefully arranged to produce an intense emotional effect. Look at the photograph on p.44 and read the following passage from the diary of an American radio correspondent and try to imagine the atmosphere.

The hall was a sea of brightly coloured flags. Even Hitler's arrival was made dramatic. The band stopped playing. There was a hush over the thirty thousand people packed in the hall. Then the band struck up the *Badenweiler March*, a very catchy tune, and used only, I'm told, when Hitler makes his entries. Hitler appeared in the back of the auditorium, and followed by his aides, Göring, Goebbels, Hess, Himmler, and the others, he strode slowly down the long centre aisle while thirty

A gathering of a group of German schoolboys belonging to the junior branch of the Hitler Youth

thousand hands were raised in salute. Then an immense symphony orchestra played Beethoven's *Egmont* Overture. Great Klieg lights played on the stage, where Hitler sat surrounded by a hundred party officials and officers of the army and navy. Behind them the 'blood flag', the one carried down the streets of Munich in the ill-fated putsch. Behind this, four or five hundred S.A. standards. . . .

In such an atmosphere no wonder, then, that every word dropped by Hitler seemed like an inspired Word from on high.

Youth movements

Many people have suggested that if the beliefs and loyalties of children and adolescents can be shaped in a particular way, they will keep these beliefs and loyalties when they grow up. Hitler certainly believed this.

In the 1930s a Hitler Youth movement was organised and eventually membership was made compulsory. They wore uniforms and were taught above all to love and obey Hitler. They also learnt practical outdoor skills. There was a special organisation for girls called the League of German Maidens.

Propaganda

Adults could not be controlled in quite the same way. They picked up information and ideas from newspapers, radio and the cinema. Hitler realised that it was vitally important to control these media. Hitler therefore appointed a Minister of Popular Enlightenment and Propaganda. (Propaganda is telling people what you want them to believe.) This man was Dr Joseph Goebbels—a short man with a limp. He was brilliant at his job. Soon newspapers, radio broadcasts and films were all telling the German people (and the rest of the world) how splendid the Nazis were! For example, the Olympic Games of 1936 were held in Berlin and were used quite deliberately as a massive propaganda exercise to show the world how prosperous and efficient Nazi Germany was.

Adolf Hitler in ſeiner hiſtoriſchen Rede im Reichstag:

„Auf allen Gebieten unſeres nationalen, politiſchen und wirtſchaftlichen Lebens iſt unſere Stellung gebeſſert worden. Ich konnte dies alles nur tun, weil ich mich nie als Diktator meines Volkes, ſondern ſtets nur als ſein Führer und damit als ſein Beauftragter gefühlt habe."

Darum am 29. März

Deine Stimme dem Führer!

A typical Nazi propaganda leaflet. This propaganda leaflet was produced to persuade people to vote for Hitler in 1936 to support his take-over of the Rhineland (see p. 61). Zeppelins were used as a publicity stunt in this campaign. The official result showed that nearly 100% of the people voted in support of Hitler!

The translation reads:

Adolf Hitler in his historic speech in the Reichstag:
'In all areas of our national, political and economic life there have been improvements.
I was only able to do all this because I have never felt myself to be the dictator of my people, but only its leader and therefore its representative.' Therefore on 29th March: Vote for the Fuhrer!

Joseph Goebbels, the Nazi propaganda minister

Hitler's achievements before 1939

We saw in Figure 2 that the popularity of the Nazi Party rose with the number of unemployed. It was clear that Hitler would not remain popular if he did not substantially reduce unemployment. Look at Figure 5 and you will see how successful he was.

How did Hitler manage this? Basically in two ways: by directing men into jobs and by the government organising production and building schemes. These were the main changes:

1 The creation of a National Labour Service. Millions of men were drafted into this to be organised for work (especially the kind of work in 3 below).

2 Conscription of men into the armed forces, which were considerably increased in size.

3 Improvements in agriculture and the building of motorways ('Autobahnen'), hospitals, schools.

4 The expansion of industry—e.g. synthetic oil and rubber; cars, including the famous Volkswagen 'Beetle'.

5 Armaments production was expanded for guns, tanks, aeroplanes, and warships.

Many people enjoyed a better standard of living; were happier as a result of these improvements in the economy; and were pleased that the chaos of the Weimar Republic was at an end. These were the people who could ignore the Gestapo, did not know that concentration camps existed, and were not worried that conscription and the build-up of armaments would mean war.

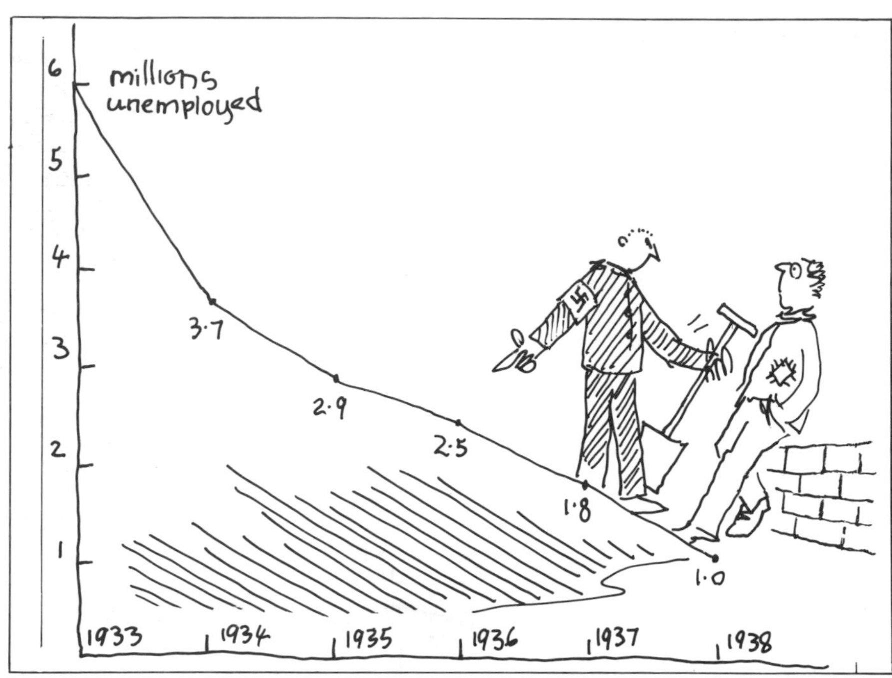

Figure 5 Hitler reduces unemployment

A parade of National Labour Service men

Time chart

Fascists and Nazis

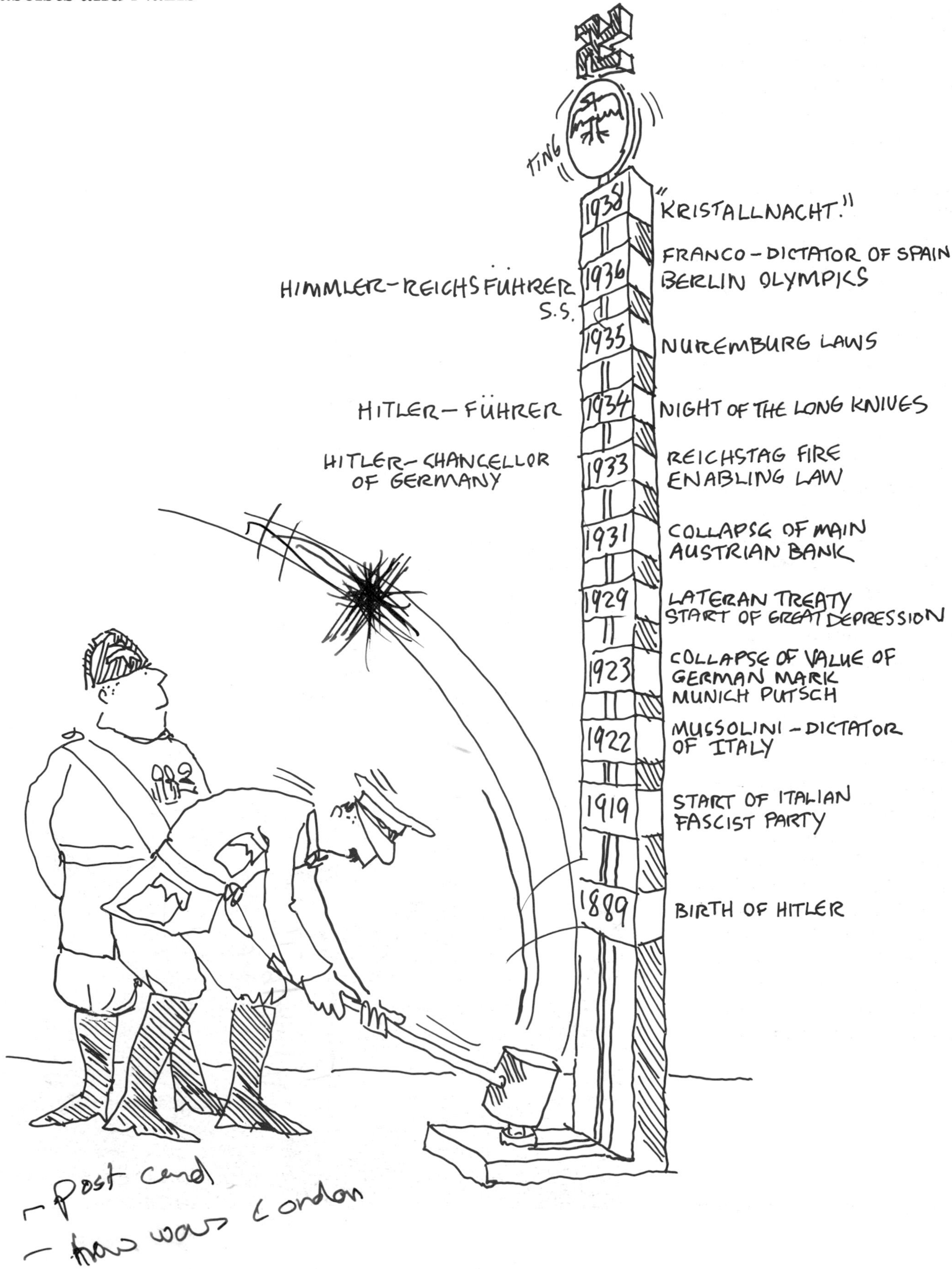

- TING
- 1938 — "KRISTALLNACHT."
- FRANCO – DICTATOR OF SPAIN
- 1936 — HIMMLER – REICHSFÜHRER S.S. — BERLIN OLYMPICS
- 1935 — NUREMBURG LAWS
- 1934 — HITLER – FÜHRER — NIGHT OF THE LONG KNIVES
- 1933 — HITLER – CHANCELLOR OF GERMANY — REICHSTAG FIRE, ENABLING LAW
- 1931 — COLLAPSE OF MAIN AUSTRIAN BANK
- 1929 — LATERAN TREATY, START OF GREAT DEPRESSION
- 1923 — COLLAPSE OF VALUE OF GERMAN MARK, MUNICH PUTSCH
- 1922 — MUSSOLINI – DICTATOR OF ITALY
- 1919 — START OF ITALIAN FASCIST PARTY
- 1889 — BIRTH OF HITLER

Questions

1 Study the statistics on Germany between the Wars and answer the questions which follow.

Unemployment in Germany, 1928–38

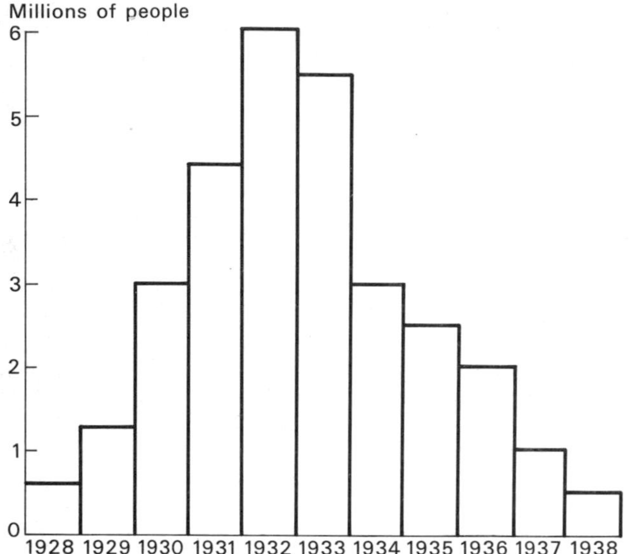

Size of parties in Reichstag

	1928	1932	1933
Nazi	12	196	233
Nationalist	60	51	53
Communists	54	100	81*
Centre Party	78	70	73
Socialists	153	121	121
Other parties	134	31	21

**Party declared illegal after election.*

a In which year did unemployment in Germany reach its peak?
b How many people were unemployed in this peak year?
c Give *one* important reason why unemployment rose so drastically after 1929.
d Which *two* political parties increased their representation during the worst years of the Depression?
e By how many millions had unemployment fallen in Germany between 1933 and 1938?
f Which political party was in power during the years 1933–38?
g Give *two* important reasons why the policy of this party helped to reduce unemployment.
h In which year did the Nazis first become the largest party in the Reichstag?
i Use the statistics to suggest *one* important reason why the Nazi party was not able to form the government in this year.
j Which political party was banned in March, 1933?
k Give *one* reason why this party was banned.
l Using the actual figures provided, show how the Nazis, in coalition with the Nationalists, were able to gain an overall majority after the 1933 election.
m Why were there no more elections in Germany after 1933?

2 Trace the stages by which Mussolini and the Fascists came to power in Italy, using the following headings.
a Mussolini's early life and career.
b The post-war situation in Italy.
c 1919 the foundation of the Fascist Party.
d 1922 The March on Rome.
e 1922–25 the establishment of the dictatorship.
Write a short paragraph to explain why Mussolini eventually fell from power in the early 1940s.

3 Write an account of events inside Germany from 1919 to 1935. You may find it useful to include in your answer:
a the formation of the Weimar Republic,
b the rise of Hitler,
c the Depression and Hitler's coming to power,
d how Hitler established Nazism in Germany.

4 Describe in detail Nazi rule in Germany 1933–39, using the following information as a guide.
The setting up of a totalitarian state—the Enabling Act;
The Night of the Long Knives;
The Gestapo—S.S.—concentration camps;
The Hitler Youth;
The Jews—Nuremberg Laws;
Economic Progress.

5 'As from today,' Hitler ordered on March 10th, 1933, 'the National Government holds executive power throughout Germany. Thus the remaining stages of the national revolution will be planned and directed from above. Where there is opposition to these orders ... this opposition must be smashed immediately.'
a (i) How had Hitler tried to influence the result of the March, 1933, election?
(ii) What was the result of the election for the Nazis?
b What did he do 'to smash the opposition'?
c How successful was he in 'planning the remaining stages of the national revolution' with regard to (i) education and youth, (ii) action against Jewish people, (iii) the economy.

Questions

6 Look carefully at Sources A–D and answer the questions below.

Source A

Source B

'The "seizure of power" by Herr Hitler's government is almost complete. Bavaria, Baden, Wurttemberg and Saxony are virtually governed by Nazi dictators or Reich commissioners with almost unlimited powers. The smaller states have been forcibly converted into Hitlerite *citadels*. In Prussia the council elections have gone in favour of the Nazi-Nationalist combination which now has a majority in most of the local administrations. In the great cities of the Rhineland the tide has turned against the centre and the left. The "purging" of the police and the civil service is still continuing, but this is no more than an incident in the swift advance of the government of the Reich to power over its states and citizens.

'Unfortunately the change has been accompanied by indiscriminate violence and persecution. The whole history of the Nazi movement made excesses probable and indeed inevitable.'
(The Times, March 1933)

Source C

'... on 14 July a new law destroyed the German people's democratic right to disagree openly with those who ruled them.

'"Law Against the New Formation of Parties
July 14, 1933

Article 1
The sole political party existing in Germany is the National Socialist German Workers' Party.

Article 2
Whoever shall undertake to maintain the organization of another party, or to found a new party, shall be punished with a sentence of hard labour of up to three years, or of prison between six months and three years, unless other regulations provide for heavier punishment"'.

Source D

THE GOOSE-STEP.
"GOOSEY GOOSEY GANDER,
WHITHER DOST THOU WANDER?"
"ONLY THROUGH THE RHINELAND—
PRAY EXCUSE MY BLUNDER!"

a (i) Who is the German politician climbing the stairs of the platform in Source A?
(ii) What name is given to the symbol on the flags and arm bands shown in Sources A and D?

b Why has the cartoonist shown a goose and referred to 'a goose step' in Source D?

c 'The Nazis feared little opposition inside Germany in the 1930's'. Is this view supported or contradicted by Sources A, B and C? Explain your answer.

d What are the disadvantages for the historian of Nazi Germany of the following sources:
(i) Photographs (as in Source A).
(ii) Newspaper reports (as in Source B).

5/The road to war

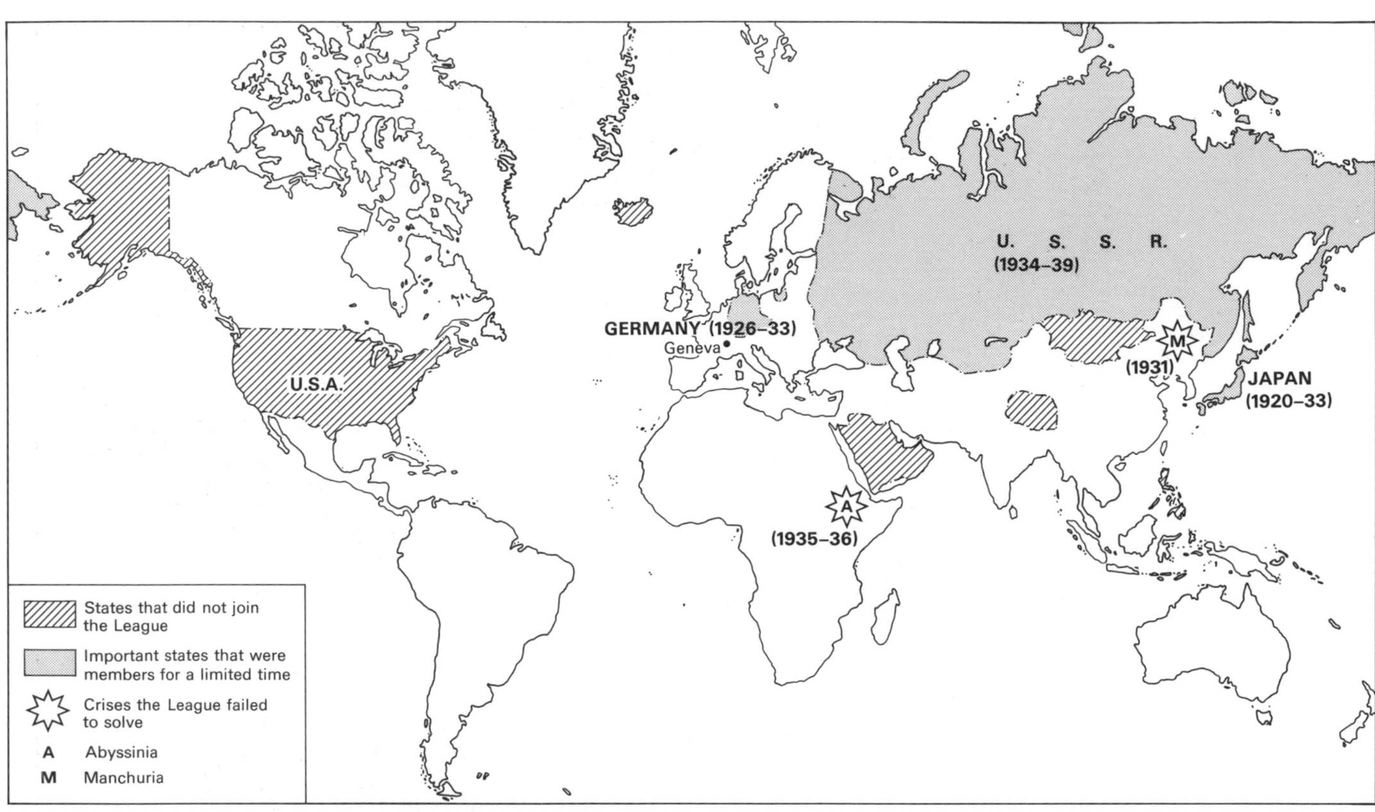

Map 1 The failure of the League of Nations

Attempts to keep the peace

The League of Nations

We saw on p.21 how the setting up of the League of Nations was part of the peace settlement at the end of the First World War. We also noticed that it was not a very strong organisation. You can see from Map 1 that the League was not supported by many of the most powerful countries. The U.S.A. was never a member; Germany and Russia joined late and left early. Only Britain and France really remained to try to keep the peace.

At first, in the 1920s, the League managed to settle some small quarrels (though it did nothing about Italy's attack on Corfu - see p.62). But, as we shall see later in this chapter, in the 1930s it proved to be quite powerless to stop a strong country conquering a weak one. The League could not stop Japan from taking over Manchuria nor Italy from taking Abyssinia.

Treaties

Britain, and more especially France, were very anxious not to be involved in another war. Why do you think this was? France was particularly frightened that Germany might attack her again. She therefore signed treaties with countries of eastern Europe. But the most important treaties for trying to keep the peace were:

1 The Treaty of Locarno, 1925. Germany and France promised not to attack each other.

2 The Kellogg-Briand Pact, 1928. The American and French foreign ministers persuaded most countries of the world to sign this agreement never to go to war.

The League of Nations in session in Geneva

Local wars in the 1930s

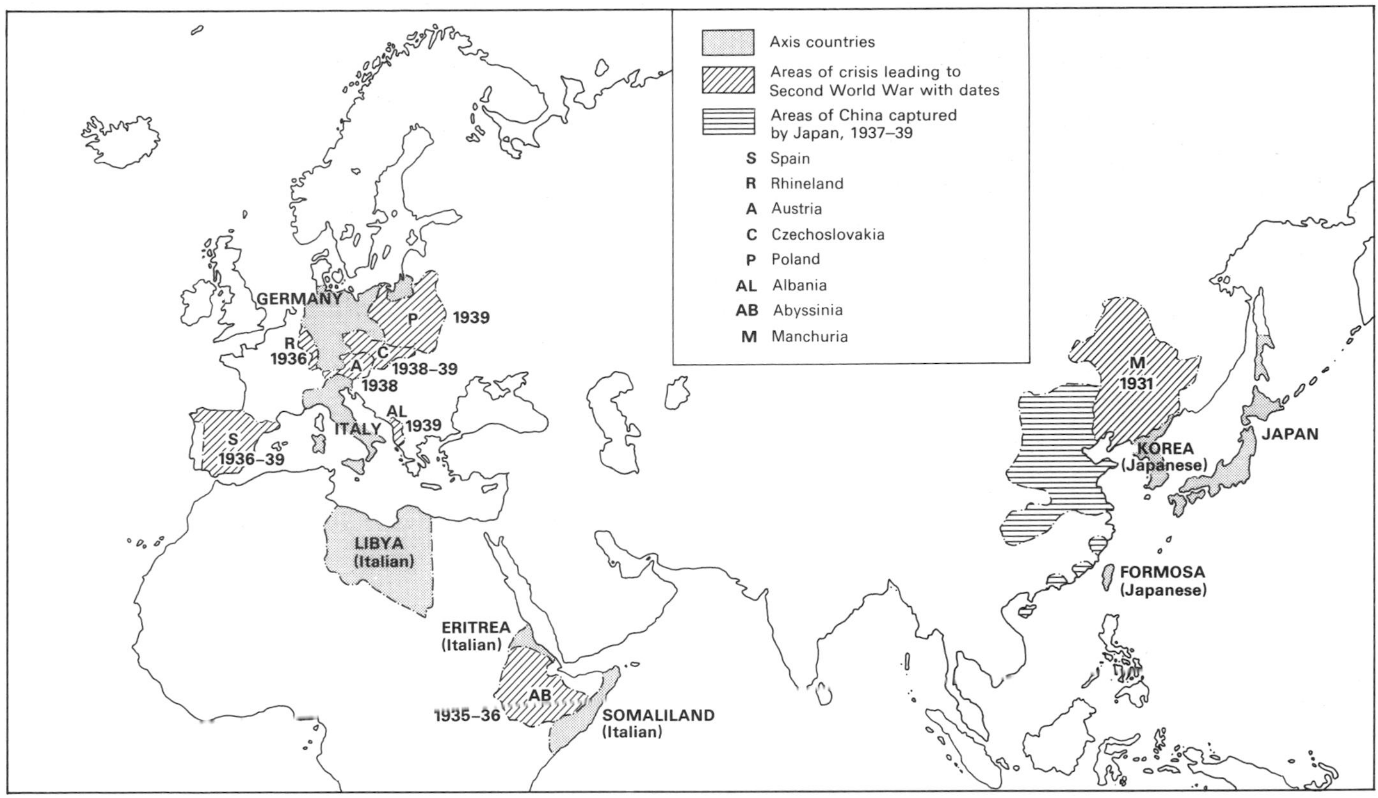

Map 2 Crises leading to the Second World War

The 1920s were comparatively peaceful. The world was recovering from the First World War. But throughout the 1930s there were a number of crises and wars, which eventually led to the outbreak of the Second World War. The most serious disturbers of the peace were Japan, Italy and Germany. You can see from Map 2 just how many local wars or conquests there were in the 1930s. The next section of this chapter deals with Germany. Here we shall describe the events involving mainly Japan, Italy and Spain.

Japan

Rise to power

In the later part of the nineteenth century Japan copied many Western ways and became a very powerful country. It came as a great surprise when she defeated Russia on both land (at Mukden) and at sea (Battle of Tsushima) in the war of 1904–5 (see p.26).

Japanese troops celebrate the capture of Peking, August 1937

Manchuria

In 1931 an explosion occurred in Mukden in Manchuria. This involved some Japanese railway property and they used the 'incident' as an excuse to invade this Chinese province. This attack was important and serious for several reasons:

1 The Japanese owned the railway and the Chinese were not keeping law and order in Manchuria. On the other hand, the Japanese had no right to capture the province. Yet the League protested in vain and was shown to be powerless. Japan left the League in 1933.

2 Japan was suffering from the world economic depression (see p.45). She was attempting to solve her problems by conquering other lands.

3 Manchuria was easily conquered and in 1932 was renamed Manchukuo. Because this was so easy the Japanese army was encouraged to attack and take over other countries during the following ten years.

War with China

In 1937 a shooting incident at the Marco Polo Bridge in Peking was used as an excuse for the Japanese army to invade China from their bases in Manchukuo. We shall see in Chapter 8 that the Chinese government at this time was very weak and involved in a civil war with the Communists. The Japanese were therefore soon able to capture large areas of north-eastern China as you can see from Map 3.

The Japanese announced a 'New Order' in the areas they captured. They promised a more efficient and just government than the corrupt Chinese officials had provided for their own people.

But it was the Japanese people who really benefited by becoming wealthier from these conquests. Large numbers of people were now, of course, employed in Japan making guns, tanks and aeroplanes for the wars. However, the Japanese army still needed to conquer other lands, especially to be sure of the vital supplies of rubber and oil. There were rich quantities of these in south-east Asia. The plan was to take over east and south-east Asia and the western Pacific and to make the whole area a 'Co-Prosperity Sphere'.

Map 3 The expansion of the Japanese Empire

Italy

Mussolini's ambitions

We saw in Chapter 4 what an ambitious man Mussolini was. He certainly was not going to be satisfied with ruling just Italy—especially as he dreamed of creating a new Roman Empire. Indeed, he boasted that he would turn the Mediterranean Sea into an Italian lake!

In 1922, as you can see from Map 4, Italy already had three colonies in Africa: Libya, Eritrea and Somaliland. In 1935–36 Mussolini added to his empire Abyssinia (also called Ethiopia) and in 1939, Albania.

Corfu

During the 1920s Italy was gradually gaining influence in Albania. This led to a quarrel with Greece. In 1923 the Italians bombarded the Greek island of Corfu because the Greeks refused to pay some money the Italians demanded. The Greeks were forced to pay.

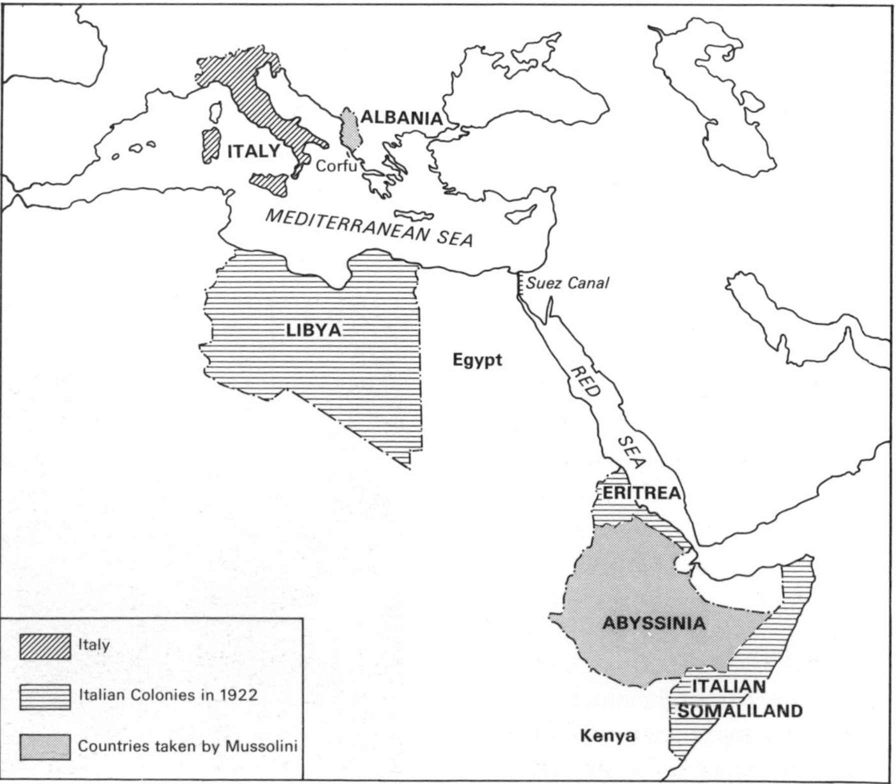

Map 4 The Italian Empire

Local wars in the 1930s

Emperor Haile Selassie of Abyssinia

The conquest of Abyssinia

The war in Abyssinia was very brutal. Tribesmen, often armed with no more than swords and spears, fought fiercely against Italian forces, armed with tanks, aeroplanes and poison gas. The Emperor of Abyssinia, Haile Selassie, went to Geneva to ask the League of Nations for help.

The League decided to impose 'sanctions'—that is, countries were asked not to trade with Italy. But it was all pathetically half-hearted:

1 The Suez Canal, a vital supply route from Italy to Abyssinia, remained open to the Italians.

2 No one stopped supplying Italy with oil. Yet without oil the Italian lorries, tanks and aeroplanes would have ground to a halt within a few days.

By early summer 1936 the Abyssinian resistance had collapsed.

The Axis

In 1936 Mussolini had a meeting with Hitler, the dictator of Germany. They agreed to work more closely together. This new friendship came to be called the Berlin-Rome Axis. They were soon co-operating in the Spanish Civil War. In 1940 the agreement was extended to a formal alliance. Japan also joined to make it a Three-Power Pact.

The Spanish Civil War

How did the war break out?

During the 1930s there was much confusion in Spain. Politicians quarrelled bitterly among themselves. Strikes and riots broke out. In 1936 a government of Socialists and Communists came to power. They were opposed by the Church, the rich people and the Spanish Fascists, called 'Falangists'. General Franco, who commanded an army in Morocco in North Africa, crossed over to Spain to overthrow the government by force. A civil war started between the Republicans (the government) and the Nationalists (followers of Franco). Other left-wing groups also fought against Franco. These included the Anarchists, who believed that government should interfere in people's lives as little as possible. The Civil War lasted for three years.

Why was the war internationally important?

The Spanish Civil War was important for three reasons:

1 Franco eventually won and became a dictator like Mussolini and Hitler. He was known by the title, 'Caudillo'.

2 The Russian government helped the Republicans and the Germans

The moment of death—a victim of the Spanish Civil War

Local wars in the 1930s

Picasso's 'Guernica'. This is one of the most famous paintings of the twentieth century to have been painted to give a political message. It shows the horror of modern war following the bombing by German aeroplanes of the Basque town of Guernica. Notice the symbols. The bull represents the brutality of the German airmen. The horse represents the savagely wounded land of Spain. The lamp represents the conscience of mankind. The torn bodies and agonised faces represent the horror of war

and Italians helped the Nationalists. This help was partly to support friends. But the war was also an opportunity for these countries to try out new weapons, especially aeroplanes, in real combat conditions. The most notorious example was the destruction of the town of Guernica by German bombers. The Spanish Civil War became something like a dress-rehearsal for the Second World War.

3 There were strong sympathies in different countries for each of the two sides. Some quite famous people went to fight on the side of the Republicans and wrote about their experiences. One of the most famous books is George Orwell's *Homage to Catalonia*. What do these two extracts tell you about the War?

. . . the aspect of Barcelona was something startling and overwhelming. It was the first time that I had ever been in a town where the working class was in the saddle. Practically every building of any size had been seized by the workers and was draped with red flags or with the red and black flag of the Anarchists. . . . Churches here and there were being systematically demolished by gangs of workmen. Every shop and café had an inscription saying that it had been collectivized. . . . Tipping was forbidden by law. . . . There were no private motor cars, they had all been commandeered.

The war was fought at a low technical level and its major strategy was very simple. That side which had arms would win. The Nazis and the Italians gave arms to the Spanish Fascist friends, and the western democracies and the Russians didn't give arms to those who should have been their friends. So the Spanish Republic perished.

A mother hurries her child to shelter as another air raid strikes Madrid

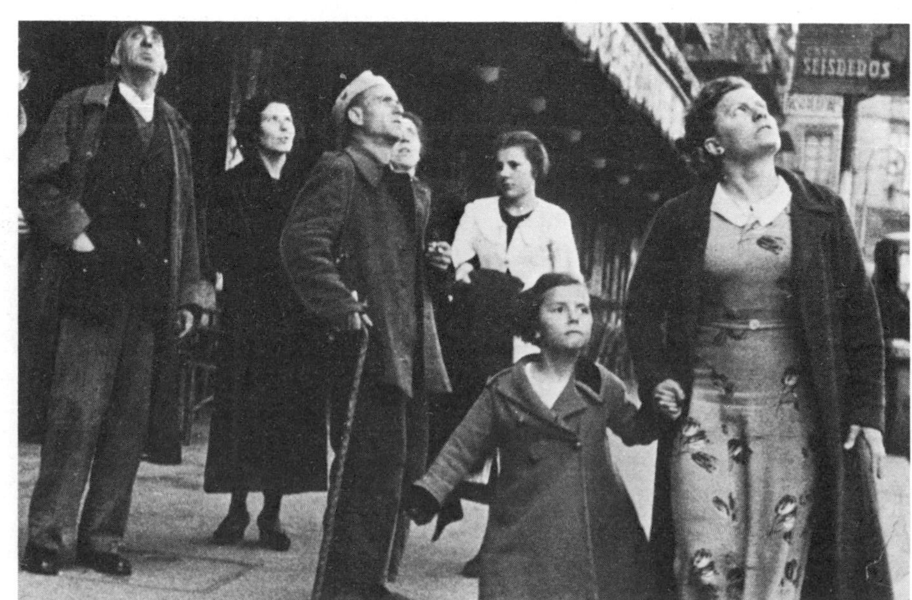

Hitler's policy of expansion

How Hitler set about undoing the Versailles Treaty

Reoccupation of the Rhineland

One of the reasons why Hitler became so popular in Germany was that he promised to undo the terms of the Versailles settlement which many people thought were unjust (although reparations payments had been almost totally discontinued from 1931).

His first very obvious step in this direction occurred in March 1936. On pp.19–20 we noted that one of the terms of the Versailles settlement was that no German soldiers should be stationed in the Rhineland. You can see this area shaded on Map 5. This arrangement was to prevent another sudden invasion of Belgium and France. Hitler now ordered troops to march into that area. It was a typical Hitler action:

1 He claimed that it was unreasonable for a country not to be allowed to station its soldiers where it wished.

2 The action broke not only the Versailles Treaty but the Locarno Treaty (see p. 60) as well.

3 The show of power—of soldiers marching across the river—was a bluff. Hitler had only a very small army ready for fighting.

4 But France merely protested. In any case, the British were not willing to help the French if they had declared war.

It has often been said since that the failure of France and Britain to stand up to Hitler in 1936 was a fatal mistake. Hitler learned that he could get away with breaking international law, even when his forces were weak. When they were stronger, France and Britain were even less prepared to risk war. You should keep this in mind while reading the rest of this chapter.

Map 5 The expansion of Germany, 1936–39

German troops marching over the Rhine, 1936

Hitler's policy of expansion

Austria

The people of Austria speak German just as the people of Germany do. In Chapter 2 we saw that frontiers were redrawn after the First World War so that as far as possible people of the same nationality should be in the same country. But the German peoples of Germany and Austria were forbidden to unite. The German word for such a joining together was 'Anschluss'. Hitler was personally especially keen on this because he was Austrian by birth himself.

By 1934 an Austrian Nazi party had become quite powerful. In that year they murdered the Chancellor (prime minister), Dolfuss, but were unable to take over power.

However, in 1938 Hitler felt strong enough to interfere. In February, he summoned the Austrian Chancellor, Schuschnigg, to Berlin. Hitler bullied him into agreeing to include Austrian Nazis in his government. The next month Schuschnigg tried to organise a vote of all the Austrian people to show that they wanted to stay independent of Germany. Hitler threatened to invade Austria if the voting went ahead. It was cancelled. Hitler ordered the invasion in any case! There was no resistance. The Anschluss was announced the next day.

Hitler's entry into Vienna, the capital of Austria, 1938

Czechoslovakia

Look at Map 5 again. You can see that, with the Anschluss, Czechoslovakia found its head inside the jaws of surrounding German land. Hitler now turned his attention to taking over this country. It proved to be a complicated and very important matter so that we shall need to describe the events in some detail.

The different peoples of Czechoslovakia

We saw in Chapter 2 how Czechoslovakia was created as a separate country at the end of the First World War. It was, in fact, a country of several nationalities. The German-speaking areas round the north-western and south-western rim were called the Sudetenland. A Nazi-type party was organised there by a man called Konrad Henlein. These Sudeten Germans complained about their treatment by the Czech government in the capital, Prague.

How did the Sudetenland become an international problem?

Throughout the spring and summer of 1938 demonstrations took place in the Sudetenland. Hitler made speeches supporting the Sudeten Germans against the Czechs. By September it looked as though Hitler might invade Czechoslovakia 'to protect' the Sudeten Germans.

The British and French governments became very worried. They felt that they should protect Czechoslovakia, yet they did not want to risk war. The British prime minister, Neville Chamberlain, flew to Germany twice in one week to discuss with Hitler possible peaceful solutions to the problem. (One of these meetings was at Hitler's private house at Berchtesgaden).

Meanwhile, preparations were made for war. The two meetings were failures. Chamberlain talked on the wireless to the people of Britain. He said:

> How horrible, fantastic, incredible it is that we should be digging trenches [that is for air-raid shelters] and trying on gas masks here because of a quarrel in a far-away country between people of whom we know nothing.

The phrase 'a far-away country ... of whom we know nothing' has since been used to criticise Chamberlain. When you have finished reading this chapter, ask yourself whether he was selfish, short-sighted or sensible.

Hitler's policy of expansion

The chief negotiators at Munich: Chamberlain, Daladier (French prime minister), Hitler, Mussolini, Ciano (Italian foreign minister).

The Munich Conference

Then, on 29–30 September, Mussolini had a brief moment of glory. He called a meeting of the German, British and French leaders with himself, at Munich in southern Germany. At that meeting, to which the Czech prime minister was not even invited, the four men agreed to let Germany have the Sudetenland. In return, Hitler gave only vague promises of making no more trouble.

Neville Chamberlain flew back to London and at the airport showed the piece of paper that he and Hitler had signed, as a separate agreement, at Munich. It referred to 'the desire of our two peoples never to go to war with one another again.' That evening, when he arrived back at 10 Downing Street, Chamberlain made a short speech to the welcoming crowd. He announced that he had brought back 'peace with honour. . . . I believe it is peace for our time.' The most determined opponent of Hitler in the British parliament was Winston Churchill. He disagreed with the prime minister's views of the Munich agreement. In a speech in the House of Commons, he said, 'All is over. Silent, mournful, abandoned, broken Czechoslovakia recedes into the darkness. . . . We are in the presence of a disaster of the first magnitude which has befallen Great Britain and France. Do not let us blind ourselves to that.'

Chamberlain arrives back from Munich with the peace agreement signed by Hitler

How was Czechoslovakia finally destroyed?

So Germany took over the Sudetenland. Then Hungary and Poland took other pieces of Czechoslovakia, as you can see from Map 5. In March 1939 the remaining provinces of Slovakia and (Czech) Bohemia-Moravia split. Bohemia-Moravia was taken over by Germany. Slovakia placed itself 'under the protection' of Germany. Czechoslovakia was no more.

Hitler's policy of expansion

Poland

How Britain and France guaranteed the safety of Poland

It was now obvious that Hitler was going to continue to take more land. Because the 'Polish corridor' and the free city of Danzig separated East Prussia from the rest of Germany, it was clear that Poland would be his next victim. The British and French governments therefore declared that they would protect Poland if attacked.

The German-Soviet Pact

But the problem was, how were British and French soldiers to get to Poland? The obvious extra ally was Russia, Poland's next-door neighbour. But the British, French and Polish governments hated Communism and thought that the Russian army was too weak to help in any case (see p.37). Then, in August 1939, to everyone's amazement, the foreign ministers of Germany and Russia (Ribbentrop and Molotov) signed a non-aggression pact. (The pact was surprising because Hitler had been so bitter in his comments about Communism and so determined about his plans for 'lebensraum' for the Master Race in Russia.) The two countries promised not to fight each other. They also agreed to share Poland between them at some future date (see p.37).

How the Second World War started

At 4.45 a.m. on 1 September German forces invaded Poland. The British and French governments demanded their withdrawal. The demand was ignored. And so, at 11.15 a.m. on Sunday morning, 3 September 1939, Mr Chamberlain broadcast to the British nation:

> This morning the British Ambassador in Berlin handed the German Government a final note stating that unless we heard from them by eleven o'clock that they were prepared at once to withdraw their troops from Poland, a state of war would exist between us. I have to tell you now that no such undertaking has been received and that consequently this country is at war with Germany.

The French declared war the same evening.

THE SCUM OF THE EARTH, I BELIEVE ?
THE BLOODY ASSASSIN OF THE WORKERS, I PRESUME ?

This British cartoon shows how Hitler and Stalin, who hated each other, agreed to partition Poland, whose body lies between them

On the eve of war. The British public reads about the German invasion of Poland

Who was responsible?

Appeasement

Was appeasement a good policy?

The policy of Neville Chamberlain and those, including the French government, who supported him was called 'appeasement'. The idea was that Hitler had certain reasonable demands and that if people gave in to him, he would eventually be satisfied and a general war would be avoided. In any case, it was believed by many that the British and French people would not be willing to fight another war; nor were their armed forces prepared. Those, like Winston Churchill, who opposed appeasement, thought that Hitler was anything but a reasonable man and that, like any other bully, the sooner people stood up to him the better.

How strong was Germany?

As soon as Hitler had secured full power in Germany in 1934 he set about building up powerful armed forces (see p.56). This was, of course, in complete defiance of the Versailles settlement (see p.19). This rapid increase in the size of the 'Wehrmacht' (the German army) particularly worried France. The creation of the 'Luftwaffe' (the German airforce) particularly worried Britain. The Luftwaffe was developed by one of Hitler's closest supporters, Hermann Goering. He had been a fighter-pilot ace during the First World War, but had since become very fat and pleasure-loving.

Reichsmarschall Hermann Goering

The French put their faith in a strategy of defence. A powerful defensive system called the Maginot Line was built along the frontier with Germany. The British gradually built up their squadrons of fighter aircraft and an early warning radar system. But many people were terrified of the likely effects of air-raids on cities and towns. As early as 1932, the British prime minister, Baldwin, had said, 'The bomber will always get through.' The success of the Luftwaffe in the Spanish Civil War, as we saw on p.64, and especially the destruction of Guernica seemed to confirm these fears.

In fact, estimates made at the time exaggerated the strength of the German forces, even as late as 1938. Even so, the figures in the table show that people were right to be afraid of German power, especially if Russia was not to be an ally of Britain and France.

What were Hitler's aims?

Hitler ignored protests from other countries. He built up strong armed forces. Does this mean that he deliberately planned the Second World War? This has been a matter of sharp disagreement among historians. The problem is, how can we know what really went on in Hitler's mind?

The argument can be clearly illustrated by quotations from two British historians, Mr A. J. P. Taylor and Professor Hugh Trevor-Roper. Who do you think is nearer the truth?

> In principle and doctrine, Hitler was no more wicked and unscrupulous than many other contemporary statesmen. The state of German rearmament in 1939 gives the decisive proof that Hitler was not contemplating general war, and probably not contemplating war at all. The war of 1939, far from being premeditated, was a mistake, the result on both sides of diplomatic blunders.

> Let us consider briefly the programme which Hitler laid down for himself. It was a programme of Eastern colonisation, entailing a war of conquest against Russia.... In order to carry it out, Hitler needed a restored German army which, since it must be powerful enough to conquer Russia, must also be powerful enough to conquer the West if that should be necessary. And that might be necessary even before the attack on Russia ... it was always possible that a war with the West would be necessary before he could march against Russia. And in fact that is what happened.

Figure 1 Armed forces, 1938–39

	U.S.S.R	U.K.	FRANCE	ITALY	GERMANY
AIRCRAFT 1938	3,050	1,053	1,195	1,301	1,820
AIRCRAFT 1939	3,361	1,750	1,234	1,531	4,210
DIVISIONS 1938	125	2	63	73	81
DIVISIONS 1939	125	4	86	73	125
BATTLESHIPS 1939	3	15	7	4	5
SUBMARINES 1939	18	57	78	105	65

Time chart

The road to war

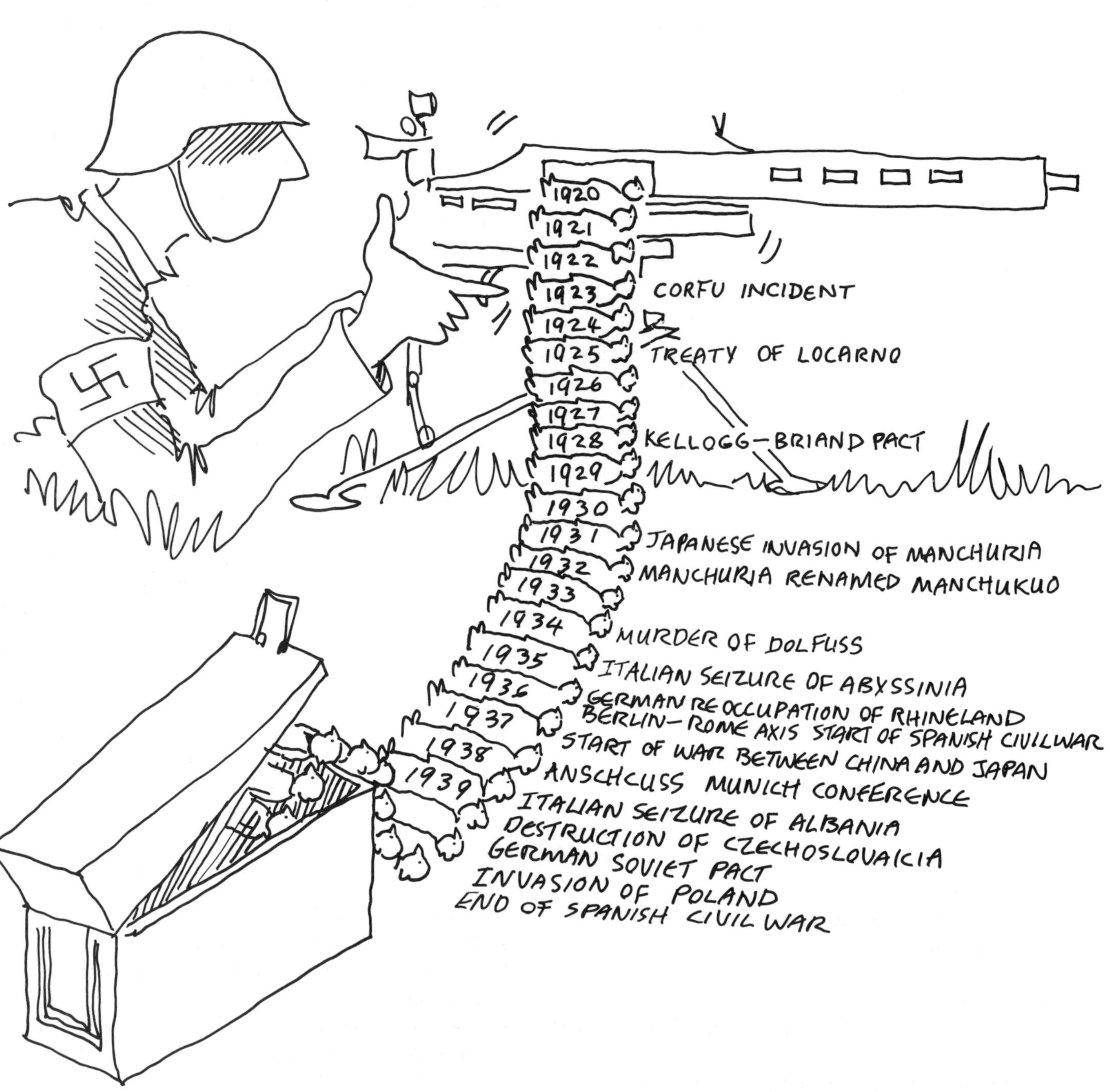

1920
1921
1922
1923 CORFU INCIDENT
1924
1925 TREATY OF LOCARNO
1926
1927
1928 KELLOGG–BRIAND PACT
1929
1930
1931 JAPANESE INVASION OF MANCHURIA
1932 MANCHURIA RENAMED MANCHUKUO
1933
1934 MURDER OF DOLFUSS
1935 ITALIAN SEIZURE OF ABYSSINIA
1936 GERMAN REOCCUPATION OF RHINELAND
BERLIN–ROME AXIS START OF SPANISH CIVIL WAR
1937 START OF WAR BETWEEN CHINA AND JAPAN
1938 ANSCHLUSS MUNICH CONFERENCE
1939 ITALIAN SEIZURE OF ALBANIA
DESTRUCTION OF CZECHOSLOVAKIA
GERMAN SOVIET PACT
INVASION OF POLAND
END OF SPANISH CIVIL WAR

Questions

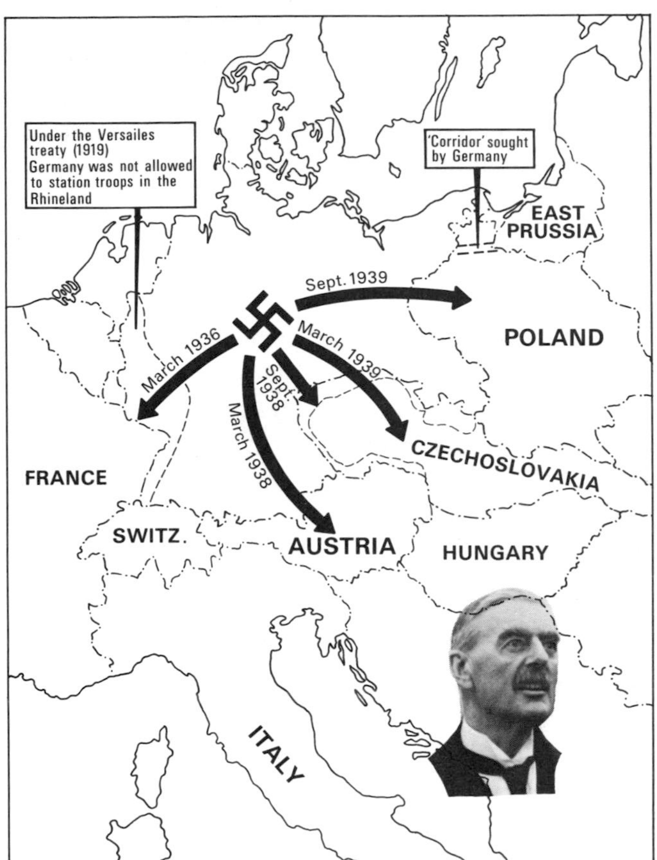

1 Use the detail provided in the map (above) to write an account of Hitler's occupation of much of Central Europe during the period 1936–39.
Describe the part played by the British prime minister (inset) in the effort to keep the peace during those difficult years.

2 Describe changes in British foreign policy 1918–39. Include in your answer:
- a Peace-making
- b Collective security
- c Appeasement.

3 Outline the rise of the Japanese empire until 1942. Include in your answer:
- a Pre-1918
- b Japan and China
- c Japanese conquests in the Second World War.

4 a Why did civil war break out in Spain in July, 1936?
- b Describe the attitude to the conflict of
  - (i) Great Britain and France,
  - (ii) the Soviet Union,
  - (iii) Germany and Italy.
- c Outline the main stages of the war.
- d What was the importance of the Spanish Civil War for the future of Europe?

5 What were the causes of the Second World War? You may find it useful to include in your answer: (a) Hitler's aims, (b) the reoccupation of the Rhineland and German rearmament, (c) the union between Austria and Germany, (d) Czechoslovakia and the Munich crisis, (e) the German threat to Poland.

6 Choose **four** of the following and write a paragraph about each, pointing out their importance in the international situation which developed in the years before 1939.
- a The Locarno Treaties of 1925.
- b The invasion of Manchuria in 1931.
- c The Spanish Civil War.
- d The Rome-Berlin-Tokyo Axis.
- e The Munich Conference of 1938.
- f The German Soviet Pact of 1939.

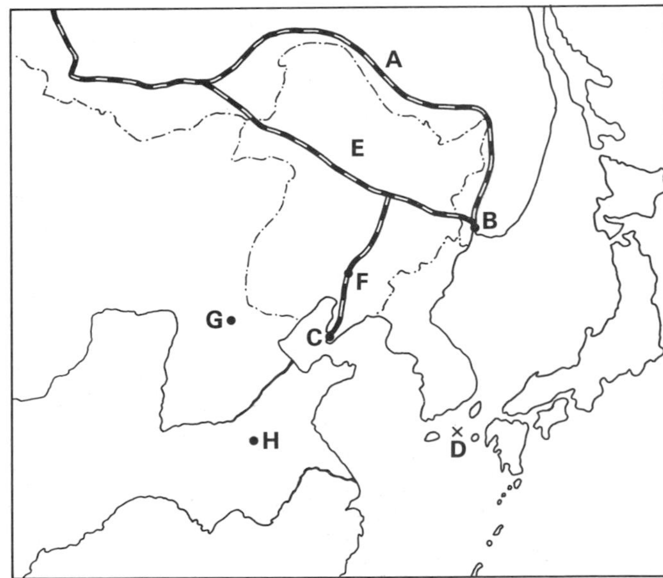

7 The map shows the Far East, 1900–39.
- a Name railway *A*, ports *B* and *C*, and battle *D*.
- b Why did Japan come into conflict with Russia in 1905 and with what results?
- c Name province *E* and town *F*. What incident happened at *F* in September, 1931, which was to lead to the Japanese invasion?
- d Why did Japan invade country *E* and what were the worldwide consequences of this?
- e Name cities *G* and *H*. Describe briefly the progress of the Japanese conquest of China.

Questions

8 Read the following extract from an eye-witness account of the bombing of Guernica and answer the questions below.

'We reached the outskirts of Guernica just before five o'clock. The streets were busy with the traffic of market day. Suddenly we heard the siren, and trembled. People were running about in all directions, abandoning everything they possessed, some hurrying into the shelters, others running into the hills . . .

'I saw an old peasant standing alone in a field: a machine-gun bullet killed him. For more than an hour these eighteen planes, never more than a few hundred metres in altitude, dropped bomb after bomb on Guernica. The sound of the explosions and of the crumbling houses cannot be imagined . . .

'The aeroplanes left around seven o'clock, and then there came another wave of them, this time flying at an immense altitude. They were dropping incendiary bombs on our martyred city. The new bombardment lasted thirty-five minutes, sufficient to transform the town into an enormous furnace . . .

'Not even the people who went into the refuges were saved; nor the sick and wounded in the hospitals. Guernica had no anti-aircraft guns, no batteries of any kind; nor were there any machine-guns.'

a What is the name of the people who live in the region of Guernica?
b In what war did the attack on Guernica take place?
c What evidence is there that Guernica was: (i) prepared for air-raids; (ii) not able to defend itself against air-raids? Why did the attack become so infamous?

9 Look carefully at these extracts and answer the questions below.

Source A
This extract concerns the Munich Agreement of September, 1938.

'We, the German Fuhrer and Chancellor, and the British Prime Minister, have had a further meeting today and are agreed in recognising that the question of Anglo-German relations is of the first importance for the two countries and for Europe.

'We regard the agreement signed last night and the Anglo-German Naval Agreement as symbolic of the desire of our two peoples never to go to war with one another again.

'We are resolved that the method of consultation shall be the method adopted to deal with other questions that may concern our two countries, and we are determined to continue our efforts to remove possible sources of difference and thus to contribute to assure the peace of Europe.'

Source B
This extract is from Churchill's speech in the House of Commons about the Munich Agreement.

'All is over. Silent, mournful, abandoned, broken, Czechoslovakia recedes into the darkness . . .

'. . . our loyal, brave people . . . should know that we have sustained a defeat without a war, the consequences of which will travel far with us along our road; they should know that we have passed an awful milestone in our history . . . And do not suppose that this is the end. This is only the beginning of the reckoning. This is only the first sip, the first foretaste of a bitter cup which will be proffered to us year by year unless, by a supreme recovery of moral health and martial vigour, we arise again and take our stand for freedom as in the olden time.'

a Name the two men who signed the Munich Agreement.
b Name two other statesmen who took part in the Munich Conference.
c What did Churchill mean by saying, 'This is only the beginning of the reckoning'? Was he right?
d Explain the differences between the two extracts. How do you account for these differences?

6/World War again

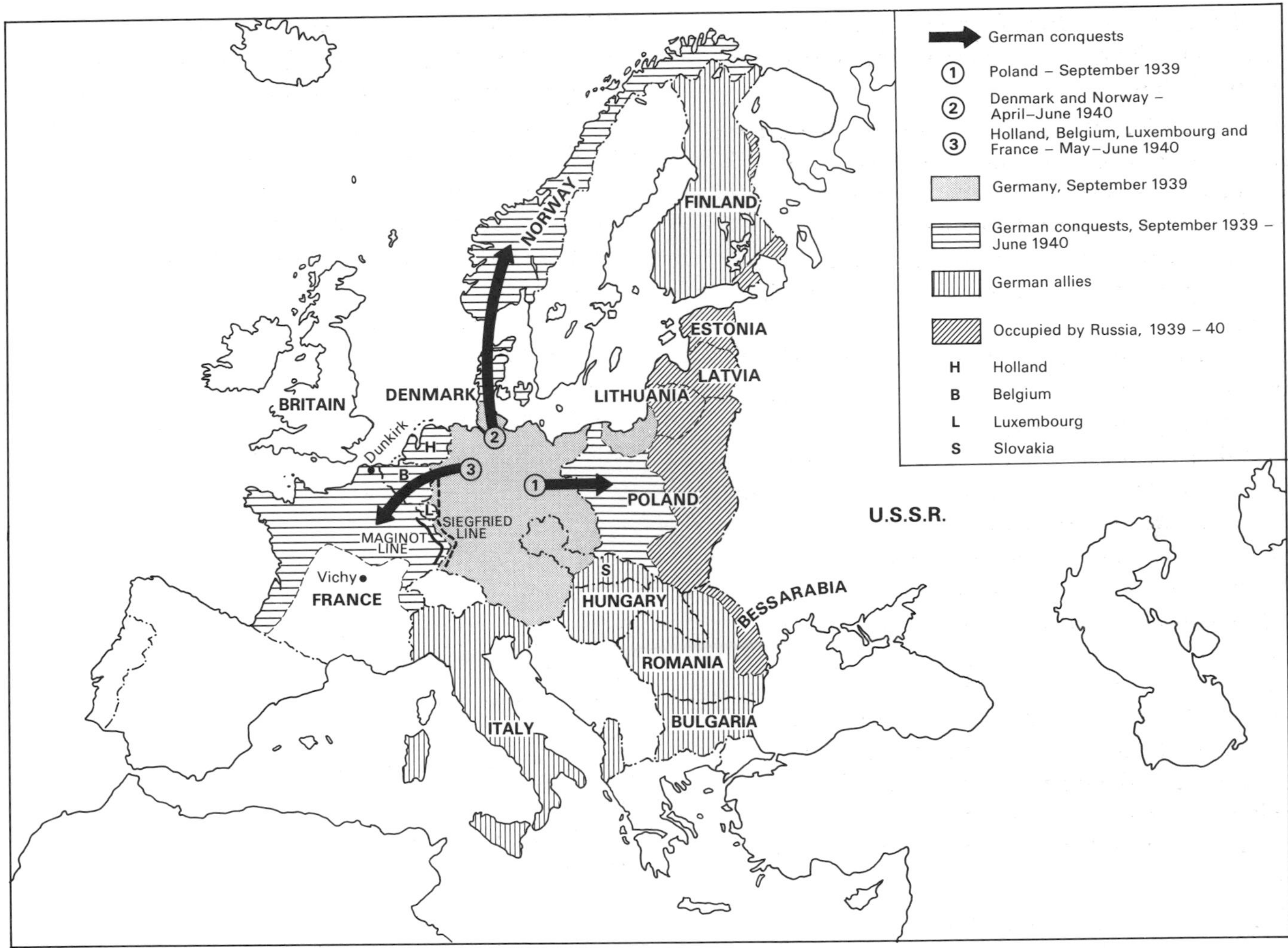

Map 1 The start of the War in Europe

The War in Europe, 1939–40

The War starts

The partition of Poland

The Germans invaded Poland on 1 September. Within a month, the Polish army had been completely defeated. The Germans had developed tactics called 'blitzkrieg' or lightning war. A combination of tanks, bombers, parachute troops and soldiers transported in lorries utterly overwhelmed the smaller, slower and less up-to-date enemy forces. The general who was most successful in using these tactics was Guderian. These tactics were completely successful in Poland.

Also, the Russians invaded Poland from the east. And so Poland was divided between Germany and Russia according to the agreement reached in August (see p.68). In fact, as you can see from Map 1, during 1939–40 Russia captured a whole strip of land from the Baltic Sea to the Black Sea to protect herself from a possible German attack. Only Finland resisted the Russians in the 'Winter War' of 1939–40.

The 'Phoney War'

Meanwhile, in western Europe nothing very much was happening. We saw on p.69 that the French hoped to prevent the Germans from again invading their land by building the Maginot Line, described by a British general as 'a battleship built on land'. (Looking at Map 1, can you see what its weakness was?) The Germans had a similar defence system called the Siegfried Line. The British Expeditionary Force (B.E.F.) was sent to France. One of their favourite songs was 'We're going to hang out the washing on the Siegfried Line'. But the British and French did not really want to invade Germany. And the Germans were not yet ready to invade France. Some people were impatient and called these months the phoney war.

Blitzkrieg in the West

The invasion of Denmark and Norway

In April 1940 Hitler struck to the north. Denmark and Norway were soon conquered. The British tried to help the Norwegians but they completely failed.

Churchill, Prime Minister of Britain

This failure brought to a head the discontent with Neville Chamberlain as prime minister of Britain. He resigned on 10 May. He was replaced by Winston Churchill, who formed a National Government from all the parties. He was a very forceful character and had had much experience in government (he first became a minister in 1911). In the years before the outbreak of the Second World War he was especially critical of the failure of the government to improve Britain's armed forces. Churchill proved to be a splendid war leader. He gave the British people confidence when the war seemed to be going disastrously and he was able to make rousing speeches. His first as prime minister contained the following famous realistic warning, 'I have nothing to offer but blood, toil, tears and sweat.'

Winston Churchill

The Fall of France

On the very day that Churchill became prime minister, German forces attacked Holland and Belgium. Then France was invaded. The German blitzkrieg tactics worked brilliantly. The Maginot Line was completely by-passed by German forces to the north. Holland and Belgium surrendered. The B.E.F. was trapped at Dunkirk. But the German army hesitated. And so, by a remarkable operation undertaken by hundreds of ships and boats—whatever could cross the Channel—over 300,000 soldiers were ferried across to England, though they had to leave all their equipment behind.

The Germans pressed on deeply into France. The prime minister, Paul Reynaud, resigned and was replaced by Marshal Pétain. On 22 June Pétain signed an armistice.

The Germans occupied the north and west of France (see Map 1). The rest was governed by Pétain from the town of Vichy.

Marshal Pétain shakes hands with Hitler and sets France off on the path of collaboration

The War in Europe, 1939–40

An artist's impression of the beaches at Dunkirk

For the next year Britain alone faced a German-controlled continent. On 18 June Churchill had broadcast one of his most heroic speeches. Here is the last paragraph:

What General Weygand called the Battle of France is over. I expect that the Battle of Britain is about to begin. Upon this battle depends the survival of Christian civilisation. Upon it depends our own British life, and the long continuity of our institutions and our Empire. The whole fury and might of the enemy must very soon be turned on us. Hitler knows that he will have to break us on this island or lose the war. If we can stand up to him, all Europe may be free and the life of the world may move forward into broad, sunlit uplands. But if we fail, then the whole world, including the United States, including all that we have known and cared for, will sink into the abyss of a new Dark Age made more sinister, and perhaps more protracted, by the lights of perverted science. Let us therefore brace ourselves to our duties, and so bear ourselves that, if the British Empire and its Commonwealth last for a thousand years, men will still say, 'this was their finest hour'.

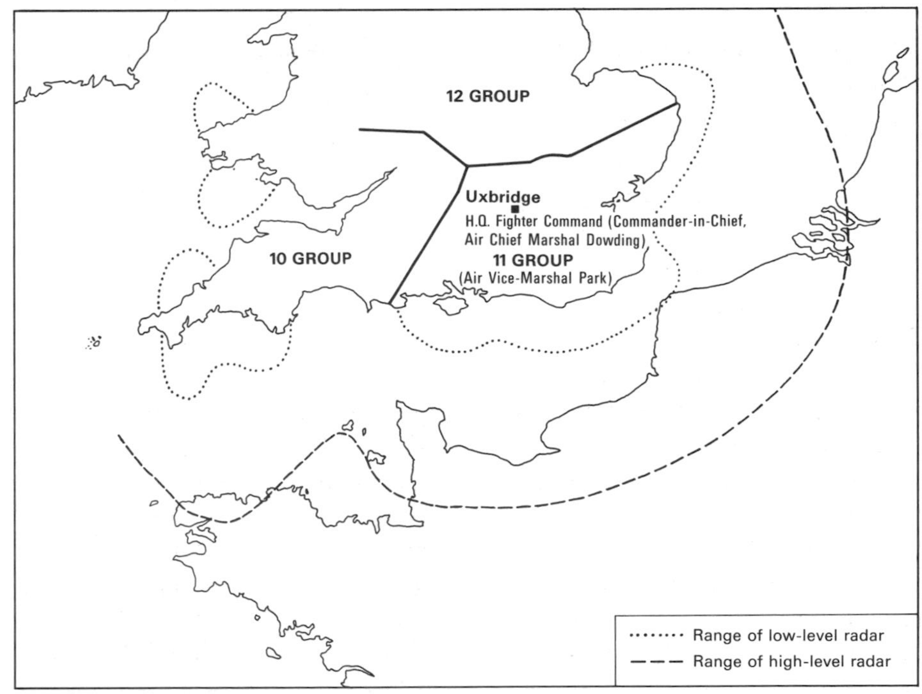

Map 2 The Battle of Britain

The Battle of Britain

Operation 'Sealion'

Hitler now prepared for an invasion of Britain. This was code-named Operation 'Sealion'. But he could not risk sending a fleet of invasion barges across the Channel if they would be attacked from the air. Goering, the chief of the Luftwaffe (airforce), therefore had the task of destroying the R.A.F. fighter aeroplanes. R.A.F. Fighter Command was commanded by Air Chief Marshal Sir Hugh Dowding. From July to September aerial fights raged over southern England: this was called the Battle of Britain.

Hawker Hurricane—the main British fighter in the Battle of Britain

Messerschmitt Me 109—the main German fighter in the Battle of Britain

Junkers Ju 87 'Stuka'—German dive-bomber used in the Battle of Britain particularly to attack ships in the English Channel

Heinkel He 111s—German bombers used in the Battle of Britain and also later in the Blitz

Aeroplanes of the Battle of Britain

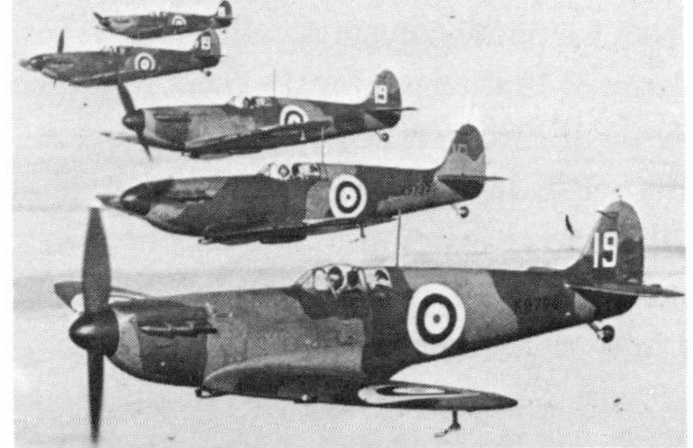

Supermarine Spitfire—British fighter. Although not many had been built in time for the Battle of Britain, it was the most famous aeroplane used in the battle, and feared by German airmen

How were the opposing airforces matched?

The Luftwaffe had well over 1,000 bombers and nearly 1,000 fighters for the battle. R.A.F. Fighter Command had about 600 fighters. The most famous German aeroplanes were the Heinkel He III bombers, Junkers Ju 87 'Stuka' dive-bombers and Messerschmitt Me 109 fighters. The most famous British fighters were the Hurricane and Spitfire. But most important for the British was the system of ground control linked to the chain of radar stations along the coast (see Map 2). The R.A.F. fighter squadrons could therefore be accurately and quickly directed to the incoming German aircraft. This British radar system was developed by Robert Watson-Watt.

Luftwaffe v. Fighter Command

The Battle of Britain was fought in three stages:

1 10 July—12 August. Attacks on British coastal shipping. To force the British fighters into the sky to defend the Channel shipping.

2 13 August—6 September. Attacks on airfields. To destroy aeroplanes on the ground and the airfield buildings. But the Germans stupidly did not try to destroy the radar stations.

3 7—15 September. Attacks on London.

Desperate dog-fights raged in the skies over southern England during that warm summer. Many more German aeroplanes were destroyed than British, though by early September the R.A.F. was becoming dangerously short of trained pilots.

But the Luftwaffe decided that its losses were too great and switched to night bombing of British cities (see p.89). Hitler gave up his plans for invading Britain and turned his attention instead to Russia (see p. 78.) Britain had been saved by her fighter pilots. In the words of Churchill, 'never in the field of human conflict was so much owed by so many to so few.'

The Mediterranean and Russia, 1940–44

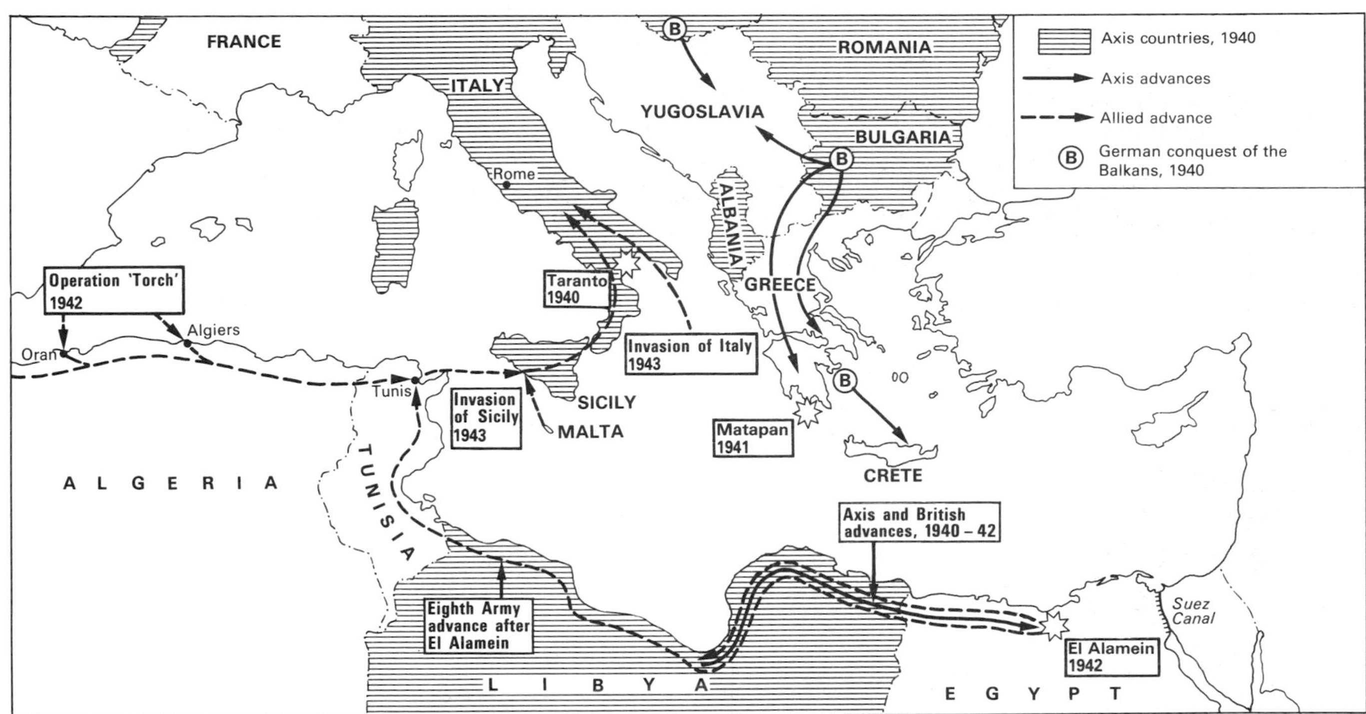

Map 3 The Mediterranean

The Balkans and the Middle East

The Germans take over the Balkans

Mussolini hesitated to enter the war on the side of his Axis friend, Hitler, until he felt sure that Germany would win. In June 1940, with France on the brink of collapse, Italy declared war. Italian armies invaded France and, later, Greece (see Map 3). But the Greeks fought back successfully in Albania, so the Germans had to come to the rescue of their ally. By the early summer of 1941 the Germans had control of almost the whole of the Balkans:

1 Romania and Bulgaria joined the Axis.
2 Yugoslavia was quickly defeated.
3 Greece was defeated, and the British troops who were sent to help, retreated to the island of Crete.
4 The Germans captured Crete.

These German successes were very serious for the British. Why do you think this was so? If the Germans came to control the Mediterranean, they would soon be able to threaten:

1 The vitally important oil-fields of the Middle East.
2 The route through the Suez Canal to India and the Far East.

But the Royal Navy produced some cheerful news. They soundly defeated the Italian navy in the Battles of Taranto (1940) and Matapan (1941).

The Desert War

Because of the importance of Middle East oil and the Suez Canal, it was vital for the British to defend Egypt from attacks from the Italian colony of Libya.

Between September 1940 and June 1942 the armies moved like a pendulum to and fro across the northern fringes of Egypt and Libya. The Axis armies pushed into Egypt

British soldiers capture a German tank near Tobruk in the Western Desert

three times and the British and Commonwealth (mainly Australian) soldiers of the Eighth Army (called the 'Desert Rats') pushed them back into Libya twice. The Italians suffered such a disastrous defeat at first that in 1941 the Germans sent the powerful Afrika Korps under its brilliant commander, General Rommel (known as the 'Desert Fox').

General Rommel

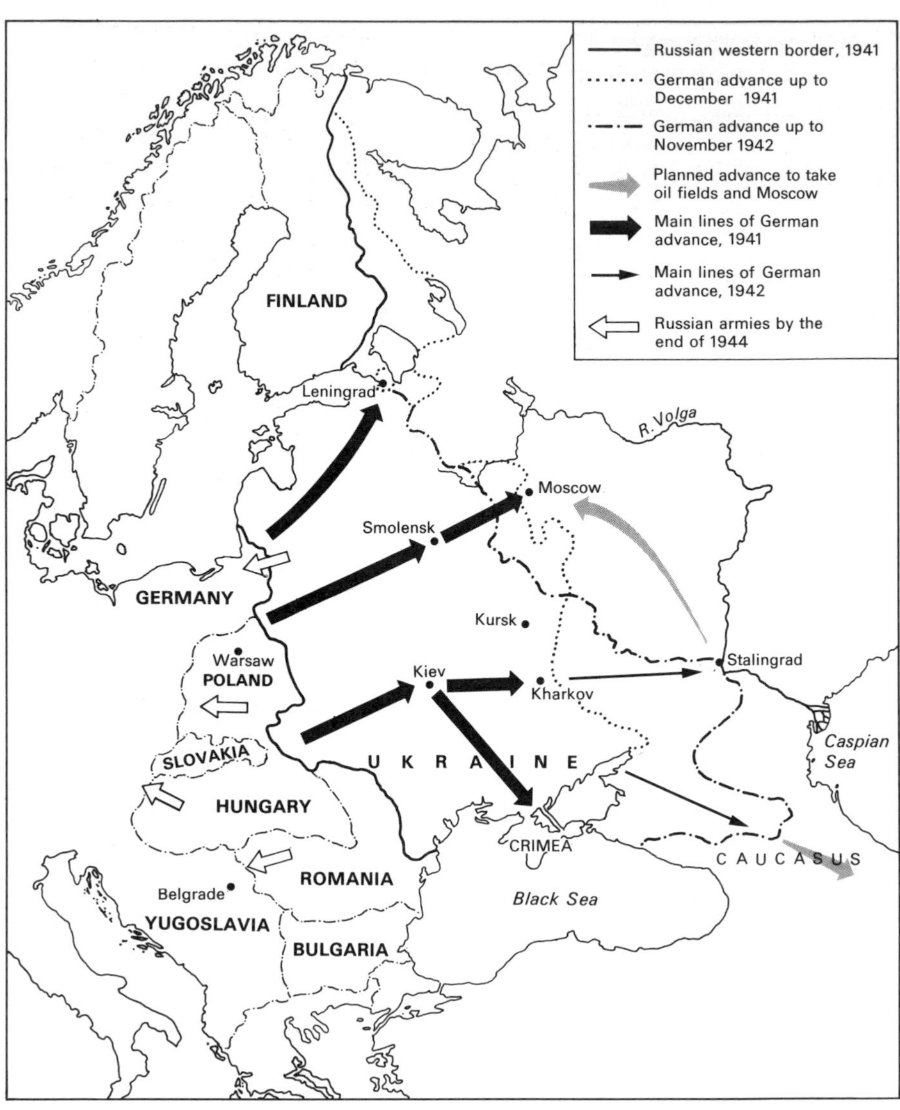

Map 4 Russia, 1941–44

During 1942 the Eighth Army was greatly strengthened and a new commander, General Montgomery, was appointed. In October the Battle of El Alamein was fought. The strength of the Afrika Korps was broken and the Eighth Army chased them as far as Tunis by May 1943, as you can see from Map 3.

Throughout the desert war, the island of Malta remained gallantly undefeated, despite heavy air attacks. British convoys could therefore sail through the Mediterranean without too many losses to carry equipment and supplies to the British forces in Egypt.

Operation 'Torch'

In November 1942 American, British and French forces, under the command of General Eisenhower (nicknamed 'Ike'), landed in Morocco and Algeria (see Map 3). They advanced eastwards into Tunisia. By May 1943 the fighting in North Africa was over.

Russia, 1941–44

Operation 'Barbarossa'

On 18 December 1940 Hitler made his greatest mistake. He issued a secret document code-named 'Barbarossa'. It contained the plans for the invasion of Russia. The invasion was launched on 22 June 1941. Hitler was putting into practice his long-held dreams of crushing the Communists and gaining 'lebensraum' (living space) in Russia (see p. 52). This scheme was a mistake because in the end the campaigns over this huge country destroyed the mighty strength of the Third Reich. Do you think that Hitler was foolish even to try to conquer Russia?

The Mediterranean and Russia, 1940–44

German advances in 1941

At first the blitzkrieg methods of the Germans seemed to work against the Red Army (as the Russian army was called). The Germans advanced deep into Russia. By the end of 1941, as you can see from Map 4, the Germans had achieved the following:

1 Captured the Baltic lands and laid siege to Leningrad.
2 Captured the rich agricultural and industrial areas of the Ukraine and reached the Black Sea.
3 Reached the suburbs of Moscow.

The Battle of Stalingrad

The German advance ground to a halt in the bitter Russian winter. In June of the following year, 1942, the German armies started to advance again—this time south-eastwards. The Germans had two aims:

1 To capture the oil-fields of the Caucasus area.
2 To encircle Moscow.

When the German Sixth Army reached the city of Stalingrad on the River Volga, Stalin gave a famous order to his troops: 'Not a step back'. The city had been named after Stalin because he had helped to defend it in the Civil War. For five months the most keenly fought and important battle of the war was fought in a city reduced to ruins in the process. Eventually, the Russian commander, Marshal Zhukov, surrounded the German army: 100,000 soldiers including 24 generals surrendered in January 1943.

The German retreat, 1943–44

The Russians now steadily pushed the Germans back. In July 1943 the greatest tank battle of the war was fought at Kursk—involving 3,000 tanks! By the end of 1944, as you can see from Map 4, Russian armies had recaptured all their lost land and were invading Germany.

What was the Russian war like?

The war in Russia was quite unlike

Marshal Zhukov

the war in other parts of the world. Everything was on such a vast scale.

1 The sizes of the armies were huge: millions of men were involved.
2 The area over which the war was fought was huge: thousands of square miles were affected.
3 The amount of destruction was

German troops retreating in the snow near Moscow

enormous. As the Russian armies retreated they used a 'scorched earth' policy. Buildings and crops were set on fire so that the Germans could not use them.

4 Whole factories were dismantled and removed eastwards out of the way of the advancing Germans.

5 The human suffering was dreadful. The German armies were not properly clothed against the bitter cold. Food was difficult to obtain from the stricken farmlands. It was a war of fierce hatred: prisoners of war were cruelly treated. It is estimated that 20 million Russians died. The agony of Russia was acted out on a small scale in Leningrad. This city was besieged for three years. One million of its people died. A British war correspondent gave this description of the plight of the people:

To fill their empty stomachs, to reduce the intense sufferings caused by hunger, people would look for incredible substitutes; they would try to catch crows or rooks, or any cat or dog that had still somehow survived....

Death would overtake people in all kinds of circumstances; while they were in the streets they would fall down and never rise again; or in their houses where they would fall asleep and never awake ... the dead body would usually be put on a handsleigh drawn by two or three members of the dead man's family; often wholly exhausted during the long trek to the cemetery, they would abandon the body half-way, leaving it to the authorities to deal with.

Italy, 1943–44

After taking over the whole of North Africa, the Americans and British decided to invade Italy. The main events were as follows:

1 Conquest of Sicily, July–August 1943.

2 Invasion of the mainland of Italy, September 1943.

3 The Italians were tiring of the war. Mussolini was imprisoned in July 1943. The new Italian government signed an armistice with the Allies.

4 The Germans took control of Italy including Rome. Mussolini was rescued by the Germans though he was captured again by Italian partisans (guerrilla fighters) and executed in 1945.

5 The fighting. The Germans put up a fierce resistance. The American and British armies were able to advance up the 'leg' of Italy only very slowly throughout 1943, 1944 and 1945. One action in 1944 that caused much controversy was the destruction of the monastery of Monte Cassino. German soldiers occupied it and Allied aeroplanes destroyed it in order to advance further.

The ruins of the Monte Cassino. The Germans made a stand in this famous monastery and it was virtually destroyed by the Allies

The Japanese War

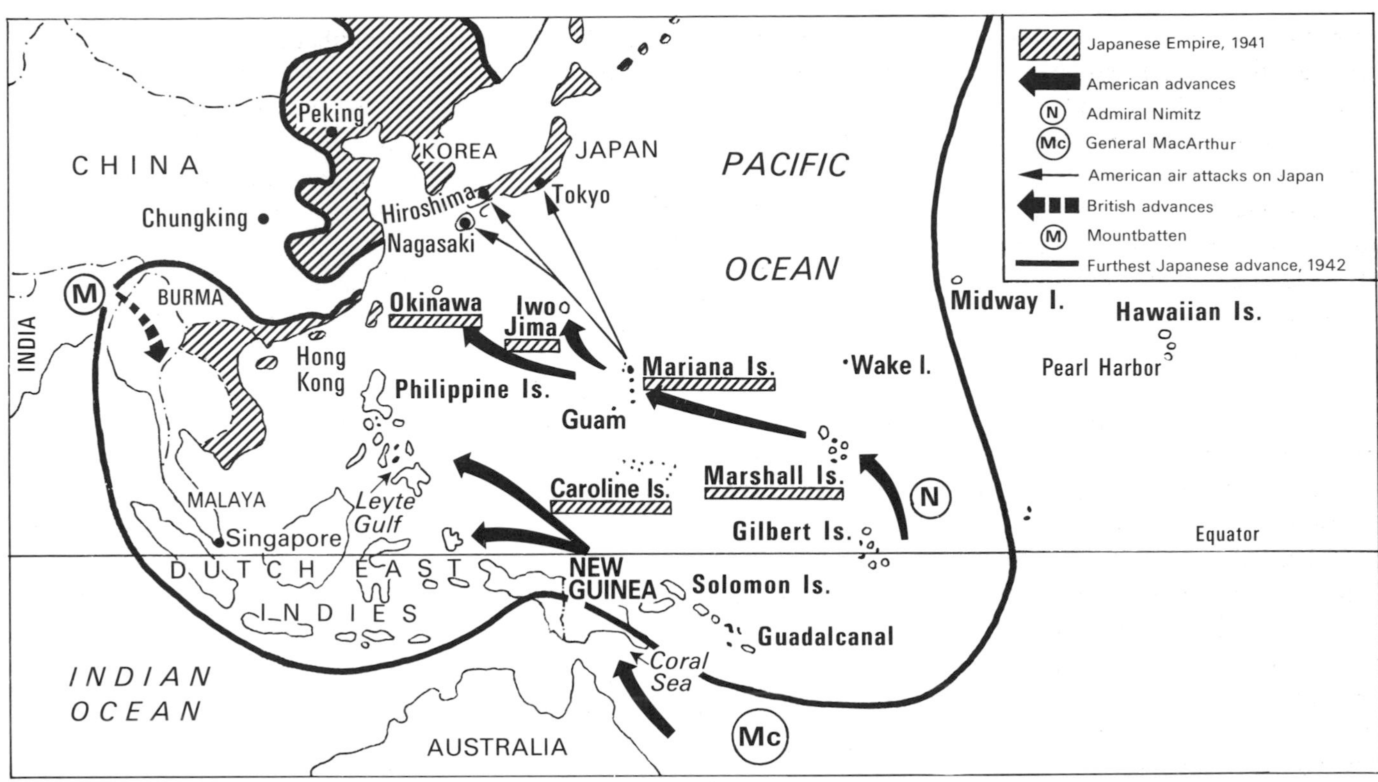

Map 5 The War in the Far East

Japan attacks

Pearl Harbor

On Sunday morning, 7 December 1941, the American Pacific Fleet lay peacefully at anchor in the Hawaiian base of Pearl Harbor. At 7 o'clock a radar operator saw blips on his screen made by approaching air-craft. It was assumed that they were American. They were, in fact, Japanese. Nearly 400 bombers had taken off from aircraft carriers and were heading for the unsuspecting and undefended American fleet. Between 8 and 10 o'clock bombs and torpedoes smashed into the American ships. Eighteen warships were sunk or severely damaged. Japan had entered the war. It had become a truly world war.

Where did the Japanese make other attacks?

Before the month of December was out, the Japanese had also:

1 Captured some small American islands in the Pacific including Guam and Wake.

2 Captured the British colony of Hong Kong.

3 Invaded the Philippine Islands.

4 Invaded Malaya.

5 Invaded Burma.

During these rapid campaigns, Japanese aeroplanes sank the British battleships, *Prince of Wales* and *Repulse*. The Allies were learning through sad experience that even the mightiest warships had to be protected from the air.

Pearl Harbor. Directly after the Japanese attack on 7th December, 1941, the U.S. battleship Nevada *burns on the shallow bottom of the harbour*

The Japanese War

Japanese conquests, 1942 Very rapidly in 1942 the Japanese followed up their first attacks. They captured the important lands shown in this diagram (see also Map 5).

The Allies fight back

What were the Allies' difficulties?

The American, British and Australian forces were at a great disadvantage in trying to stop and reverse the Japanese advance:

1 President Roosevelt of the U.S.A. understood that Hitler was very dangerous. Before the Japanese attack the Americans supplied Britain with warships and aeroplanes under a scheme called Lend-Lease. The Allies now agreed to concentrate on defeating Germany first. Most of the men and the best equipment were therefore concentrated in Europe.

2 The Japanese had captured huge areas of south-east Asia and the Pacific.

3 The Japanese fought with fanatical courage believing that they would be blessed if they died for their god-emperor, Hirohito. Soldiers would not surrender and often had to be burned to death with flame-throwers. Kamikaze (suicide) pilots damaged American warships by crashing their bomb-laden aeroplanes into them.

The fighting

Fighting to regain what the Japanese had captured took place in four main areas:

1 China. Government forces under Chiang Kai-shek and Communist forces under Mao Tse-tung (see pp.117 and 118).

2 Burma. British and Commonwealth forces under Admiral Lord Mountbatten.

3 North Pacific. U.S. navy and marines under Admiral Nimitz. In June 1942 the U.S. navy defeated a Japanese attempt to capture Midway Island. This was the turning-point in the war against Japan. The Americans started now to recapture all the many islands occupied by the Japanese.

4 South-west Pacific. Forces under General MacArthur. Japanese navy defeated in the great air/sea battles of the Coral Sea (March 1942) and Leyte Gulf (October 1944).

General Douglas MacArthur

The War at Sea

A Short 'Sunderland'—A British flying-boat used for patrolling the seas

Japanese 'Zero' fighters—these were flown from aircraft carriers and were particularly feared by American airmen in battles in the Pacific

An American battle fleet—notice how the wings of the aeroplanes on the aircraft carriers are folded for storage below decks

A destroyer—a fast warship, used to defend bigger warships and convoys

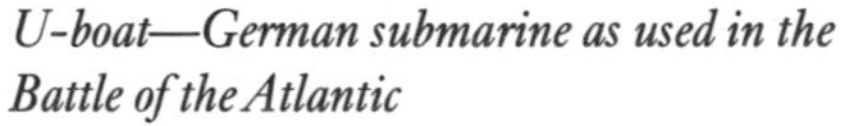

U-boat—German submarine as used in the Battle of the Atlantic

The ships and aeroplanes

All kinds of passenger and merchant ships were used especially by the Allies to transport soldiers, equipment, food and fuel to wherever they were needed for the fighting. The convoy system that had been introduced in the First World War (see p.14) was used to try to protect them against attack by submarines.

Warships

1 Battleships. These had many large guns, but, as the fate of the *Prince of Wales* and *Repulse* showed (see p.81), they could be easily attacked by aircraft.
2 Aircraft carriers. These were very important in the Pacific because of the great distances involved. Fleets in this way had their own air defence and their own means of aerial attack. For example, in the Battle of the Coral Sea, the ships of each side did not even see each other—all the attacks were made by aircraft.
3 Destroyers. Fast, small ships important for protecting both convoys and the bigger, capital, ships. Their weapons included depth-charges for use against submarines.
4 Submarines. The Germans especially built up a large fleet of U-boats, based in splendidly defended pens on the Atlantic coast of France. They sometimes hunted merchant ships in 'wolf-packs'.

Aeroplanes

1 Fighters. These flew from aircraft carriers to fight off attacking bombers.
2 Short-range bombers. These flew either from aircraft carriers or land. Some carried bombs, others carried torpedoes. The most famous British torpedo-bomber was the Swordfish. This was a very old-fashioned looking biplane, but it was very successful in several attacks on German warships.

3 Long-range reconnaissance. Landplanes and seaplanes were used for patrolling over the oceans. They often carried depth-charges for attacking submarines.

Detection equipment

1 Asdic. This was an instrument that detected submerged submarines by sending out sound impulses and receiving back the echoes.
2 Radar. Both ships and reconnaissance aircraft were eventually equipped with radar sets.

Main areas of naval warfare

The Pacific

As we have already seen, the biggest naval battles took place in the Pacific Ocean between the Japanese and American navies (see p.82, also later p.91)

Convoys

1 Mediterranean. We have already seen how supplies for the British Eighth Army were shipped through the Mediterranean Sea (see p.78).
2 Russia. Supplies, especially lorries, tanks and aeroplanes, were sent from Britain via the Arctic Ocean to Russia.
3 Atlantic. Britain relied on supplies of food, petrol and aeroplanes being shipped from the U.S.A. After the U.S.A. entered the war American soldiers were carried across the Atlantic to prepare for the invasion of France (see p.90). German battleships and U-boats tried to sink these ships. This fighting was called the 'Battle of the Atlantic' and was so important for Britain that we need to describe it separately.

A British convoy

The War at Sea

The Battle of the Atlantic

A typical incident

The novel, *The Cruel Sea*, by Nicholas Monsarrat describes this part of the war very vividly. Here is a short extract.

. . . the men who sailed in oil-tankers . . . lived, for an entire voyage of three or four weeks, as a man living on top of a keg of gunpowder: the stuff they carried—the life-blood of the whole war—was the most treacherous cargo of all; a single torpedo, a single small bomb, even a stray shot from a machine-gun could transform the ship into a torch. . . .

Appropriately, it was an oil-tanker which gave the men of *Compass Rose*, as spectators, the most hideous hour of the whole war. . . .

She was torpedoed in broad daylight on a lovely sunny afternoon . . . and in a minute the long shapely hull was on fire almost from end to end. . . .

There were about twenty men on the fo'c'sle . . . they [began] to jump. . . .

[But] the oil, spreading over the surface of the water and catching fire as it spread, was moving faster than any of the men could swim.

. . . one by one they were overtaken, and licked by flame, and fried, and left behind.

Famous battles

In December 1939 the German battleship *Graf Spee* was chased by three British cruisers into a South American harbour at the mouth of the River Plate where the captain scuttled (i.e. sank) her.

In May 1941 a great battle was fought in the North Atlantic against the German battleship *Bismarck*. She was eventually sunk, though not before she had destroyed the British battleship H.M.S. *Hood*.

Losses

Look at the following table. Which was the worst year for the Allies? How do you think the Allies succeeded in sinking more U-boats?

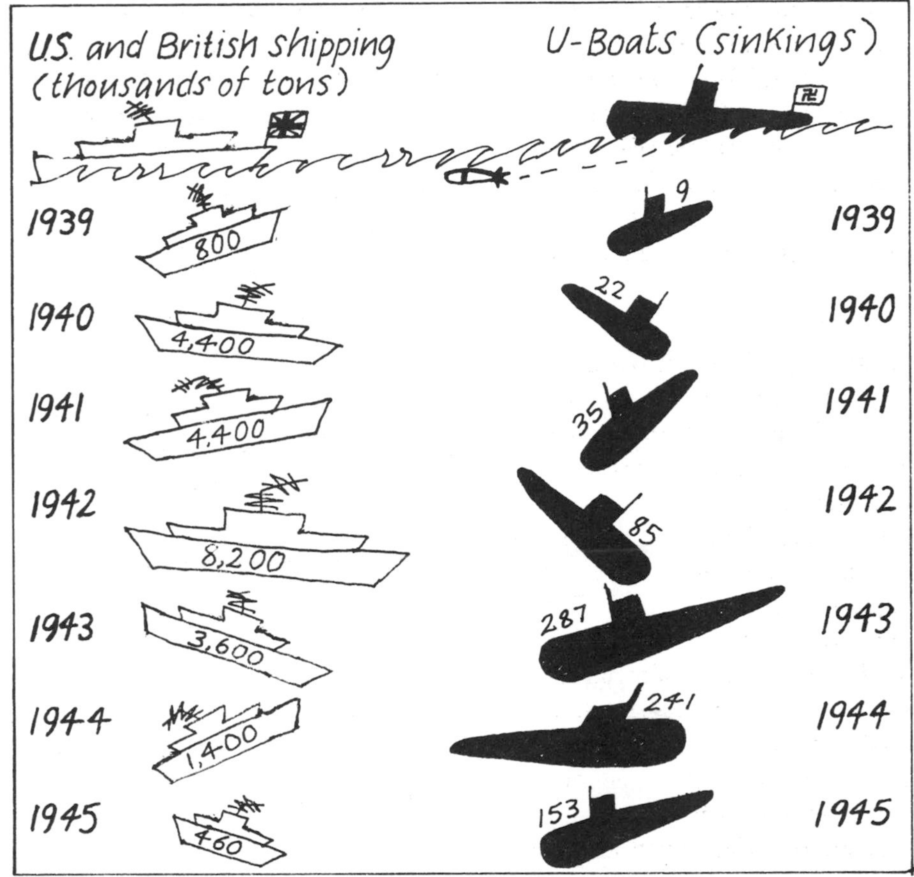

Figure 1 The U-boat war (The Battle of the Atlantic)

The British battlecruiser, H.M.S. Hood

The wherewithal to fight

Total war

Until recent times wars were fought by armies and navies and the civilians were hardly involved. In the Second World War almost everyone contributed and was affected. Civilians worked in factories to produce weapons or on the farms to produce food. Civilians were bombed in attacks from the air.

What were the problems of production?

The war put a huge strain on the economies of the countries in the following ways:

1 Millions of men were needed for the armed forces. This meant that there were very few to work on the farms or in the factories.

2 Large numbers of workers were needed to make uniforms and weapons for the armed forces.

3 There was not so much food in some countries as in peacetime for the following reasons: the armies had to be fed; farming was affected especially where battles were fought over the farmlands; and trading between countries was interrupted.

How were the problems solved?

1 Men were conscripted into the armed forces and in some countries, like Britain and Germany, into civil defence forces such as the fire service.

2 To replace the men, many women worked on the farms and in factories.

3 Strict rationing was introduced for food, clothes and petrol. Factories were changed to make war goods: guns instead of sewing-machines; tanks instead of cars; uniforms instead of civilian clothes.

A woman welder in a wartime factory

Digging for victory. This family is turning a bomb site into a vegetable garden

Map 6 Hitler's Europe, 1942

Life and death in Hitler's Europe

Slave labour

We saw in Chapter 4 how the Nazis organised concentration camps. The dreadful slaughter of the death camps reached its height in 1944–5. But the prisoners in some of the camps were used as slave labour instead. In fact, able-bodied men from the occupied countries were drafted into working for the German war effort in many ways.

Resistance movements

As you can see from Map 6, by 1942 Hitler had gained control over most of the continent of Europe. In a number of countries, the people did not accept their fate, but organised resistance movements.

Guerrilla warfare was fought against the Germans in the mountains of Yugoslavia (now divided into Croatia and Serbia) by the Partisans organised and led by Tito.

Marshal Tito with some of his partisan comrades in a cave in the mountains

Guerrilla warfare was fought against the Germans in the occupied lands of Russia.

In western Europe, particularly France, resistance groups helped Allied airmen who were shot down and attacked factories and German transport systems. The French resistance was called the *Maquis*. Britain helped by setting up the Special Operations Executive which flew in agents and received intelligence reports by secret radio messages.

By 1944 opposition to Hitler was growing inside Germany itself. In July of that year a plot to blow up Hitler failed. Some of the conspirators were executed in a most horrible way—hung up and strangled by piano wire. Field Marshal Rommel was involved, but was allowed to commit suicide by poison.

The bombing of cities

Why were cities bombed?

During the course of the war German bombers attacked British cities, Allied bombers attacked German cities and American bombers attacked Japanese cities. They did this for two main reasons:

1 To destroy the factories, railways and harbours which were making and carrying war supplies.

2 To weaken the morale of the civilian population and therefore their will to continue the war.

Bombing during day-time was, of course, much more accurate than night bombing as the crews could see their targets. But fighters could also see the bombers. Both the Germans and the British sent their bombers out at night to avoid the huge losses of day-light bombing. Because precision bombing was not possible at night, the targets were whole cities. Air Chief Marshal 'Bomber' Harris of R.A.F. Bomber Command put into operation the idea of 'area bombing'. As a result, many German cities were devastated and many civilians were killed and maimed (see p.89). But neither in Britain nor in Germany was the spirit of the people broken by the air-raids.

The weapons used

The most famous Allied bombers were the British Lancaster and the American Flying Fortress. They dropped both high explosive and incendiary (fire) bombs.

Radar became important for accurately navigating the way to the target.

In 1944 the Germans produced V-weapons ('Vengeance'). The V-1 was a jet-propelled pilotless bomb. The V-2 was a rocket. They were used to attack southern England.

Allied bombers, The British Lancaster (above) and the American B-17 Fortress (below)

The V-I

The Blitz

When the Luftwaffe admitted defeat in the Battle of Britain (see p.76), they turned to night bombing. This was called 'the blitz'. It lasted from September 1940 to May 1941. London was the main target, though other cities, including Coventry and Plymouth also suffered heavily. Over 40,000 people were killed.

R.A.F. raids on Germany

British raids on Germany gradually built up in size. In May 1942 the first thousand-bomber raid was made—on Cologne.

In July 1943 a most horrific raid was made on Hamburg. Incendiary bombs were used that created an intense 'fire storm'. The heat generated in the centre of the fire reached 1,000° C. As the hot air rose a powerful suction effect was caused. The winds that were whipped up raged through the streets at 150 m.p.h., uprooting trees and carrying them and people bodily into the furnace of the fire. Hamburg was turned into a huge crematorium.

Many other German cities including Berlin were reduced to ruins. In February 1945, as the war in Europe was rapidly coming to an end, the beautiful city of Dresden was destroyed. It was at the time the sanctuary of refugees fleeing from the battling German and Russian armies. Do you think this attack was right?

The RAF also tried a few precision raids. One of the most famous was undertaken by Lancasters to destroy dams on the important industrial area of the Ruhr. An inventor named Barnes Wallis produced bombs which bounced on the water so that they could accurately hit the dam walls.

The Blitz. The docks burn behind the Tower and London Bridge, 7 September, 1940

A London Underground platform used as an air raid shelter during the blitz

What protection was there against air-raids?

Fire-fighting, rescue and ambulance services were, of course, very important in the attempts to keep damage and casualties as low as possible.

Sirens were sounded to warn people of the approach of bombers. People slept in air-raid shelters or ran to them when the sirens sounded. In Britain there were several kinds of shelters:

1 Anderson: corrugated steel huts covered with earth in gardens and back yards.

2 Morrison: steel tables for use indoors.

3 Underground railway platforms: many Londoners slept in the underground as the best protection.

Defeat of the Axis

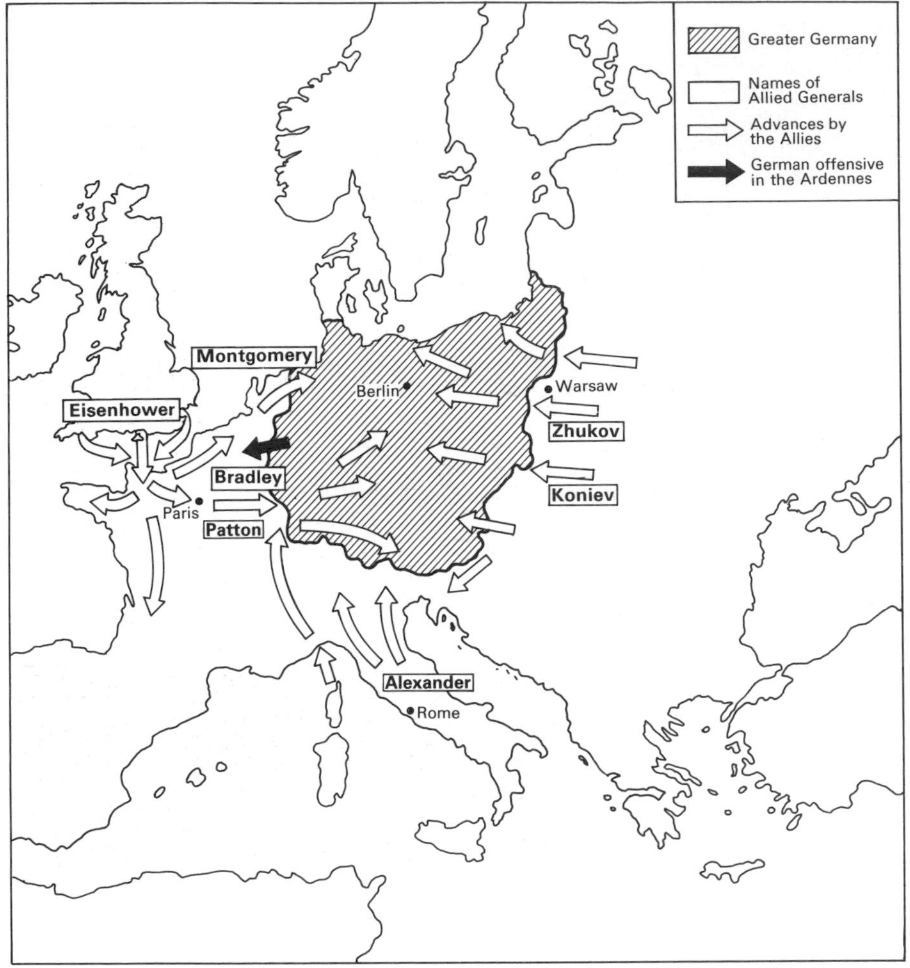

Map 7 The defeat of Germany, 1944–45

The liberation of Western Europe

By September 1944 the Allies had freed France and Belgium of the Germans. The Allies had two set-backs:

1 In September British paratroops tried to capture the bridge over the River Rhine at Arnhem in Holland, but they were defeated.

2 In December–January, as you can see from Map 7, the Germans made a vigorous counter-attack in the Ardennes area of Belgium. But by the spring of 1945 the Allied armies crossed the River Rhine (the Americans made the first crossing at Remagen). Then they advanced into the heart of Germany.

Russian advance

Throughout 1944 and into 1945 the Red Army continued to advance through Poland and Czechoslovakia and into the heart of Germany. An uprising in Warsaw took place in 1944 before the Russians could provide help. The Germans devastated the city and killed about 300,000 Poles.

The defeat of Germany

D-Day

On 6 June 1944 American, British and Canadian soldiers landed on the beaches of Normandy. Operation 'Overlord' for the invasion of western Europe was under way.

It was a huge and complicated operation. An armada of over 5,000 ships transported men and equipment across the Channel. The whole operation was directed by General Eisenhower of the U.S. army. The Germans had built powerful defences along the coast of France. The Allied troops suffered heavy casualties before they could advance inland.

General Eisenhower (centre) and Field-Marshal Montgomery (right)

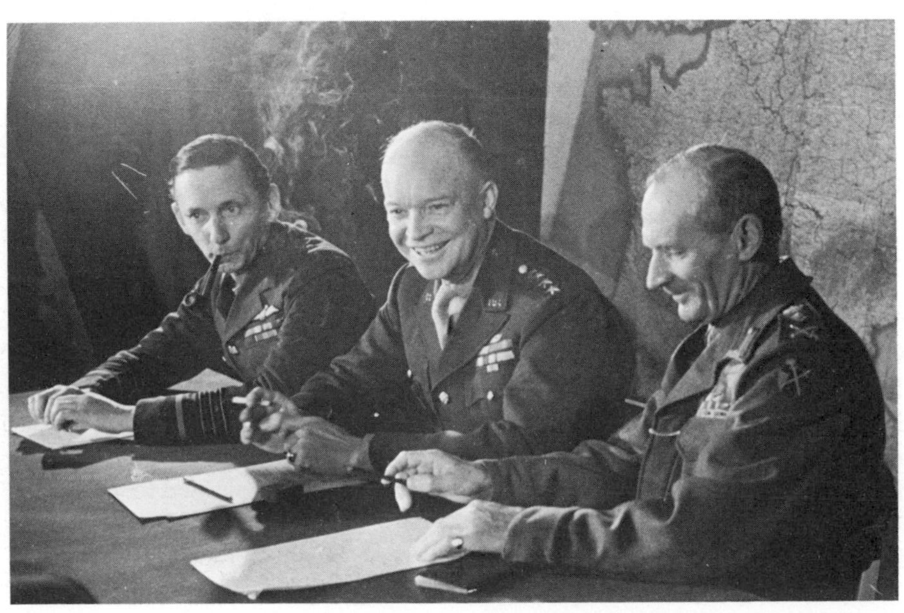

Defeat of the Axis

The surrender of Germany

The Red Army reached the outskirts of Berlin in April 1945. Hitler took refuge in an underground bunker. On 1st May, when it was obvious even to him that the final defeat was very near, he shot himself. Goebbels took poison at the same time. On 7 May the formal German surrender was signed at Reims. The war in Europe was at an end. Hitler's Third Reich was no more.

Victorious Russian troops on the roof of the Reichstag raise the red flag over the ruins of central Berlin

The defeat of Japan

The problem of how to defeat Japan

We saw on p.82 how the Japanese had reached the limit of their conquests by the summer of 1942. For the next two years, as you can see from Map 5, the Allies gradually advanced across the Pacific and into the East Indies and Burma.

Japanese cities suffered huge destruction from American bomber raids. And fierce naval and land battles were fought in the spring and summer of 1945 as the Americans captured the island of Okinawa near to the Japanese homeland. But it seemed obvious that Japan itself would have to be invaded to force them to surrender. The casualties on both sides in such an operation were likely to be enormous. Was there another way?

Nagasaki, one month after the atom bomb was dropped

The atomic bomb

For several years secret research had been going on, mainly in the U.S.A., to produce a powerful bomb by splitting atoms of the highly radioactive element uranium. By the summer of 1945 such an atomic bomb had been successfully tested. But the full effects of using a bomb of this kind on a city were not all that clear. Should it be used to bring about the quick defeat of Japan? This was the dilemma facing the new American president, Harry S. Truman. But he did not hesitate.

Hiroshima and Nagasaki

On the morning of 6 August 1945 an atomic bomb was dropped by an American Superfortress bomber on to the Japanese city of Hiroshima. The city was obliterated; 60,000 people were killed; 100,000 people were injured, many suffering the agonies of radiation burns and sickness. An American author, John Hersey, wrote a famous description of the city after the attack. In the following extract, he describes the experiences of one of the survivors, a Jesuit priest.

On 18 August, twelve days after the bomb burst, Father Kleinsorge set out on foot for Hiroshima from the Novitiate with his papier-maché suitcase in his hand.... By now he was accustomed to the terrible scene through which he walked on his way into the city: the large rice field near the Novitiate, streaked with brown; the houses on the outskirts of the city, standing but decrepit, with broken windows and dishevelled tiles; and then, quite suddenly, the beginning of the four square miles of reddish-brown scar, where nearly everything had been buffeted down and burned; range on range of collapsed city blocks, with here and there a crude sign erected on a pile of ashes and tiles ('Sister, where are you?' or 'All safe and we live at Toyosaka'); naked trees and canted telephone poles; the few standing, gutted buildings only accentuating the horizontality of everything else; ... and in the streets a macabre traffic—hundreds of crumpled bicycles, shells of street cars and automobiles, all halted in mid-motion.... About half-way there, he began to have peculiar sensations. The more or less magical suitcase, now empty, suddenly seemed terribly heavy. His knees grew weak. He felt excruciatingly tired ... and the next morning the rector, who had examined Father Kleinsorge's apparently negligible but unhealed cuts daily, asked in surprise, 'What have you done to your wounds?' They had suddenly opened wider and were swollen and inflamed.

Even after the destruction of Hiroshima the Japanese still hesitated to surrender. But another atomic bomb, dropped on Nagasaki, persuaded them. On 14 August 1945 the Second World War came to an end.

Conferences of the Allied leaders

During the war high-level conferences of the Allied leaders were held to discuss the best ways of winning the war and of organising the world afterwards. The most important were as follows.

Tehran, November 1943

Roosevelt, Stalin and Churchill. Agreement to invade western Europe the following year.

Yalta, February 1945

Roosevelt, Stalin and Churchill. Arrangements to divide Germany into zones of occupation after the war and for Poland to give up some land to Russia and gain some land from Germany. The new western boundary of Poland was to be along the Oder and Neisse rivers.

Potsdam, July 1945

Stalin, Truman (Roosevelt had died in April) and Churchill (replaced by Attlee after Churchill's defeat in the general election). Little agreement. It was clear that Russia was determined to control eastern Europe (see p.128).

The Yalta Conference. Churchill, Roosevelt and Stalin

The world at the end of the War

Death and destruction

Large areas especially of Europe had been laid waste by the fighting. Huge sums of money had been spent. And about 50 million people had been killed. What does the graph on the right tell you about the varying intensity of the fighting in different parts of the world? And how do the figures compare with the First World War? (See p.15.)

Refugees

Many millions of people in Europe were uprooted from their homes either because they fled from the battlefields or because governments sent them off for slave labour. The problems of housing and feeding them were very difficult in 1945.

BRITAIN 0·4
USA 0·4
FRANCE 0·6
JAPAN 2
POLAND 6
GERMANY 6
RUSSIA 20
CHINA 20

The figures are in millions.

Some of the figures are very rough estimates and include civilians and those who died in concentration and prison camps as well as the armed forces. The figure for Poland is approximately $\frac{1}{6}$ of its population in 1939 and for Russia and Germany, approximately $\frac{1}{10}$

Figure 2 Deaths in the Second World War

The United Nations Organisation

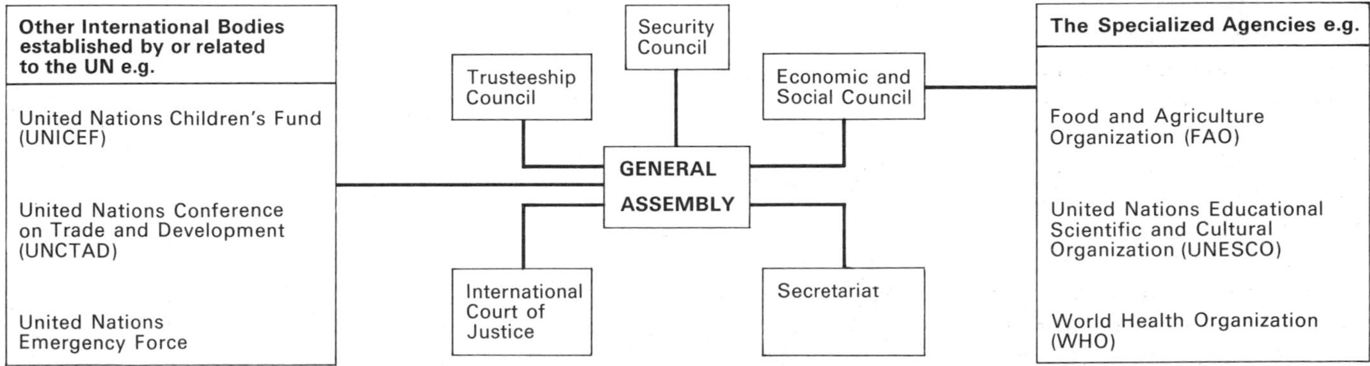

1 Foundation. The League of Nations had failed to prevent the Second World War (see p.60). It was decided to create a new international organisation.
2 Dumbarton Oaks Conference, 1944. Arrangements were discussed for the setting up of a United Nations Organisation.
3 Then in 1945 at a conference in San Francisco, the U.N. Charter was signed by 51 countries.

Structure. The U.N. operates from a 39-storey building in New York. The diagram shows you how the U.N. is organised. Every member is represented in the General Assembly (there were 159 by 1985). The Security Council consists of five permanent members (U.S.A., U.S.S.R., Britain, France and China) and others in turn. Much of the detailed work is undertaken by the secretariat under the Secretary-General (since 1981 — Perez de Cueller). Most of the important work of the United Nations is done by the Specialised Agencies such as the Food and Agriculture Organisation (FAO) and the World Health Organisation (WHO).
5 Peace-keeping. The U.N. has been involved in a number of operations to try to stop fighting. Some examples are mentioned in other chapters: Palestine (p.163), Kashmir (p.179), Korea (p.132), Egypt (p.166) and the Congo (pp.183–4).

Time chart

World War again

Questions

1 A 'At the beginning of July, Britain stood alone with no more than a narrow strip of sea separating her from the victorious armed forces of Hitler's Germany. Had the Germans been able to follow up their success by an immediate invasion, they might have succeeded. It is sometimes forgotten that the object of the R.A.F. was not simply to defeat the German air attacks but also the destruction of Hitler's plan for the invasion and conquest of Britain'.
'History of the 20th Century.' *Purnell.*

B 'We ran into them at 18,000 feet, twenty yellow-nosed Messerschmitt 109's about five hundred feet above us.... In two vital seconds they had lost the advantage.... For a second he seemed to hang motionless, then a jet of red flame shot upwards and he spun out of sight'.
'The Last Enemy' *Richard Hillary.*

C 'A small team of scientists under Watson-Watt secretly developed the first equipment. It became known as Radio Detection and Ranging and made use of radio echoes. The heart of the system was at Fighter Command, Stanmore and, from here, details of the position, strength and direction of the raiders were noted and plotted'.

D '... undaunted by odds, unwearied in their constant challenge and mortal danger, are turning the tide of war.... Never in the field of human conflict was so much owed by so many to so few'.
Prime Minister in a speech to the House of Commons.

Carefully read the four extracts above and then answer the following questions.

a Name the 'narrow strip of sea' mentioned in Extract A.
b Name two of the countries that had already been defeated by the Germans early in the war so that, by July 1940, 'Britain stood alone'.
c What was the R.A.F. trying to achieve at that time?
d Name any R.A.F. fighter plane that might have fought against the German Messerschmitts.
e What name is usually given to the battle of which the events described in Extract B were a part?
f What nickname was usually given to the equipment developed by Watson-Watt (Extract C)
g What great advantage did this equipment give the R.A.F. at this time?
h In Extract D, who exactly were the 'many' and the 'few'?
i Which British prime minister made this speech (Extract D) to the House of Commons?
j What were the long term consequences of the fialure of the Germans to win the battle against the R.A.F. in the skies over Britain?

2 Given below is a list of outstanding events in 1940:
Norway occupied
Churchill Prime Minister
Holland defeated
Dunkirk
Fall of France
Battle of Britain.
Write an account of the events in 1940. You may base your account on the list above, but you can add anything else you know about. Your account should explain why the Germans were very successful for most of the year, and why they were checked in 1940.

3 Give an account of the various types of air attack made on Britain from October 1940 to the end of the war, answering the following questions about each type of attack.
a What was the purpose of the attack?
b What type of plane or weapon was used?
c How successful was the attack?
d How was it countered by the British?

4 Outline in a paragraph (10–20 lines), the chief problems faced by the conquered population of Hitler's Europe.

5 Write a paragraph on each of any **two** of the following to show its importance in the Second World War:
a the Battle of Britain;
b the German invasion of Russia;
c the Japanese attack on Pearl Harbour;
d the Battle of the Atlantic;
e the Normandy landings.

6 The fighting in the Second World War was spread over the world. Write out the following list of battles, and against each one, write the names of the main countries involved.
a Matapan;
b Stalingrad;
c Midway Island;
d El Alamein;
e Arnhem:
f Okinawa.
Write accounts of any **two** of these battles explaining why the battle was fought, giving details of the fighting and the effects of the battle on the rest of the war.

Questions

7 The following extracts are from an official book entitled *Front Line 1940–41* about the work of the Civil Defence forces in Britain during the 'Blitz'. Study them carefully and then, using the information, write an imaginary account of the work of the Civil Defence during and after an air-raid.

Source A

'By 6 o'clock the day raiders had gone. There was a two-hour break in the attack. At ten minutes past eight the night raiding force appeared, guided straight to its targets by huge riverside fires which it set out to stoke with high explosive and incendiary bombs. Until 4.30 next morning the droning process went on. Some 250 bombers were over the city. When the last departed there were, as product of the day and night attack, nine conflagrations (huge spreading areas of flame), nineteen fires that would normally have called for thirty pumps or more, forty ten-pump fires, and nearly a thousand lesser blazes, . . .

'In the dockside boroughs thousands of houses were destroyed or damaged by bomb and fire, though many of them not irreparably. The factories that sprinkle London and the railway lines that run so plentifully near the river had their inevitable share of hits. Three of the main line terminal stations were out of action.

'Four hundred and thirty men, women and children lost their lives and 1,600 were seriously wounded. Fire did little of this slaughter: it was wreaked by collapsing walls and ceilings, by the direct impact of bombs, by flying brick and stone, by swift javelins of splintered glass.'

Source B

'Mrs A. was a district warden in charge of seven unusually large posts, having under her 250 wardens, and 25,000 people . . .

'"I'm not brave," she said. "When the warning goes or a bomb falls, my inside turns over and I have to get a grip of myself. But when I go out and can see what's going on and have something to do, I'm all right." She was grateful to the senior wardens with whom she worked when she first joined the service. They took her about, showed her when to duck, and taught her never to feel depressed however wretched the prospect. One of her difficulties was to make recommendations for gallantry awards, for she was usually so absorbed in her job as to be quite unaware of the colleagues next to whom she might be working.'

Source C

	Personal and social needs (the succour and protection of human beings)	Material needs (the defence and restoration of the physical basis of life)
During attack	The police The wardens' service The rescue service The casualty services	The Fire-fighting Services Fire prevention (the Fire Guard)
After attack	Immediate after-care (Rest Centres) Emergency feeding Information and instruction Rehousing and billeting Money compensation Salvage and replacement of personal possessions	Food: maintenance of supplies Factories: repair and reconstruction Housing: repair Communications: repair or restoration of roads, railways, telephone, telegraph and postal facilities Essential services: repair of gas, water and electricity mains and sewage pipes Salvage of damaged materials for further use

7/Wealth & poverty in the New World

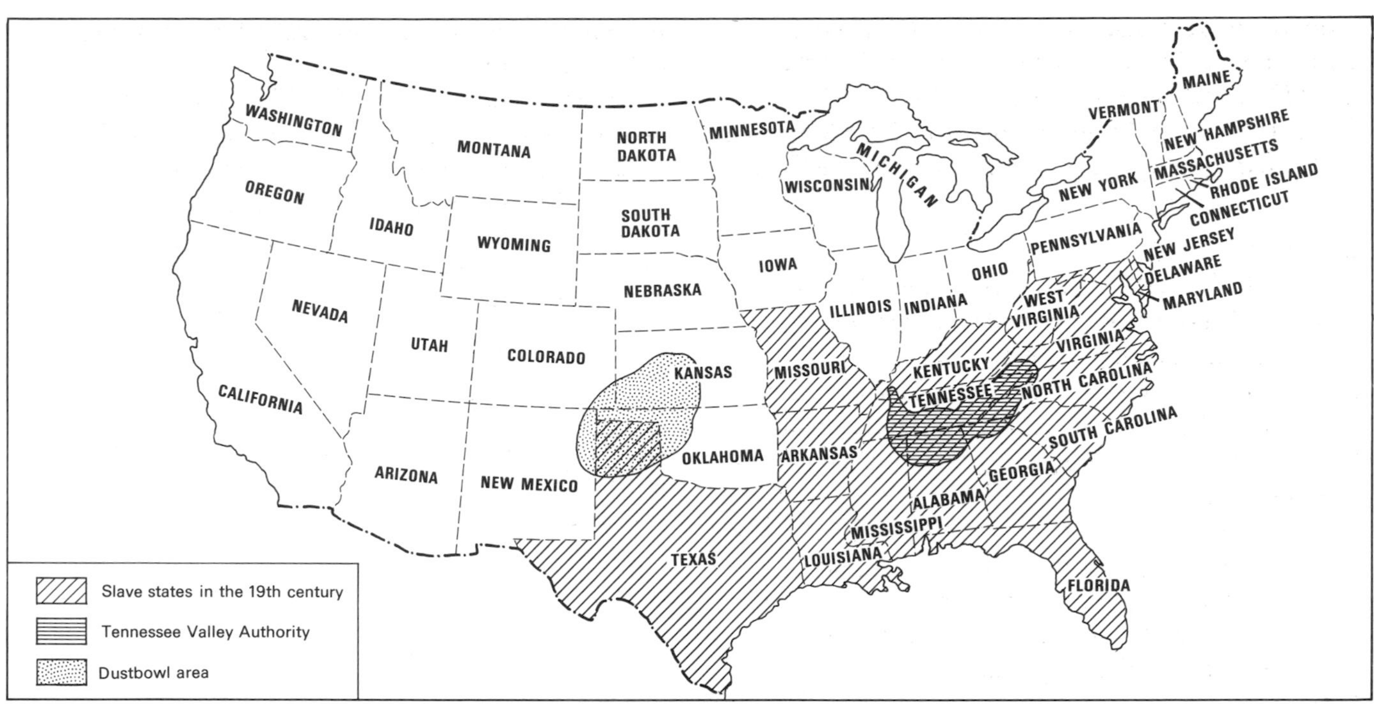

Map 1 The U.S.A., 1900–40

The U.S.A. at the beginning of the century

The land and the people

The size and wealth of the country

The U.S.A. is almost a continent in its size and variety. At the beginning of the twentieth century there was very little that the Americans could not produce for themselves. Railways, oil-drilling, steel-production and wheat and beef farming were all well developed and had made some people very wealthy. There was a general feeling that no one need be poor if he had sufficient energy and initiative. And there was a common belief that the government had no need to concern itself about the many people who were in fact very poor.

Immigrants arriving from Europe, 1890

'The melting pot'

Its rapidly expanding industries and vast open prairies for farming gave the U.S.A. the reputation of being a land of splendid opportunities. Meanwhile, in the late nineteenth and early twentieth centuries there was much poverty and misery in Europe. As a result millions of people emigrated to the U.S.A. from Europe. In 1910 over one-seventh of the population of 92 millions had not been born in the U.S.A. Many of these people were very poor—they arrived in America with next to nothing. Most of them were not even able to speak English. Gradually, however, they, or at least their children, fully adapted to the American way of life.

The U.S.A. at the beginning of the century

Blacks

Another group with many disadvantages were the blacks. Black people had been brought to American from Africa to work as slaves (see Map 1). Slavery was abolished in 1863. But the black people suffered many disadvantages until quite recently, especially in the southern states. At the beginning of the century these were some of the disadvantages. (Compare these conditions with South African apartheid, p.187).

1 Segregation. For example, black and white children had to attend different schools and black people had to sit apart from white people in buses and restaurants.

2 Discrimination. Black people were not given well-paid or important jobs.

3 Disenfranchisement. After the abolition of slavery negroes were meant to be able to vote in elections just like white men. But round about 1900 campaigns were organised in the southern states to prevent black people from voting. This was done by introducing tests which the blacks could not pass such as the ability to read. (They could not read because they had no good schools.)

4 Persecution. Black people were still treated very brutally. Some fanatical white men organised themselves into a secret society called the Ku Klux Klan. They tortured and even killed blacks.

The Ku Klux Klan initiation ceremony

The American Empire

Towards the end of the nineteenth century and in the early part of the twentieth century the U.S.A. started to increase her influence in Central and South America and across the Pacific Ocean. The U.S.A. took the following lands (see Map 2):

1 Puerto Rico, Philippines, Hawaiian Islands and several other Pacific Islands including Guam and Wake Island (in the Spanish-American War, 1898).

2 Panama Canal Zone (bought from Panama in 1903 in order to build the Canal which was opened in 1914).

Theodore Roosevelt (President 1901–9) was especially keen on extending American influence.

Map 2 The American Empire, 1900

The U.S.A. at the beginning of the century

Government

The President

The President of the U.S.A. is both the Head of State (like the British monarch) and Head of Government (like the British prime minister). Neither he nor his cabinet are members of Congress, quite unlike the British system where ministers must be members of one of the houses of parliament.

Congress

1 House of Representatives. Members, known as Congressmen, are elected in constituencies. The two main parties are Republicans and Democrats.

2 Senate. More important than the House of Representatives. Two senators are elected to represent each state irrespective of its size. Since 1959, when Alaska and Hawaii became states, there have been 100.

The federal system

The President and Congress work in Washington, the capital city of the U.S.A. But they do not do all the work of governing the country. The U.S.A. is a union of states. Each state (see Map 1) has control over some of its own affairs like police and education.

Elections

1 The President is elected for a period of four years. He can be re-elected, though since 1951 only for one extra term.

2 Congressmen are elected for two years.

3 Senators are elected for six years. Because these elections are held separately it is possible for the President to be of a different party from that holding a majority in one or both houses of Congress.

The White House—the President

The Capitol Building—Congress

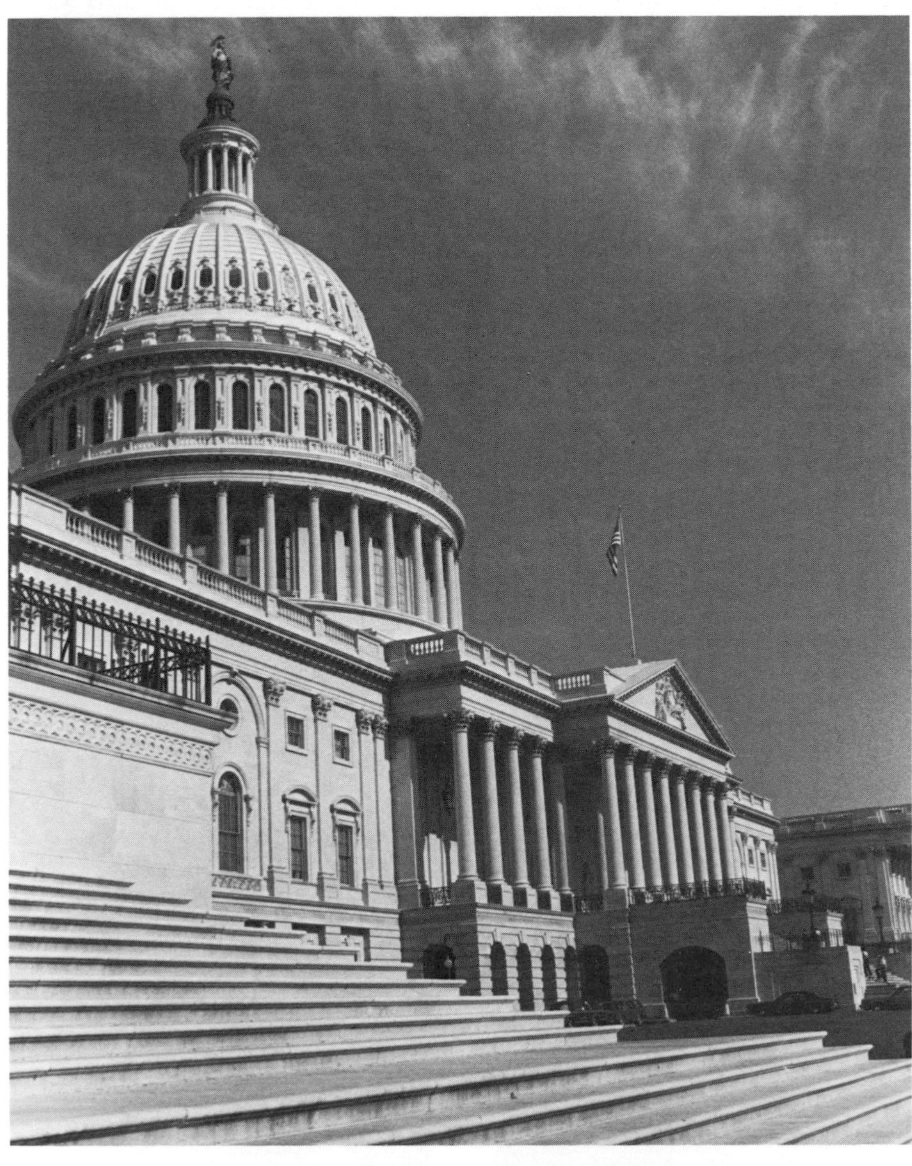

The 1920s

Post-war America

Return to peace

As we saw in Chapter 2 the U.S.A. fought in the First World War. But immediately the war was over there was a strong feeling among Americans that they wished to have nothing more to do with Europe. This policy was called 'isolationism'. The U.S.A. did not join the League of Nations. Also a series of laws drastically reduced the number of immigrants who could now enter the U.S.A. But the 1920s were exciting years, sometimes called 'The Roaring Twenties'. It was the great jazz age and the years when the cinema industry developed. The early 1920s were also years of great scandal as corruption was uncovered among members of the government.

Prohibition and gangsters

In 1920 the eighteenth amendment to the U.S. Constitution became law. This prohibited 'the manufacture, sale, or transportation of intoxicating liquors.' The law was repealed (withdrawn) in 1933. These thirteen years were the years of prohibition. But in an attempt to stamp out drunkenness, the American government found that it had encouraged gangsterism. This became the age of illegal bars called 'speakeasies'; of 'bootleggers' who supplied illegal liquor; of protection rackets; and of rival gang warfare.

Al Capone—a notorious gangster

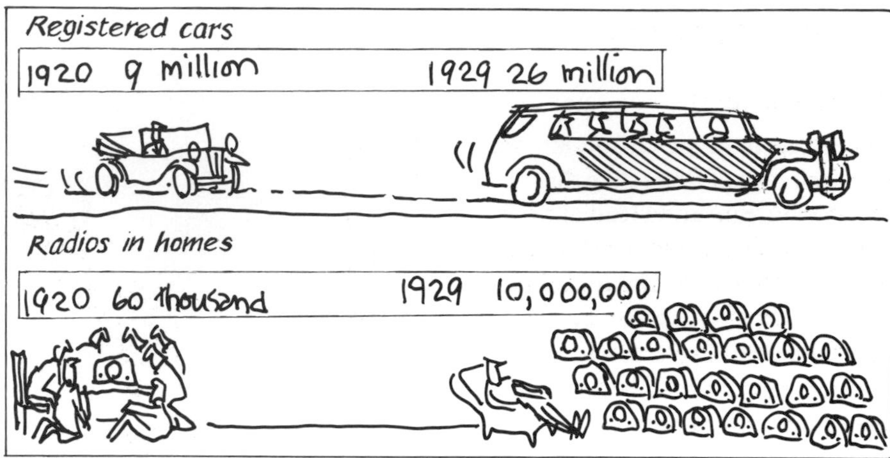

Figure 1 Increase in cars and radio ownership 1920–29

Industry

Meanwhile American industry was booming, taking advantage particularly of mass-production techniques and hire-purchase arrangements. Figure 1 provides just two examples to show how Americans benefited from this boom.

Wealth

While Coolidge was President (1923–29) America seemed on the verge of ridding itself of the curse of poverty. Some people became fabulously rich. A famous novel called *The Great Gatsby* by Scott Fitzgerald gives a vivid description of the wealth some people enjoyed in the 1920s.

On weekends his Rolls-Royce became an omnibus, bearing parties to and from the city between nine in the morning and long past midnight. . . . And on Mondays eight servants . . . toiled all day . . . repairing the ravages of the night before.

Every Friday five crates of oranges and lemons arrived from a fruiterer in New York. . . .

At least once a fortnight a corps of caterers came down. . . .

By seven o'clock the orchestra has arrived, no thin five-piece affair, but a whole pitful . . . the cars from New York are parked five deep in the drive.

The Roaring Twenties

Economic problems

The Great Crash

But the whole economic system was based on the confidence of the investor. People invested money in stocks and shares and made money when the companies made profits. Sales started to decline in the late 1920s. In 1929 investors became nervous. Some started to sell their shares, then many more followed. On 29 October ('Black Tuesday') more than 16 million shares were sold on the New York Stock Exchange in Wall Street. Nervousness had turned to panic. Shares became worthless. Some banks had to close. Many businessmen were ruined in the Wall Street crash. The dream of perpetual growth in wealth had turned into the nightmare of the Depression.

Unemployment

As firms went bankrupt men were thrown out of work. And not just in the towns: there were difficulties in rural areas as farmers were unable to get loans from banks. Unemployment rose alarmingly from 1930 to 1933, as you can see from the graph

While Hoover was President (1929–33) millions of men became idle, bitter and destitute. Many even turned to begging as the song 'Brother, Can You Spare a Dime?' showed (a dime is a ten-cent coin):

> Once I built a railroad, made it run,
> Made it race against time.
> Once I built a railroad,
> Now it's done—
> Brother, can you spare a dime?

These economic problems in the U.S.A. were experienced in many European countries as well. So American firms also found it difficult to sell goods abroad.

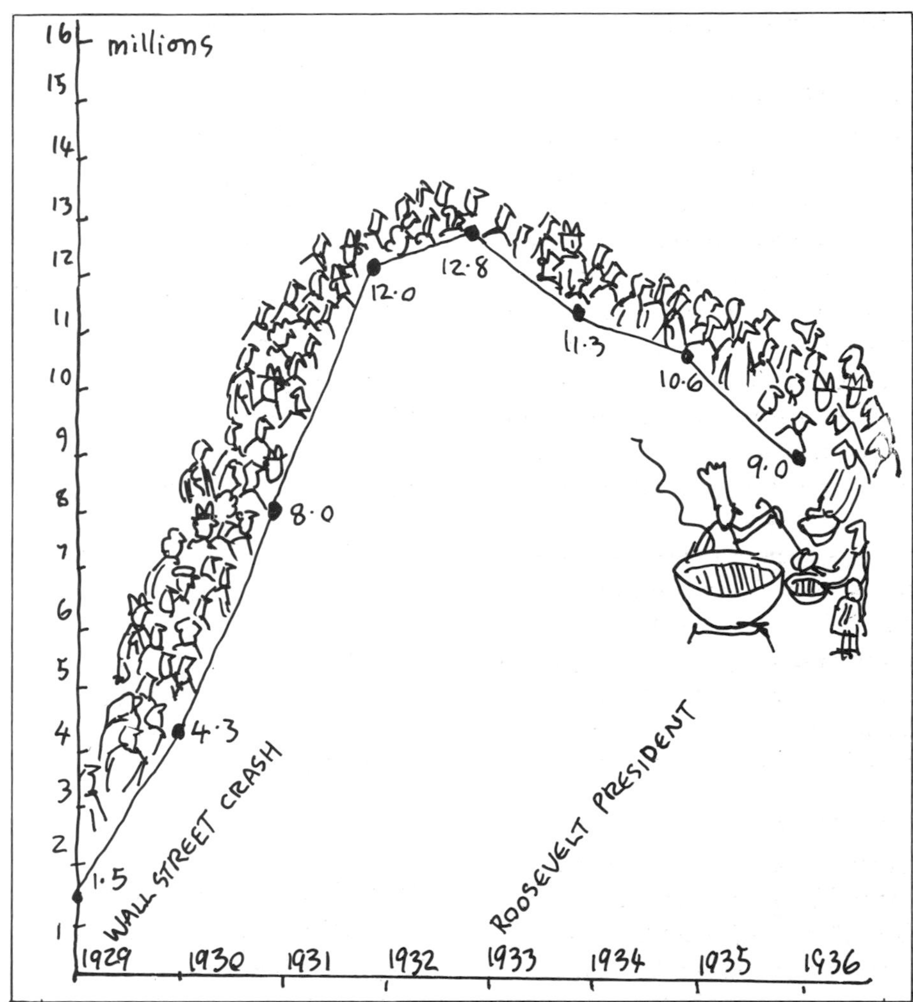

Figure 2 Unemployment in 1930s (in millions)

A queue of unemployed workers, 1932

The New Deal

Roosevelt as President

In 1932 Franklin Delano Roosevelt, the Governor of New York, was nominated by the Democrats as their candidate for the presidential election. He pledged himself to give America 'a new deal'. He won the election and remained President for a record length of time, from 1933 until his death in 1945. Although he had been crippled by polio in 1921, he was a man of great energy and determination.

President Franklin D. Roosevelt

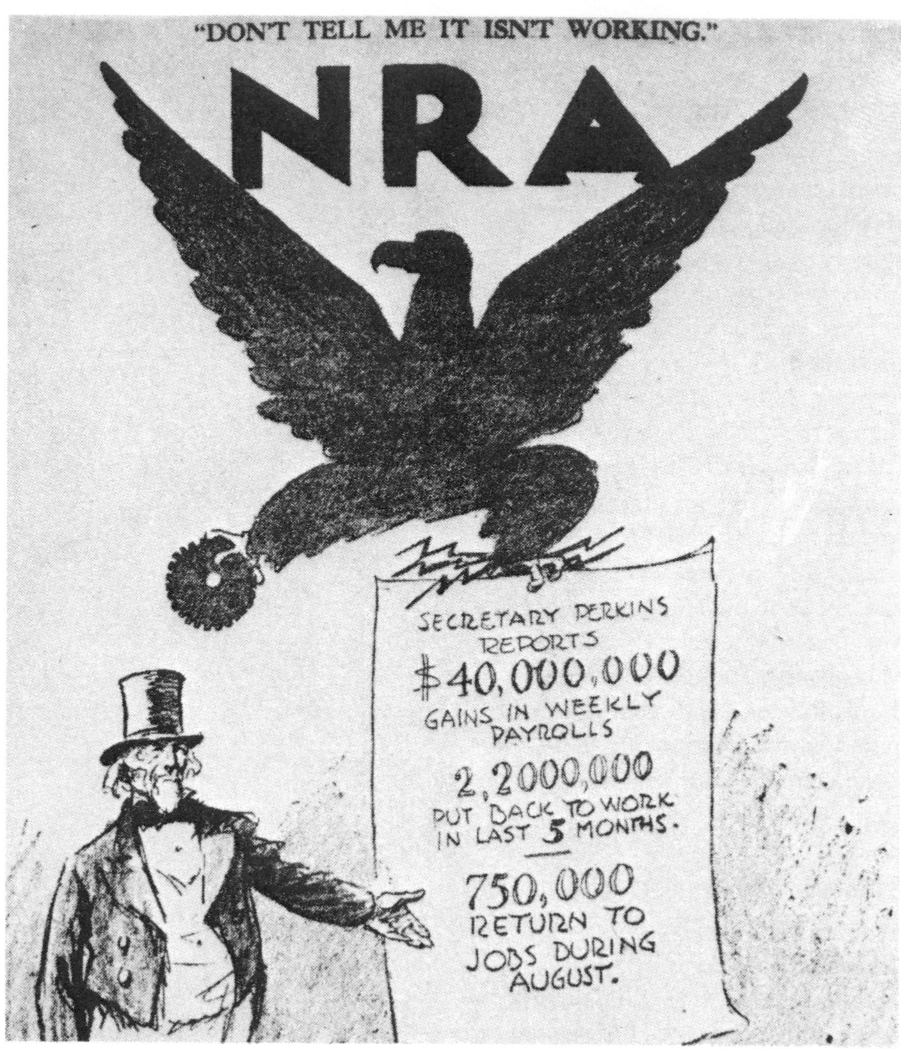
"DON'T TELL ME IT ISN'T WORKING."
NRA
SECRETARY PERKINS REPORTS
$40,000,000
GAINS IN WEEKLY PAYROLLS
2,2000,000
PUT BACK TO WORK IN LAST 5 MONTHS.
750,000
RETURN TO JOBS DURING AUGUST.

A newspaper cartoon praising the work of the N.R.A., 18 September 1933

The New Deal policy

During his first hundred days in office Roosevelt arranged for a number of laws and schemes to be introduced in order to pull America out of the Depression. These were followed up by more and more schemes during the next five years. He spoke in 'Fireside Chats' over the wireless to explain what he was doing. He recruited enthusiastic and vigorous men to put the policies into effect. The policy had two aims:

1 to revive businesses, industry and farming;

2 to help the unemployed find jobs and in the meantime give them food and money.

Some of the schemes

1 Agricultural Adjustment Administration (A.A.A.). To plan food production and to guarantee reasonable prices for farmers.

2 Civilian Conservation Corps (C.C.C.). Unemployed young men were organised for projects such as reforestation and restocking rivers with fish.

3 National Recovery Administration (N.R.A.). Workers and management to agree on prices for goods and working conditions.

4 Public Works Administration (P.W.A.), Civil Works Administration (C.W.A.), Works Progress Administration (W.P.A.). To provide work schemes for the unemployed. Many new schools, hospitals, roads, ships and airfields were built.

5 Home Owners' Loan Corporation (H.O.L.C.). To help people who were unable to keep up with mortgage payments.

6 Social Security Act. The start of 'welfare state' schemes, e.g. old age pensions.

7 Tennessee Valley Authority (T.V.A.). The most famous of all the New Deal Schemes. A huge scheme covering a great area of south-east America (see Map 1)

where poverty and unemployment were particularly serious. Dams were built to control flooding and provide cheap hydro-electric power.

What was achieved?

The New Deal revived American industry and agriculture; it saved millions from destitution; it helped to modernise public buildings and services; and, as you can see from the Graph on p.101, it reduced the unemployment figure. An enormous amount had been achieved by about 1935. But serious problems remained and Roosevelt suffered some bitter criticism.

Continuing problems

The Dustbowl

The work of the A.A.A. did not by any means benefit all farmers. And it was most severely tested when, in the mid-1930s, a combination of drought and soil erosion turned the vast area shown on Map 1 into a great dust bowl, from where all life fled or died. A great novel called *The Grapes of Wrath* by John Steinbeck is about a family who migrate from Oklahoma because of these conditions. Here is part of the opening description:

> Little by little the sky darkened by the mixing dust, and the wind felt over the earth, loosened the dust, and carried it away....
>
> All day the dust sifted down from the sky, and the next day it sifted down. An even blanket covered the earth. It settled on the corn, piled up on the tops of the fence posts, piled up on the wires; it settled on roofs, blanketed the weeds and trees.

Opposition to the New Deal

The New Deal meant more government interference in the life of the country than ever before. This policy was quite contrary to the tradition of individual self-reliance (see p.97). It also weakened the power of the states in comparison with the central, federal government (see p.99) and greatly strengthened the power of the President. Many came to hate Roosevelt because of this. He was called a Communist and a Fascist. Germany had very similar economic problems to the U.S.A. at this time. Compare the way Hitler tackled them (p.56) to Roosevelt's way. Which do you think was preferable? Do you think that it would have been possible to tackle America's economic problems without increasing the powers of the government?

The Second World War

When the Second World War broke out the U.S.A. kept to its policy of isolationism. As we have seen in Chapter 6, the U.S.A. entered the war when the Japanese attacked in December 1941. Roosevelt became one of the most important Allied leaders. But earlier in 1941 he had already shown by three actions that he opposed the Axis.

Four freedoms, January 1941

Roosevelt declared that by the end of the war the peoples of the world should enjoy freedom of speech, of worship, from want and from fear.

Lend-lease Act, March 1941

Urgently needed military supplies were made available first to Britain, then later to Russia.

Atlantic Charter, August 1941

Drawn up by Roosevelt and Churchill on board the British battleship H.M.S. *Prince of Wales*. It looked ahead to a free and prosperous world after the end of the war.

A typical dustbowl scene. The shack has been deserted by its owners who have probably moved to the nearest city. Notice the dead trees

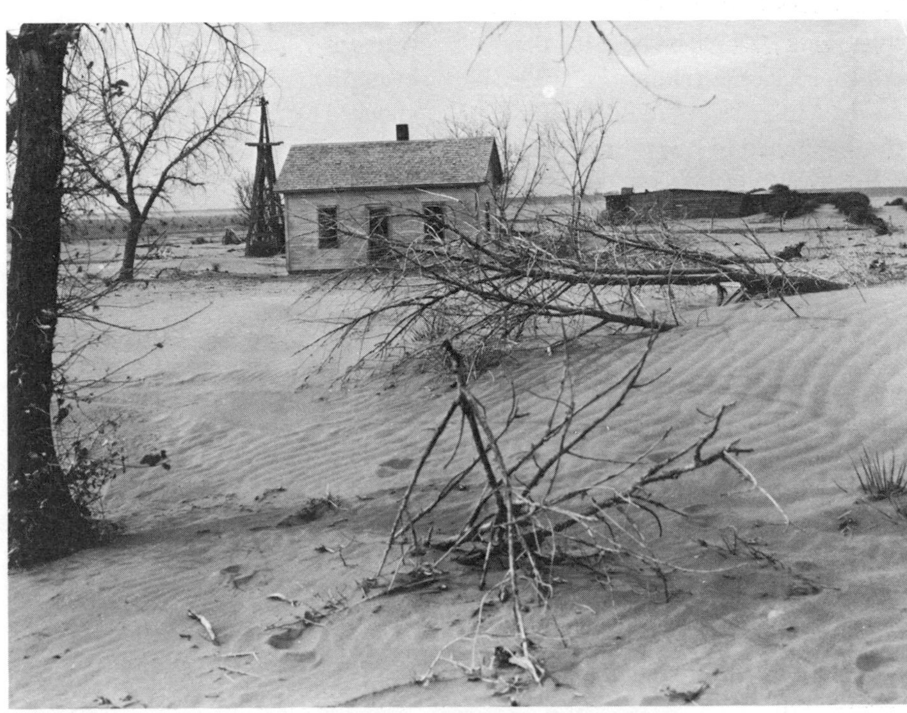

The U.S.A. since 1945

Presidents and their problems

Truman and Eisenhower

When Roosevelt died he was succeeded by his Vice-President, Harry S. Truman. The next President was Dwight D. Eisenhower. Both of these Presidents were very much concerned with the Cold War (see Chapter 9).

Kennedy

John F. Kennedy won the Presidential election in 1960 by a very narrow majority. But he soon became very popular. He was the youngest man ever to be President (he was 43 when he took office in 1961). He tried to stir up enthusiasm to tackle the 'New Frontier'—scientific and social problems that needed to be solved. Why do you think that he chose this particular phrase? He spent much effort trying to solve the Cold War struggle with Russia (see p.137) and on the race problem within the U.S.A. (see p.106). In order to show that the Americans were technically more advanced than the Russians, he ordered that an American man should be landed on the Moon before 1970 (in fact, this happened in July 1969 when Neil Armstrong set foot on the Moon's surface).

Assassination of Lee Harvey Oswald, the assumed killer of President Kennedy.

Kennedy had little time to tackle the problems he wished to solve. In November 1963 he was shot and killed. This happened in Dallas, Texas, while he was touring the southern states. Exactly why he was killed is still a mystery. It is thought that a man called Lee Harvey Oswald fired the shots but he in turn was killed before he could be brought to trial. Many people were shocked by this evidence of the violence in American society.

Johnson

Immediately on the death of Kennedy his Vice-President, Lyndon B. Johnson, became President. He became a very unpopular President because it was during this time that America became increasingly involved in Vietnam (see p.141). Serious demonstrations broke out in many parts of the U.S.A. demanding that American forces be withdrawn.

But in many ways Johnson's unpopularity was unfair. His slogan was the 'Great Society'. More reforms were passed than at any time since the New Deal, though admittedly they were not as successful as he had hoped. The most important were:

1 Civil Rights Act (1964) to enable black people to use their right to vote.

2 Office of Economic Opportunity (1965) to help the poor with services and advice.

3 Medicare Act (1965) to provide cheap medical treatment for old people.

Nixon

Richard Nixon will be remembered for his efforts to build up a closer relationship with China (see p.124).

An anti-Vietnam War march. This march in San Francisco was one of thousands that took place all over the world in the mid- to late 1960s

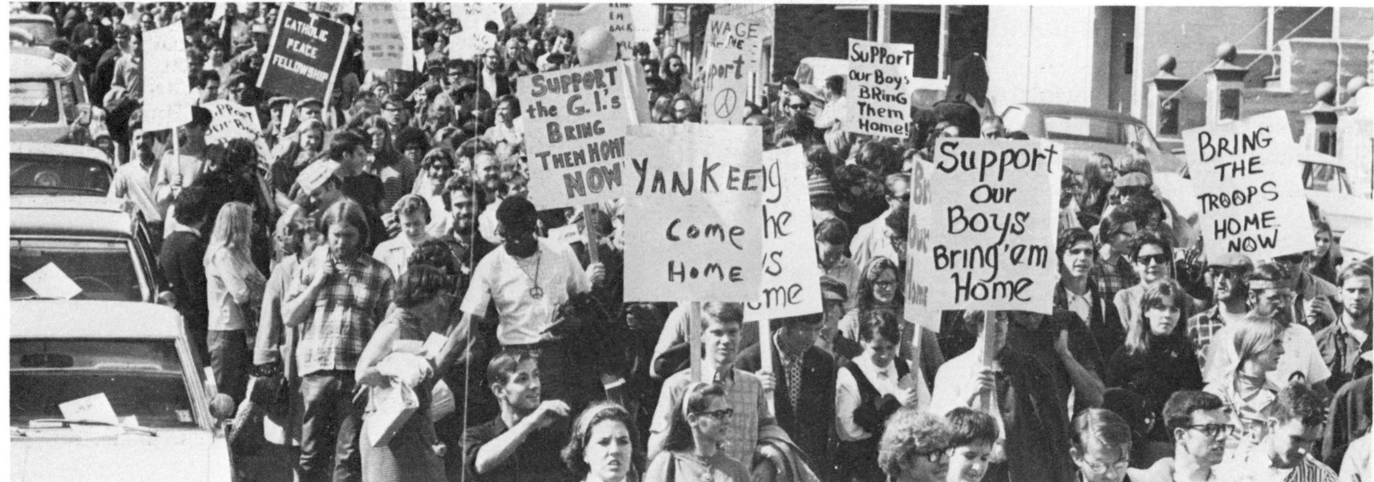

But he will also be remembered for a most embarrassing scandal. During the 1972 presidential election campaign Nixon was the candidate of the Republican Party for re-election. The Democratic Party's headquarters in the Watergate Building in Washington were 'bugged' by electronic listening devices. It became clear that some of Nixon's closest advisers were involved. Nixon denied that he knew anything about this spying. He was lying. He was forced to resign in shame. He was succeeded as President for the rest of his presidential term by his Vice-President, Gerald Ford.

Carter

Jimmy Carter, who became President in 1977, seemed a very honest and sincere man in contrast to Nixon. He had many problems to cope with including the crises in Iran (see p.171) and Afghanistan (see p.142). He also recognised the very serious nature of the energy crisis even though he was unable to do anything very effective about it. America was using huge quantities of oil, yet the earth's supplies were rapidly being exhausted. He was defeated in the presidential elections of November 1980 by Ronald Reagan.

Reagan

Before entering politics Ronald Reagan (pronounced Ray-gan) spent many years as a film-actor. He is the oldest man ever to have been President of the U.S.A. and had a reputation for not understanding the details of his work. Nevertheless, he was very popular, for the following reasons:

1945–53 Truman Democrat

1953–61 Eisenhower Republican

1961–63 Kennedy Democrat

1963–69 Johnson Democrat

1969–74 Nixon Republican

1974–77 Ford Republican

1977–81 Carter Democrat

1981–89 Reagan Republican

American Presidents since the end of the Second World War

1 He has a friendly manner, is effective on television, and claims to uphold Christian principles.

2 He promised a 'tough' policy against Communism and increased spending on weapons.

3 While many people have become poorer in the 1980s in the U.S.A., many others have become richer.

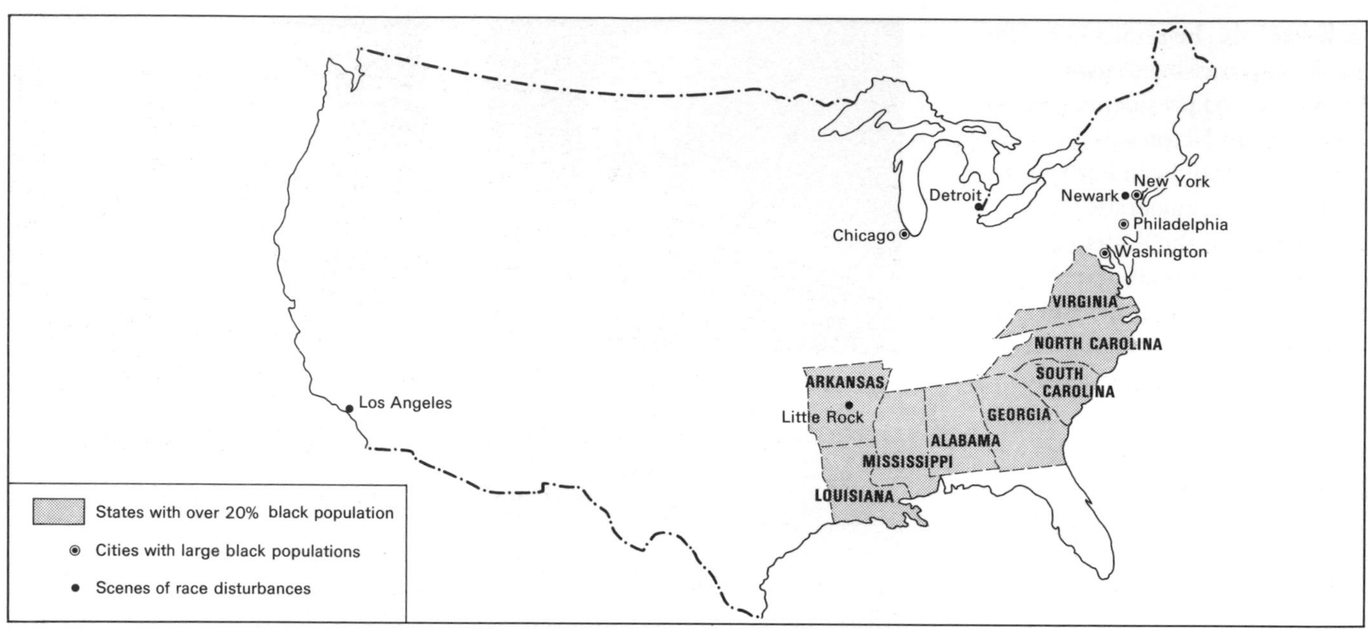

Map 3 The distribution of blacks in the U.S.A. in the 1960s

Race

What was the problem?

We saw on p.100 that at the beginning of the century the American black people suffered many disadvantages. Half a century later their condition was not much better although they numbered over one-tenth of the total population. But a larger proportion were now living in the northern cities. They had moved there to seek a better life, though most lived in slum ghetto areas. Also, the black people were no longer willing to accept these conditions.

Martin Luther King (1929–68), black civil rights leader

Peaceful demonstrations

The most important black leader in the 1960s was Dr Martin Luther King. He was a clergyman and insisted that his people should demonstrate for reforms without using violence. Black people protested, for example, by occupying seats reserved for white people in buses and restaurants. One of Dr King's most bitter opponents was George Wallace, a southern politician who became Governor of Alabama in 1963. He did everything in his power to keep segregation.

In 1963 Dr King organised a massive demonstration attended by a quarter of a million people in Washington. The meeting was to demand Civil Rights, that is equal political and legal rights with white people. Dr King made a famous speech. He said, 'I have a dream that one day this nation will rise up and live out the true meaning of its creed: "We hold these truths to be self-evident, that all men are created equal."' He was very successful in persuading people that what he was demanding was just. He was awarded the Nobel Peace Prize in 1967. The next year he was assassinated by a white man.

The U.S.A. since 1945

Violence

Not all American blacks agreed about using only peaceful methods.

The Black Power movement grew in the 1960s. They were prepared to use violence to obtain their rights and to keep themselves proudly different from the white people. Some became Muslims to emphasise their rejection of white man's Christianity. One of the most famous was the world heavy-weight boxing champion, Cassius Clay, who took the new name, Muhammed Ali.

Serious race riots, causing deaths and huge damage to property, broke out in the 1960s. The most serious were in the Watts district of Los Angeles, Newark and Detroit, all in 1965 (see Map 3).

The National Guard escorts black students into the High School at Little Rock, Arkansas

Black children playing on the streets of Harlem

What reforms were introduced?

Several laws were passed in the 1960s to make discrimination against black people illegal. The most important was the Civil Rights Act passed in 1964.

In 1954 the Supreme Court ruled that it was contrary to the Constitution to have separate white and black schools. This ruling was tested in 1957 when President Eisenhower sent armed men to a school in Little Rock, Arkansas, to escort some black children into a mainly white school.

The position of the black people improved considerably in the 1970s. For example, segregation in schools and public places was quickly reduced, more black people obtained important jobs and black people secured the right to vote.

Nevertheless, as unemployment increased in the early 1980s it was clear that the minority groups in the U.S.A. were still underprivileged. The proportion of Mexican and Puerto Rican immigrants, as well as Blacks, who were unemployed was well above the national average.

Daniel Ortega (left), President of Nicaragua, 1985–90, and his brother Humberto, Army Chief

Fidel Castro, who overthrew the hated dictator of Cuba, Batista, in 1959

U.S. relations with Latin America

The poverty of Latin America

The countries of Central and South America are called 'Latin America' because the people speak Spanish or Portuguese – languages derived from Latin.

Until quite recently most of the people were peasants and most of these were very poor. However, in recent years the populations of some of the big cities have grown enormously. For example, by 1985 the populations of Buenos Aires (Argentina), Rio de Janeiro and Sao Paulo (both Brazil) together totalled 15 million; and Mexico City, the largest capital in the world, had 18 million. Many of their citizens lived in slum 'shanty-towns' on the outskirts.

The great majority of the people of Latin America are poor; and the four countries with the biggest international debts in the world in 1985 were Latin American – Brazil ($105 bn), Mexico ($93 bn), Argentina ($47 bn), Venezuela ($35 bn).

Politics in Latin America

In most Latin American countries throughout the twentieth century dictators have been in control and have generally prevented the discontent of the poor people from breaking out into violence. Often the government has been a group of army officers. This 'committee of dictators' is called a *junta*.

The history of Argentina is particularly interesting because the government of the dictator Peron and his wife Eva was very popular from 1946–52. There followed many years of unstable and unhappy government, often by generals. From 1981 to 1982 the dictator was General Galtieri. He was unpopular; and to try to improve his popularity he invaded and captured the Falkland Islands, a British colony. The British government sent a task force to recover the islands. This war increased the popularity of Mrs Thatcher, the British prime minister, but Galtieri was forced to resign.

Revolutionary movements have developed in some countries. As a result there have been left-wing governments in Chile (under Salvador Allende, 1970–73), Cuba (under Fidel Castro, since 1959) and Nicaragua (under the Sandinista movement, 1979–91).

U.S. influence

We saw on p.98 how the U.S.A. gained influence in Central America at the turn of the century. Since then, many important American companies have invested a great deal of money in a number of Latin American countries. Since 1945 especially the U.S. government has protected Latin American governments that would not interfere with these firms.

In 1948 the Organisation of American States was set up. The U.S.A. and most Latin American

Contrasts in wealth in Rio de Janeiro

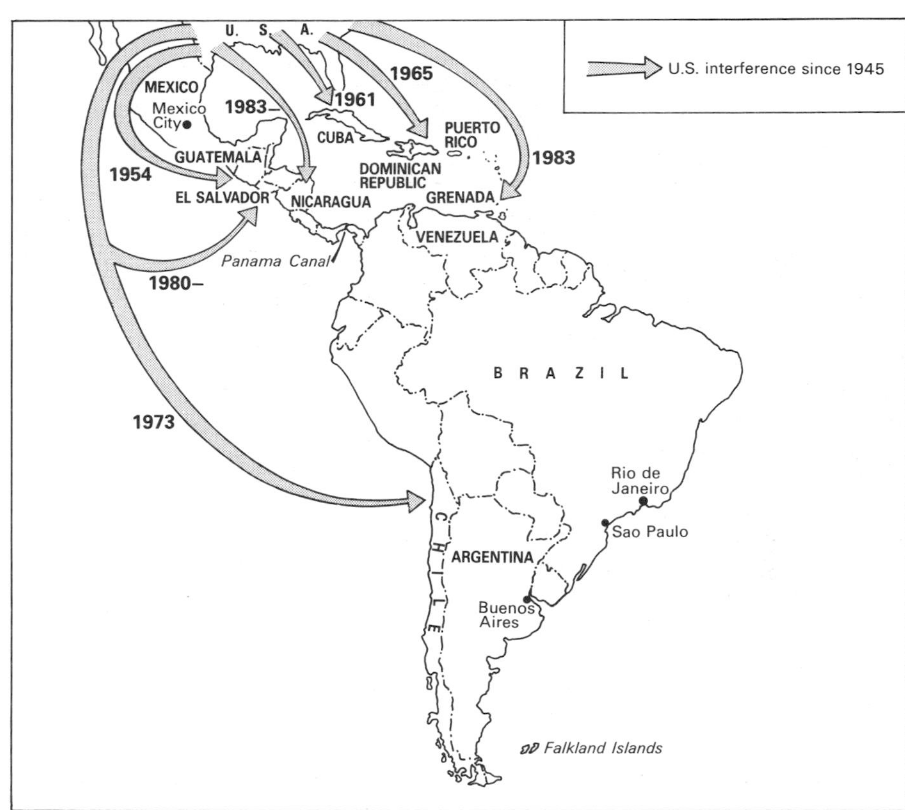

Map 4: Latin America since 1945

countries have been members. In theory the organisation is to help the countries co-operate with each other. In practice, it has helped the U.S.A. to keep its influence.

The U.S. secret service, the Central Intelligence Agency (C.I.A.) has been very active in many Latin American countries to try to prevent revolutions from breaking out.

American troops in the Dominican Republic, 1965

U.S. interference, 1945–80

1 Guatemala, 1954. A reforming government was overthrown with the help of the Americans.
2 Cuba, 1961. In Chapter 9 we shall see how the Americans failed to overthrow Fidel Castro's Communist government.
3 Dominican Republic, 1965. Thousands of U.S. troops were sent to crush a revolution.
4 Chile, 1973. From 1970 to 1973 Salvador Allende was prime minister. He was a Communist and nationalised some American-owned firms. The Americans helped to overthrow him.

U.S. interference since 1980

President Reagan became particularly concerned about the increasing influence of Communism in Central America and the Caribbean.

1 The U.S.A. has supported several cruel governments in Central America. Especially notorious was its support for the government of El Salvador during the start of the civil war there in 1980–81.
2 The Americans increased their support in 1983 for rebels fighting against the left-wing Sandinista Government in Nicaragua.
3 U.S. troops landed on the island of Grenada in 1983 to overturn a brutal left-wing government.

The U.S.A. in the 1980s

The U.S.A. is the richest country in the world, one of the two most powerful and a country where people enjoy a great deal of freedom. Yet each of its achievements has had an accompanying problem.

The U.S.A. produces a great deal of wealth on its farms and in its factories. But a large number of people do not enjoy a share of this wealth, especially the non-white people – Blacks, chicanos (Mexicans and Puerto Ricans), for example. Many Mexicans are still entering the U.S.A. despite attempts to patrol the frontier along the Rio Grande river. In the cities these poor people are living in dilapidated ghettos. Also, although the black people have become equal in theory, in practice a large number are still poor.

Furthermore, not enough of the wealth is being used to repair the dilapidated towns. And so the economist J. K. Galbraith has coined the phrase 'private affluence; public squalor'.

American people own more cars and electrical goods than any other. But although they produce a lot of their own oil, they are having to import increasing quantities and there are serious worries about what will happen when the supplies of oil dry up.

The Americans are proud of living in the freest country. But freedom includes the freedom to own guns and the number of murders in the U.S.A. each year is horrifying.

For many years the U.S.A. has been the most powerful country in the world. But by 1980 Russia had become just as powerful. Also the Americans had felt powerless during the 1970s to help the non-Communist governments in Indo-China (see pp.141–2) or even to help their own people held hostage in Tehran (see p.171). These changes hurt American pride.

A petrol queue in California during the energy crisis caused by the revolution in Iran in 1979. The owner of the filling station is running out of petrol and has put this sign on the car

Time chart

Wealth and poverty in the New World

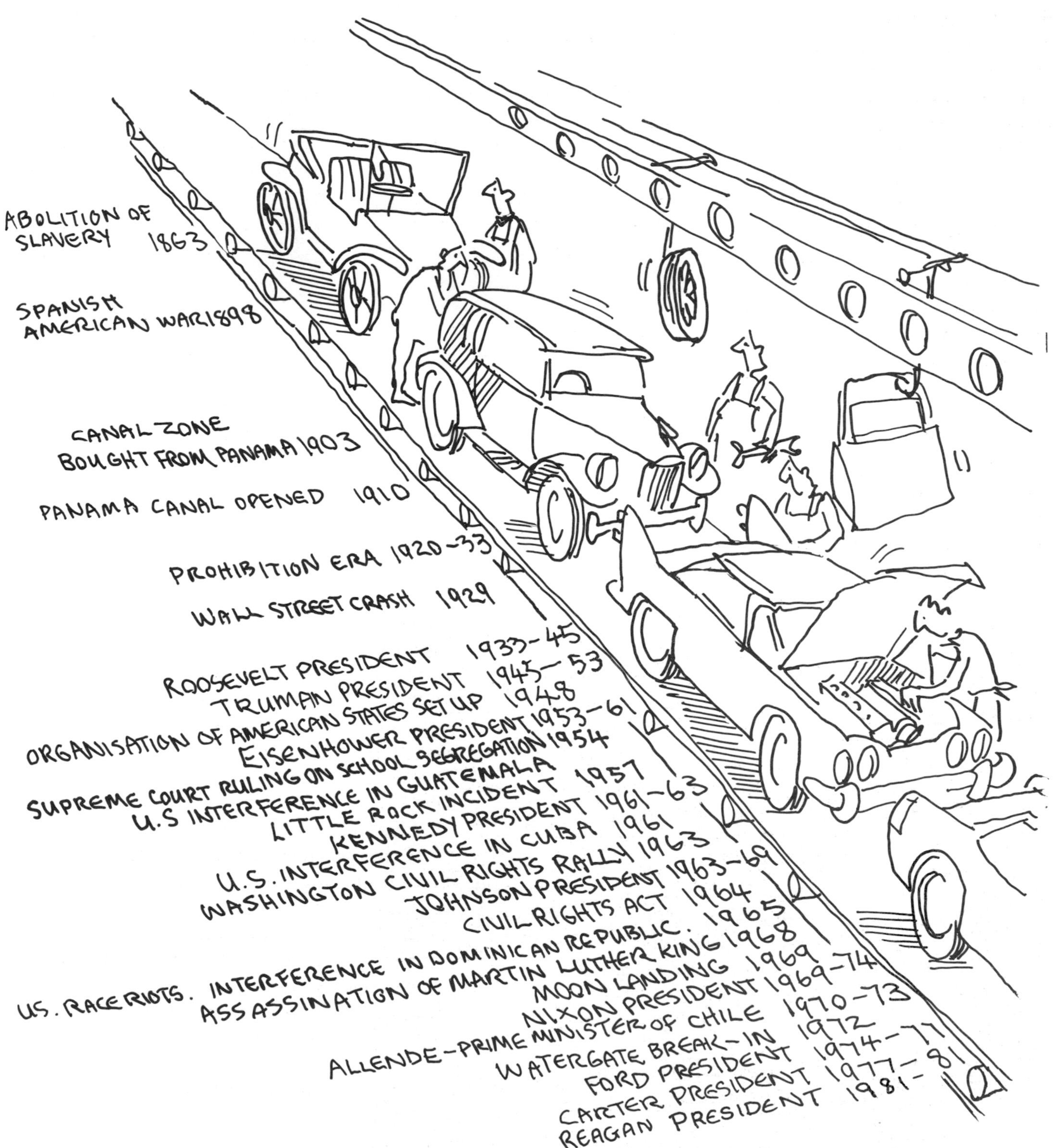
ABOLITION OF SLAVERY 1863
SPANISH AMERICAN WAR 1898
CANAL ZONE BOUGHT FROM PANAMA 1903
PANAMA CANAL OPENED 1910
PROHIBITION ERA 1920-33
WALL STREET CRASH 1929
ROOSEVELT PRESIDENT 1933-45
TRUMAN PRESIDENT 1945-53
ORGANISATION OF AMERICAN STATES SET UP 1948
EISENHOWER PRESIDENT 1953-61
SUPREME COURT RULING ON SCHOOL SEGREGATION 1954
U.S INTERFERENCE IN GUATEMALA
LITTLE ROCK INCIDENT 1957
KENNEDY PRESIDENT 1961-63
U.S. INTERFERENCE IN CUBA 1961
WASHINGTON CIVIL RIGHTS RALLY 1963
JOHNSON PRESIDENT 1963-69
CIVIL RIGHTS ACT 1964
US. RACE RIOTS. INTERFERENCE IN DOMINICAN REPUBLIC. 1965
ASSASSINATION OF MARTIN LUTHER KING 1968
MOON LANDING 1969
NIXON PRESIDENT 1969-74
ALLENDE-PRIME MINISTER OF CHILE 1970-73
WATERGATE BREAK-IN 1972
FORD PRESIDENT 1974-77
CARTER PRESIDENT 1977-81
REAGAN PRESIDENT 1981-

Questions

A

B

C

1 a Name the **three** Presidents of the U.S.A. marked A, B and C in the pictures.
President A
President B
President C
b How did President A die?
c Where did he die?
d Who was accused of his death?
e What political office was held by President B when President A died?
f Name the scandal in which President C was involved.
g How did President C end his period of office?
h Who succeeded him?

2 During the 1920s, known as the 'Roaring Twenties', life for Americans had never been more exciting. They were richer, had more spare time and enjoyed life to the full. It was an age of great optimism—soured by crime, gangsterism and prejudice.
a What made life so exciting and enjoyable for Americans during the 'Roaring Twenties'?
b What had been the result of the passing of the Eighteenth Amendment in 1919 and why did it lead to 'bootlegging' and 'speakeasies'?
c In what ways did Americans show their prejudices during those years?
d What steps were eventually taken to reduce crime and gangsterism in the United States?

3 Describe in a paragraph (10–20 lines), why America became isolationist after the First World War and why she entered the Second World War.

4 Write detailed accounts of **two** of the following:
a The causes and events of the Wall Street Crash (October 1929).
b the world-wide effects of the 'Crash' and the misery caused by the Depression in the United States.
c President Roosevelt's 'New Deal'.

5 a Up to the 1960s, negroes living in the Southern states had the segregation laws, and the Ku Klux Klan to keep them in a lowly position. Write paragraphs about these laws and the Ku Klux Klan.
b 'To escape these conditions Negroes began to move from the South to the North.' Describe the extent of this movement and the conditions the Negroes found in the Northern towns.
c 'Protests for civil rights began in the South, and the Negroes found a national leader in Martin Luther King.'
1 What are civil rights?
2 Write a paragraph about Martin Luther King.
d 'In the North protest took a more extreme form as the Black Power movement made itself felt.'
1 Describe the Black Power movement.
2 What was the more extreme form which protest took in many northern cities in the late 1960s?
e What position has the American Negro gained in the United States in the 1970s?

6 Briefly describe in a paragraph (10–20 lines) the career of **either** Richard Nixon **or** John F. Kennedy.

7 Read the following extract and answer the question below.

'Those in charge of relief have never known actual

hunger and want, have never lain awake at night worrying about unpaid rent, or how to make a few groceries do for the seemingly endless seven days till the next week's order of groceries . . . It gives me the nightmare, but I'm used to it.

'But we are supposed to have faith in our government. We are told to keep cheerful and smiling. Just what does our government expect us to do when our rent is due? When we need a doctor? When we need clothes? We haven't had a tube of toothpaste in weeks and have to check off some item of needed food when we get soap. I can only do my washing every two weeks, because that is as often as I can get oil for the oil stove to heat wash water and laundry soap with which to do my washing.

'But we are supposed to fall down on our knees and worship the golden calf of government when we are in dire need.

'It is always the people with full stomachs who tell us poor people to keep happy. I should love to have some new clothes, and I should enjoy a radio the same as anybody. But try to get them!

'No work, no hope; just live from one day to the next. Maybe better times are coming. Personally, I doubt it.' (Letter to an American newspaper during the Depression.)

Whom does the writer blame for her misery? Explain whether you think that she is justified or not.

8 Read the following extract and, using the information it contains, write an imaginary letter by an American Black to the President of the U.S.A. demanding better conditions.

'More than two decades after President Lyndon Johnson's great society legislation set the stage for black economic advancement the problem for minorities of all kinds in the United States, with the possible exception of women, remains deepseated. By most accounts "affirmative action," the process under which American corporations are all but forced, through government contracts, regulations and the courts, to discriminate positively in favour of their minority employees has not worked in the way the civil rights activists had hoped.

'Black unemployment in the United States remains criminally high. At 15 per cent of the workforce it is some 2.3 times that of whites. Among teenagers it is even worse: for Hispanic youth the jobless rate is 21 per cent and for Blacks it is an alarming 41 per cent. While the rest of America flourishes black America, and the inner-cities in particular, remain in deep depression.

'Indeed, there is growing evidence that despite "affirmative action" the position of black Americans is deteriorating fast. Black poverty is triple that of whites, black infant mortality twice that of whites and the country has reached the point where more than 50 per cent of black children are born out of wedlock. Federal state prisons are stuffed with Blacks and at most high schools across the country the black dropout rate has reached 30 per cent.'
(Alex Brummer, 'The Great Society fails to deliver the jobs', *The Guardian* 15 October 1985.)

8/A quarter of mankind

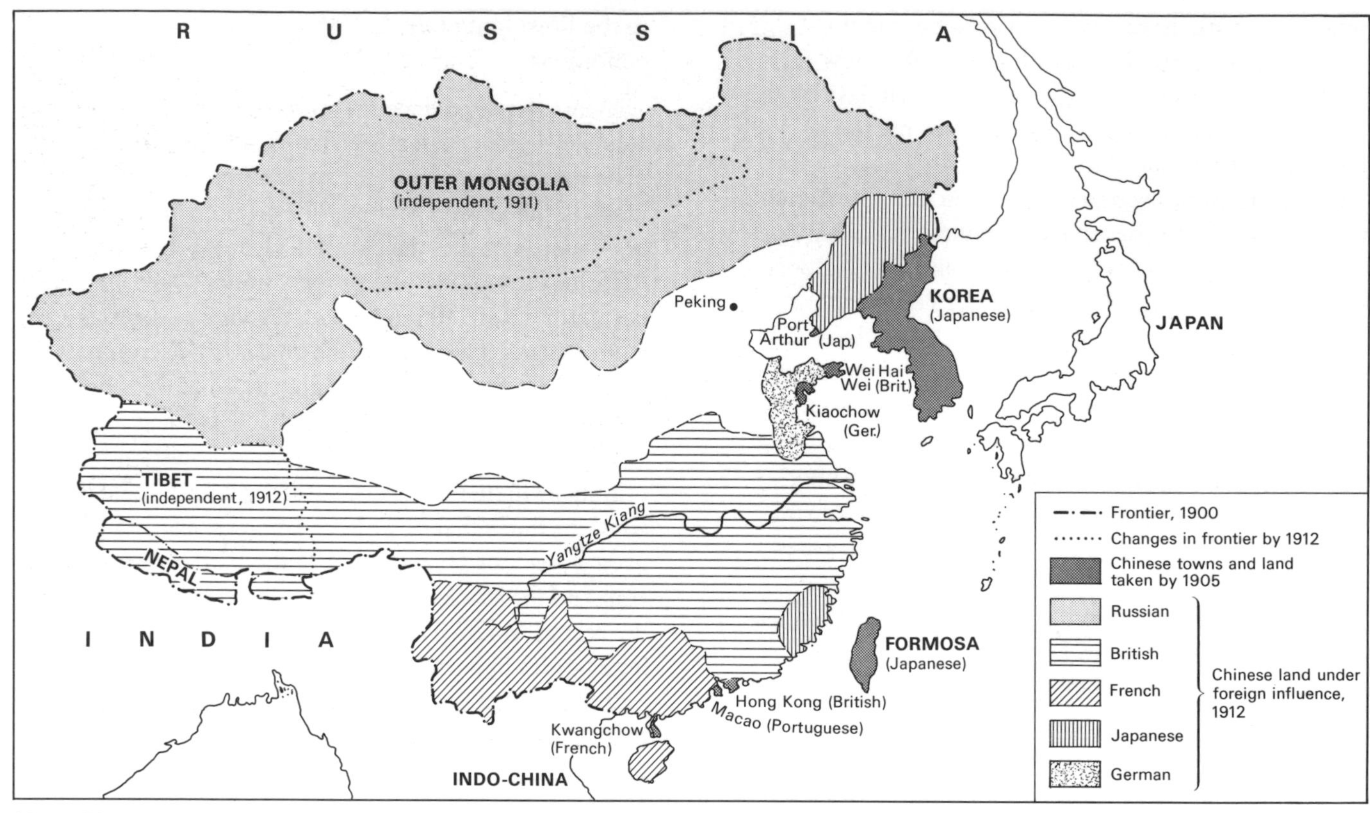

Map 1 China at the beginning of the twentieth century

The collapse of the Chinese Empire

China at the beginning of the century

The Land and the people

In 1900 the population of the world was estimated to be roughly 1,660 millions. Of these, about 430 millions were Chinese. (By 1985 China had about one-fifth of the world's population, which by then was roughly 5 billions.) The vast majority of these people worked on the land. Many lived in the direst poverty and millions died when drought or flood caused serious famine.

The great majority of the people of China lived in the eastern third of the country. The desert lands of the north and the mountainous areas of the west are not very suitable for human settlement.

The Government

At the beginning of the century China was still ruled by the Manchu royal family. From 1861 to 1908 the country was ruled by the Dowager Empress, Tzu Hsi. (Dowager means that she had been married to the Emperor, who was now dead.) During her reign officials became corrupt, the government barely controlled the more remote provinces, and there were serious rebellions. The Chinese government tried to cling to their old traditions, refusing to have anything to do with modern western ways. They bitterly resented increasing foreign influence but could do little to stop it.

The Dowager Empress Tzu Hsi

The collapse of the Chinese Empire

Foreign control

The Chinese considered western peoples to be barbarians and were so suspicious of them that they tried not to trade with Europe or America. But the western merchants realised that great profits could be made by such trade and forced the Chinese to open some of their ports to them. By the early years of the century other countries had gained so much influence and special privileges in the areas shown on Map 1 that it appeared that China might be divided up into colonies like Africa (see p.181).

In 1900 the Boxer Rebellion broke out. This was provoked by hatred of foreigners and their Christian religion being introduced by missionaries. There was much brutality on both sides as European armies suppressed the rebellion.

Throughout the first half of the century China suffered much brutality and fighting. Many people were executed as this picture, taken in 1927, shows

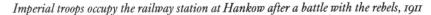

Imperial troops occupy the railway station at Hankow after a battle with the rebels, 1911

The Revolution of 1911

What were the causes?

The population was rising faster than any increase in food production. The ordinary people became even poorer and more discontented.

The national pride of the educated people was hurt by the foreign influence in the country.

Some Chinese men went abroad for their education. They picked up ideas about democracy and reform. Secret organisations were set up in China to plot the overthrow of the Imperial government.

The Empress Dowager was blamed for the chaos in the country and for failing to prevent the increasing foreign influence. She died in 1908 and was succeeded by a child. But the country needed a strong leader: people were not willing to be loyal to a child.

What were the main events?

A rebellion broke out in central China on 10 October 1911 and was therefore known as the 'Double Tenth'. It spread very rapidly. In February 1912 the child Emperor abdicated. China became a republic.

The Republic 1912–49

The Kuomintang

The Kuomintang Party

The Kuomintang (National People's Party) was by far the strongest political party in 1911. Its leader was Sun Yat-sen. He summed up its aims in his Three Principles:

1 Nationalism: freedom from foreign interference.
2 Democracy: ordinary people should have a say in the government.
3 People's Livelihood: a fairer sharing out of wealth, and especially of land.

The Leaders

1 Yuan Shi-kai. The president from 1912 to 1915 was Yuan Shi-kai. But he was a great disappointment because he acted as though he wanted to be emperor.

Sun Yat-sen (1867–1925)

2 Sun Yat-sen. Sun was educated abroad as a doctor. He was the leader of the government in 1912 and again from 1917 until his death in 1925.
3 Chiang Kai-shek. Chiang came from a wealthy family and was a general. He became leader of the Kuomintang on the death of Sun.

Chiang Kai-shek (1887–1975)

He was head of the Chinese government until he was defeated by the Communists in 1949 (see p.118).

What were the problems facing the Kuomintang?

1 Warlords. We have already seen how weak the Manchu government was. The Empress Dowager had certainly not been able to control the whole of such a vast country as China. Local warlords organised their own armies and were almost totally independent of the government. These warlords were not willing to be controlled by the Kuomintang. Both Sun and Chiang spent much time and effort trying to win over or defeat the warlords. It was not until 1928, for example, that Chiang was able to enter the old capital city of Peking.
2 Poverty. Because there was no effective government the peasants suffered. The warlords as well as the government taxed them. Also the government neglected to keep the dykes and irrigation systems in good repair. Floods, bad harvests and starvation increased. In 1929 an American journalist was shocked at the scenes in north-west China:

> How many people starved to death in those years I do not accurately know, and probably no one will ever know. . . . I am not inclined to doubt . . . estimates ranging as high as 6,000,000.
>
> Have you ever seen a man . . . when he has had no food for more than a month? It is a most agonizing sight.
>
> Children are even more pitiable, with their little skeletons bent over and mis-shapen . . . Women lie slumped in corners, waiting for death, their black

Peasants being evicted for non-payment of rent. A Communist propaganda woodcut of the Second World War

blade-like buttocks protruding, their breasts hanging like collapsed sacks. But there are, after all, not many women and girls. Most of them have died or been sold.

3 Japanese attacks and 4 The Communists. These were so important that they need separate sections.

Japanese attacks

Manchuria

A third problem for the Kuomintang government was the continuing interference of Japan. Turn back to Map 1. You can see that Japan had already gained land and influence by the time of the revolution. Then, in 1931, the Japanese took over Manchuria and renamed it Manchukuo (see p.62).

The war with Japan, 1937–45

Six years later the Japanese again attacked and immediately captured the Chinese capital of Peking. Chiang moved the government to Chungking. Fighting continued until, after 1941, the war between Japan and China became part of the Second World War (see p.62 and p. 82). Despite help from America, the Kuomintang armies were not very successful.

The Communists

The Chinese Communist Party

The Kuomintang was eventually completely defeated and replaced by the Communists. How this happened is a very important story.

We saw in Chapter 3 how the Communist Party in Russia organised a revolution in November 1917. In 1920 a Communist Party was set up in China. At first the two Communist parties in Russia and China kept in close touch and the Chinese tried to organise uprisings in big towns like Shanghai just as the Russian Communists had organised their revolution in Petrograd and other big towns. But Chiang's army was too strong.

Japanese troops entering Manchuria in 1931

Mao Tse-tung

One of the first members of the Communist Party was Mao Tse-tung. He came to believe that the Communist revolution was more likely to be successful in China by organising the peasants. After all, they were wretched enough and had not really benefited from the Kuomintang government. Sun's third Principle (People's Livelihood) had not been put into effect. Mao organised his own Red Army in a part of south-east China. He introduced land reforms there. He called this area the Kiangsi Soviet—almost a little independent country within China (see Map 2). In 1934 Chiang decided to destroy it and sent an army to surround the area.

The Long March

The Red Army managed to break through Chiang's encircling army. But how could they really escape? For a year they, or rather an ever-decreasing number of survivors, undertook one of the most remarkable treks in all history.

These peasant-soldiers marched 6,000 miles. They fought desperate battles; they climbed rugged mountains; they crossed raging rivers and treacherous marshland; they starved, froze in bitter cold and sweltered in intense heat. It is a fantastic story of human determination and selfless heroism. Here are two descriptions by soldiers who took part:

> The rain pelted down mercilessly; . . . the water made [the path] slick as oil. . . . We rolled rather than marched forward.
>
> Even under these conditions, men kept dozing off. . . . Finally, the men simply unwrapped their puttees and tied themselves together in a long chain, each pulling the other along. . . .
>
> In twenty-four hours, besides fighting and repairing wrecked bridges, we had marched 240 *li* [that is, 80 miles].

The last peak in the range . . . was terrible. Hundreds of our men died there. They would sit down to rest or relieve themselves, and never get up. All along the route we kept reaching down to pull men to their feet only to find that they were already dead.

At last, as you can see from Map 2, the survivors reached Yenan in the province of Shensi. The Soviet there now became the new Communist base.

Guerrilla warfare

During the war with Japan the Communists fought rather more successfully than the Kuomintang. Why do you think this was so? Mao taught his soldiers the importance of the guerrilla tactics that he had perfected on the Long March:

The enemy attacks, we retreat;
The enemy camps, we harass;
The enemy tires, we attack;
The enemy retreats, we pursue.

Civil war

After the defeat of Japan in 1945 the struggle between the Communists and the Kuomintang for the control of China continued. The Communists became increasingly popular compared with the Kuomintang. By 1949 the Kuomintang armies were retreating. On 1 October Mao announced the creation of the new People's Republic of China. Chiang fled with the remnants of his army to the island of Taiwan (sometimes called Formosa). He declared that he would one day return to 'free' China from the Communists and made an alliance with the U.S.A. He died in 1975.

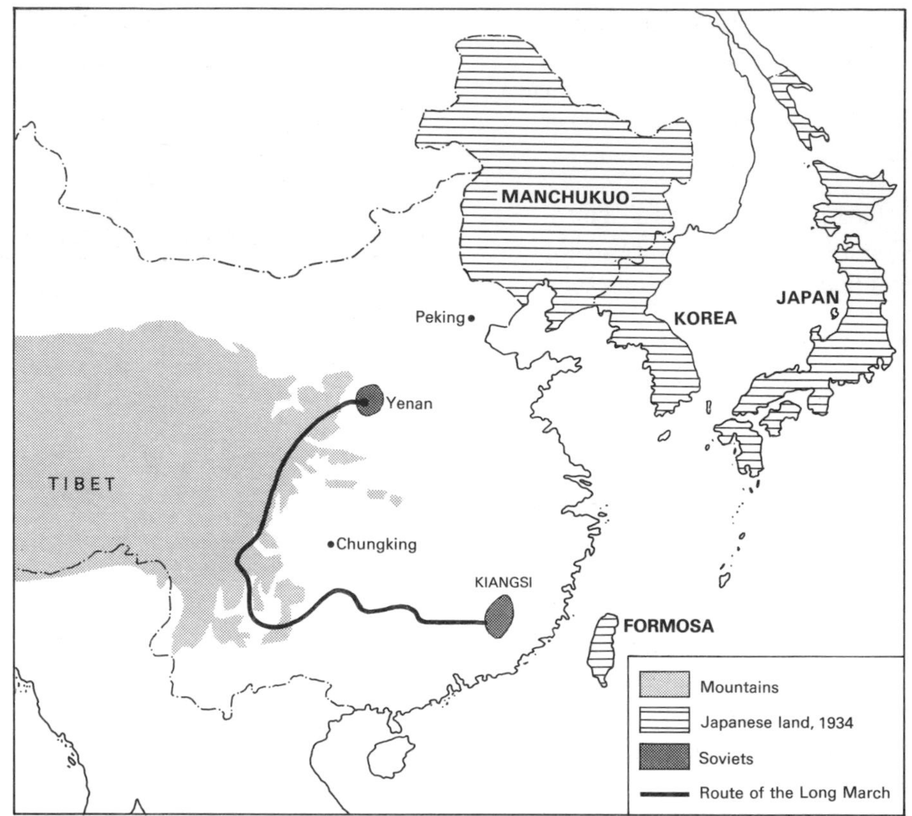

Map 2 The Long March 1934–35

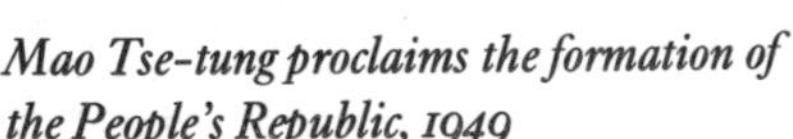
Mao Tse-tung proclaims the formation of the People's Republic, 1949

Changes made by the Communists

The speed of change

Once the Communists were in charge of the government they set about introducing reforms that changed the way people lived at an incredible speed. To manage so much was really amazing considering the size of the country and the size of the problems.

Land reform

The first and most important task was land reform. Party members travelled round the villages to organise this. Land and animals were taken from the rich landlords and given to the poorest peasants. Many landlords were tried for their bad treatment of the peasants and some were shot.

Then the peasants were encouraged to form 'co-operatives'. A group of peasants would share the work and the use of their animals.

In 1955 Mao urged peasants to go one stage further and form 'collectives'. In these the peasants were not allowed to own land or animals privately at all.

Revolution in the towns and in industry

The revolution in the towns was more gradual. Businessmen and government officials were fined, then allowed to continue their work.

In 1953 a five-year plan laid the foundations for a huge increase in Chinese industry and a great improvement in the country's wealth. The graph shows some examples of what was managed.

Standard and condition of life

In the ordinary matters of life—in housing, food and clothing—the people gradually came to enjoy im-

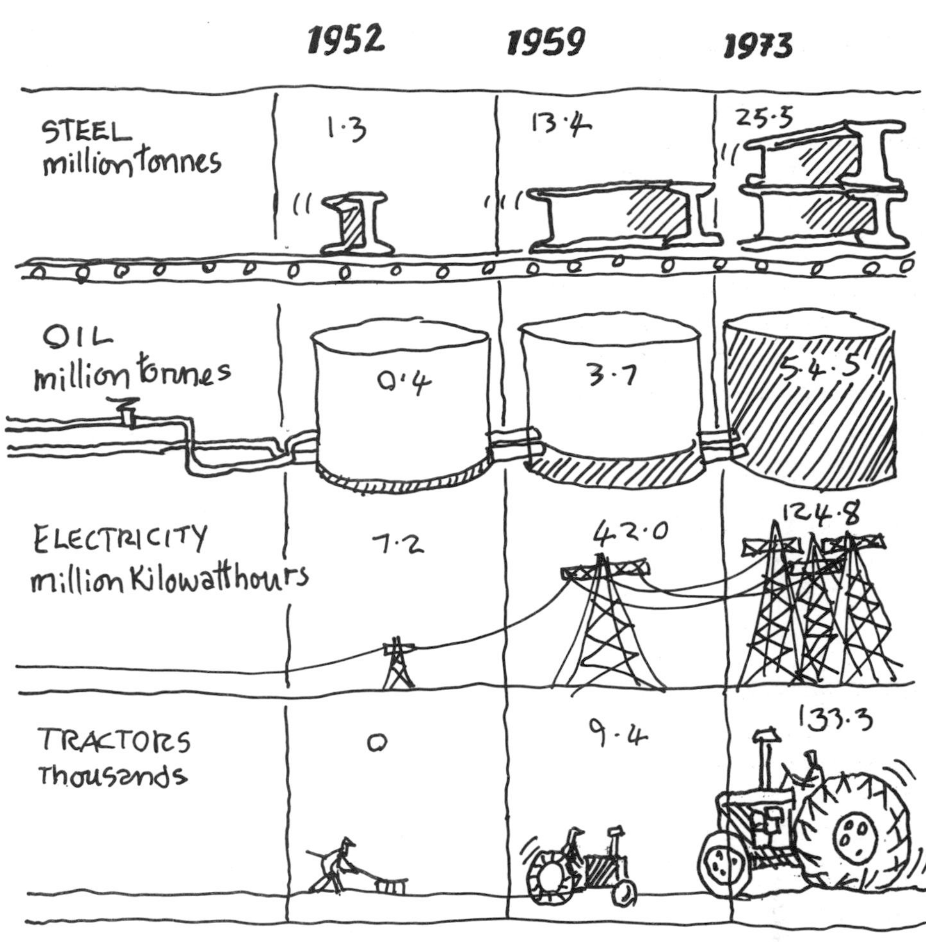

Figure 1 Industrial production in China, 1952, 1959 and 1973

provements. The new wealth was spread quite evenly. Even by 1980 the people of China were still poor by European standards, but they had been freed from their former wretchedness.

Medical and education services were also much improved. The people became healthier and the illiteracy rate dropped considerably. In much of Chinese life the policy was that of 'walking on two legs', that is, combining traditional Chinese ways with modern western ways. Medicine was a good example of this. Traditional Chinese medicine such as acupuncture was found side by side with western drugs.

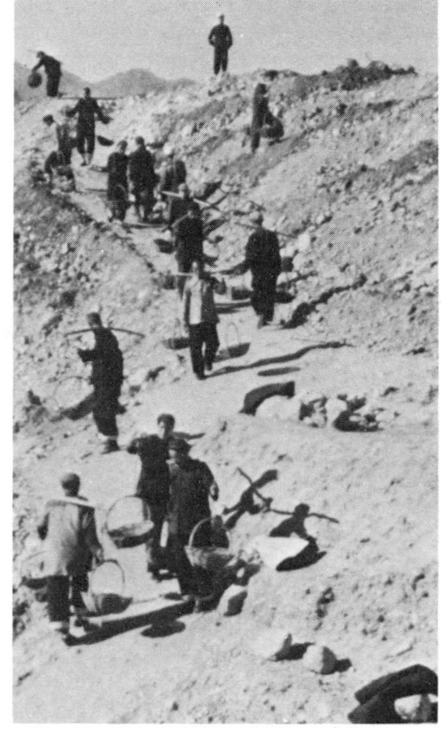

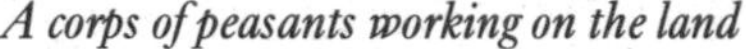

A corps of peasants working on the land

Government

The Government and Party systems

Since 1949 China has been run by two separate systems—the government of ministers and civil servants, and the Communist Party. The Prime Minister from 1949 to 1976 was Chou En-lai. The Chairman of the Party from 1935 to 1976 was Mao Tse-tung.

Membership of the Communist Party has been a sought-after honour reserved for a small proportion of the population. And it has been very difficult for anyone to gain a senior position in the government, army or industry, for example, without being a member.

Criticism and conversion

But it was a few, ordinary peasant and soldier members of the Party that made all the rapid changes possible. These people were called 'cadres'. They were the enthusiastic leaders. They persuaded the ordinary people to work hard and accept changes by argument and by their own example. The aim was to overcome opposition by persuasion rather than by killing. Estimates of the number of executions vary between 100,000 and 1,000,000, mainly landlords. Compare this figure with the deaths after the Russian Revolution, taking into account the different sizes of the populations (see p.36).

Chou En-lai (1898–1976)

It became common for groups to be formed in villages and factories for sessions of criticism and self-criticism. Hard work and honesty were encouraged in this way.

Experiment and uncertainty

'The hundred flowers', 1956

But did people really believe that the changes were for the best? In 1956 Mao decided to encourage people to express their criticisms of the government. 'Let a hundred flowers blossom,' he said. 'Let a hundred schools of thought contend.' However, the criticism was much harsher than Mao had expected. He quickly clamped down and people were punished for their outspokenness.

A group discussion of Commune workers. Such meetings of 'mass criticism and repudiation' were common during the Cultural Revolution

'The Great Leap Forward', 1958

The next experiment was to try to force the pace of China's economic improvement to a break-neck speed. Agricultural and industrial production were to be enormously increased.

The main method for bringing this about was to be the commune. Villages were clustered together. The peasants were organised to work in the fields. Then, in the slack agricultural seasons, they were employed in local workshops. Women also worked alongside the men. The workers ate in communal dining halls and young children were looked after in communal nurseries. Mao claimed that the system not only made the best use of the workforce, but was closer to true Communism than any other country had managed.

At first there was great enthusiasm. Massive irrigation works were undertaken, for instance. But the experiment was not generally a success, for these main reasons:

1 Food production dropped seriously in 1959–61 due largely to severe drought. At least 25 million peasants died of starvation.
2 The peasants did not like giving up their own little plots for growing vegetables and rearing chickens.
3 The quality of the products from the workshops was poor.
4 The communes contained on average 250,000 people. The managers did not have sufficient skill to organise them efficiently—an enormous task in any case.

At the height of the Cultural Revolution. All the delegates to the congress of the Chinese Communist Party hold up their 'little red books' (the Thoughts of Chairman Mao) as a sign of their approval

'The Cultural Revolution', 1966–76

Mao's reputation suffered from the set-backs of the 'Hundred Flowers' and 'Great Leap Forward' campaigns. It almost looked as though other men would replace him.

In the mid-1960s Mao struggled to restore his own authority. Posters were made showing him almost as the saviour of his people. Extracts from his writings were collected into a little red-bound book and hundreds of millions of copies were distributed. The Little Red Book was read privately and publicly rather like the Bible.

In 1966 Mao launched the Cultural Revolution. The idea was to keep the revolutionary enthusiasm alive. Suspicion was cast upon all kinds of 'experts' for hindering progress. Young people were organised into units called Red Guards. Mao's opponents were denounced. Schools and universities were closed and students and teachers were sent to the countryside to do manual work. Peasants and factory workers were stirred up to protest against inequalities. Few people dared stand up to the fanatical Red Guards. The result was considerable chaos throughout China.

By about 1968 some order was restored, largely because of the influence of Chou En-lai. However, many townspeople were still kept forcibly working on the land. Also some of the better and simpler ideas of the Cultural Revolution continued into the 1970s—for example, 'bare-foot' doctors, who were sent with a little training to give simple medical treatment in villages.

The Cultural Revolution finally came to an end with the death of Mao in 1976. The period is sometimes referred to as 'the Eleven Years'.

China since Mao

Change of leaders

Opposition to Mao

Mao became much less popular and even made enemies by his extreme policies. In 1971 Marshal Lin Piao tried unsuccessfully to seize power and was killed in an air crash while trying to escape from China.

Possible successors, 1976

1 Chou En-lai. But he died a few months before Mao.
2 Jian Quing, Mao's widow. She and three supporters, known as the 'Gang of Four', planned to take power and continue the Cultural Revolution.

Jiang Qing (widow of Mao Tse-tung) at her trial

3 Hua Kuo-feng. He succeeded Chou as prime minister, 1976–80 and Mao as party chairman, 1976–81. He had the Gang of Four arrested, tried and imprisoned.

4 Deng Xiaoping. In all this manoeuvring, however, the man who became the real leader was Deng Xiaoping, although he was only Vice-Chairman of the party. He is a short man and was already quite old (71) when Mao died.

Deng Xiaoping, the most important Chinese leader since 1979

Policy of Deng

Population

If the increase in the Chinese population is not slowed down, China could suffer calamity by the turn of the century. Since *c.*1980 the government has made great efforts to persuade couples to have only one child.

The 'Four Modernizations'

Until his death Mao continued to emphasise the importance of peasant agriculture. The new government recognised that many improvements were needed to bring the country up to date – especially the four modernizations in agriculture; industry; science and technology; and the armed forces.

Relaxation of tension

The harsh policies of 'the Eleven Years' have been relaxed. For example, the townspeople who were forced to work on the land were allowed to return home, 1977–80 and political prisoners were released. Also, people stopped wearing the blue 'uniform' of 'Mao suits' and caps.

Private profit

One of the most surprising changes since 1976 has been to allow individuals, especially peasants, to sell a certain amount for private profit. This has encouraged greater production.

A modern Chinese street scene

Communist China in the world

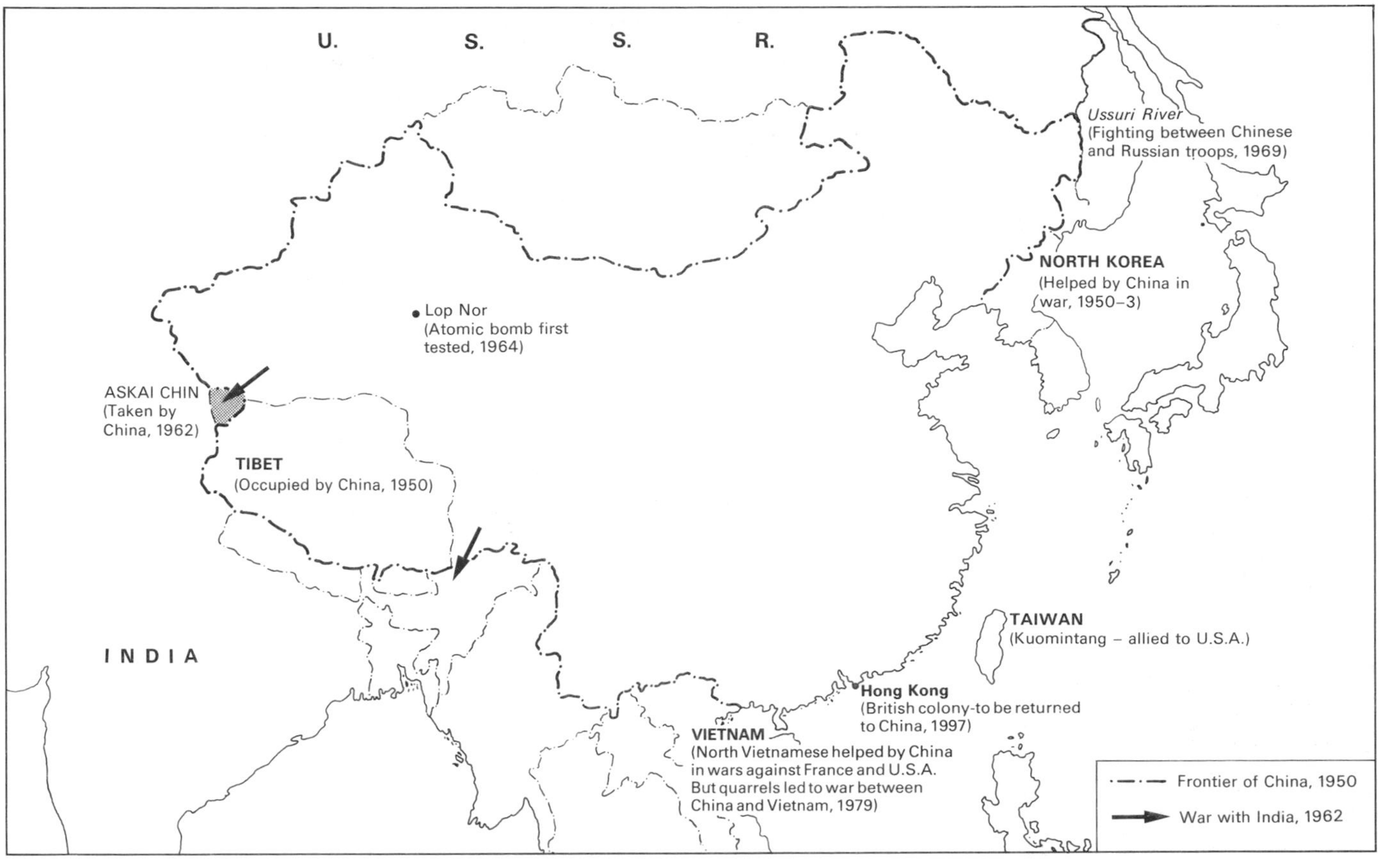

Map 3 China and her neighbours

The Cold War

Korea and Vietnam

Both Korea and northern Vietnam were parts of the Chinese Empire in previous ages. It is not surprising therefore that the Communist government took a great interest when war broke out in these countries. As we shall see in Chapter 9 China helped both the North Koreans and the Vietminh.

Taiwan

We have seen (p.118) how Chiang Kai-shek and his supporters fled to Taiwan in 1949. Because the Americans disliked the Communist government, they signed an alliance with Chiang. In 1945 China had been made a permanent member of the Security Council of the United Nations Organisation (see p.93).

On the frozen Ussuri River Chinese troops (on foot) confront Russian troops on an armoured car

Communist China in the world

From 1949 to 1971 this seat was occupied by Taiwan because the U.S.A. would not allow Communist China to take it.

Russia

After the Communists took over control of China the Russians helped them. But by about 1960 the two countries started to quarrel. There were two main reasons for this:

1 After the death of Stalin in 1953 Mao thought that he should be recognised as the senior world Communist leader. But the Russians continued to treat the Chinese as junior partners. The Chinese, as we have seen (p.119), organised their revolution in ways different from the Russians. The Russians thought that they were wrong.

2 Russia and China share the longest land frontier in the world (about 4,000 miles). In the nineteenth century the Tsars of Russia had taken some Chinese land. The Chinese now thought that this should be returned. There was even some small-scale fighting, most severely on the Ussuri River in 1969 (see Map 3).

The Third World

China as a revolutionary leader

Because China is a comparatively poor and an Asiatic country, the Chinese leaders claimed that China could help the countries of Africa and Asia better than Russia. They claimed that their ways of revolution and reform were more suitable. Several countries, Tanzania in the 1960s and Kampuchea in the 1970s for example, were helped by China.

India

But China and India have not been friendly. This was partly because of disputed frontiers (see Map 3). War broke out between them in 1962. China took a small piece of land called Aksai Chin so that they could build a military road to connect the provinces of Sinkiang and Tibet.

Friendship with the West

During the period of the Cold War, America's relations with China were as poor as they were with Russia. Throughout the 1970s, however, China became increasingly friendly with America and with the West in general. President Nixon, wishing to have a reputation as a peace-maker, visited China in 1972.

A change in direction. President Nixon and Chairman Mao meet in Peking

Why have the Chinese become friendly with the West?

1 The Chinese felt that they had no reason to quarrel with the U.S.A. after the Americans had withdrawn from Vietnam (see p.141). The Chinese were pleased to be friendly with the U.S.A. in order to join the U.N. The Americans allowed Communist China to take the permanent seat instead of Taiwan in 1971.

2 The Chinese were becoming increasingly frightened of Russia and did not wish America and western Europe to be enemies as well.

3 The failure of the Great Leap Forward showed that China could not develop her heavy industry quickly by herself. She wanted to buy goods and machinery from the western countries.

Hong Kong

During the nineteenth century Britain acquired the island of Hong Kong and a lease on the nearby mainland territory. This lease expires in 1997. In 1984 an agreement was reached for Britain to hand over the whole of the colony in 1997 while the Chinese promised that it could keep its own distinctive way of life as a Special Administrative Region (S.A.R.).

Time chart

The world's largest nation

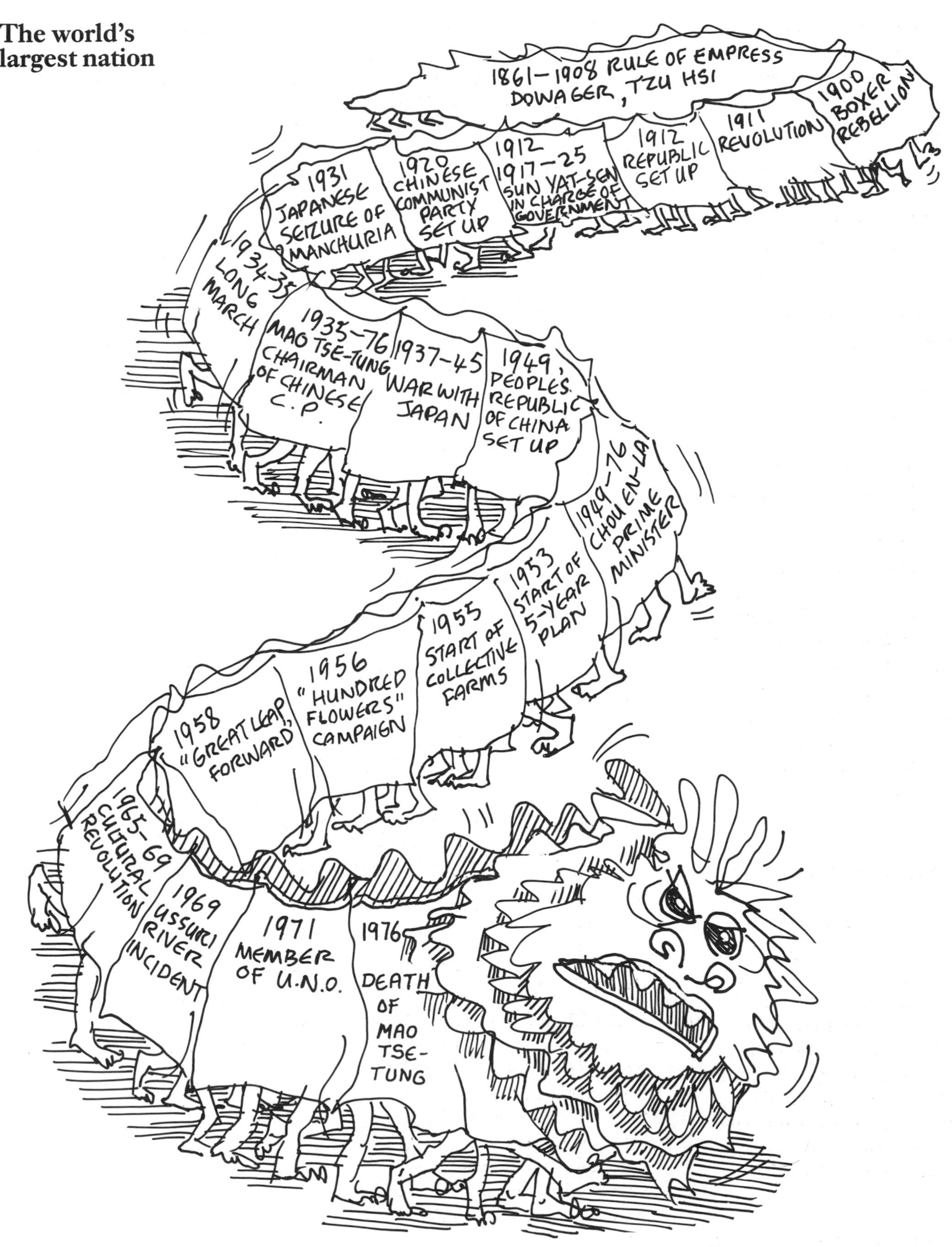

1861–1908 RULE OF EMPRESS DOWAGER, TZU HSI
1900 BOXER REBELLION
1911 REVOLUTION
1912 REPUBLIC SET UP
1912 1917–25 SUN YAT-SEN IN CHARGE OF GOVERNMENT
1920 CHINESE COMMUNIST PARTY SET UP
1931 JAPANESE SEIZURE OF MANCHURIA
1934–35 LONG MARCH
1935–76 MAO TSE-TUNG CHAIRMAN OF CHINESE C.P.
1937–45 WAR WITH JAPAN
1949, PEOPLES REPUBLIC OF CHINA SET UP
1949–76 CHOU EN-LAI PRIME MINISTER
1953 START OF 5-YEAR PLAN
1955 START OF COLLECTIVE FARMS
1956 "HUNDRED FLOWERS" CAMPAIGN
1958 "GREAT LEAP FORWARD"
1965–69 CULTURAL REVOLUTION
1969 USSURI RIVER INCIDENT
1971 MEMBER OF U.N.O.
1976 DEATH OF MAO TSE-TUNG

Questions

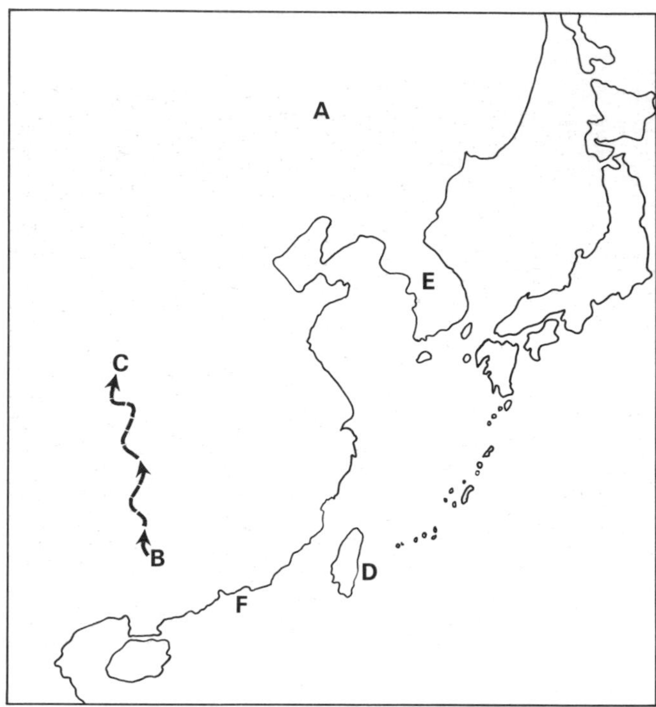

1 a Name area A, seized by Japan in 1931. What action did the League of Nations take?
  b The Communists went from B to C in 1934. What was this event called? Name area C.
  c Name island D, ruled by Japan till 1945. Which leader fled there in 1949?
  d Name area E, divided into two in 1945. Name F, which is still a British Crown Colony.
  e Name **two** prominent members of China's Communist Party since 1949.

2 Describe the life and achievements of Chiang Kai-shek. Include in your answer:
  a Youth and character
  b Struggle for control of China
  c War against Japan
  d Taiwan.

3 Write an account of the careers of Chiang Kai-shek and Mao Tse-tung between 1919 and 1939. The following information should help you.
  Foundation of the Communist Party 1921;
  Death of Sun-Yat-sen 1925;
  Fall of Peking to the Kuomintang 1928;
  The Long March.

4 Write an account of the main changes and developments in China from 1949 to the death of Mao Tse-tung.

5 Imagine you are Mao Tse-tung writing his memoirs. Write about your life and achievements under the following headings.
  a The struggle for survival against the Kuomintang—The Long March.
  b The war against Japan.
  c Civil War, 1945–49.
  d The Great Leap Forward.
  e The Cultural Revolution.

6 a Why did the 1911 Revolution take place in China?
  b Write a paragraph about the work of Sun Yat-sen in the years after the Revolution.
  c What did Japan do in China in the 1930s which made the work of the Kuomintang even more difficult? What were their reasons for these actions?
  d Describe the part played by Chiang Kai-shek in this period up to 1945.

7 In a paragraph (10–20 lines) describe China's relations with the outside world since 1949.

8 Write an account of the events in Chinese history that followed the collapse of the Manchu dynasty in 1911. What part was played by Sun Yat-sen and Chiang Kai-shek in those events?

Why did the Chinese Communists embark on 'The Long March' during 1934–35?

Outline the troubles that beset the Chinese people after 1937 until the country was overtaken by the events of the Second World War (1941).

9 a Why was Mao Tse-tung able to defeat Chiang Kai-shek by 1949?
  b What did Mao do for China when he was her ruler?

10 Read the following extracts from speeches made by the Communist leaders in China. Then answer the question which follows them.
'Let a hundred flowers blossom'.—Mao Tse-tung, 1956.
'The great proletarian cultural revolution'—Mao Tse-tung, 1965.
Explain the meaning of these two extracts and the importance to China.

11 Look carefully at Sources A–C and answer the questions below.

Source A Report by an Austrian journalist.

'Years later, Mao was to say of that period between

the Great Leap Forward (1957) and the Great Proletarian Cultural Revolution (1966) "At that time most people disagreed with me. Sometimes I was alone. They said that my views were out of date". Compared with the quivering tension you feel everywhere today, China in 1957 was almost boring. On 16 July, 1966, when Mao emerged from the Yangtze River – or more precisely, on 25 July, when the press announced that he had swum nine miles down river in sixty-five minutes, thus proving to the world that his health was excellent – he took his place as the leader of his nation.'
(From *China Today*, by K. Mehnert.)

Source B The view of the Central Committee of the CCP.

'Although the bourgeoisie has been overthrown, it is still trying to use the old ideas, culture, customs and habits of the exploiting classes to corrupt the masses, capture their minds and endeavour to stage a come-back. The Proletariat must be the exact opposite: it must meet head-on every challenge of the bourgeoisie in the ideological field and use new ideas, culture, customs and habits of the proletariat to change the mental outlook of the whole society. Since the Cultural Revolution is a revolution, it inevitably meets with resistance. This resistance comes chiefly from those in authority who have wormed their way into the Party and are taking the Capitalist road. It also comes from the force of habits from the old society. What the Central Committee demands of the Party Committee at all levels is boldly arouse the masses, encourage those comrades who have made mistakes but are willing to correct them to cast off their burdens and join in the struggle.

'A most important task is to transform the old educational system.'
(From *Peking Review*, August 1966)

Source C

The Red Guards and their Little Red Books

a Who were the Red Guards (Source C)?

b Explain what is meant by
  i) 'the proletariat' (Source B)?
  ii) 'the bourgeoisie' (Source B)?

c The Central Committee (Source B) state that 'a most important task is to transform the old education system'.
  i) What evidence is given in Source B to explain why that statement is made?
  ii) What methods were used 'to transform the old education system'?

d What doubts would the historian of Communist China have about using the following sources as evidence?
  i) Reports of journalists (as in Source A).
  ii) Official statements (as in Source B).
  iii) Photographs (as in Source C).

9/Neither war nor peace

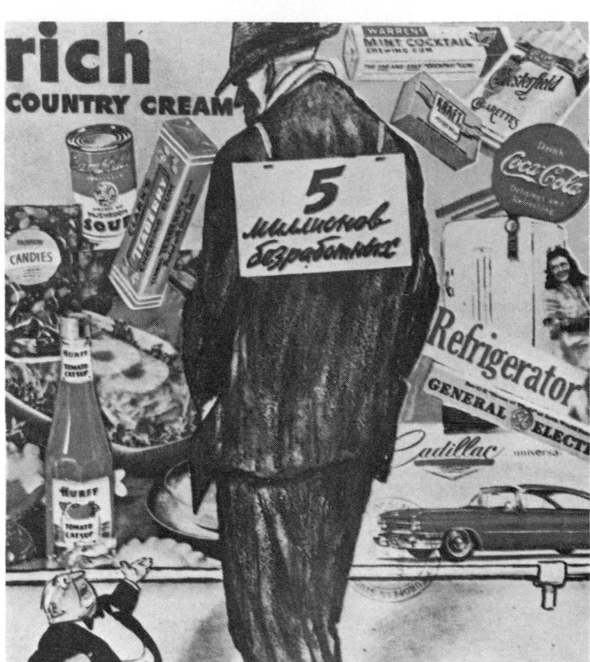

Left The West's view of the Russians. A French poster about Stalin's forcible seizure of Poland, Czechoslovakia, Bulgaria, Baltic countries, Hungary, Romania, half of Germany, and China; and his threat to France.

Right Russia's view of the West. Poverty in the affluent U.S.A. The label reads '5 million unemployed'.

The start of the Cold War

The background

Communism v. Capitalism

Karl Marx, the founder of modern Communism, believed that working-class people throughout the world would rise up in rebellion against what he thought were unjust governments (see p.29). When the revolution took place in Russia in 1917 many important Communists sincerely believed that they should help similar revolutions to take place in other countries. The governments of several countries, especially Britain and France, were frightened that this would happen and so helped the White Armies against the Communists in the Russian Civil War (see p.32).

In countries like the U.S.A. and Britain many businesses and industries are run with the aim of making a profit for the owners. People who support this system believe that this leads to competition and efficiency. The system is called capitalism. Communists believe that businesses and industries should be run for the good of all and that wealth should be more evenly shared out than in capitalist countries.

Ever since 1917 Communist and Capitalist countries have been suspicious of each other, each suspecting that the one is planning to destroy the other. The dislike has remained at the level of fear and suspicion without breaking out into all-out 'hot' war between the main countries on the two sides. The phrase 'cold war' is therefore used to describe particularly the relations beween the Soviet Union (Russia) and the U.S.A. (America) since 1947.

How did the wartime allies start to quarrel?

From 1941 to 1945 Britain, the U.S.A. and Russia were allies fighting together against Nazi Germany in the Second World War (see Chapter 9). But, as the war came to an end Britain and America started to quarrel with Russia. The Russians had suffered dreadfully during the war and naturally wanted to make sure that there were governments friendly to them in the countries of eastern Europe. At the Yalta meeting (see p. 92) the western allies agreed that Russia should have influence in eastern Europe. However, they objected to the way the Red Army and Communist Parties took over complete control. The quarrel was very obvious at the Potsdam Conference (see p.92).

The 'Iron Curtain'

The Red Army remained in control of the countries of eastern Europe

The start of the Cold War

and it became very difficult for people from the west to visit them. In 1946 Churchill made a speech in which he said:

From Stettin, in the Baltic, to Trieste, in the Adriatic, an iron curtain has descended across the continent. Behind that line all the capitals of the ancient states of central and eastern Europe . . ., and the populations around them, lie in the Soviet sphere and are subject in one form or another, not only to Soviet influence, but to a very high and increasing measure of control. . . . This is certainly not the liberated Europe we fought to build up.

The American reaction, 1947

The Truman Doctrine

President Truman of the U.S.A. was also worried, though without any real evidence, about possible Russian control of the eastern Mediterranean. In 1947 a civil war was being fought in Greece between the government and the Communists. Truman also feared a possible take-over by Russia of Turkey. He therefore made a speech in 1947 in which he announced that America would be giving economic aid to

Iron Curtain, 1949
Germany, 1945
Zones of occupation, Germany and Austria
American
British
French
Russian
Russian satellites with dates of complete Communist control
Communist but expelled from the Cominform
Lands taken from Germany
Stettin
Berlin
GERMANY
POLAND 1947
CZECHOSLOVAKIA 1948
AUSTRIA
HUNGARY 1949
ROMANIA 1947
Trieste
YUGOSLAVIA 1945
BULGARIA 1946
ALBANIA 1946

Map 1 Central and Eastern Europe, 1945–49

President Harry Truman (left) and George Marshall after whom the Marshall Plan was named (see p.130)

Greece and Turkey. He also said that the U.S.A. would support peoples trying to keep their political freedom. This came to be called the Truman Doctrine. In practice Truman was telling Russia that America would resist any attempts by the Russians to gain influence in any more countries. The Cold War had really begun.

The start of the Cold War

The Marshall Plan

The Americans believed that poverty breeds Communism. Many European countries were struggling with serious economic problems. The U.S. Secretary of State (that is, foreign minister), George Marshall, announced in 1947 that America would provide aid. The Russians were very suspicious—they thought that America wanted to use aid to interfere in eastern Europe. But the countries of western Europe did accept the plan and the money proved very important for their recovery (see p.152).

Crises in Central Europe

How did the Communists come to control eastern Europe, 1945–48?

1 The Red Army freed most of eastern Europe from the Germans and stayed on after 1945.
2 The Russians set up the Cominform in 1947 to co-ordinate the Communist parties in various countries (see p.40).
3 Yugoslavia, led by Tito (see p. 87), refused to take orders from Russia. Yugoslavia, though remaining Communist, was expelled from the Cominform in 1948.
4 The Communist parties took over complete control of the governments of the countries of eastern Europe in the years shown on Map 1. These countries came to be called Russian satellites.

How the Communists came to control Czechoslovakia, 1948

But the Communist party in Czechoslovakia was weaker than those in other east European countries. Masaryk, the Foreign Minister, was a powerful anti-Communist influence in the government. On the morning of 10 March 1948 his body, clothed just in pyjamas, was found beneath an open window of his Ministry building. Soon afterwards the Communists took control.

The Berlin Blockade, 1948–49. An American aeroplane brings supplies

The Berlin Blockade, 1948–49

We now need to turn our attention to Germany. Turn back to Map 1 and note the following:
1 Germany was reduced in size compared with its frontiers in 1938. Poland took large areas.
2 Germany was also divided into four zones of occupation.
3 But the city of Berlin, itself divided into four occupation sectors, was in the heart of the Russian zone of Germany.

In June 1948 the Russians closed all the roads and railways linking the western sectors of Berlin to the western zones of Germany. The Russians were frightened that the western zones would be united. Were they trying to force the Americans, British and French out of Berlin? If the western countries wanted to stay, how could they keep western Berlin supplied, with essential food and fuel especially? The answer was an incredible airlift. Hundreds of transport aircraft shuttled back and forth supplying the people of Berlin with all they needed. At the height of the airlift, aeroplanes were landing in western Berlin night and day at the rate of one every 45 seconds. In May 1949 the Russians admitted defeat and reopened the roads and railways.

Later in 1949 the western zones were joined to become the new West Germany and the Russian zone became the new East Germany. The German people were split in two.

The start of the Cold War

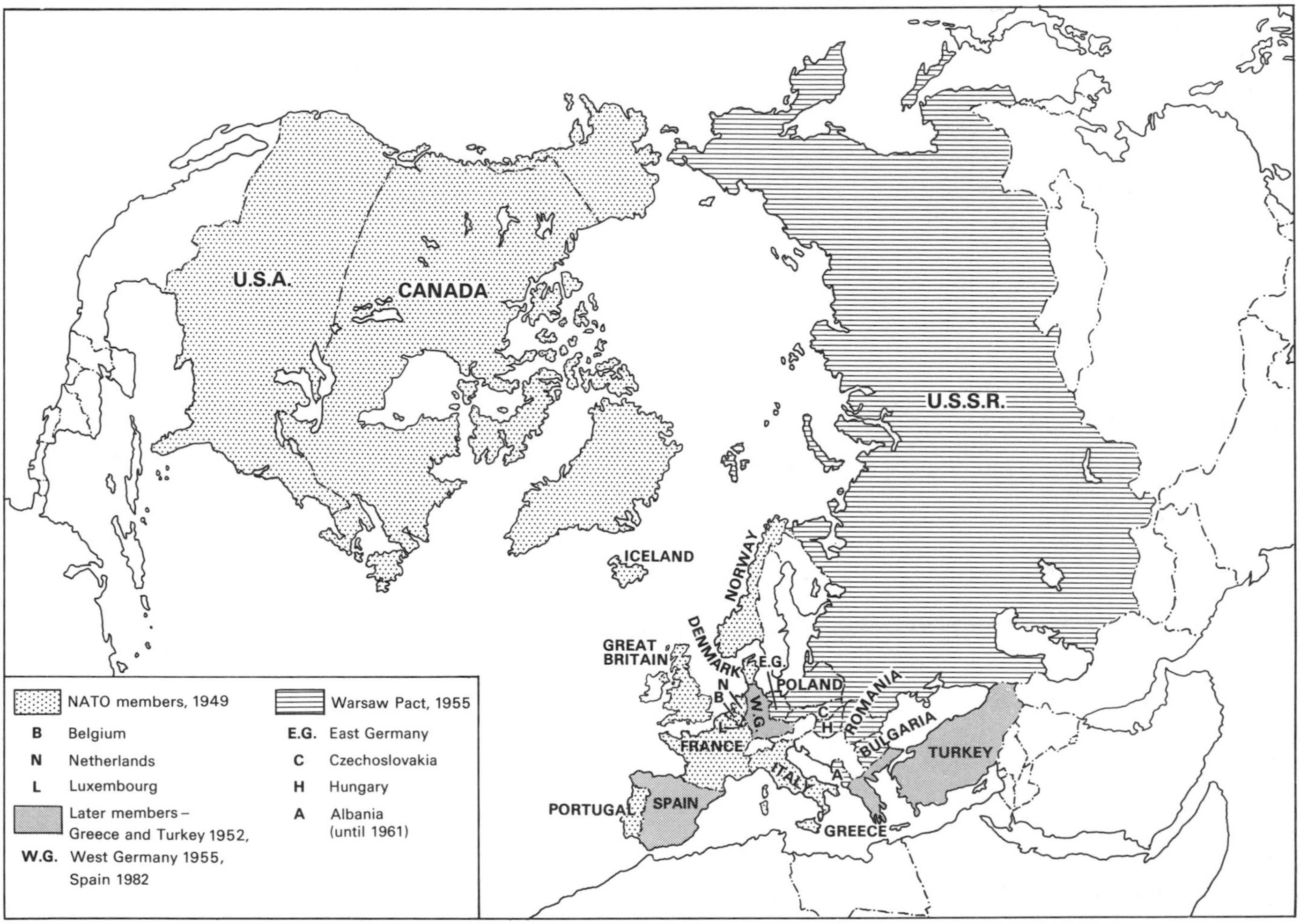

NATO members, 1949

- B Belgium
- N Netherlands
- L Luxembourg

Later members – Greece and Turkey 1952, West Germany 1955, Spain 1982

- W.G. West Germany

Warsaw Pact, 1955

- E.G. East Germany
- C Czechoslovakia
- H Hungary
- A Albania (until 1961)

Map 2 NATO and the Warsaw Pact

NATO and the Warsaw Pact

In the meantime, many people in western Europe and the U.S.A. were worried that there were very large armies in eastern Europe. Were the Russians preparing to take over western Europe?
Perhaps the American fear of Russia was exaggerated. At any rate, the Americans organised an alliance to defend the western world. It was called the North Atlantic Treaty Organisation (NATO) and came into being in April 1949. The first commander of its forces in Europe was General Eisenhower (see p.90). You can see from Map 2 which countries were the original members and which countries joined later. In 1955 the Russians set up a similar organisation in eastern Europe, called the Warsaw Pact. They were particularly angry and frightened by West Germany becoming a member of NATO in that year.

No country has left NATO as an alliance. However, French forces have not been under its command since 1966; nor the Spanish since they joined. The Greek forces were withdrawn, 1964–80.

VIGILANCE
the price of LIBERTY

Vigilance the price of liberty. The figure is composed of the flags of the member countries of NATO. NATO claims to be a defensive *alliance: it is a* shield *against attack, as this shows. What do you think the caption means?*

The Cold War spreads to Asia

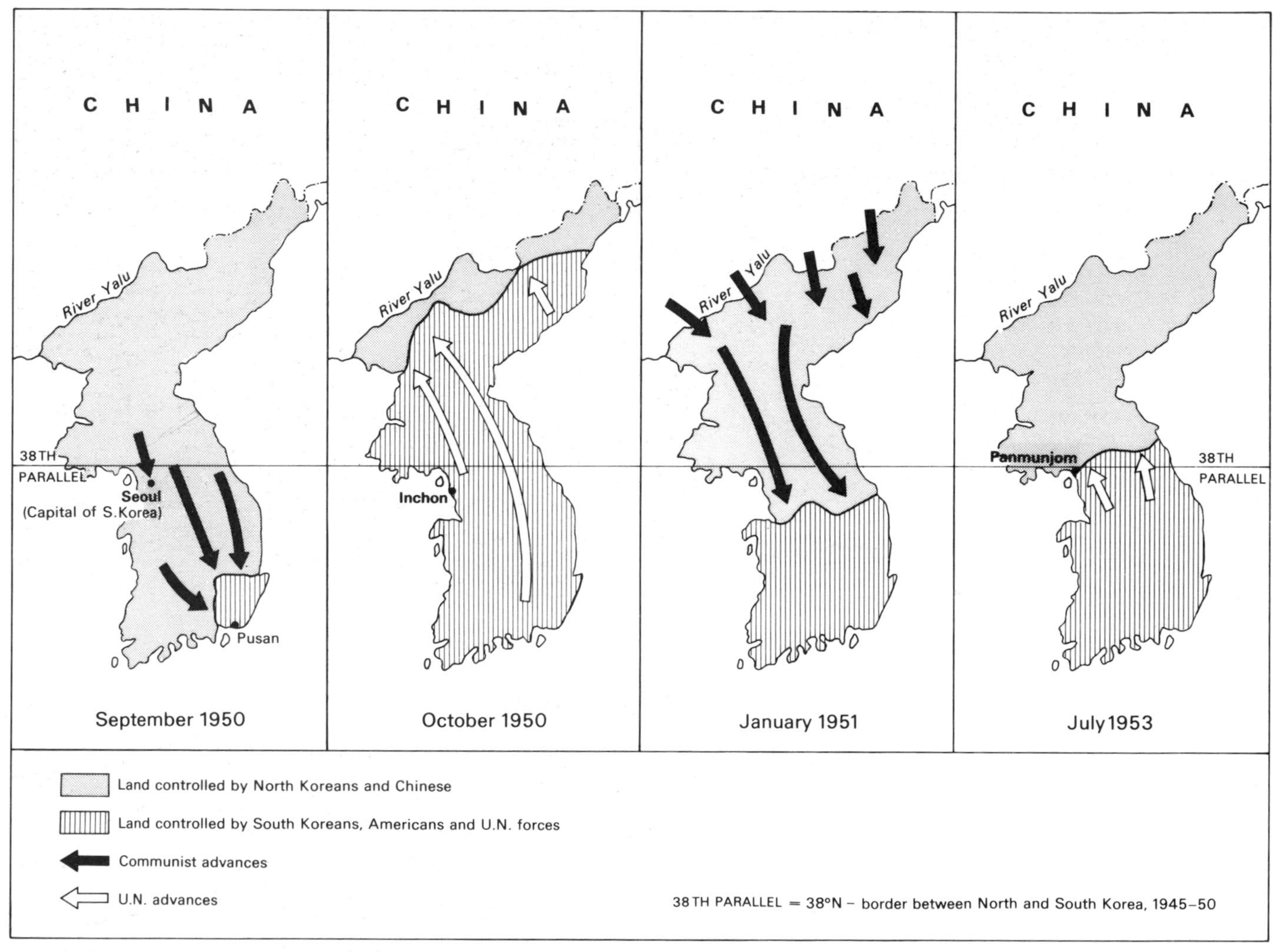

Map 3 The Korean War, 1950–53

The Chinese Revolution

As we have seen in Chapter 8 the Communist party finally took over control of China in 1949. The Chinese and Russian Communists have never been very friendly with each other. But many people in the west, and especially in America, became very worried by this new Communist victory. These people emphasised the huge areas of land now under Communist control in Europe and Asia. The Americans promised to defend Chiang Kai-shek on the island of Formosa (Taiwan)(see p.118). The American fear of Chinese Communism was strengthened by the Korean War.

The Korean War, 1950–53

The partition of Korea

Korea is a peninsula, roughly the size of England, jutting out from China towards Japan. Japan controlled it for many years and in 1945, rather like Germany, it was partitioned along the 38th parallel of latitude. The Russians set up a Communist government in the northern half. The Americans set up a government friendly to themselves in the south.

The start of the War

At dawn on 25 June 1950 the North Korean army invaded South Korea. They soon captured the capital, Seoul. The South Korean and American forces were swept back very quickly until they were boxed in to a small corner of the country round Pusan. You can follow the various stages of the war on Map 3. The Americans arranged that the war be discussed in the United Nations. As a result, South Korea was supported by the U.N. and several member-countries sent soldiers to fight there. The commander of all these forces was the American General MacArthur (see p.82).

The Cold War spreads to Asia

American soldiers firing on North Korean troops

Senator Joseph McCarthy describing his theory of a nation-wide Communist conspiracy

The Chinese become involved

MacArthur made a bold landing at Inchon and was soon forcing the North Koreans to retreat. The U.N. forces advanced to the Yalu river, which forms the frontier between North Korea and China. Large numbers of Chinese soldiers then crossed over to Korea and fought on the side of the North Koreans. The Communist forces advanced southwards once again. By early 1951 the front-line was again roughly at the original border between North and South Korea. It was stalemate.

General MacArthur wanted to attack China. But President Truman was frightened that such an action might well trigger off a new world war. He dismissed MacArthur from the command. Peace was eventually signed at Panmunjom in 1953, leaving Korea still divided. The human suffering of the people of Korea had been dreadful as the armies and airforces fought back and forth, destroying their land and homes.

McCarthyism

These events in Asia had serious side-effects in America. Many people became violently anti-Communist. Senator Joseph McCarthy particularly made wild accusations that there were Communists in important positions in America. Loyal Americans were placed under suspicion in a 'witch-hunt' for people he accused of having Communist sympathies. The whole country seemed gripped by this hysteria.

The Western Hemisphere, 1953–68

Some of the leaders

Americans

From 1953 to 1961 the President of the U.S.A. was Dwight D. Eisenhower. He tried to reach agreement with the Russians by holding talks. But his Secretary of State, John Foster Dulles, wanted to be 'tough'. He said that he was willing to go to the brink of all-out war with Russia. This policy came to be called 'brinkmanship' and frightened many people because it was so dangerous.

In 1961 John F. Kennedy became president. Although he tried to continue talks, it was during his time that the most serious crisis of all happened—the Cuba missile crisis (see p.137).

Russians

The most important Russian leader from 1953 to 1964 was Nikita Khrushchev (see pp.38-9)—a stubby man with a colourful character. In 1956 he made a speech urging 'peaceful coexistence'. The idea was that Communism and Capitalism should compete with eath other but should avoid all-out war because, with nuclear weapons, this would be suicidal.

From 1964 to 1982 Leonid Brezhnev was the most important Russian leader. In 1968, at the time of the uprising in Czechoslovakia (see p.136), he announced what came to be called the Brezhnev Doctrine. This declared that Russia would not allow any of the east European satellite countries to set up a non-Communist government.

The German problem and summit conferences

Germany

We saw on p.130 how the post-war zones of occupation in Germany became two separate countries: West Germany (the Federal German Republic) and East Germany (the German Democratic Republic). During the 1950s and 1960s there were four main problems:

1 Many Germans still hoped that their country would be reunified.
2 The Russians were frightened that a new strong Germany might again threaten them. The Russians still remembered the dreadful suffering of the Second World War (see p.80).
3 The people of East Germany were envious of the much higher standard of living enjoyed in West Germany.
4 There was still the problem of Berlin, divided and embedded in the heart of East Germany.

The Geneva 'Summit' Conference, 1955

Stalin died in 1953. Hopes were then raised that agreement between the two sides of the Cold War might now be easier—especially over the problems of Germany and Berlin. The leaders of Russia, America, Britain and France met at Geneva in 1955. This was called a 'summit' conference because the 'top' people attended. It was very friendly, though nothing was agreed.

Nikita Khrushchev at the Paris Summit Conference, 1960. He is attacking the Americans about the U-2 incident

The Paris 'Summit' Conference, 1960

The next summit meeting was held in Paris. It broke up in disorder. The reason was as follows.

The Americans felt that they needed more information about Russian weapons. It is remarkable how much information can be gathered by skilled interpreters from photographs taken from high-flying aeroplanes (for an example, see p. 137). By 1960 the Americans had developed an aeroplane called the U-2 for this purpose. They believed that it flew so high that it could not be shot down. On 1st May one of these aeroplanes *was* shot down—near Sverdlovsk in the middle of Russia. At Paris Khrushchev asked Eisenhower to apologise for using 'spy planes'. He refused. Khrushchev was naturally furious and left Paris in a great rage.

The Berlin Wall. On the right, East Berlin. On the left, West Berlin

The U-2 aeroplane

The Berlin Wall

During the 1950s and 1960s the people of East Germany were very unhappy. From 1945 to 1961 over 3 million fled to West Germany. The border between East and West Germany was guarded by watch-towers, barbed-wire fences and mine-fields. But people could still pass freely from East Germany into West Berlin, and from there to West Germany. In 1961 this route for refugees was closed by the building of the Berlin Wall. The Wall became a dreadful symbol of the hatred of the two sides in the Cold War and the lack of freedom in eastern Europe.

One of the most famous spy stories written about the Cold War is John Le Carré's *The Spy Who Came in from the Cold.* At the end of the book, the British spy, Leamas, is trying to help a friend, Liz, across the Wall into the safety of West Berlin:

> Before them was a strip of thirty yards. It followed the wall in both directions. Perhaps seventy yards to their right was a watch tower; the beam of its search-light played along the strip....
>
> They were almost at the wall when the beam darted to the north leaving them momentarily in total darkness. Still holding Liz's arm, Leamas guided her forward blindly, his left hand reaching ahead of him until suddenly he felt the coarse, sharp contact of the cinder brick. Now he could discern the wall and, looking upwards, the triple strand of wire and the cruel hooks which held it.... Leamas pulled himself quickly upwards until he reached the top of the wall....
>
> Laying himself flat he reached down, grasped her outstretched hand and began drawing her slowly upwards....
>
> Suddenly the whole world seemed to break into flame; from everywhere, from above and beside them, massive lights converged, bursting upon them with savage accuracy....
>
> Then came the hysterical wail of sirens, orders frantically shouted....
>
> Then they fired—single rounds, three or four and he felt her shudder. Her thin arms slipped from his hands.

The Russians control Eastern Europe

The problem of Eastern Europe

We saw on p.128 how Stalin was determined to have friendly governments in the countries of eastern Europe. And that meant Communist governments. But the Communists would not necessarily have been able to gain and keep control of these governments if the Red Army had not stayed in these countries. Even so, there were several desperate uprisings. We have just seen how unhappy were the people of East Germany. They rose in rebellion in 1953. Russian soldiers and tanks restored control.

The Hungarian uprising, 1956

The most famous uprising occurred in Hungary in 1956. The Hungarians were so successful that they took control of their capital city, Budapest, and the Russians withdrew. A new government was set up. But the Russian tanks returned. There was desperate fighting in the streets. No other country seemed able to help the Hungarians, partly because the attention of the western countries was concentrated on the Suez crisis (see pp.165–6).

The Prague spring, 1968

Twelve years later, very similar events happened in Czechoslovakia. In the spring of 1968 a new government was set up by Alexander Dubček (pronounced doob-check). He wanted more freedom for his people. He wanted, he said, 'socialism with a human face.' Again, Russian tanks restored Communist control.

Poland

In contrast, the Poles managed to achieve changes and avoided Russian interference. Strikes and demonstrations took place in 1956, 1970 and 1980. In each year political leaders were replaced and reforms introduced. In 1980 a free trade union called 'Solidarity' was set up by Lech Walesa (pronounced Va-wen-sa).

Many people were worried that the Russians might invade Poland in 1981 as they had crushed the reforming governments in Hungary in 1956 and Czechoslovakia in 1968. This did not happen, though a very firm government was set up by General Jaruzelski. Walesa was arrested and kept imprisoned until the end of 1982. In 1983 he received the Nobel Peace Prize.

Budapest, 1956. Burnt out Russian tanks with their dead crew members. For a short while it seemed that the Hungarian uprising might have succeeded. Then the Russians returned

Fidel Castro in 1959 just after his victory over the Dictator, Batista, with some of his followers. For three years he had fought from a mountain stronghold (see p.137)

Lech Walesa, leader of Solidarity and President of Poland since 1990

The Western Hemisphere, 1953–68

Cuba

The Bay of Pigs invasion

Just as the Russians wanted friendly governments in eastern Europe, so the Americans wanted friendly governments in the Caribbean, Central and South America. The U.S. secret service, the C.I.A. (Central Intelligence Agency) have supported brutal dictators in many countries for fear that they might be replaced by Communists.

But in 1959 a Communist government was set up in Cuba by Fidel Castro. Two years later a motley band of invaders, organised by the C.I.A., landed in the Bay of Pigs (see Map 4). Their aim was to overthrow Castro. They were easily captured by the Cuban army. The 'invasion' was a fiasco. President Kennedy of the U.S.A. was very embarrassed.

The missile crisis, 1962

But there followed the most serious crisis of the Cold War so far.

On 14 October 1962 photographs taken by U-2 aeroplanes showed that Russian rockets were being set up in Cuba. Map 4 shows you how dangerous these missiles might be to America. Also Russian ships carrying more missiles and aeroplanes were sailing towards Cuba. What was to be done? President Kennedy could not ignore this danger. Yet if he ordered a bombing or an invasion of Cuba, he might spark off a nuclear war with Russia. He therefore ordered a naval blockade of Cuba and exchanged letters with Khrushchev. Khruschchev also saw the danger. He agreed to remove the missiles if Kennedy agreed not to invade Cuba. The world breathed a sigh of relief.

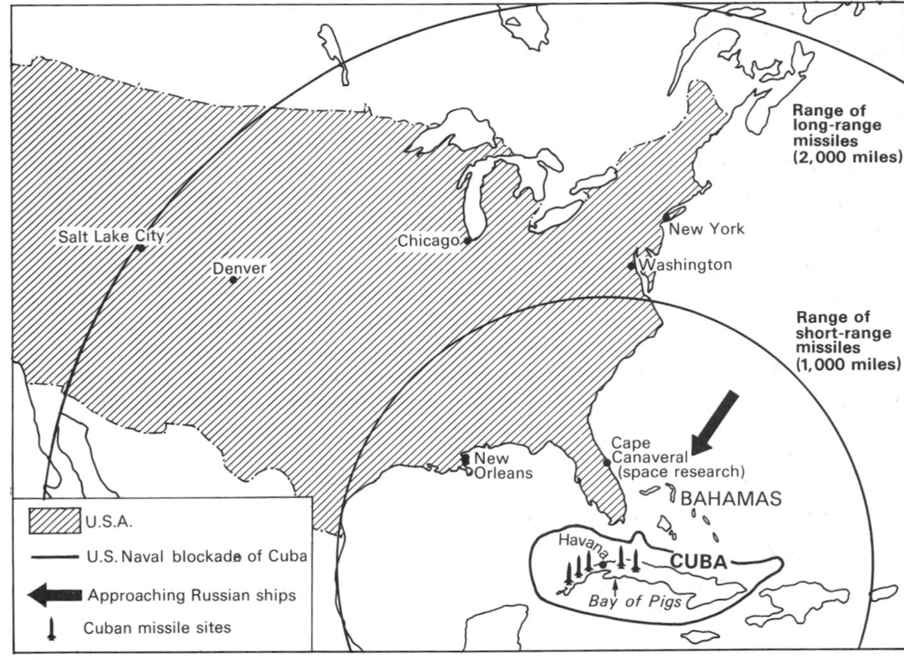

Map 4 The Cuban missile crisis

Who do you think had won? Khrushchev announced that he had saved Cuba from an American invasion. Kennedy claimed that he had saved the world from nuclear war.

An aerial photograph of a Cuban missile base

An enlargement to show the missile sites more clearly

Nuclear weapons

The weapons of the Cold War

A nuclear submarine firing a missile

The Russian 'Backfire' swing-wing bomber

A B-52 bomber—shown releasing a Hound Dog missile

The Arms Race

The weapons

Look at this selection of weapons developed for the Cold War. Compare them with the weapons of the two World Wars on pp.16, 76, 83, and 88. Since 1945 many wars have been fought with, for example, tanks and machine-guns not basically different from those used in the Second World War. The really big change has been in the development of nuclear weapons and missiles. These are some of the main weapons developed in the 1960s and 1970s:

1 Nuclear weapons. Atomic bombs are like the bomb dropped on Hiroshima (p.92). the explosion is caused by the splitting of atoms of uranium or plutonium. Hydrogen bombs are even more powerful. The explosion is caused by the bringing together of atoms of hydrogen. Both kinds can be fitted as warheads to missiles as well as carried by aeroplanes in the form of bombs.

2 Strategic bombers. Long-range heavy bombers, e.g. the American B-52.

3 Medium-range bombers. Small and fast, but still able to carry nuclear weapons, e.g. the Russian 'Backfire'.

4 Intercontinental ballistic missiles (I.C.B.Ms). Long-range rockets, e.g. American 'Minuteman', Russian SS-9. Many are housed in heavily protected underground chambers (or 'silos').

5 Submarine launched ballistic missiles (S.L.B.Ms). These have the advantage that they can be launched from under the sea anywhere in the world.

6 Multiple independently-targeted re-entry vehicles (M.I.R.Vs). A missile carries several warheads and releases them on to different targets.

Nuclear weapons

The build-up of nuclear weapons

In 1945 the U.S.A. was the only country with nuclear weapons. The Russians were frightened that the Americans might use this advantage to bully them. They therefore hurried to produce their own. Other countries followed. Look at the following table and Figure 1.

Dates of Test Explosions

	Atomic	*Hydrogen*
U.S.A.	1945	1952
U.S.S.R.	1949	1957
U.K.	1952	1957
France	1960	1968
China	1964	1968
India	1974	—

What do they tell you about (a) the speed with which countries developed atomic and hydrogen bombs? (b) the development of missiles? Why do you think missiles are so much more important and dangerous than bombers?

Huge sums of money have been spent since 1945 in producing weapons, a large proportion because of the Cold War. By the 1980s the world was spending well over $500,000,000,000 a year on armed forces and weapons!

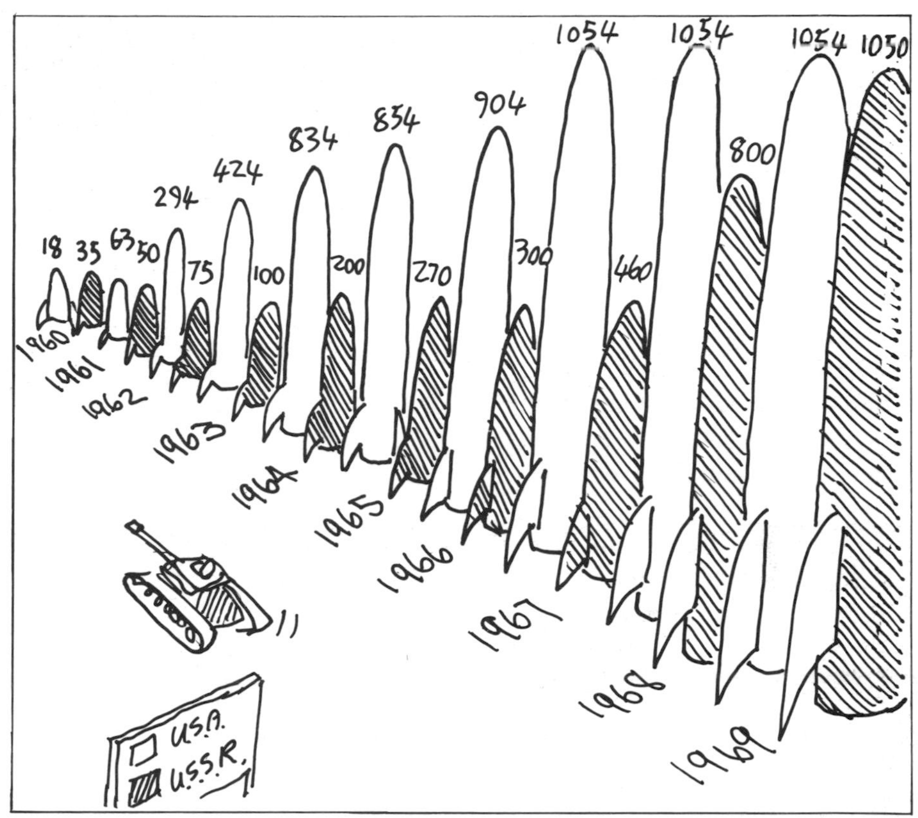

Figure 1 The growth of missiles in the 1960s

Détente

The fears

The destruction, death and human suffering at Hiroshima, were terrible enough (see p.92). But as the years went by the weapons became more powerful and more plentiful. Many people became very worried at the prospect of nuclear war. The Cuban missile crisis was a particular shock: war seemed so near (see p. 137). In the 1960s people spoke of a 'thaw' in the Cold War. In the 1970s the word used was *'détente'* meaning relaxation of tension.

On the other hand, military leaders have said that nuclear weapons have been a 'deterrent', that is, they have made people hesitate to provoke war. Do you think this is a good argument?

Arms control

Several important agreements have been reached to help control the spread of nuclear weapons and reduce the likelihood of war:

1 Hotline, 1963. Direct teleprinter link between the American and Russian leaders.

2 Partial test-ban treaty, 1963. No nuclear tests to be made except underground. Over 100 countries signed, including America and Russia.

3 Non-Proliferation Treaty, 1968. Those who signed made the following promises. Countries without nuclear weapons promised not to buy or make them. Countries with nuclear weapons promised to negotiate to reduce their numbers.

4 Strategic Arms Limitation Treaties. A treaty was signed in 1972, generally called SALT-I. At the same time America and Russia signed the ABM treaty. By this they promised not to set up more than one site each for Anti-Ballistic Missile defence, i.e. missiles to destroy missiles.

Talks continued and another treaty, SALT-II, was signed in 1979. But it was not confirmed by the American Senate and the opportunity for further agreement was lost in the quarrel over Afghanistan (see p.142).

The new Cold War

From 1979 relations between America and Russia again became very tense. *Détente* was at an end.

Nuclear weapons

The world entered the period of the New Cold War, though the American and Russian leaders did meet for talks at Geneva 1985. Who was responsible for this change? There were, in fact, faults on both sides.

Russian responsibility

Russia took two kinds of action which frightened the West:

1 She threatened two of her neighbours, Afghanistan (see p. 142) and Poland (see p. 136), and even sent troops into Afghanistan.

2 She started to deliver new missiles, SS-20s, to sites in eastern Europe. These were a much more dangerous threat to western Europe than the missiles they replaced.

American responsibility

On the other hand there were many critics of *détente* in America. These people believed that America had been cheated by the Russians who used the time to build up their forces so that by about 1980 Russia was just as strong as America.

Reagan was elected as President in 1980 largely because he promised to resume the build-up of America's nuclear weapons.

New weapons

The following new weapons have been developed by the Americans. Very similar ones have been developed by the Russians.

1 MX. Very accurate ICBM.

2 Pershing II. Very accurate intermediate-range missile.

3 Cruise. Pilotless aeroplane with a nuclear warhead.

4 Trident. Very accurate SLBM.

Nuclear arms talks

1 INF (Intermediate-range Nuclear Forces); Geneva, 1981–83.

2 START (Strategic Arms Reduction Talks); Geneva, 1982–83.

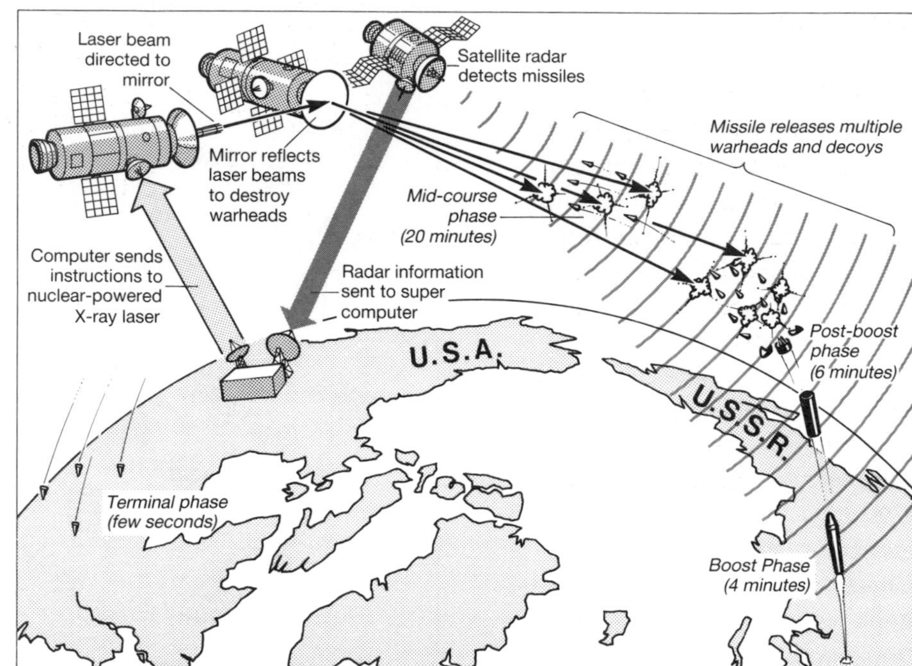

Star Wars: how the Strategic Defense Initiative (S.D.I.) might have worked

(Russian negotiators brought both of these to an end because they believed that the Americans were not treating them seriously.)

3 Nuclear arms reduction talks – Geneva, from 1985.

Star Wars

In 1983 President Reagan ordered research to be started on the Strategic Defense Initiative (SDI). This was a scheme to develop methods of destroying Russian satellites and attacking missiles in flight. And so it was nick-named 'Star Wars'.

The theory was that nuclear weapons would become useless if they could all be destroyed immediately after launching. In practice, many scientists believe that such a system is impossible; and the Russians accused Reagan of speeding up the arms race.

Nuclear disarmament movements

The collapse of *détente* revived fears that a nuclear war might start. Many people in Europe and America joined protest movements. In Britain the Campaign for Nuclear Disarmament (CND), formed in 1957, was revived. Most famous of all in the early 1980s was the demonstration of women who camped at Greenham Common in Berkshire to protest against the basing of American cruise missiles there.

A CND demonstration

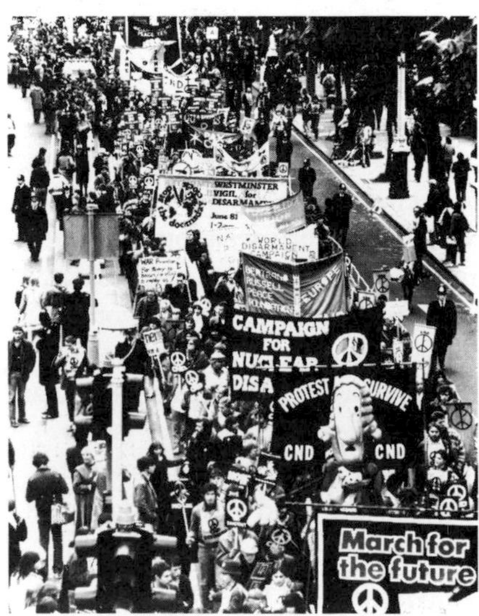

Indo-China

The defeat of the French

Indo-China is a land on the south-east corner of Asia, to the east of Thailand and to the south of China. During the nineteenth century the various countries of Indo-China became French colonies. During the Second World War the land was occupied by the Japanese. When the French tried to take over again in 1945 a war broke out because many of the people wanted their countries to be independent. By this time, Indo-China was divided into three colonies: Laos, Cambodia and Vietnam. Fighting against the French was particularly fierce in the northern part of Vietnam, where the Vietnamese fighters were brilliantly led by the Communist Ho Chi Minh. In 1954 the French army was surrounded at Dien Bien Phu and surrendered. The politicians met at Geneva and agreed that Indo-China could be independent. But Vietnam was divided into two along the 17th parallel of latitude, with a Communist government in North Vietnam and a government friendly to the west in South Vietnam. Hanoi became the capital of North Vietnam and Saigon of South Vietnam.

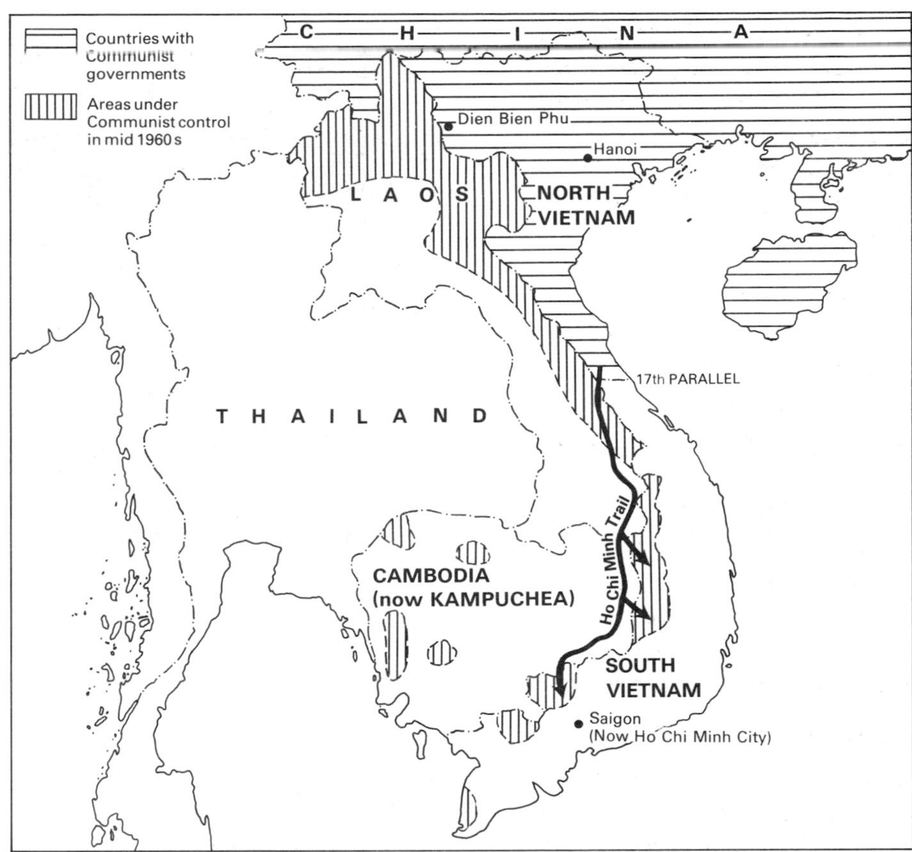

Map 5 The wars in Indo-China, 1945–75

Ho Chi Minh

How the Americans became involved

A Communist organisation called the Vietcong was then set up in South Vietnam and in 1957 a civil war started between them and the government. The Americans became frightened that South Vietnam might be taken over by the Communists. They thought that then other countries in south-east Asia would in turn collapse to Communism like a line of dominoes. This fear was called the domino theory. First of all the Americans sent a few advisers to help the South Vietnamese. But by the mid-1960s American soldiers and airmen were fighting in a most terrible war against Vietnamese Communist armies. The Vietcong were supplied from North Vietnam along the Ho Chi Minh trail through thick forests (see Map 5). This war lasted until 1973, when the Americans withdrew. By 1975 all three countries of Indo-China were Communist.

The horrors of the War

Both sides committed terrible atrocities.

1 The Vietcong terrorised villages to force them to support the Communist cause.

2 The Americans used aircraft to drop high explosive bombs. More bombs were dropped in the war in Vietnam than in the whole of the Second World War. Hanoi suffered huge attacks. Napalm (fire) bombs were used against people and chemicals were used to destroy trees.

3 Huge numbers of Vietnamese men, women and children were killed or maimed.
4 The Americans also made massive bombing attacks on Cambodia because the Vietcong were using that nearby country as a base.
5 Many people, including Americans (see p.104), were horrified by the American involvement in Vietnam. There were many organised protests.
6 For many years after the war came to an end the countries of Indo-China remained in a most wretched condition. Refugee 'boat people' fled in leaky vessels from Vietnam. Cambodia (renamed Kampuchea) suffered a most brutal government and became a devastated, starving land.

A U.S. Air Force aeroplane spraying 'defoliants' on the jungle. Although the Americans claimed otherwise, these chemicals had a harmful effect upon people and animals

Map 6 Afghanistan

Afghanistan

During the 1970s the Americans and Russians were becoming rather more friendly. This was the time of détente. Then, in 1979, strong Russian forces invaded Afghanistan. The Russians did this to support the Communists there whose government was becoming unpopular. The Afghans showed how they hated the Russian invaders by fighting them wherever possible.

Many people throughout the world were shocked by the Russian action. The Americans were also frightened, because they thought the Russians might be advancing towards the precious supplies of oil in the Persian Gulf area. At the same time the Americans were having difficulties with Iran (see p. 171). In 1980 the Olympic Games were held in Moscow. Many countries refused to send athletes as a means of protesting. The Cold War had become decidedly chilly once again.

Who was to blame?

Compare the following statements by two American diplomats.

As soon as the defeat of the Nazis appeared certain, the Soviet Union began to abandon the policy of wartime cooperation to which it had turned for self-protection ... the historical record is clear. As soon as the Soviet Government saw no further military need for the wartime coalition, it set out on its expansionist adventures. ... [This] forced those nations determined to defend their freedom to take measures in their own self-defense.

The image of a Stalinist Russia poised and yearning to attack the West, and deterred only by our possession of atomic weapons, was largely a creation of the Western imagination, against which some of us who were familiar with Russian matters tried in vain, over the course of the years, to make ourselves heard.

Who was really to blame for the Cold War—Russia or America? Read again pages 38, 92, and 128-31. Was Russia really planning to conquer Europe in the late 1940s? Or was she utterly exhausted from the Second World War and frightened of the American atomic bomb?

Time chart

Neither war nor peace

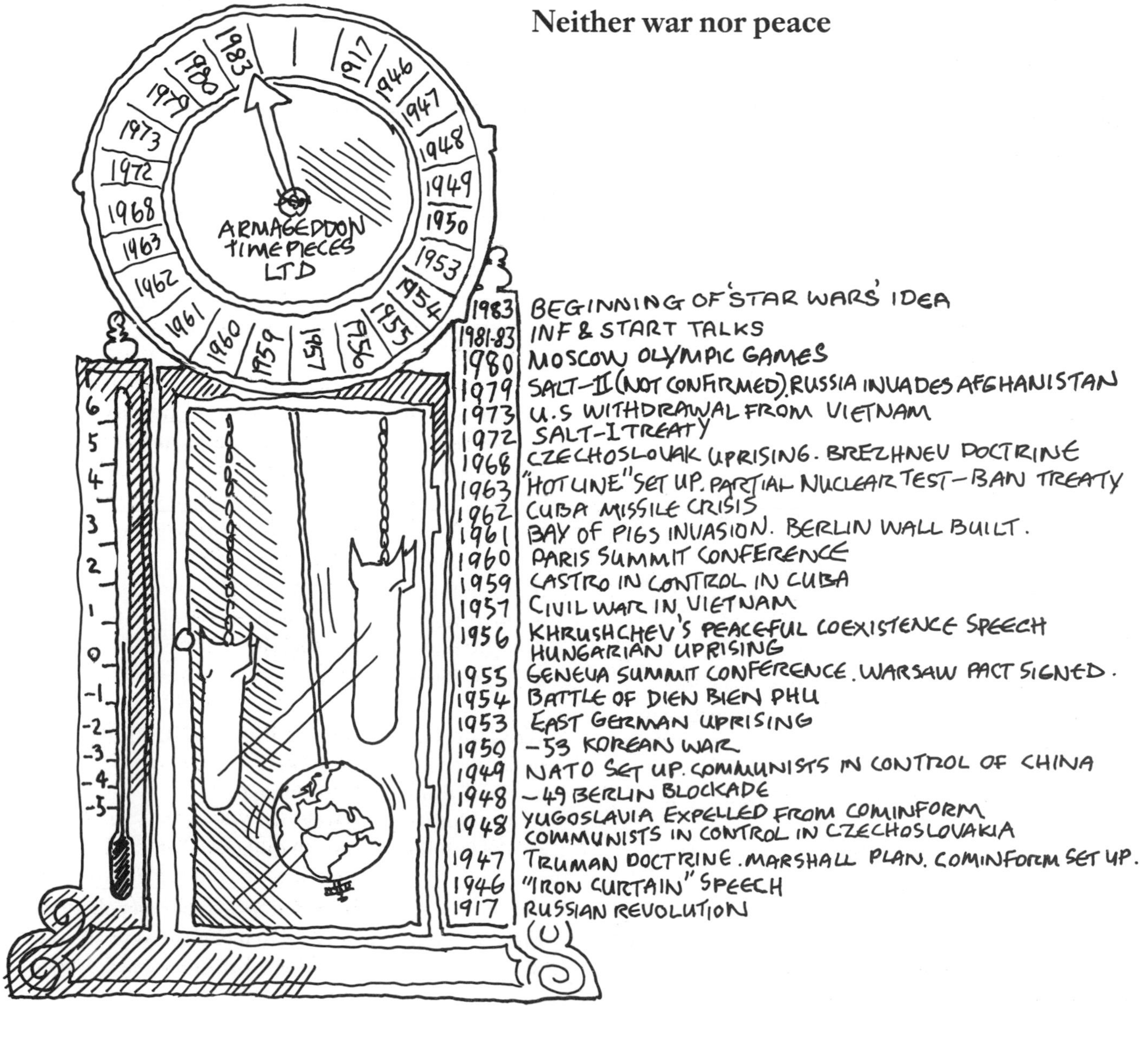

ARMAGEDDON TIMEPIECES LTD

1983 BEGINNING OF 'STAR WARS' IDEA
1981-83 INF & START TALKS
1980 MOSCOW OLYMPIC GAMES
1979 SALT-II (NOT CONFIRMED). RUSSIA INVADES AFGHANISTAN
1973 U.S WITHDRAWAL FROM VIETNAM
1972 SALT-I TREATY
1968 CZECHOSLOVAK UPRISING. BREZHNEV DOCTRINE
1963 "HOT LINE" SET UP. PARTIAL NUCLEAR TEST-BAN TREATY
1962 CUBA MISSILE CRISIS
1961 BAY OF PIGS INVASION. BERLIN WALL BUILT.
1960 PARIS SUMMIT CONFERENCE
1959 CASTRO IN CONTROL IN CUBA
1957 CIVIL WAR IN VIETNAM
1956 KHRUSHCHEV'S PEACEFUL COEXISTENCE SPEECH
HUNGARIAN UPRISING
1955 GENEVA SUMMIT CONFERENCE. WARSAW PACT SIGNED.
1954 BATTLE OF DIEN BIEN PHU
1953 EAST GERMAN UPRISING
1950 -53 KOREAN WAR
1949 NATO SET UP. COMMUNISTS IN CONTROL OF CHINA
1948 -49 BERLIN BLOCKADE
1948 YUGOSLAVIA EXPELLED FROM COMINFORM
COMMUNISTS IN CONTROL IN CZECHOSLOVAKIA
1947 TRUMAN DOCTRINE. MARSHALL PLAN. COMINFORM SET UP.
1946 "IRON CURTAIN" SPEECH
1917 RUSSIAN REVOLUTION

Questions

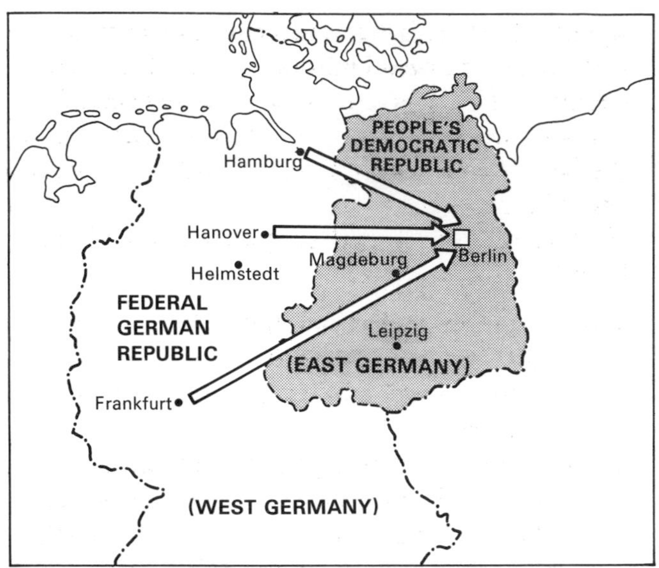

1 What exactly is meant by the 'Cold War'? For what reasons did it start?

Use the map (above) to help explain why Berlin became a major crisis point during the Cold War. Write notes that explain the importance of the event illustrated in the picture.

2 a Suggest reasons for the Cold War between the U.S.S.R. and the Western Allies since 1945.
b Describe and explain the issues involved in any **three** main international clashes which have occurred between these two power blocks since 1945.

3 'From Stettin in the Baltic to Trieste in the Adriatic an iron curtain has descended across the continent.'
(British politician in 1946)
a Who said this?
b What did he mean by the Iron Curtain?
c Name **three** countries behind the Iron Curtain.

4 The Truman Doctrine of 1947 said:
'It must be the policy of the United States to support free peoples who are resisting attempted subjugation by armed minorities or by outside pressures.'
a What political office did Truman hold in 1947 and in what circumstances had he gained this office in 1945?
b How was the Truman Doctrine put into effect in the years 1947–49 by George Marshall?
c Write an account of **two** important conflicts since 1947 into which the United States has been drawn in order to carry out the Truman Doctrine.

5 a Why was NATO established in April, 1949, and what were its aims?
b Name **three** of the original members.
c Which country became a member in 1955? Why was there controversy about this?
d Give an account of the attitude of the Soviet Union to the formation of NATO and the action taken by the Soviet Union in 1955.
e What have been NATO's achievements since 1949?
f What political problems have beset NATO in the 1970s?

6 Explain how the Cold War affected Europe between 1945 and 1961. You may find it useful to bear in mind the following:
a 1945: Europe divided and Germany zoned;
b 1947: Truman Doctrine and Marshall Aid;
c 1948: Berlin Blockade;
d 1949: formation of N.A.T.O.;
e 1955: Warsaw Pact formed;
f 1956: Hungarian uprising;
g 1961: Berlin Wall built.

7 Write **three** chapters in the history of Berlin after 1945 under the following headings:
a the division of the city in 1945;
b the blockade of the city in 1948–9;
c the building of the wall in 1961.

8 Outline the main changes in Soviet foreign policy since 1945. You may find it useful to include in your answer:
a Cold War b Thaw c Brezhnev and Kosygin.

Questions

9 Read the following extracts and answer the questions below.

Source A
'From Stettin in the Baltic to Trieste in the Adriatic, an iron curtain has descended across the continent. Behind that line lie all the capitals of the ancient states of central and eastern Europe. Warsaw, Berlin, Prague, Vienna, Budapest, Belgrade, Bucharest, and Sofia, all these famous cities and the populations around them lie in the Soviet sphere and all are subject, in one form or another, not only to Soviet influence but to a very high and increasing measure of control from Moscow . . .

'. . . in a great number of countries, far from the Russian frontiers and throughout the world, Communist fifth columns are established and work in complete unity and absolute obedience to the directions they receive from the Communist center . . . the Communist parties or fifth columns constitute a growing challenge and peril to Christian civilization.'
(Winston Churchill's 'Iron Curtain' speech, 5 March 1946.)

Source B
'The following circumstances should not be forgotten. The Germans made their invasion of the USSR through Finland, Poland, Rumania, Bulgaria, and Hungary. The Germans were able to make their invasion through these countries because, at the time, governments hostile to the Soviet Union existed in these countries. As a result of the German invasion the Soviet Union has lost irretrievably in the fighting against the Germans, and also through the German occupation and the deportation of Soviet citizens to German servitude, a total of about seven million people. In other words, the Soviet Union's loss of life has been several times greater than that of Britain and the United States of America put together. Possibly in some quarters an inclination is felt to forget about these colossal sacrifices of the Soviet people which secured the liberation of Europe from the Hitlerite yoke. But the Soviet Union cannot forget about them. And so what can there be surprising about the fact that the Soviet Union, anxious for its future safety, is trying to see to it that governments loyal in their attitude to the Soviet Union should exist in these countries? How can anyone, who has not taken leave of his senses, describe these peaceful aspirations of the Soviet Union as expansionist tendencies on the part of our state?'
(Stalin's reply to Churchill's speech, in *Pravda*, 13 March 1946.)

a In what country did Churchill make his speech (Source A)?
b Name the countries whose capital cities Churchill lists (Source A).
c Write a paragraph to explain the following statement in Stalin's speech: '. . . these colossal sacrifices of the Soviet people which secured the liberation of Europe from the Hitlerite yoke'. (Source B).
d Explain how important these two extracts are for understanding the start of the Cold War.

10 In 1960 the following cartoon appeared in *Crocodile*, a Soviet magazine.

a The man shown in the cartoon is President Eisenhower of the U.S.A. Why is he re-painting the aeroplane?
b After 1953 there were signs of a thaw in the Cold War. What were these signs and how did the events of May 1960 affect this thaw?
c Why, in the 1960's, did American and Soviet leaders pursue a policy of *détente?*

10/The European get-together

A painting by Ben Shahn entitled 'Liberation' (1945)
What does this tell you about the state of Europe in 1945? Notice the damaged building and rubble, the condition of the children's clothes and their looks. Why do you think the artist entitled the picture, 'Liberation'?

Western Europe after the Second World War

Damage

Try to imagine the destruction, desolation and despair in Europe in 1945. The fighting had come to an end, it is true. But the fighting in Germany, Italy, the Low Countries and northern France had been very fierce on land. And Allied aeroplanes had made constant attacks from the air. As a result, many cities were reduced to little more than heaps of rubble; factories were gutted; and railway and road bridges were demolished. How could millions of homeless people be given shelter? How could the towns be supplied with food? A return to normal life seemed almost impossible in the most seriously affected regions. Then, to make matters worse, as the continent was slowly recovering, the winter of 1947 was one of the most severe in living memory.

German refugees fleeing from the advancing Russian army

People without homes

Rebuilding and repairing would have been easier if there had not been so many homeless people in western Europe, especially in the western parts of Germany. Some of these refugees or 'displaced persons' (D.Ps.) were people whose homes had been destroyed or who had been removed from their homes during the war. Others were people who had left their homes because they were too frightened to stay. They were fleeing from the fighting or frightened of the advancing Russians. Altogether there were about eight million displaced persons in Europe in 1945.

Three important countries

The trial of Nazi war criminals at Nuremberg. The man in dark glasses on the left is Hermann Goering. Next to him is Hess

West Germany

De-Nazification

We saw in Chapter 9 how Germany was divided into zones of occupation. One of the first tasks for the occupying countries was to place non-Nazis in important positions. The most important Nazi leaders were put on trial in a special court set up in Nuremberg. They were accused of 'war crimes' such as murdering Jews and other civilians. Eleven were sentenced to death, others to imprisonment.

Creation of the Federal German Republic

In 1949 the Federal German Republic was formed by joining together the U.S., British and French zones of occupation. The new country was 'federal' because it was subdivided into nine states (Länder), each with its own local government.

In the elections the new Christian Democrat party won a majority of the seats in the parliament (Bundestag). Their leader therefore became Chancellor (the equivalent of prime minister). This was Dr Konrad Adenauer. He remained Chancellor until 1963 when he retired at the age of 87. Adenauer led West Germany in two fine achievements. One was the creation of a successful democratic system of government in place of the Nazi dictatorship. The other was what came to be called 'the economic miracle'.

Konrad Adenauer

Germany's Economic Miracle

Within a short time West Germany was transformed from the most devastated country of western Europe to one of the most prosperous. Here are a few examples of what the West Germans achieved.

By 1960 West Germany had the second biggest steel production in the whole of Europe (Russia had the biggest). By 1960 West Germany had the second biggest car production in the world (U.S.A. had the biggest). From 1948 to 1964 industrial production increased sixfold. From 1952 to 1965 unemployment dropped from 9 per cent to 0.4 per cent of the population.

Relations with East Germany

We saw in Chapter 9 how people in East Germany were envious of the West Germans. For many years the two governments were not very friendly. But when Willy Brandt was Chancellor of West Germany (1969–74) he signed treaties with several countries of eastern Europe including East Germany.

Willy Brandt at an election meeting. On the right is his successor, Helmut Schmidt, Chancellor from 1974 to 1982

France

The Fourth Republic

France, too, had to create a new system of government—to replace the Vichy government of the Second World War. The new system was called the Fourth Republic (the First Republic was set up during the French Revolution in 1792, the Third was the one that collapsed in 1940). It came into being in 1947. Although France recovered from the war remarkably well during the Fourth Republic, the politicians were constantly quarrelling and resigning. There were 25 separate governments in 12 years!

Algeria

We shall see in Chapter 12 how the European colonies in Africa gained their independence. The struggle between the Algerians and the French was one of the most bitter in the whole continent. The French had started to settle in Algeria in the 1830s and the country came to be considered as part of France—it just happened to be on the other side of the Mediterranean. By the 1950s there were about one million French 'colons' (settlers) living in Algeria.

But the Arab and Berber majority of the population wanted independence from France. They organised a liberation movement, the F.L.N. From 1954 to 1962 a vicious and complicated war was fought in Algeria. These were the main events:

1 Both the F.L.N. and the notorious French paratroops fighting against them used brutal terrorist and torture methods.

2 In 1958 the leaders of the army and 'colons' in Algeria forced the collapse of the government in France. General de Gaulle came to power as President of France.

3 De Gaulle showed that he was preparing to give the Algerians independence. The French in Algeria therefore set up their own secret army (O.A.S.) to try to prevent this by terrorism. They even tried to assassinate de Gaulle.

4 By a treaty signed at Evian in 1962, Algeria became independent.

French paratroopers in the streets of Algiers, 1961

General de Gaulle (1890–1970)

De Gaulle

General Charles de Gaulle was President of France from 1958 to 1969. He set up a new system of government, the Fifth Republic, giving more power than before to the president.

De Gaulle was a tall, impressive-looking man. He was also intensely proud. He had been the leader of the Free French forces fighting against the Germans from 1940 to 1945. He believed that France should again be a great nation and dreamt of a Europe united under French leadership, free of any influence from America and Britain. He thought that France should:

> Lead the states bordering on the Rhine, Alps, and Pyrenees to unite politically, economically, and strategically. Create of this entity the third planetary power and, if necessary, become one day the arbiter between the Anglo-Saxons and the Soviet camp ('arbiter' means umpire or judge).

What do you think his attitude was to the Common Market? (See p.154.)

May 1968

1968 was a year of student demonstrations and riots in many countries. The most serious were in Paris. There were serious clashes with the police. This is how two British journalists described the fighting:

> The main weapon on the rabble side was the *pavé*—the cubic French cobblestone weighing about three pounds, easily prized from the roadway by determined men. . . . Barricades of *pavés*, as high as a man, were thrown up with incredible speed, providing almost unlimited supplies of ammunition. Some of the worst police casualties were caused by *pavés* received in full face or chest, sometimes thrown from balconies with punishing effect. The police riposte was almost as traditional: the truncheon, the gas grenade, and on rare occasions high-pressure water-jets, which can knock a man down or even toss him several yards.

Discontent soon spread and millions of workers throughout France went on strike. But de Gaulle called new elections and received massive support. Yet he was shaken and retired the following year.

France in the 1970s and 1980s

France became more prosperous and settled in the 1970s under two less colourful presidents—Pompidou (1969–74) and Giscard d'Estaing (1974–81). They were followed by the Socialist, Mitterrand.

François Mitterand, President of France since 1981

May 1968, Barricades of paving stones and upturned cars block a main road

Three important countries

Britain

Party politics

The Conservative and Labour Parties have alternated as governments of Britain since 1945, as the table on the right shows.

The Conservative Party has been supported by businesses and the Labour Party by the Trade Unions. But many working class people have voted Conservative and middle class people, Labour.

Since 1982 there has been an important new group – the SDP/ Liberal Alliance (the Social Democratic Party was formed in 1981).

1945–51 Labour
Clement Attlee

1951–55 Conservative
Winston Churchill

1955–57 Conservative
Anthony Eden

1957–63 Conservative
Harold Macmillan

1963–64 Conservative
Alec Douglas-Home

1964–70 and 1974–76
Labour, Harold Wilson

1970–74 Conservative
Edward Heath

1976–79 Labour
James Callaghan

1979–91 Conservative
Margaret Thatcher

Britain's governments and prime ministers since 1945

The Welfare State

During the Second World War the British government was already planning for better standards of living after the war. The most important scheme was the Beveridge Plan. This set down the main ideas for the modern welfare state. This extract from the Beveridge Report mentions the arrangements by which your family is now protected from poverty and the effects of ill-health.

The Report on Social Insurance and Allied Services which I presented to His Majesty's Government in November 1942, takes Freedom from Want as its aim, and sets out a Plan for Social Security to achieve this aim. Want is defined as lack of income to obtain the means of healthy subsistence—adequate food, shelter, clothing and fuel. The Plan for Social Security is designed to secure, by a comprehensive scheme of social insurance, that every individual, on condition of working while he can and contributing from his earnings, shall have an income sufficient for the healthy subsistence of himself and his family, an income to keep him above Want, when for any reason he cannot work and earn. In addition to subsistence income during interruption of earnings, the Report proposes Children's Allowances to ensure that, however large the family, no child need ever to be in want, and medical treatment of all kinds for all persons when sick, without a charge on treatment, to ensure that no person need be sick because he has not the means to pay the doctor or the hospital.

From 1945 to 1951 the Labour Party formed the government. Mr Clement Attlee was Prime Minister. This Government put the ideas of the Beveridge Report into Practice. The main reforms were the Family Allowances Act (1945), National Insurance Act (1946) and the setting up of the National Health Service (1946). They also nationalised many industries, that is, the government took over their control: the Bank of England, Coal, Civil Aviation, Electricity, Railways, Gas and Iron and Steel.

Three important countries

Immigration

During the 1960s Britain became a multi-racial country. Many families immigrated to Britain from the West Indies, East Africa, Pakistan and India—parts of the old British Empire. These coloured people have done important work for example in hospitals, on the buses and on the London underground. But many white people disliked these immigrants and their habits. Eventually laws had to be passed:
1 to restrict the numbers of coloured people entering Britain;
2 to make it an offence to discriminate against people on the basis of race.

Figure 1 Britain's Economic decline (over different periods of time)

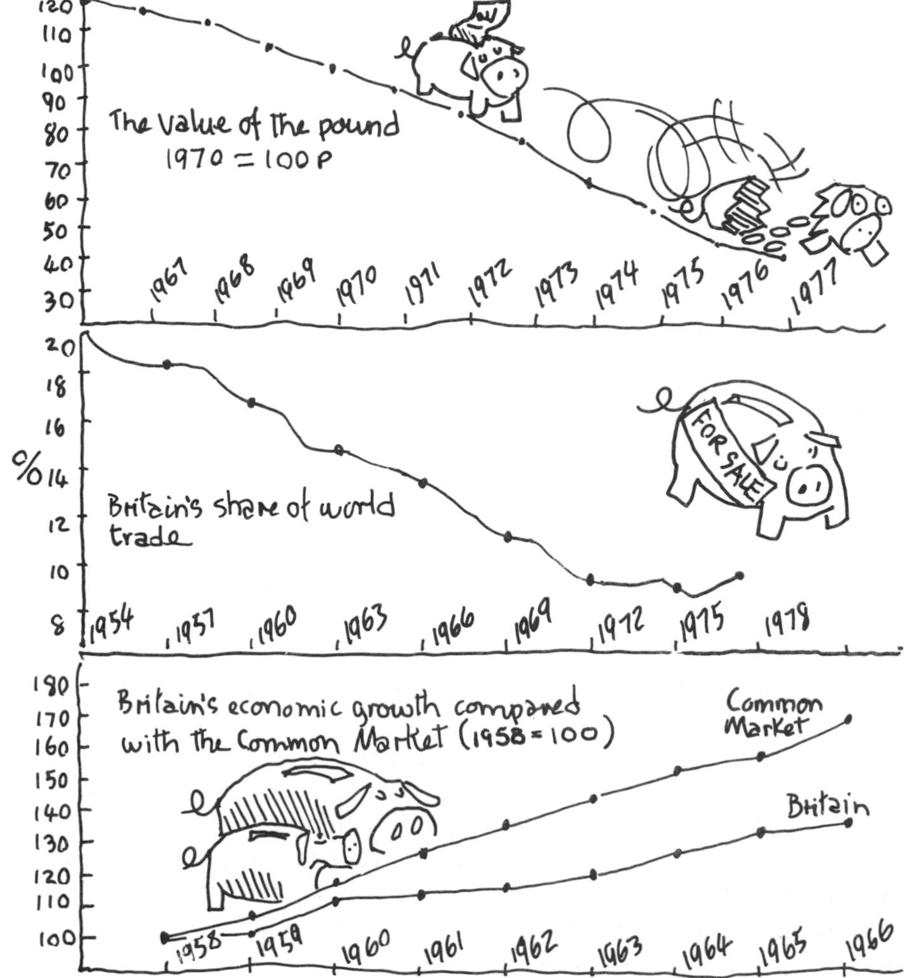

Ireland

Most of the people of Ireland are Roman Catholic by religion. But many in the north-east corner, the province of Ulster, are Protestant. In 1921 Ireland was partitioned. Six counties in Ulster remained part of the United Kingdom and the rest of Ireland became independent.

But many people disliked this arrangement. The Irish Republican Army (I.R.A.) has used terrorism to try to force the re-unification of Ireland. The Protestants of Ulster are frightened of this possibility. The Roman Catholics of Ulster have been treated badly by the Protestants. Since 1969 there has been much violence, bloodshed and destruction in Ulster. British soldiers have tried to keep law and order.

British troops on active service in Northern Ireland

Economic decline

During the 1960s British people enjoyed quite a high standard of living compared with most countries of Europe. But during the 1970s Britain suffered many economic troubles:
1 Inflation. Prices kept rising. Savings therefore lost their value.
2 Low productivity. British industries were much less efficient than the industries of other manufacturing countries—that is, more workers took longer to produce an article than in other countries.
3 Strikes. There were many quarrels about wages and working conditions.

Look at the graphs on the left. Do you think that Britain's economic problems started in the 1970s?

Troubles in the 1980s

1 Unemployment. In the early 1980s over 3 million people were out of work.
2 Disorders. Serious clashes with the police occurred in 1981 in several cities and in 1984 in connection with a long coal strike.

European co-operation

Map 1 West European economic co-operation since 1957

Figure 2 Marshall Aid

The background

Why should the countries of Europe co-operate?

We have seen in chapters 2 and 6 how the countries of Europe suffered because they fought each other in deadly wars. Some people came to believe that if something like a United States of Europe were organised these kinds of wars would be prevented.

There was a feeling that the different European nations had much in common in their traditions and ways of life. In 1949 the Council of Europe was set up in Strasbourg to discuss social and cultural matters.

Mass production methods have made it more efficient to sell to a large number of customers. Industry and trade would therefore benefit if the comparatively small countries of Europe joined together.

Because of the Cold War (see Chapter 9) some of the countries of western Europe felt that they should co-operate closely to defend themselves against Russia.

American help

As we saw on p.130, the Americans provided aid in the form of the Marshall Plan to help the countries of western Europe recover from the destruction of the Second World War. Over 13 billion dollars was provided from 1948 to 1951. The money was made available through a new organisation called the Organisation for European Economic Co-operation (O.E.E.C.). There were 16 member-countries when it was set up in 1948. But the bulk of the money went to only four countries (see Figure 2).

The Americans also took the lead in organising the defence of western Europe by creating NATO (see p. 131).

European co-operation

Creation of the Common Market

Important men

The closest co-operation that the countries of Western Europe have managed has been in the Common Market. The most important man behind this scheme was the Frenchman Jean Monnet. But he worked behind the scenes. Politicians had to persuade their peoples and parliaments to approve. The most important of these were Konrad Adenauer, Chancellor of West Germany from 1949 to 1963 and Robert Schuman, Foreign Minister in several French governments of the Fourth Republic.

The European Coal and Steel Community

What is usually called the Common Market in fact developed as three separate organisations. The first was the European Coal and Steel Community (E.C.S.C.), set up in 1952. The scheme was called the Schuman Plan, though it was really worked out mainly by Monnet. Six countries (see Map 1) gave up their individual control of their coal and steel industries to a nine-member committee called the High Authority.

The Rome treaties

In 1957 the same six countries signed treaties to set up two other organisations:

1 European Atomic Energy Community (Euratom). This is for co-operation in nuclear research.

2 European Economic Community (E.E.C.). This has come to be by far the most important European organisation. The aim was to abolish customs duties between the member countries and to set up common policies for agriculture and food.

Jean Monnet

Robert Schuman

Cartoon from Die Zeit. *This shows De Gaulle as a sentry preventing the entry of Mr Wilson to the Common Market in 1967. Wilson is weighed down by responsibilities of the Commonwealth, military commitments in the Middle and Far East and balance of payments problems.*

Britain and Europe

Britain remains aloof

Britain had the opportunity to join the Six in 1952 and in 1957. But she kept apart for three reasons:

1 Britain felt separate from the continent and felt more important in the world than even France or West Germany.

2 Trade with the Commonwealth countries was still important. This would have to decrease if Britain became a member of the E.E.C.

3 British politicians thought that the country had a 'special relationship' with the U.S.A. This would be lost if Britain gave up its complete independence.

EFTA

Britain realised, however, that economic co-operation was very important. Therefore in 1959 she created the European Free Trade Association (E.F.T.A.—see Map 1). Seven countries were loosely linked together.

Negotiations to join

But the British prime minister, Harold Macmillan, believed that it was in Britain's interests to join the Common Market. Figure 1 shows how weak the British economy was becoming (see p.151). But we have also seen (p.149) that President de Gaulle of France did not like the

'Anglo-Saxons' (that is, the Americans and British). In 1960 he prevented Britain from becoming a member. In 1967 the Labour Prime Minister, Harold Wilson, started talks again. Again, de Gaulle refused to allow Britain to enter.

In 1970 Edward Heath became prime minister. He believed very strongly that Britain should be a member of the Common Market. By this time de Gaulle was dead. The negotiations succeeded. Britain became a member in 1973. At the same time Ireland and Denmark also joined. When the Labour Party again formed a government in 1974, some of the arrangements were re-negotiated. Then, in 1975, the government asked the people of Britain to vote in a referendum whether to stay a member or leave. Three-quarters of the votes cast were in favour of staying a member.

The E.E.C. Headquarters in Brussels

Map 2 Regional Development areas in the E.E.C., 1973

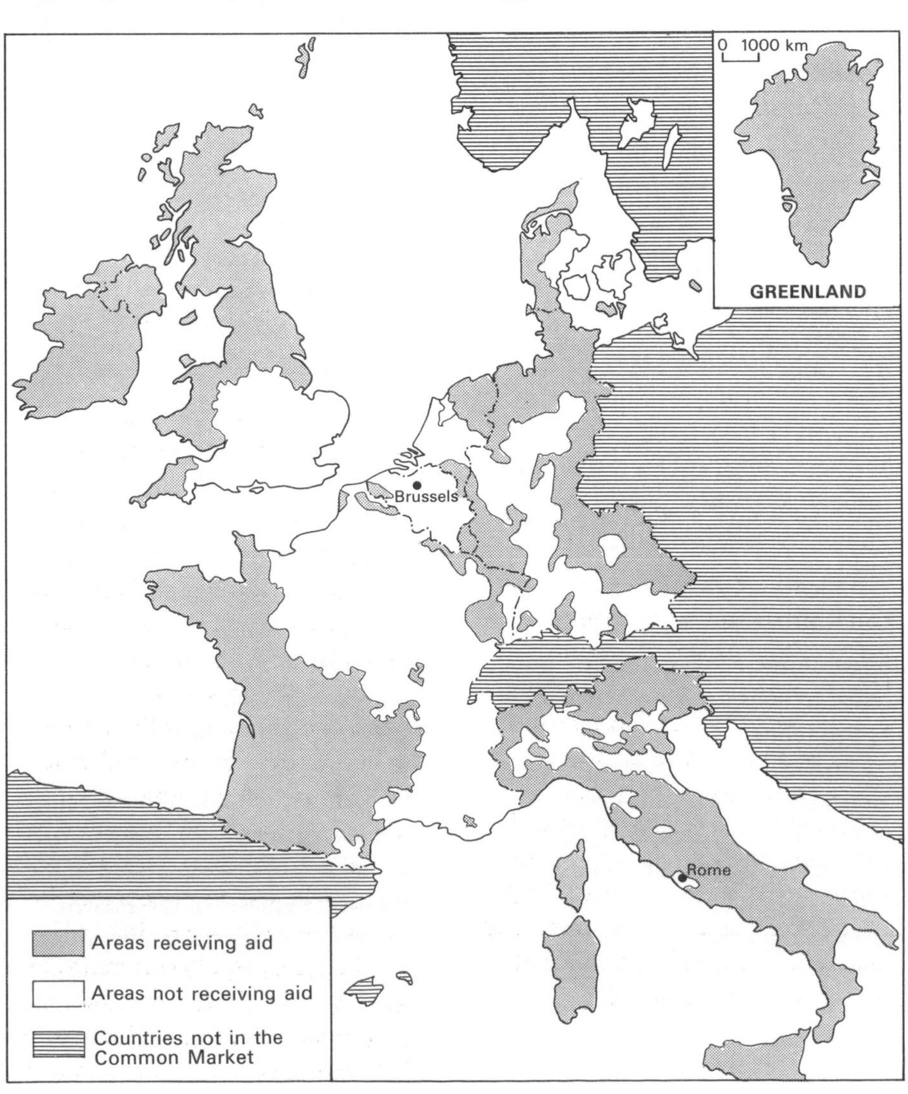

The Common Market in the 1970s

How the Common Market works

From 1957 to 1967 there were three different communities (E.C.S.C., Euratom and E.E.C.). In 1967 these were joined into one Community which is now usually referred to as the Common Market. This Community has since expanded to twelve members. The diagram on p. 156 shows you how it works.

The most important part is the Commission. Each Commissioner deals with a particular task, for example, agriculture or help for the poorer regions. The Commissioners hold their jobs for four years. They are very important because they decide what matters are presented to the Council of Ministers for decision. The chairman is called the President of the European Commission. The detailed work is done by thousands of civil servants (sometimes called 'Eurocrats'!) in the large European Commission building in Brussels.

Developments and problems in the 1970s and 1980s

1 Regional Development Fund. This was set up in 1973. Money is provided to help the poorer regions (see Map 2) to improve their industries, railways and roads.
2 Lomé Convention. This was signed in 1975 by 46 A.C.P. countries—former colonies of the Common Market countries in Africa, the Caribbean and the Pacific. Customs duties between the A.C.P. countries and the Common Market were gradually abolished and they have been given financial and technical help. The Convention is renewed every five years. Lomé III, signed by 65 A.C.P. countries, lasts from 1985 to 1990.
3 Common Agricultural Policy (C.A.P.). One of the main aims of the Treaty of Rome was to ensure a good supply of food at the same price in every member country of the Common Market. The C.A.P. was set up to do this. One arrangement has been to guarantee to farmers certain prices for their products. This was largely for the benefit of French farmers who are not as efficient as the farmers in some other countries. A result of this system is that huge stocks of some food have been built up and then sold off cheaply to other countries or to make animal feed. People have talked about the enormous cost and inefficiency of butter and beef 'mountains' and wine 'lakes'.

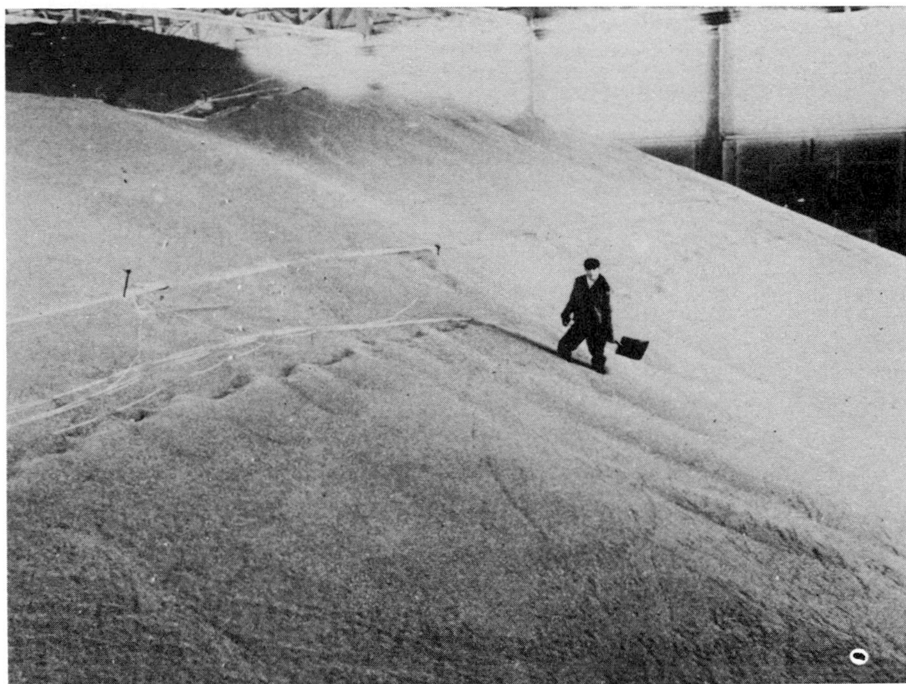

A Common Market 'barley mountain' in Lincolnshire

New members

By 1986 three extra countries were members. These were Portugal, Spain and Greece. How do you think their membership might change the Common Market?

Pros and cons

By 1985 the experiment in West European economic co-operation was a generation old. There had been many changes over the years. The following points may help you to make up your mind whether the Common Market has been a benefit to the member countries.
1 The 'Eurocrats' sometimes seem to make regulations without fully understanding the very real differences between the various countries. It seems to some people that they make regulations for the sake of regulations and create conformity for the sake of conformity.
2 The European Parliament is too weak to control the Commission. In theory the parliament, which meets in Strasbourg, is the democratic part of the Community. But the first direct elections for members took place as recently as 1979. Can it be taken more seriously and be more important?
3 The Common Agricultural Policy is notoriously inefficient, as we have seen. Many people in Britain ask why tax-payers' money should be used to help French farmers to produce more food than they can sell.
4 All customs duties are being gradually abolished on goods sold between member countries. Customers do not have to pay extra for some products made in another member country. This should lead to better choice and quality.
5 Co-operation among trade unions, businessmen, professional people and politicians has increased enormously. It is difficult to imagine now another war breaking out between, say, France and Germany. Co-operation is surely better than conflict?

European institutions

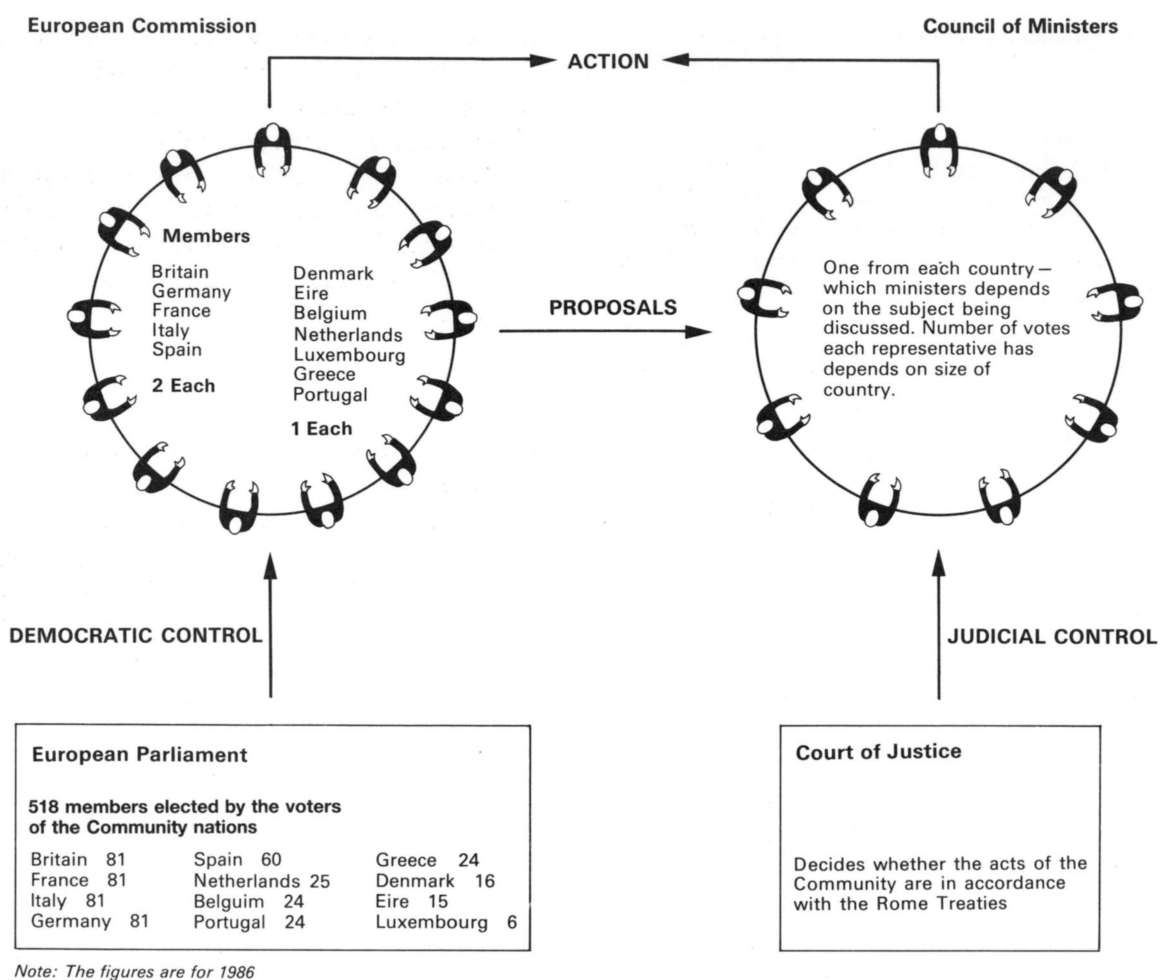

Note: The figures are for 1986

Questions

1 a Name the Treaty, signed in March, 1957, which set up the European Economic Community. Name one of the countries which signed the Treaty at this time.

b Name one country which joined the E.E.C. at the same time as Britain.
Which European politician kept Britain out of the E.E.C. in 1963 and 1967?

c Where is the Headquarters of the European Commission?
Where does the E.E.C. Assembly (Parliament) meet?

d What do the letters E.C.S.C. stand for?
Who is the present President of the Commission of the E.E.C.?

e Name the Prime Minister who took Britain into the E.E.C.
Name the Prime Minister who held a referendum on Britain staying in the E.E.C.?

2 Outline the moves towards unity in western Europe since 1945. Include in your answer:

a Marshall aid
b European coal and steel community
c E.E.C. and E.F.T.A.

3 Write a paragraph (10–20 lines) about the problems faced by West Germany in 1945 and explain how she has overcome them.

4 Write a paragraph (10–20 lines) about the benefits the E.E.C. has brought to Western Europe, and the problems facing the E.E.C. today.

5 Explain how the Common Market has developed in Europe. What advantages and disadvantages have there been for Britain since joining the E.E.C.?

Questions

6 Read the following extracts and answer the questions below:

Source A

'In these pages various severe statements, based on events of the moment, are set down about General de Gaulle, and certainly I had continuous difficulties and many sharp antagonisms with him . . . I understood and admired, while I resented, his arrogant demeanour. Here he was – a refugee, an exile from his country under sentence of death, in a position entirely dependent upon the goodwill of the British Government, and also now of the United States. The Germans had conquered his country. He had no real foothold anywhere. Never mind; he defied all. Always, even when he was behaving worst, he seemed to express the personality of France – a great nation, with all its pride, authority, and ambition.'
(Winston Churchill, *The Hinge of Fate*, 1951, p. 547)

Source B

'The *"Moi, Général de Gaulle"* (first introduced to France by the B.B.C. during the war) is, in the General's view, the incarnation *[embodiment]* of France, which is the most important country of the most important continent of the world. Not for de Gaulle the "cowardly modesty" he notes in lesser men. The General indeed has never hesitated to compare himself with the greatest figures of French history – Joan of Arc, Louis XIV, Napoleon, Clemenceau – unperturbed by the sardonic *[scornful]* laughter evoked by these comparisons, especially the first.'
(Norah Beloff, *The General Says No*, 1963, p. 22)

Source C

'De Gaulle's greatest political weapon – and he knows it – is television; and he has spared no pains to attain the position of France's foremost video star.

'He takes all the trouble to write out his text, to learn it off by heart (his memory is stupendous), to make the most of his mannerisms which, in the end, move rather than irritate people. He rehearses his TV speeches in front of a mirror and with the help of a tape-recorder. He even took lessons in diction from an eminent actor of the Comédie Française, and knows all the right cadences, and is aware of the gestures and intonations to avoid.'
(Alexander Werth, *De Gaulle*, 1965, p. 361)

a Explain in your own words what these extracts tell you about the character of de Gaulle.

b All three extracts are taken from British writers. Do you think French writers might give a different view of de Gaulle? Explain the reasons for your answers.

c Using your own knowledge explain what de Gaulle achieved for France. Do you think that his personality was important? Give reasons for your answers.

7 Look at the map and decide which statements are true and which false.

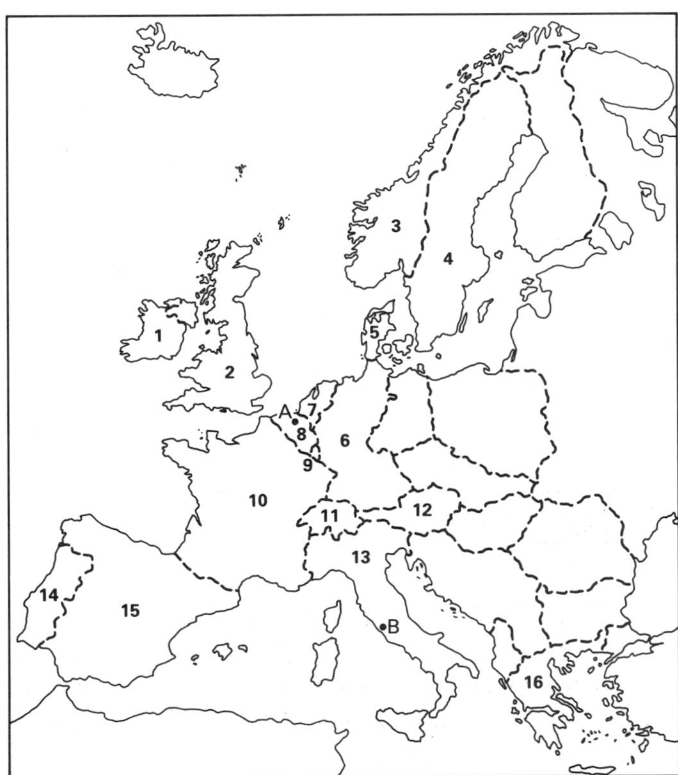

a All the numbered countries had become members of the European Economic Community by 1986.

b Countries 14 and 15 were the last countries to join the European Community.

c The Treaty which created the European Economic Community was signed in city A.

d Countries 1, 2, 3, 4, 11, 12 and 14 were the original members of the European Free Trade Association.

Time chart

The European get-together

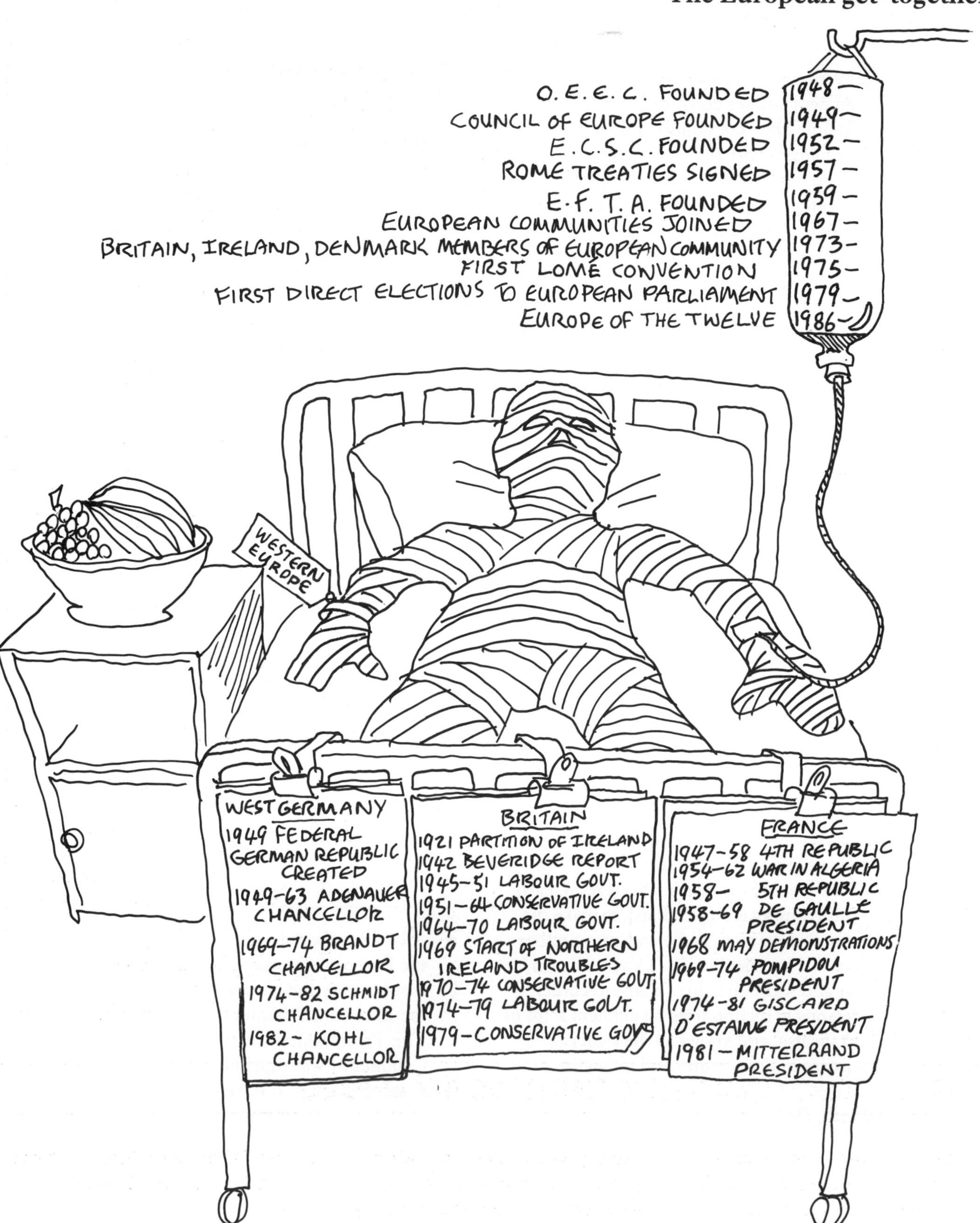

O.E.E.C. FOUNDED 1948
COUNCIL OF EUROPE FOUNDED 1949
E.C.S.C. FOUNDED 1952
ROME TREATIES SIGNED 1957
E.F.T.A. FOUNDED 1959
EUROPEAN COMMUNITIES JOINED 1967
BRITAIN, IRELAND, DENMARK MEMBERS OF EUROPEAN COMMUNITY 1973
FIRST LOMÉ CONVENTION 1975
FIRST DIRECT ELECTIONS TO EUROPEAN PARLIAMENT 1979
EUROPE OF THE TWELVE 1986
WESTERN EUROPE
WEST GERMANY
1949 FEDERAL GERMAN REPUBLIC CREATED
1949–63 ADENAUER CHANCELLOR
1969–74 BRANDT CHANCELLOR
1974–82 SCHMIDT CHANCELLOR
1982– KOHL CHANCELLOR
BRITAIN
1921 PARTITION OF IRELAND
1942 BEVERIDGE REPORT
1945–51 LABOUR GOVT.
1951–64 CONSERVATIVE GOVT.
1964–70 LABOUR GOVT.
1969 START OF NORTHERN IRELAND TROUBLES
1970–74 CONSERVATIVE GOVT.
1974–79 LABOUR GOVT.
1979– CONSERVATIVE GOVT.
FRANCE
1947–58 4TH REPUBLIC
1954–62 WAR IN ALGERIA
1958– 5TH REPUBLIC
1958–69 DE GAULLE PRESIDENT
1968 MAY DEMONSTRATIONS
1969–74 POMPIDOU PRESIDENT
1974–81 GISCARD D'ESTAING PRESIDENT
1981– MITTERRAND PRESIDENT

11/Arabs and Israelis

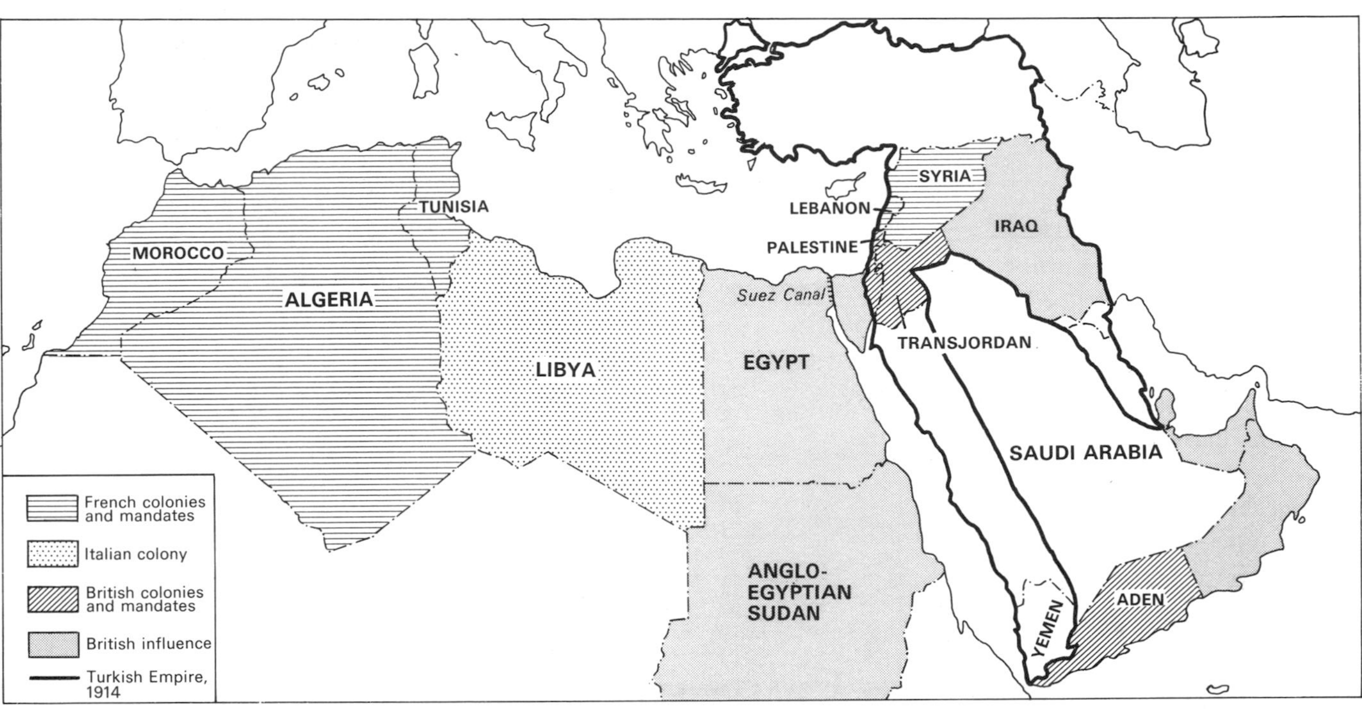

Map 1 The Arab countries between the two World Wars

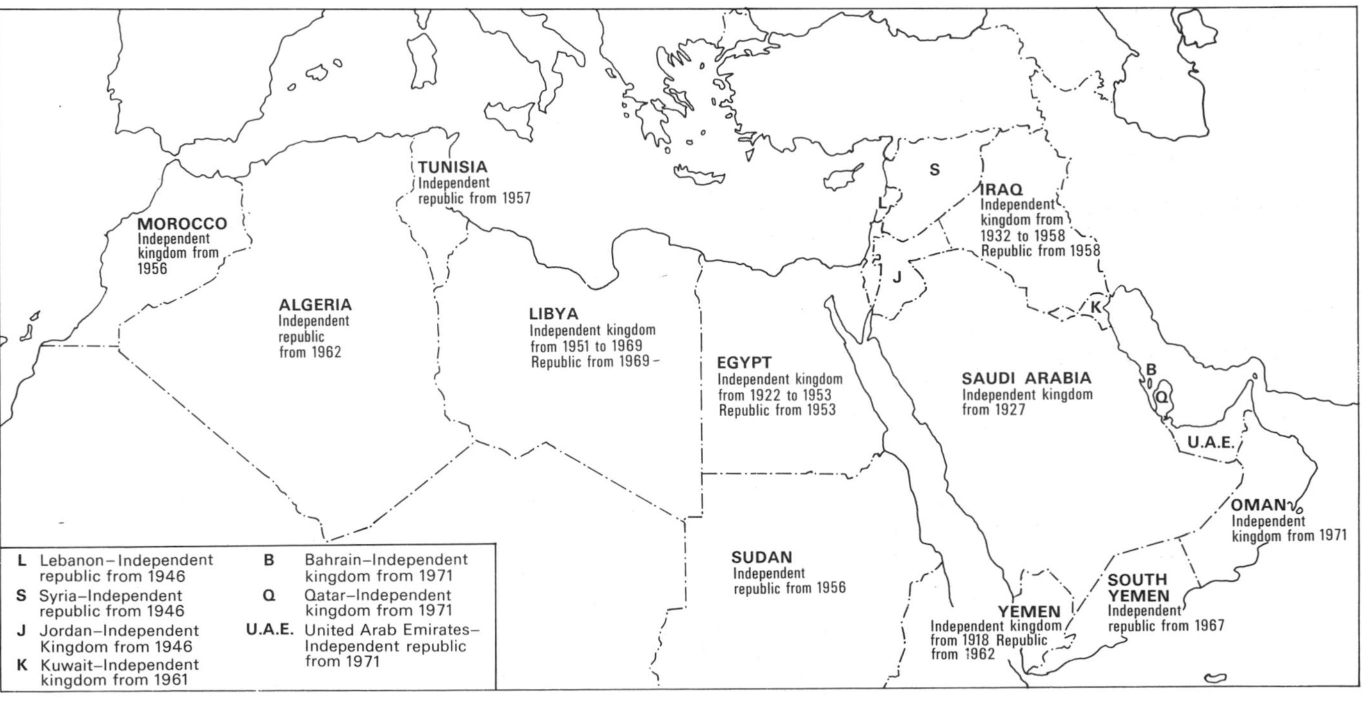

Map 2 Members of the Arab League

The Middle East in modern world affairs

Just by comparing these two maps you can learn some important basic facts about the Arab countries of the Middle East in the twentieth century. What other countries or peoples controlled much of the area in the early part of the century? When did this control come to an end? Where and when were kings overthrown in revolutions?

The Middle East in modern world affairs

Some important features of the Middle East

The Suez Canal

Before the Suez Canal was opened in 1869 journeys between Europe and Asia were very long indeed. The Canal therefore became a convenient and very busy route for trade and communications. The European country that used it most in the nineteenth and early twentieth centuries was Britain—because of her control of India. From 1875 to 1956 the Canal was managed by an international company in which Britain had a controlling interest. But, as you can see from Map 1, the Canal cuts through Egypt. Britain was therefore anxious to have a friendly government in Egypt. In fact, Britain governed Egypt herself from 1882 to 1922 and had troops stationed in a strip called the Canal Zone for another 32 years after that.

We have seen in Chapter 6 how important the area was during the Second World War. Later in this chapter we shall see that the Canal was the centre of a serious international crisis in 1956. By that time it had become very important for the shipping of oil from the Persian Gulf to Europe.

Oil

Think of all the vital every-day uses of oil—generating electricity; fuelling transport; heating; making plastics and fertilisers. The graph (above, right) shows how oil consumption has increased. This increase has been a dramatic one since about 1960. In 1978 world oil consumption for the first time exceeded 3,000 million tonnes! About one-sixth of all oil supplies now come from the Middle East, particularly the countries round the Persian Gulf. Map 3 shows which are the biggest producers.

Figure 1 The rise in oil production in the twentieth century

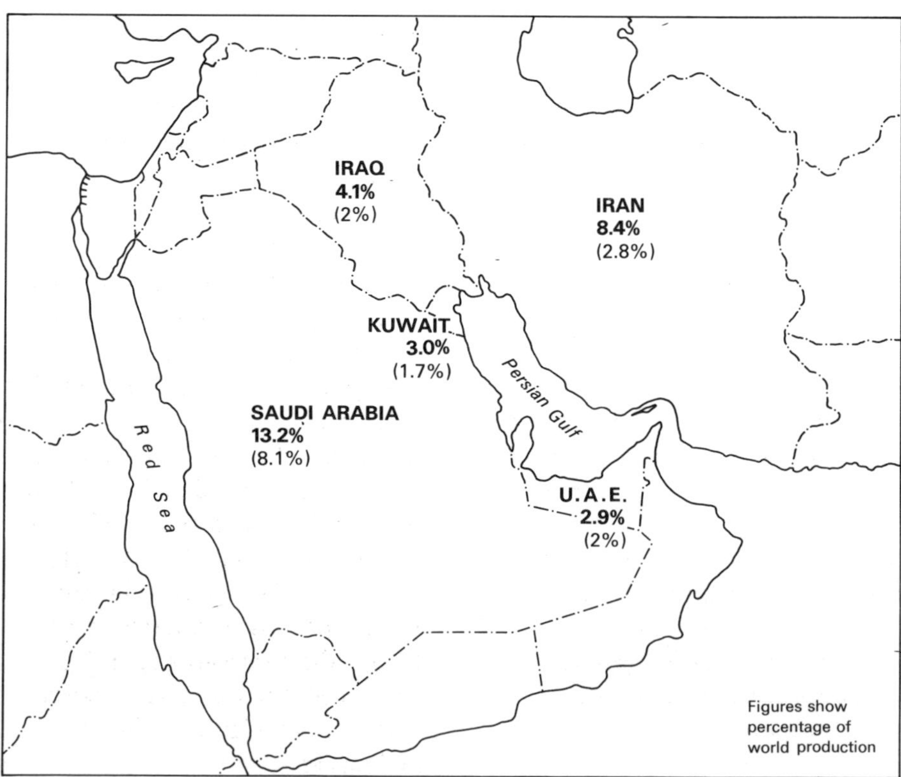

Map 3 The five biggest producers of oil in the Middle East, 1978 (1984 figures in brackets)

The Middle East in modern world affairs

Muslims at prayer. Devout muslims pray several times each day. They kneel facing in the direction of the Holy City of Mecca

The rest of the world has therefore come to depend increasingly on these countries for a steady flow of this vital source of energy. Here are three examples of the way other parts of the world have been affected:

1 In 1956 the Suez Canal was blocked (see p.166) and oil supplies were disrupted. The British government had to introduce petrol rationing.

2 In 1973 the main oil-producing countries (O.P.E.C.—the Organisation of Petroleum Exporting Countries) increased the price of oil nearly four times. This caused serious economic problems in countries that had to import all or most of their oil.

3 In 1978–9 oil production in Iran was interrupted during a revolution (see p.171). This led to serious shortages in the U.S.A. where motorists queued for hours at petrol-stations (see p.110).

Religion and nationalism

The Middle East is the birthplace of three of the world's great religions—Judaism (the religion of the Jews), Islam (the Muslim religion) and Christianity. There have been many quarrels about who should own Jerusalem because it is a holy city for all these religions. In 1980 the Israelis angered the Arabs because they announced that they would make it their capital city.

Judaism is very important for the following reasons:

1 Although the Jews originally lived in Palestine they became scattered over many parts of the world. But wherever they live their common faith gives them a sense of belonging together.

2 Because the Holy Land of Palestine was their traditional homeland, the idea developed at the end of the nineteenth century that a Jewish state should be recreated in Palestine so that Jews could return to the land of their ancestors. This idea was called Zionism. It is the basis and strength of modern Israeli nationalism.

Islam was created by the prophet Mohammed in the seventh century. The holy book of Muslims is called the Koran. Devout Muslims believe that all aspects of life should be governed by the teachings of the Koran.

The following extract from the Koran gives you an idea of the detailed instructions it contains:

> Men have authority over women because Allah has made the one superior to the other, and because they spend their wealth to maintain them. Good women are obedient. They guard their unseen parts because Allah has guarded them. As for those from whom you fear disobedience, admonish them and send them to beds apart and beat them. Then if they obey you, take no further action against them. Allah is high, supreme.

As a result women have a very inferior place in some Muslim countries. Because of the Koran's teaching, alcohol is forbidden, and punishments for breaking the law are very harsh, such as flogging and even executions in public.

Islam is the faith of many millions of people in countries stretching in a wide band across Africa and Asia, from the West African coast to the islands of Indonesia.

The Middle East in modern world affairs

Arab nationalism is more complicated than Israeli nationalism. It has the following main elements:

1 Islam. Most Arabs are Muslims. This gives them a common bond and a feeling of superiority over the non-Muslim 'infidels'. Western ways are thought to be corrupting. The governments of Libya and Saudi Arabia have especially emphasised the importance of religion.

2 Anti-colonialism. Arabs have resented being ruled by foreign countries and have fought for their independence. The dates on Map 2 show you when they succeeded in becoming free.

3 Opposition to Israel. The creation of a Jewish state of Israel has made many Arabs very angry. Because most of the Jewish settlers have come from Europe or America, the Arabs see Israel as another foreign colony. As we shall see later in this chapter there has been much fighting because of this.

4 Pan-Arabism. Arab people have much in common—a common language, Arabic, as well as a common religion as we have seen. There have therefore been ambitious plans to join Arab countries together, though none has yet been successful.

Main events between the World Wars

After the First World War

Refer back to p.21 in chapter 2 and to Map 1 at the beginning of this chapter. You will see that at the end of the First World War all of the Turkish Empire outside Asia Minor was taken away. Syria and Lebanon became French mandates and Palestine and Transjordan became British mandates. Saudi Arabia became the main independent Arab country.

British troops in the Suez Canal Zone. The British supervised this area from 1936 to 1954

Arab anger at Britain

As you can see from Map 1 Britain controlled many Arab countries. The Egyptians and Iraqis especially disliked British rule. Riots and fighting broke out. The British were forced by the nationalist Wafd Party to give Egypt independence in 1922. But in practice the British still held so much influence behind the scenes that the Egyptians remained angry. Eventually, in 1936, another agreement was signed giving Egypt almost complete freedom, though British troops were allowed to stay in the Canal Zone. The story of Iraq was very similar. Britain gave the country independence in 1932, though again kept a great deal of influence that many Iraqis resented.

Palestine

In 1917 the British foreign minister, A. J. Balfour, issued the following statement that came to be known as the Balfour Declaration:

> His Majesty's Government view with favour the establishment in Palestine of a national home for the Jewish people, and will use their best endeavours to facilitate the achievement of this object, it being clearly understood that nothing shall be done which may prejudice the civil and religious rights of existing non-Jewish communities in Palestine, or the rights and political status enjoyed by Jews in any other country.

What is more, the setting up of a national home for the Jewish people in Palestine was written into the terms of the British mandate under the League of Nations. Yet at the end of the First World War ninety-three per cent of Palestinians were Arab and only seven per cent, Jews. As you can imagine, the Arabs were very angry with the Balfour Declaration.

During the 1930s Jews immigrated to Palestine, especially after the Nazis started their persecution. By 1939 Jews made up twenty-eight per cent of the population of Palestine. Arab anger boiled over into serious anti-Jewish riots throughout the years 1936–39.

Arab-Israeli wars

The creation of Israel

The United Nations solution

In the years immediately before and after the Second World War Britain tried to ease the rising tension between Arabs and Jews in Palestine by restricting the number of Jews to be allowed into the country. But in 1945 the full horrors of the Nazi massacre of the Jews were known (see p.53). This conscience of Britain, and much of the rest of the world, would allow no further delay in settling the problem.

But the British felt that they could not solve the problem themselves. They therefore asked the United Nations Organisation to take over. They produced a plan in 1947 to partition Palestine into a Jewish and an Arab country, as you can see on Map 4.

The Arab countries attack

The new state of Israel was proclaimed on 14 May, 1948. The next day the five neighbouring Arab countries of Egypt, Transjordan, Iraq, Syria and Lebanon attacked in an attempt to destroy it. The Arab armies were not very well organised. On the other hand, the Israelis fought so fiercely to preserve their new country that when the war came to an end the following year the Israelis (as you can see from Map 4) had even more land than the U.N. had allocated to them. (Note: in the U.N. plan Jerusalem, a holy city to three religions, was to have been a neutral area. The Jews very much wanted it to be their capital. They managed to capture the western half in the war.)

The British restricted the entry of Jews into Palestine, but many entered illegally such as 700 people in this boat, which was grounded on the beach off Tel Aviv

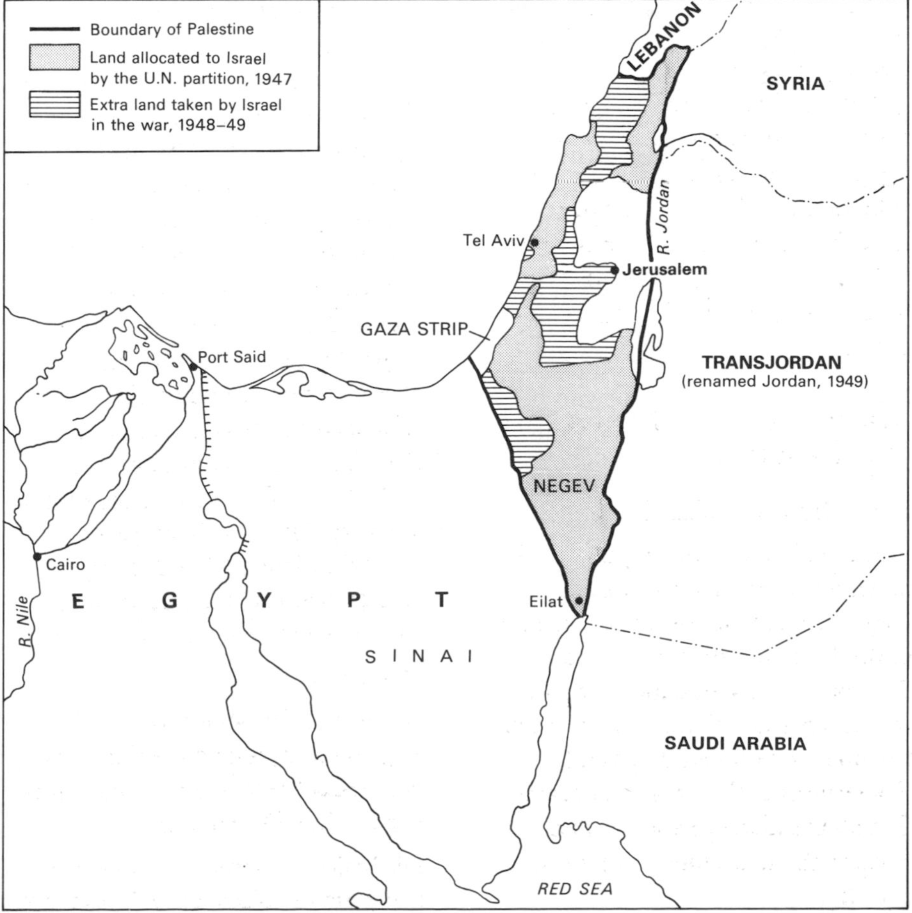

Map 4 Israel, 1947–49

Many thousands of Arabs fled from the lands that the Israelis now held. They became refugees in the neighbouring Arab countries, many in the Gaza Strip. They lived wretched lives, waiting for the day when they could return to an Arab-ruled Palestine. They, and their descendants, are still waiting in the mid-1980s. Their plight has made relations between Israel and the Arab countries even more tense.

Young Palestinians in a refugee camp, 1956. These youngsters grew up to regard Israel as their rightful home, from which they had been unjustly expelled by the Jews

David Ben Gurion (1886–1973), Israeli prime minister, 1948–53, 1955–63

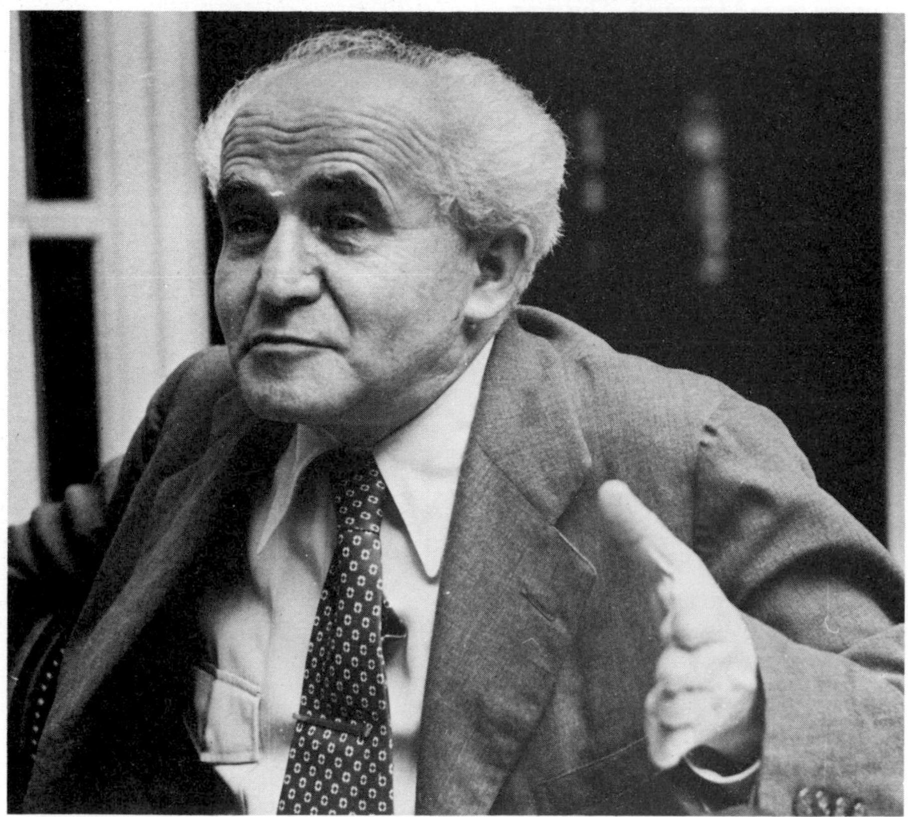

The Suez war

Israel starts life

The Israelis now settled down to build their new country. Their leader, who was prime minister for most of the period from 1948 to 1963, was David Ben-Gurion. He was a powerful, inspiring personality.

One of the most urgent needs was for more people: the total population of Israel in 1949 was only 800,000. The Law of Return was passed in 1950 allowing all Jews the right to immigrate into Israel. By 1964 the population was nearly 2½ million. The Israelis worked extremely hard to develop and cultivate the land, much of it arid desert. They were also given generous help by other countries, especially the U.S.A.

Israel under siege

But the Arab countries did not give up their desire to destroy Israel. Egypt blockaded Eilat, Israel's only outlet to the Red Sea, and prevented Israeli ships from using the Suez Canal. All the Arab countries tried to strangle Israel's trade. And fighting continued. The Palestinian refugees, especially those in the Gaza Strip and Sinai, organised groups of guerrilla fighters, called 'fedayeen'. Guerrillas are soldiers who fight in small groups, not as a large army and rely on speed and surprise to attack stronger enemies. The fedayeen made raids across the Israeli border.

Colonel Nasser

From 1954 until 1970 Egypt was led by one of the greatest and most popular politicians in the modern history of the Middle East—Colonel Gamal Abdel Nasser. We shall see on p.170 how he came to power and what he did for the Egyptian people. Here we are interested in the part he played in the Arab-Israeli wars.

Nasser believed that Egypt should be the leading country among the Arab states. He therefore had to try to achieve the following:

1 Make Egypt's armed forces stronger. He bought modern weapons from Czechoslovakia and accepted Russian help.

2 Bring the separate Arab countries together in a Pan-Arab union. He wrote about this in his booklet, *The Philosophy of the Revolution.*

3 Restore Palestine to the Arabs. This, of course, would mean fighting Israel.

The Suez crisis develops

One of Nasser's great schemes was for the building of a large dam on the river Nile at a place called Aswan. This would provide water for irrigation and generate electricity. Such a dam would, naturally, cost a great deal of money. The Americans promised to help, but then withdrew their offer. Nasser was very angry at this humiliation. He therefore took over control of the Suez Canal in order to use the dues paid by ships to help finance the Aswan High Dam.

Palestinian commandos or 'Fedayeen', listening to the leader of their group before setting out on an operation against enemy units

Colonel Nasser (right), with King Saud of Saudi Arabia

After the 1956 war. The Suez Canal blocked with sunken ships

The war for the Suez Canal

The Israelis, French and British were all angry with and frightened by Nasser:

1 The Israelis because of Egypt's increasing armed strength.

2 The French because Nasser was helping the Algerians, who were fighting for their independence against France (see p.148).
3 The British because the Suez Canal was so important to them, as we saw on p.160

In late October 1956 war broke out. The Israelis invaded Egypt. Then the British and French governments asked both sides to keep their forces away from the Canal. Nasser refused. British and French forces then attacked Egypt. Nasser sank ships in the Canal to block it to all traffic. Many people throughout the world, and especially the American government, were horrified at the Anglo-French invasion of Egypt. Russia even threatened war. The British and French were therefore forced to withdraw their soldiers. A United Nations force was sent to act as a buffer between the Egyptians and Israelis to prevent them fighting again.

There are two important questions about this short Suez war:
1 Why did the British and French invade Egypt?
2 Were they in a plot with Israel?
The prime minister of Britain at the time was Anthony Eden. In the 1930s he had believed that Britain should have stood up more firmly against Hitler and Mussolini. He believed now that Nasser was a similar threat—that *The Philosophy of the Revolution* was as clear a plan for the control of the Middle East and Africa as *Mein Kampf* was for Hitler's control of Europe (see p. 50). But he denied there was any plot ('collusion' as it was called) with Israel. He lied. M. Pineau, who was the French Foreign Minister at the time, revealed in a B.B.C. interview ten years later that there had been a secret meeting in France:

Pineau : The definite arrangements between the French, the English and the Israelis were made about 24, 25 October during a special meeting.

Interviewer : ... am I right in saying this: that there was a special meeting, and it did take place and that is as far as you wish to go at the present time?

Pineau : Yes. Personally I was present, Mr Ben-Gurion was present, and that is all.

Interviewer : That's all you want to say?

Pineau : Yes, that's all.... It was absolutely necessary for everybody to keep the secret in this period. A treaty like the Anglo-French-Israeli Treaty was necessarily secret, because the circumstances were very difficult.

Anthony Eden (later Lord Avon)

Map 5 The Six-Day War (see p.167)

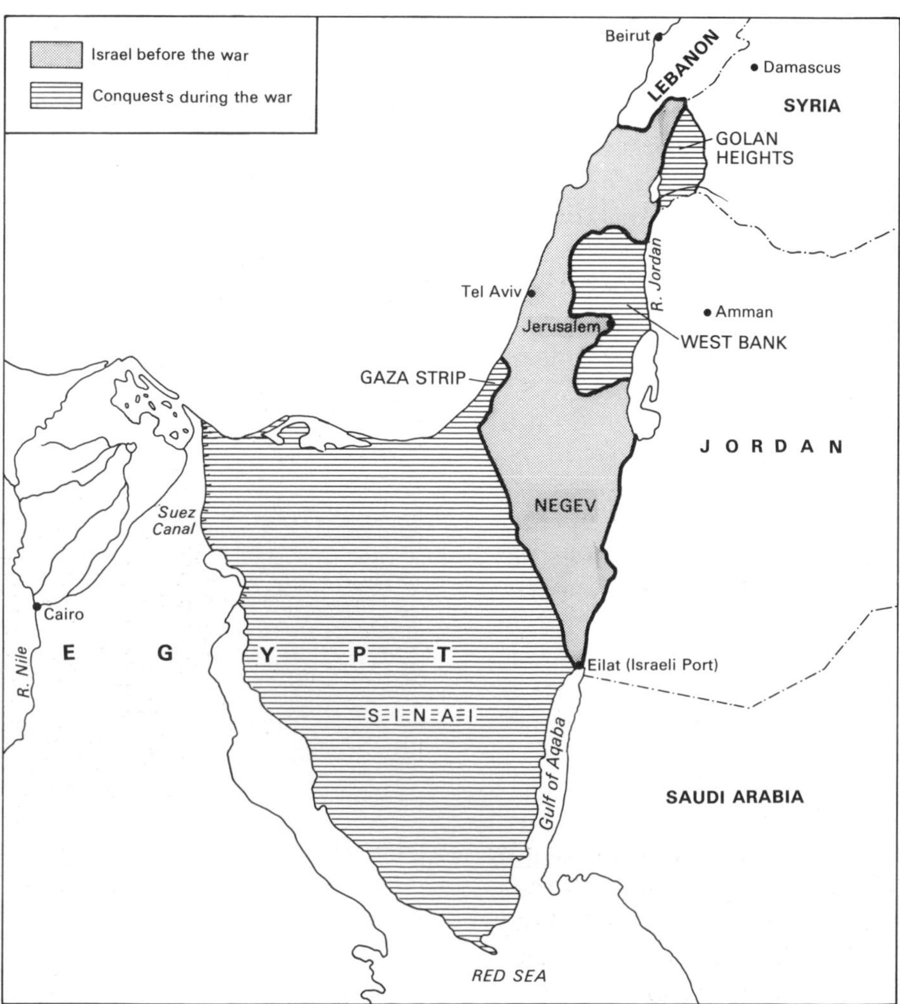

The Six-Day War

Continuing border fighting

Despite the United Nations force on the Israeli-Egyptian border, fighting continued. Well-trained Palestinians raided across the borders from camps further north in Syria, Lebanon and Jordan. Israel organised counter-attacks into these countries.

Tension mounted. In 1967 Nasser ordered the United Nations forces out of Egypt and closed the Gulf of Aqaba to Israeli ships. Israeli troops were outnumbered by three-to-one; so Israel decided to strike first.

The war

Israeli aircraft took off on the morning of 5 June. At exactly 7.45 nine separate flights of four aeroplanes struck nine separate Egyptian airfields. Follow-up attacks were made on ten other air bases. The Egyptian air force was crippled.

The Israeli army made lightning attacks on three fronts. Within just six days, as you can see from Map 5, they had captured:

a The Golan Heights from Syria.
b The land to the west of the river Jordan from Jordan.
c The Sinai peninsula from Egypt.

Israel was now in a much stronger position to defend herself. But her occupation of the West Bank of the Jordan was to cause great trouble.

The Yom Kippur War

The frustration of the Palestinians

The success of Israel in the Six-Day War made the plight of the Palestinians worse. Those who were living in Sinai, the Gaza Strip and in the lands on West Bank of the River

Yassir Arafat, P.L.O. leader

Jordan were now ruled by Israelis, their sworn enemies. And the Israelis made matters far worse by establishing Jewish settlements on the West Bank lands captured from the Kingdom of Jordan. Some Israelis believed that they had a right to these lands because they had been so important to the Jews in biblical times.

The Palestinians were also now much better organised. The Palestinian Liberation Organisation (P.L.O.) was formed in 1964. Its leader, Yassir Arafat, became a very respected defender of the Palestinians' cause. Other groups believed that dramatic, violent demonstrations were necessary to bring the misery and injustice suffered by their people to the attention of the world. They therefore committed acts of terrorism. These included kidnapping, murder and hi-jacking airliners. One of the most notorious of such events was the killing of eleven Israeli athletes at the Munich Olympic Games in 1972. Such tactics shocked the world.

Map 6 The Yom Kippur War of 1973 and Camp David Agreements, 1978

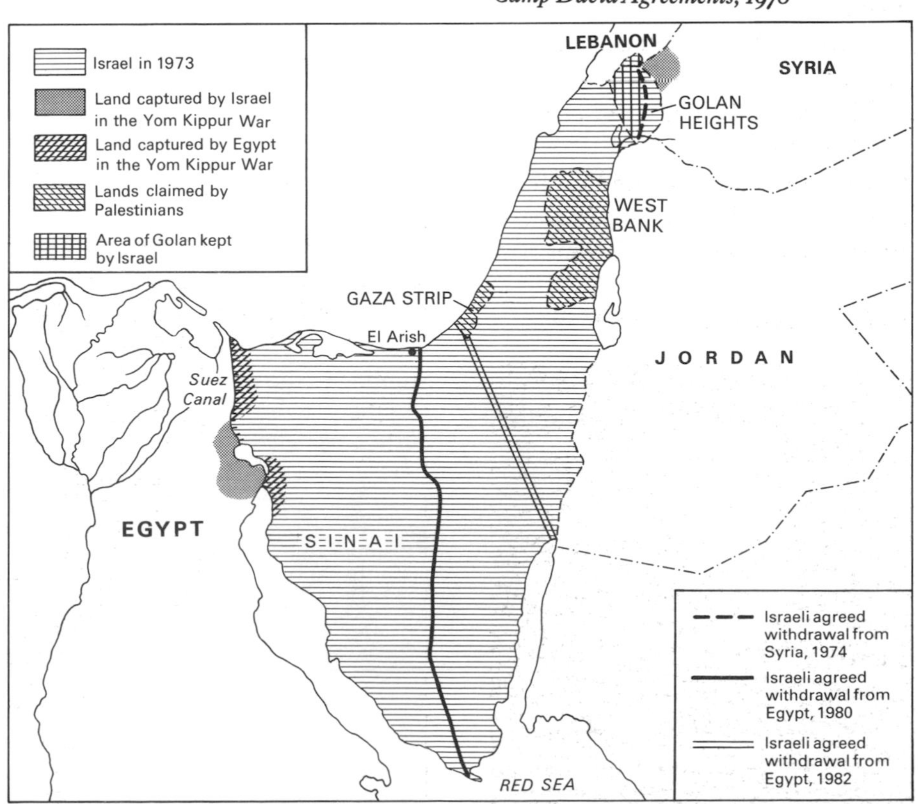

The fourth Arab-Israeli War

In 1970 President Nasser of Egypt died, at the age of 52, worn out by all his hard work. He was succeeded by Anwar Sadat, a less colourful personality. Sadat tried unsuccessfully to persuade Israel to give up some of the land she had captured in the Six-Day War. He therefore launched a sudden invasion of Israel in October 1973. He achieved maximum surprise by attacking during the Jewish religious festival of Yom Kippur. Syria also attacked in the north.

This time the two sides were more evenly matched: the Arab forces were better led and were equipped with up-to-date Russian weapons. It was a fierce, quick war and within a fortnight the two sides were exhausted. Map 6 shows you the land that was taken by Israel and Egypt.

Golda Meir (right) Israeli Prime Minister, 1969–74, and General Moshe Dayan, Minister of Defence, 1967–74 (i.e. during two wars)

The search for solutions

Why were solutions now sought more seriously?

From 1948 to 1973 there had been a quarter of a century of war between Israel and her Arab neighbours. At last, after the Yom Kippur War, everyone seemed to be taking seriously the need to find a peaceful solution. Why was this?

1 Other countries, especially the U.S.A., were very worried about the situation. At one point in the war it looked as though America and Russia might be drawn in to the fighting. Also, the huge rise in oil prices (see p.161) had very serious effects on the economies of other countries.

2 Israel realised that the Arab countries were now very much stronger. Also, she could not rely any longer on total support from the U.S.A. because the Americans dared not offend the oil-producing Arab countries.

3 The Palestinians realised that many people throughout the world had been disgusted by their terrorist methods. Yassir Arafat particularly recognised the importance of talks and compromise.

4 The presence of Palestinian bases in the Lebanon was a great strain for that country which suffered a violent civil war between Christians and Muslims in 1976.

5 President Sadat had the personal ambition of producing a peaceful solution to the problem.

Begin, prime minister of Israel, 1977–83

Camp David Agreements

There were three major problems (see Map 6):

1 Israel would need to evacuate Sinai and the Golan Heights captured from Egypt and Syria in 1967.

2 The Arab countries would need to reassure Israel that she would not be overwhelmed by a sudden attack in the future.

3 The Palestinians, especially those on the West Bank and in the Gaza Strip, needed some form of independent government.

In 1977 Jimmy Carter became President of the U.S.A. and Menachem Begin became Prime Minister of Israel. Together with President Sadat of Egypt they held many talks and produced plans for a peaceful settlement. In December 1977 Sadat visited Israel. In September 1978 President Carter invited the two Middle Eastern leaders to a meeting at Camp David, the official presidential 'country house' in the hills of Maryland. Here, they agreed to a plan to deal with all three problems.

Mubarak, president of Egypt since 1981

After Camp David

As promised at Camp David, Israel gradually handed back Sinai to Egypt (see Map 6). However, many people in the Arab countries, including Egypt, objected to the Camp David arrangements because the solution to the problem of the Palestinians was left vague. Some Egyptians who thought that Sadat had behaved treacherously assassinated him in 1981. He was succeeded as President by Hosni Mubarak.

In fact, it soon became clear that Begin had no intention of allowing the Palestinians any independence in the West Bank. Indeed, he referred to these lands by their biblical names of Judaea and Samaria. He also so speeded up the creation of Jewish settlements there that by 1982 about 40 per cent of all the land was inhabited by Israelis.

The Lebanon

Religious divisions

After the First World War Lebanon became a French mandate (see p. 21). It became an independent country in 1944. Although it is only a small country the people are divided into many different religions and sects. The main ones are:

1 Maronite Christians;
2 Sunni Muslims;
3 Shi'ite Muslims;
4 Druzes.

These divisions made Lebanon a difficult country to govern. Then, in 1970, Yassir Arafat and the P.L.O. set up camps in the country, adding a further complication.

Civil war

From 1975 to 1976 a bitter civil war raged between the Christians on the one side and the Palestinians and some Lebanese Muslims on the other. Syria sent in troops to restore order. But fighting has broken out on many occasions since, especially in the capital, Beirut, which is divided between Christian and Muslim sectors.

Israeli occupation, 1982–85

For many years the P.L.O. attacked the northern parts of Israel. Therefore, in 1982 the Israelis invaded Lebanon and captured much of the country. The P.L.O. were besieged in Beirut and eventually left Lebanon. Israel had succeeded in breaking the P.L.O. as a serious military threat to her.

However, during the fighting the Israeli army and the Lebanese Christians who were its allies acted very brutally and many Muslim civilians were killed. Begin, already suffering ill-health, resigned. And eventually, three years later, the Israeli army withdrew from Lebanon.

Map 7: Lebanon, 1975–82

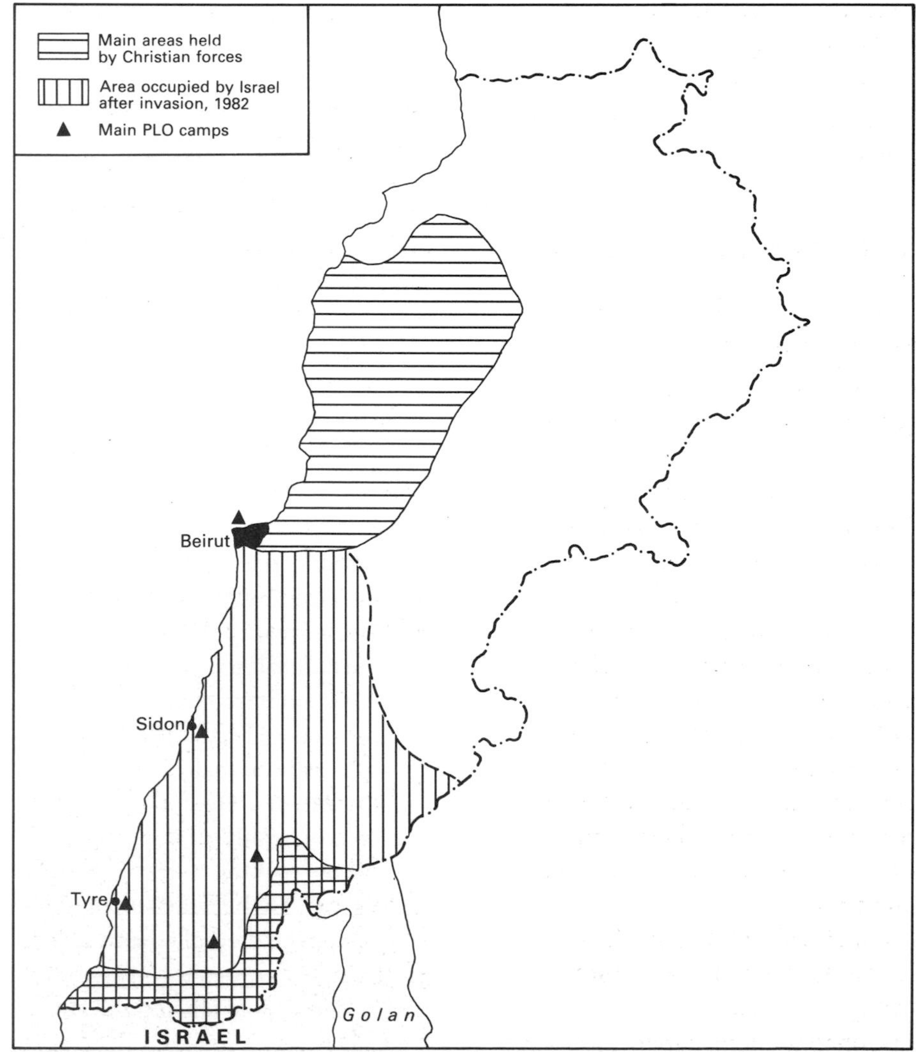

Revolution in the Middle East

Look back again at Map 2. You will see that in 1945 many Middle East countries were ruled by foreign states or by monarchs (kings, emirs or sheikhs). By about 1970 they had all become independent and in many cases the monarchs had been replaced by republican forms of government. These new governments tried to rid their countries of western influence and also introduced many reforms. It is interesting to look at what happened in three countries as examples.

Egypt

The Free Officers Revolution

Egypt is in many ways the most important Arab country: it has the largest population, geographically it is in the centre of the Arab world and it has historical traditions stretching back for thousands of years. Events in Egypt have therefore considerably influenced other Arab countries.

After the first Arab-Israeli war many officers in the Egyptian army felt humiliated by their defeat. They also resented the continued presence of the British soldiers in the Suez Canal Zone. The government of King Farouk was notoriously weak and corrupt. A Free Officers Movement was set up. In 1952 they seized control of the government and sent the king away into exile.

Nasser's reforms

The leader of the Free Officers was General Neguib. But the most important was Colonel Nasser. He took over control of the government in 1954 and ruled Egypt for sixteen years. As we have seen (pp.165–7), he fought two wars with Israel. But during the middle years, 1956–64, he introduced a great number of changes into Egypt. Egypt has many millions of poor peasants (fellahin) and no natural riches such as oil to pay for great improvements. Nasser confiscated and redistributed land. He nationalised many industries and businesses. He improved education and health services. And, of course, he had the Aswan Dam built (see p.165). He became so popular that, when he died of a heart attack at the age of 52, vast throngs of mourning people choked the streets of Cairo.

The Aswan High Dam under construction. Note the Russian and Egyptian flags flying together in the foreground

Libya

Colonel Qaddafy

The revolution in neighbouring Libya started in a similar way to Egypt. In September 1969 King Idris was deposed by a group of army officers. But their leader was a very different kind of man from Nasser. He was Captain (later Colonel) Qaddafy (sometimes spelt Gadafy), only 27 years old at the time. He is thought by many people to be rather eccentric and dangerous. He has supported many terrorists including Palestinians and the murderous dictator of Uganda, Idi Amin (see p. 184). He has produced some wild schemes for extreme changes in Libya. And he is very, puritanically religious.

Reforms

Yet he has brought about many beneficial changes, using the country's wealth from oil. He has stamped out the corruption of the old government. He has tried to involve the ordinary people in the running of their own affairs in many committees and congresses. And he has considerably improved the standard of living, education and health services in Libya.

Colonel Qaddafy of Libya

Iran

The Government of the Shah

Although the Iranian people are not Arabs, Iran is very much a Middle Eastern country: it borders Turkey, Iraq and the Persian Gulf; its people are Muslims; and it produces a great deal of oil (see Map 3).

The Shah of Iran (1919–80)

From 1941 to 1979 Iran was ruled by Shah Mohammed Reza Pahlevi. For most of his reign Iran had close connexions with western countries, especially Britain and the U.S.A. Serious discontent arose in the late 1970s for the following reasons:

1 The huge wealth enjoyed by the royal family.
2 The savage treatment by the political police organisation, Savak, of people who dared criticise the government.
3 The American influence in the country.

The Ayatollah Khomeini

In the late 1970s a great religious revival swept the country and reinforced the hatred of corrupt western ways. The leader of this movement was the Ayatollah Khomeini. In late 1978 to early 1979 strikes, riots and massive demonstrations shook Iran. In January 1979 the royal family fled to exile. Khomeini became effectively the ruler of Iran. The fabulously rich Shah, commander of the most formidable armed forces in the Middle East, was deposed by a simple, devout 78-year-old religious leader.

Important questions raised by the events in Iran

1 Was religion, and particularly Islam, becoming again an immensely powerful force in political affairs?
2 There was considerable interruption in the work of the oilfields during the revolution (and exports were further affected by a war which started in 1980 between Iran and Iraq). Were the economies of oil-importing countries to be affected by this disorder? (see p. 110).
3 Violently anti-American crowds besieged the U.S. embassy in Tehran and kept the Americans inside hostage for over a year. Was the internationally accepted diplomatic system now at risk, with the most powerful nation in the world unable to rescue its own diplomats?

By the 1970s the Middle East had become the most important and dangerous region of the world.

The Ayatollah Khomeini acknowledges the waves of his supporters

Time chart

Arabs and Israelis

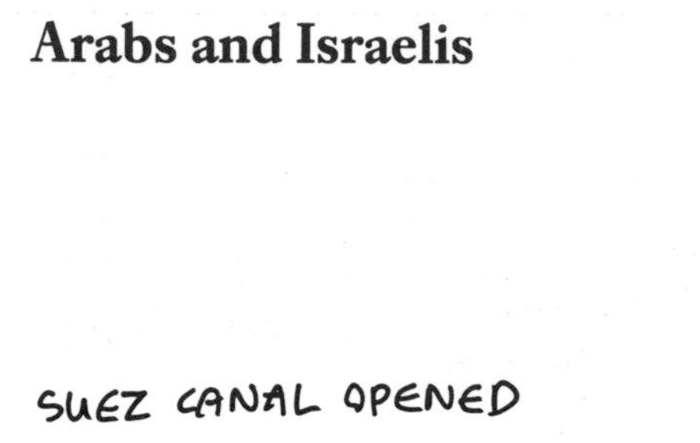
1869 SUEZ CANAL OPENED
1882–1922 BRITISH OCCUPATION OF EGYPT
1917 BALFOUR DECLARATION
1932 IRAQ INDEPENDENT
1936–39 ANTI-JEWISH RIOTS IN PALESTINE
1947 U.N. PARTITION OF PALESTINE
1948–49 FIRST ARAB–ISRAELI WAR
1949 BEN-GURION BECOMES PRIME MINISTER OF ISRAEL
1954–70 NASSER PRIME MINISTER, THEN PRESIDENT, OF EGYPT.
1956 SUEZ WAR
1964 P.L.O. FOUNDED
1967 SIX-DAY WAR
1969 LIBYAN REVOLUTION
1970 – SADAT PRESIDENT OF EGYPT
1972 MUNICH OLYMPICS
1973 YOM KIPPUR WAR
FIRST MAJOR INCREASE IN OIL PRICES
1975 START OF CIVIL WAR IN LEBANON
1977–83 BEGIN PRIME MINISTER OF ISRAEL
1978 CAMP DAVID TALKS
1978–79 IRANIAN REVOLUTION
1980 START OF IRAN–IRAQ WAR
1981 ASSASSINATION OF SADAT
1982 ISRAELI INVASION OF LEBANON

Questions

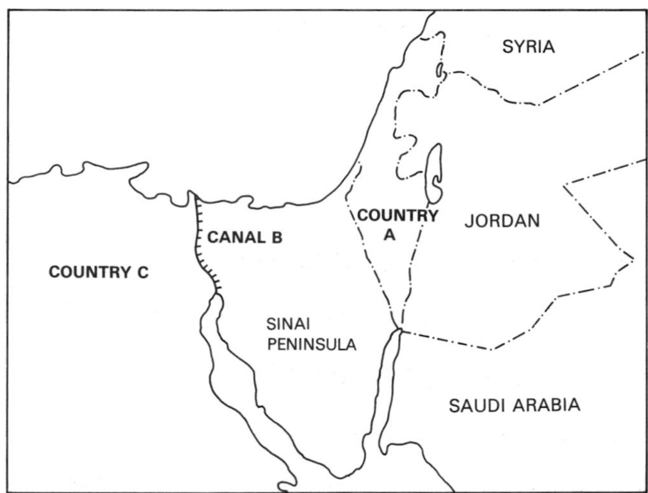

1 Look at the map of the Middle East 1949–76 and then answer the following questions:
- a Name Country A which was formed in 1948. Which people came from all over the world to settle in Country A?
- b Name Canal B
- c Name Country C and its ruler in 1956. Name two European powers which attacked Country C in 1956.
- d Why did these European powers attack, and what was the result of this attack?

2 How was the 1917 Balfour Declaration carried out. Include in your answer:
- a British mandate in Palestine
- b Unrest after 1936
- c Exodus and the foundation of Israel in 1948

3 In a paragraph (10–20 lines) describe the causes, course and effects of the 1967 war.

4
- a Write a paragraph about the policy of a 'National home for the Jews' begun in 1917.
- b What was meant by the Palestine Mandate?
- c What has been the attitude of Israel's neighbours towards this new state? Explain this attitude.
- d Write a short paragraph about the special position of Jerusalem.
- e How did Israel come to occupy the Golan heights and the left bank of the Jordan? Why are the Israelis very anxious to retain these areas?
- f What progress has been made in establishing a lasting peace in the area since 1973?

5 Study the following statements made during the Suez Crisis of 1956 and answer the questions which follow:

Speaker 1: 'We have nationalised the canal and it will be run just as efficiently by our people.'

Speaker 2: 'This is an imperialist invasion of a peaceful country. If necessary we will use nuclear weapons to halt it.'

Speaker 3: 'All war is wrong. We must not fight over this or any other issue.'

Speaker 4: 'If we are successful in this invasion it will reduce the Arab threat to our country.'

Speaker 5: 'This is a police action to prevent a war between Israel and Egypt.'

Speaker 6: 'Let us make no mistake. This is an unjustified act of aggression by our country.'

Speaker 7: 'We cannot support our allies over this matter. The invaders must withdraw and an international peace keeping force be sent to the area.'

- a Which speaker expresses the view of President Nasser of Egypt?
- b Which speaker is a pacifist?
- c Which speaker expresses the views of a British opponent of the invasion?
- d Which **two** speakers support the Anglo-French action at Suez?
- e Which speaker puts forward the Israeli point of view?
- f Which speaker puts forward the view of the Russian Government?
- g Which speaker wants the problem to be settled by the United Nations Organisation?
- h Which speaker expresses the view of the British Prime Minister, Anthony Eden?
- i Which speaker puts forward the view of the Government of the U.S.A.?

6 What are the underlying reasons for the continued conflict between the Arabs and Israelis in the Middle East?

7 What exactly happened at the time of the Suez Crisis in 1956?

8 Write briefly about **two** of the following:
- a the Abadan crisis of 1951.
- b the 'Six Days War' of June 1967.
- c the war of 'Yom Kippur' in 1973.
- d the problem of the Palestinian Arabs.

Questions

9 Read the following extract and then write an imaginary speech by a Palestinian Arab putting his people's point of view.

'In the first year we made the Defence Army: we met and mastered the invaders; we opened wide the gates of the Homeland to all the people of Israel. We enlarged our bounds, even unto Elath and the Red Sea, held tight the approaches to Jerusalem and peopled her hills, restored its services to the young State and set them in motion. We won for Jewry international and sovereign status and Israel became a State-member of the United Nations Organisation, with full participant rights and obligations.

'The endeavours of three pioneer generations and of our defenders for seventy years prepared the way for twin achievements that posterity will see as a glorious symbol and fulfilment of justice; Israel reborn and its soldiers triumphant. More than once in our long annals, storied both in rise and fall, a lost independence was regained, and even two thousand years ago warriors of Israel were victorious in the field. But never before, in our strange and separate history, has the world seen the miracle of the ingathering . . .

'Four hundred thousand exiles have come back since the founding of the State, almost as many as entered in the thirty years of Mandate. Some two hundred settlements have been established, almost as many as in the entire period of Zionism's first colonization.'
(David Ben-Gurion, a radio broadcast on Independence Day, 1950)

10 Look at this photograph taken at the Camp David meeting in 1978 and answer the questions below.

a Name the two men shaking hands and the man, smiling, with them.
b What happened to the man on the left in 1981?
c In what country did this meeting take place?
d Why do you think that the meeting was important?

12/Freedom for the colonies

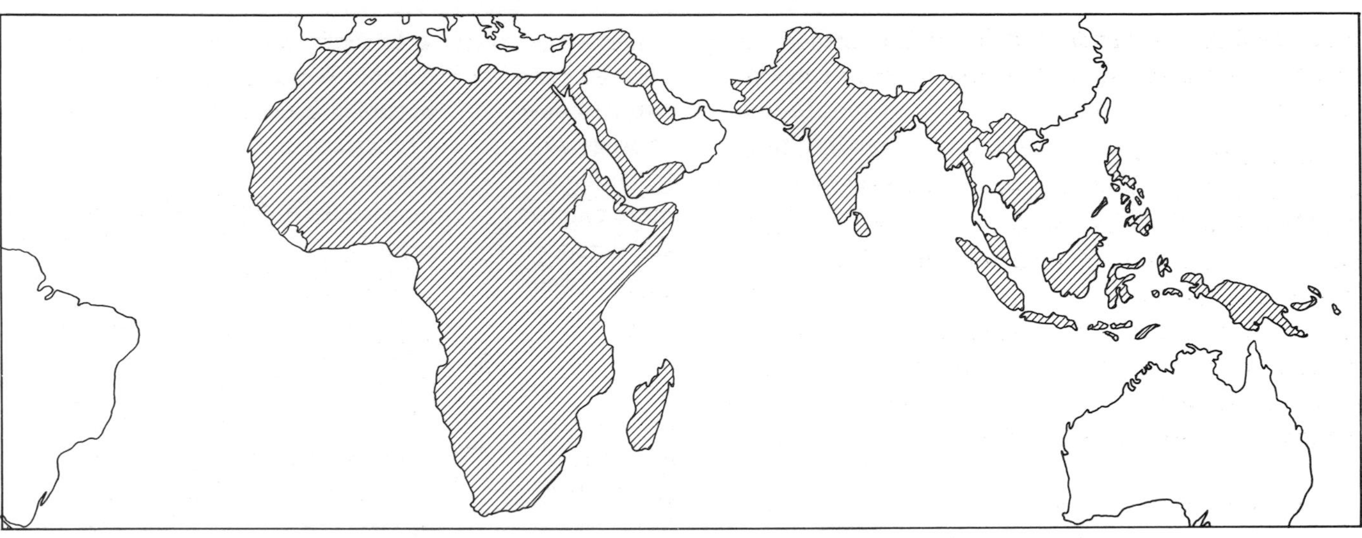

Map 1 White or foreign control in Asia and Africa in 1914

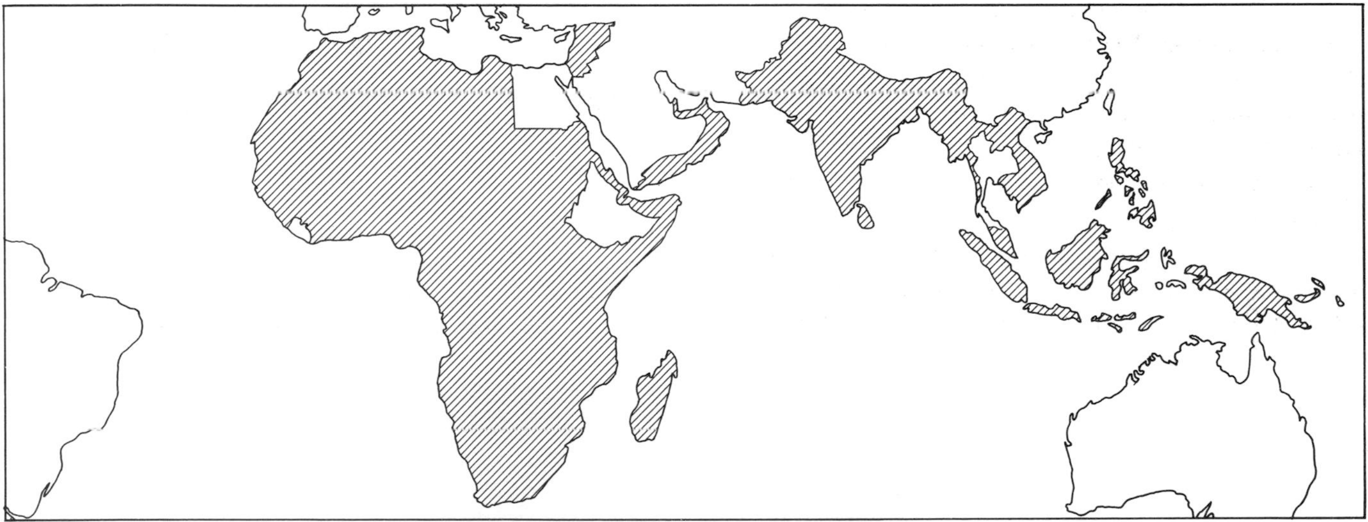

Map 2 White or foreign control in Asia and Africa in 1945

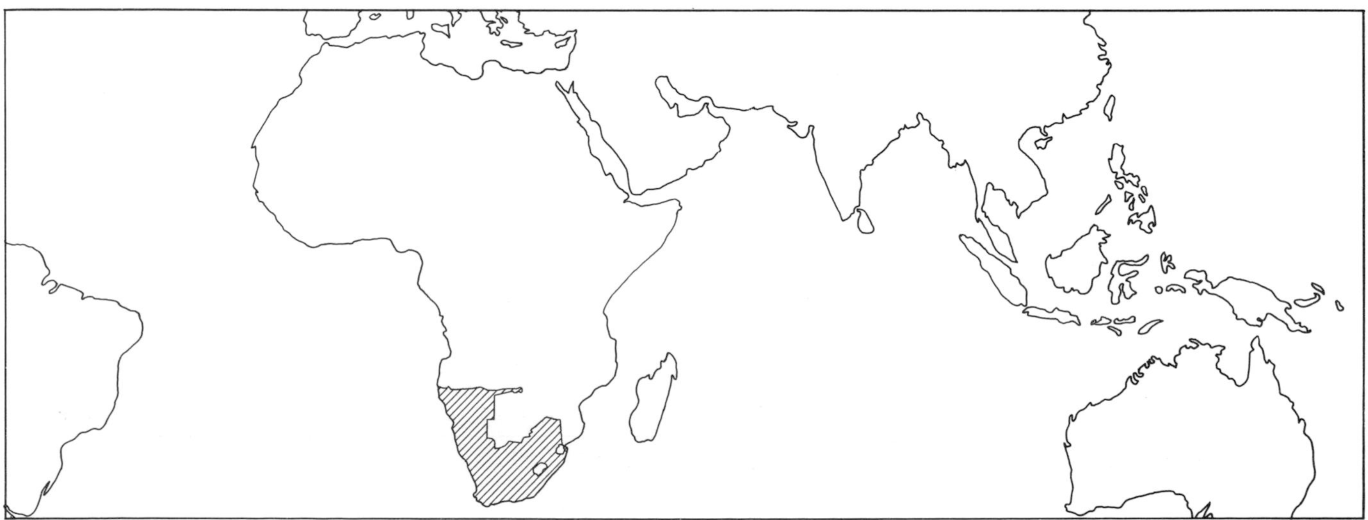

Map 3 White or foreign control in Asia and Africa in 1980

From empires to independence

The speed of freedom

A glance at Maps 2 and 3 will show you what a large proportion of Asia and Africa were colonies at the beginning of the century and how quickly independence was gained by these colonies after 1945.

The speed of these events, particularly in Africa, was commented on by the British prime minister, Harold Macmillan. In a famous speech in South Africa in 1960 he said:

In the twentieth century. . . . We have seen the awakening of national consciousness in peoples who have lived for centuries in dependence on some other power.

Fifteen years ago this movement spread through Asia. Many countries there of different races and civilisations pressed their claims to an independent national life. Today the same thing is happening in Africa. The most striking of all the impressions I have formed since I left London a month ago is of the strength of this African national consciousness. In different places it may take different forms, but it is happening everywhere.

The wind of change is blowing through the continent.

Why did the independence movements occur?

The spread of European control over large areas of the globe during the sixteenth to the nineteenth centuries was historically very important. The rapid removal of that control in the twentieth century has been just as important. How do you think that the peoples of Asia and Africa were able to gain their freedom so quickly? These were the main reasons:

1 Many people were becoming educated in European ways—to become civil servants, teachers and lawyers. In India they were sometimes insultingly called 'wogs'—Westernised Oriental Gentlemen. They also learned western political ideas about freedom and democracy. They therefore came to want these advantages for their own countries.

2 On the other hand, scholars were showing how important and different from the west the cultures of Asia and Africa had been in the past. Many people in these lands wanted to revive their own traditions.

3 Many Asian and African men fought in the Allied armies during the two World Wars. Again, they learned about European ideas. Also, it was said that these wars were fought to defend freedom. If so, they thought, surely their own countries should enjoy this right?

4 In south-east Asia during the Second World War the Japanese occupied many British, Dutch and French colonies (see pp.81–2). The peoples of those countries had no wish for their colonial masters to return.

5 Once some colonies were given independence, the others wanted independence too. India was by far the biggest and most important colonial country. Britain gave India independence in 1947. This set the scene for the rest of Asia and Africa.

6 After the Second World War the main imperial countries—Britain, France and Holland—were exhausted. They did not have the strength to resist for long people who were determined to fight for their freedom. The British and French managed to keep up loose links with their former colonies: the British through the Commonwealth and the French through their Community.

Harold Macmillan in Africa, 1960. It was during this trip that he made his famous 'Wind of Change' speech

The Viceroy of India receiving a deputation. Behind him is a full length portrait of the Empress of India, Queen Victoria

India at the beginning of the century

In 1901 Queen Victoria died. She was not only Queen of Great Britain but had also been Empress of India from 1877. Until 1947 the monarchs of Britain continued to be emperor or empress of India as well. The population of India at the beginning of the century was about 300 million. This huge country was administered by only a few thousand British officials. At the head of this government was the Viceroy, ruling on behalf of the Emperor.

The sub-continent of India contains many different peoples with different languages and different religions. However, a large majority are either Hindus or Muslims. The British allowed princes to continue to rule in some Indian states.

These princes were fabulously rich. But the huge mass of the people of India were wretchedly poor.

The English author, E. M. Forster, wrote a famous novel called *A Passage to India*, which gives a very vivid picture of the relations between the Indians and the British. In one scene, a British official explains his point-of-view:

> I have had twenty-five years' experience of this country—he paused, and twenty-five years seemed to fill the waiting-room with their staleness and ungenerosity—and during those twenty-five years I have never known anything but disaster result when English people and Indians attempt to be intimate socially. . . . I have been in charge of Chandrapore for six years, and if everything has gone smoothly, if there has been mutual respect and esteem, it is because both peoples kept this simple rule.

The struggle for independence

The early days

By the end of the nineteenth century educated Indians started to believe that India should be free of British control. The Indian National Congress was organised to bring this about. And we have already seen that fighting in the First World War strengthened these feelings. Meetings and demonstrations took place. In 1919 a peaceful demonstration in Amritsar in the Punjab was put down and nearly 400 Indians died. The local commander responsible for this massacre, General Dyer, was praised by many people in Britain. But he was dismissed from the army for this dreadful atrocity.

Mahatma Gandhi

Fortunately the story of India's early movement to independence contains very little violence. This good fortune is owed to the leadership of a most remarkable man, Mahatma Gandhi. Gandhi was born in 1869. (Mahatma was a title, meaning 'Great Soul', which he earned later.) He became a lawyer and practised in South Africa. He believed in the power of 'Satyagraha'. This word means 'soul force pure and simple'. It was the belief that by constant and peaceful demonstration of the justice and strength of your cause you could force your enemy to submit. Gandhi organised massive meetings and marches. The most famous occurred in 1930 in protest against the salt-tax. When arrested, he went on hunger-strike. He personally led a very simple life, dressing in a plain robe and sandals.

In 1931 Gandhi had talks with the Viceroy about the possibility of independence for India. The very idea was fiercely opposed by many. Winston Churchill said that he was revolted by 'the nauseating and humiliating spectacle of this one-time Inner-Temple lawyer, now seditious fakir, striding half-naked up the steps of the Viceroy's Palace there to negotiate and parley on equal terms with the representative of the King-Emperor'. Nevertheless, these talks were followed up by a Round Table Conference in London.

But no agreement had been reached by the time of the outbreak of the Second World War. During the War the Congress organised a 'Quit India' campaign. Riots and demonstrations broke out frequently. The leaders, including Gandhi, were imprisoned.

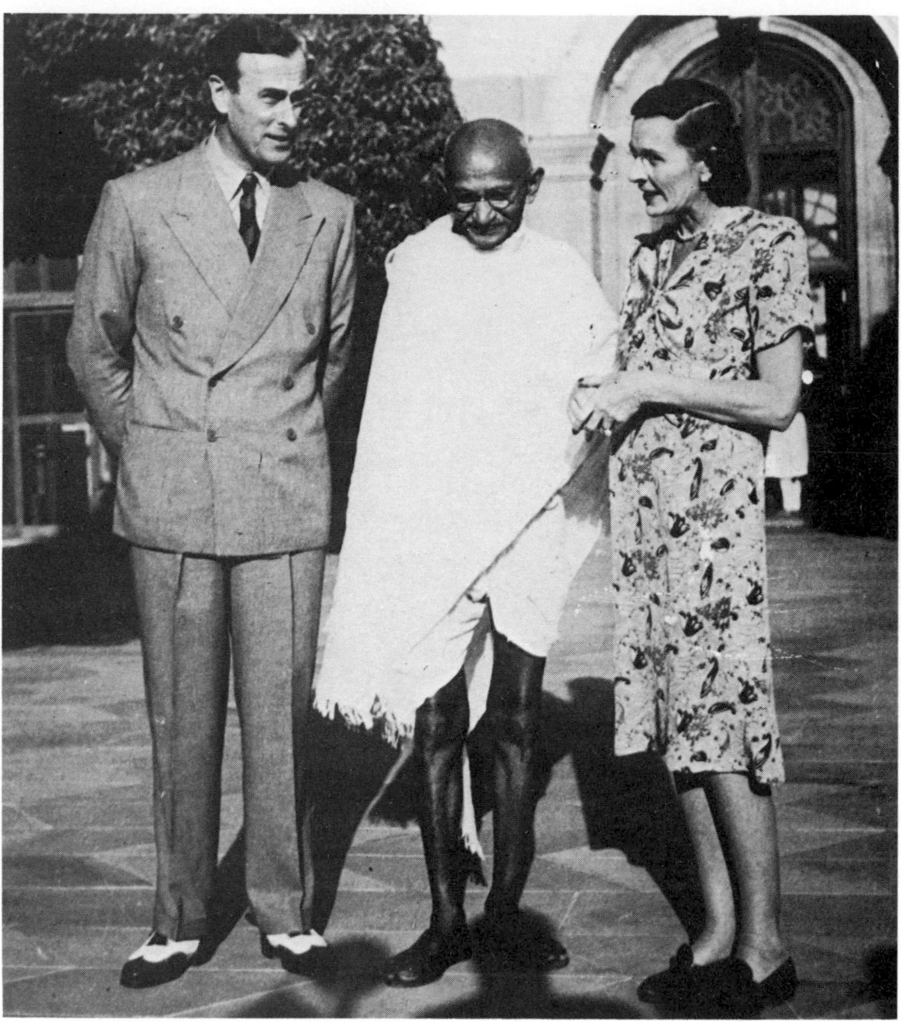

Lord Mountbatten, the last Viceroy, with Mahatma Gandhi and Lady Mountbatten

Independence

By 1945 it was clear that Britain would grant independence to India, for the following reasons:

1 The new Labour government under prime minister Clement Attlee was more willing than Churchill and the Conservatives to agree to Indian independence.

2 Britain was not strong enough to continue governing a country seething with discontent.

But timing independence was very tricky, for the following reasons:

1 The British wanted to be sure that arrangements had been properly made. A new Viceroy, Lord Mountbatten, was appointed in 1947. He needed time to make the arrangements.

2 But the Indians themselves were becoming very impatient indeed.

3 The whole matter was complicated by the division between Hindus and Muslims. Mohammed Ali Jinnah was the leader of the Muslim League. They wanted a separate country (to be called Pakistan) because they were frightened about how they would be treated after independence by the Hindu majority. Bloody communal clashes between Hindus and Muslims forced the British government to give independence quickly.

The Indian sub-continent

Partition

On 15 August 1947 Britain ceased ruling India. The sub-continent was divided into a Hindu India and a Muslim Pakistan (itself split into two parts), as you can see from Map 4. Mr Jinnah became governor-general of Pakistan. Mr Pandit Nehru became prime minister of India.

But, of course, it was quite impossible to draw the boundaries in such a way that all Hindus found themselves in India and all Muslims in Pakistan. Millions fled in order to be in the country of their religion. Crowds met. A huge wave of violence and slaughter swept the sub-continent. Gandhi was horrified by the violence, but was himself assassinated by a Hindu in Delhi in 1948. No one knows exactly how many people died in all this violence – perhaps a million.

Muslim refugees fleeing from Indian troops in Kashmir. The partition of India and Pakistan caused much human misery. These Muslim refugees are fleeing from the Indian army which took over complete control of the south-eastern half of Kashmir in 1947.

Wars since 1947

Kashmir

In 1947 it was undecided whether Kashmir should be part of India or part of Pakistan. The two countries fought over it. Then, in 1949, the U.N. established a cease-fire line, dividing the province between the two countries. But the people in the Indian-controlled part were Muslims and disliked being ruled by India. The two countries therefore went to war again over the fate of Kashmir in 1965, though nothing was changed as a result.

China

The frontier between India and China had never been clearly defined in the nineteenth century. In 1962 the Chinese invaded India and captured some land (see Map 4 and p.124).

Bangladesh

The people of the eastern part of Pakistan did not like being ruled from far-away western Pakistan. In 1971 they rebelled and created the new country of Bangladesh. People were so terrified by the atrocities in the war that nearly 10 million became refugees, fleeing to India. India helped the Bangladeshis by declaring war on Pakistan. The first prime minister (1971–75) was Mujibur Rahman.

Goa

India took over the Portuguese colony of Goa on the west coast in 1961.

Pandit Nehru in the centre with Presidents Nasser (left) and Tito (right). These three statesmen were behind the development of the 'non-aligned' group of nations, neither pro-Communist nor pro-West

The Indian sub-continent

The government of India and Pakistan

Indian democracy

India and Pakistan have not just been rivals internationally. They have had different forms of government. Pakistan has been governed for most of its history by the army. India, on the other hand, is the largest democracy in the world. Although many of the people are illiterate, elections have been held regularly. People can recognise the parties by the use of photographs of politicians and symbols. For example, the symbol of the Congress Party has been the bullock. The name of the Indian 'House of Commons' is 'Lok Sabha'.

Indian leaders

Pandit Nehru was prime minister of India from 1947 to 1964. He worked hard to ensure that India developed as a democratic country. He also speeded up industrialisation. From 1966 to 1977 Nehru's daughter, Mrs Indira Gandhi was prime minister. The strength of India's democracy was shown when she was forced to resign in 1977 because it was thought she had been acting illegally. But she remained popular and other politicians could not govern very effectively. So she became prime minister again in 1980.

Sikhs and Mrs Gandhi

Sikhs are a small but important religious group in India. Most live in the north-western state of Punjab. Some want their own independent country there (to be called Khalistan). A group gathered at their Golden Temple at Amritsar in 1984. Soldiers were sent to attack and many Sikhs were killed. A few months later two Sikhs assassinated Mrs Gandhi in revenge. The new prime minister was her son, Rajiv Gandhi, who had the huge problem of trying to prevent Hindus and Sikhs from killing each other.

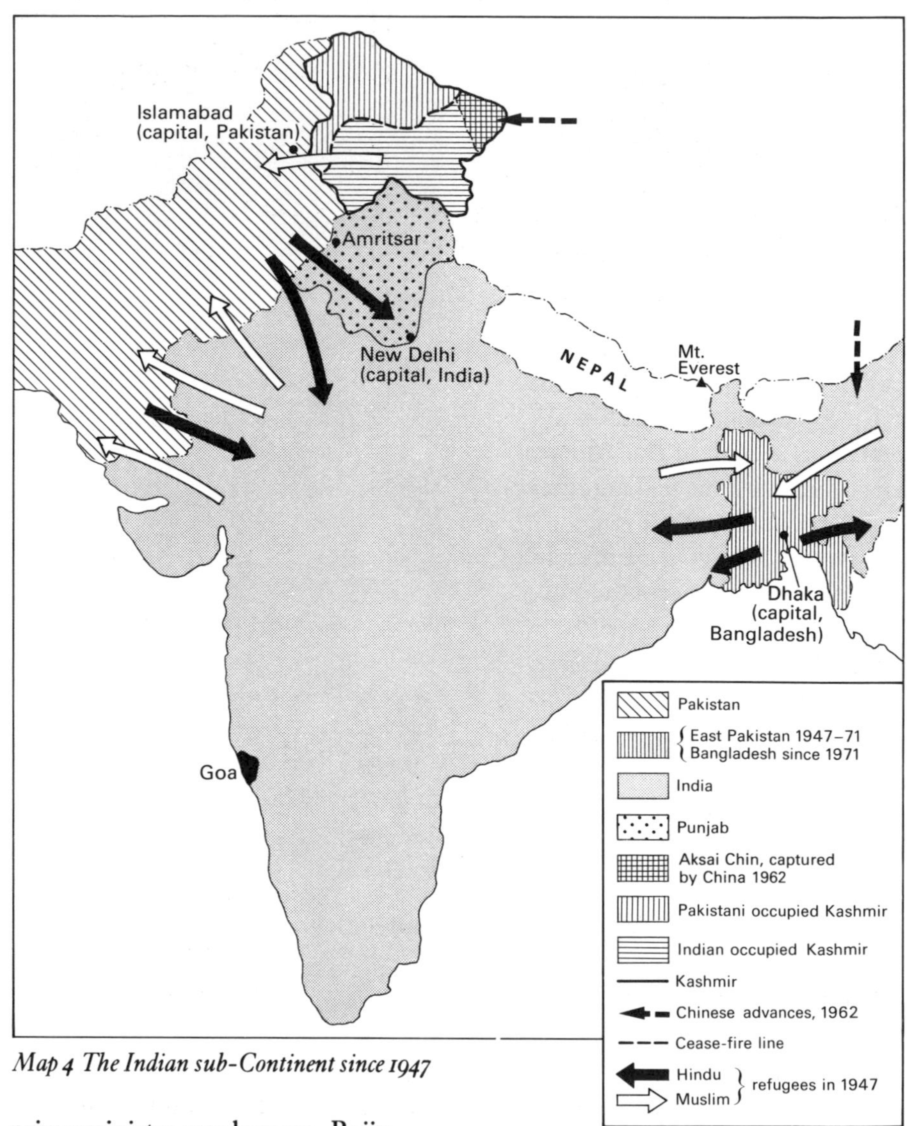

Map 4 The Indian sub-Continent since 1947

Rajiv Gandhi, Prime Minister of India assassinated in 1991

Pakistan's leaders

The first proper elections were held in Pakistan in 1970. From 1971 to 1977 Pakistan had civilian presidents. During that period Zulfikar Ali Bhutto was president (until 1973), then prime minister. But, more often, soldiers have been in charge of government, such as Field Marshal Ayub Khan (1958–69) and General Zia ul-Haq (1977–88). General Zia had Bhutto executed in 1979 and has ruled harshly since. He has introduced punishments according to the law of the Koran, as has happened in several other Muslim states.

The struggle for freedom in Africa

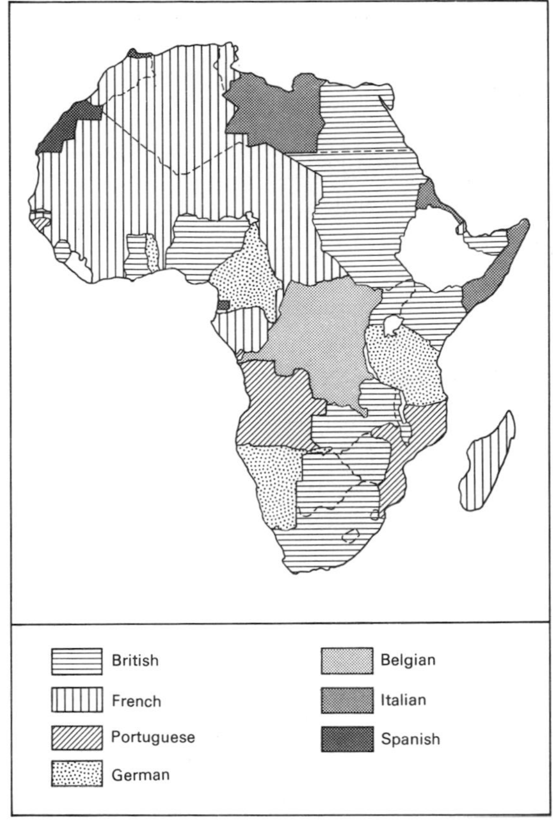

Map 5 European Empires in Africa 1914

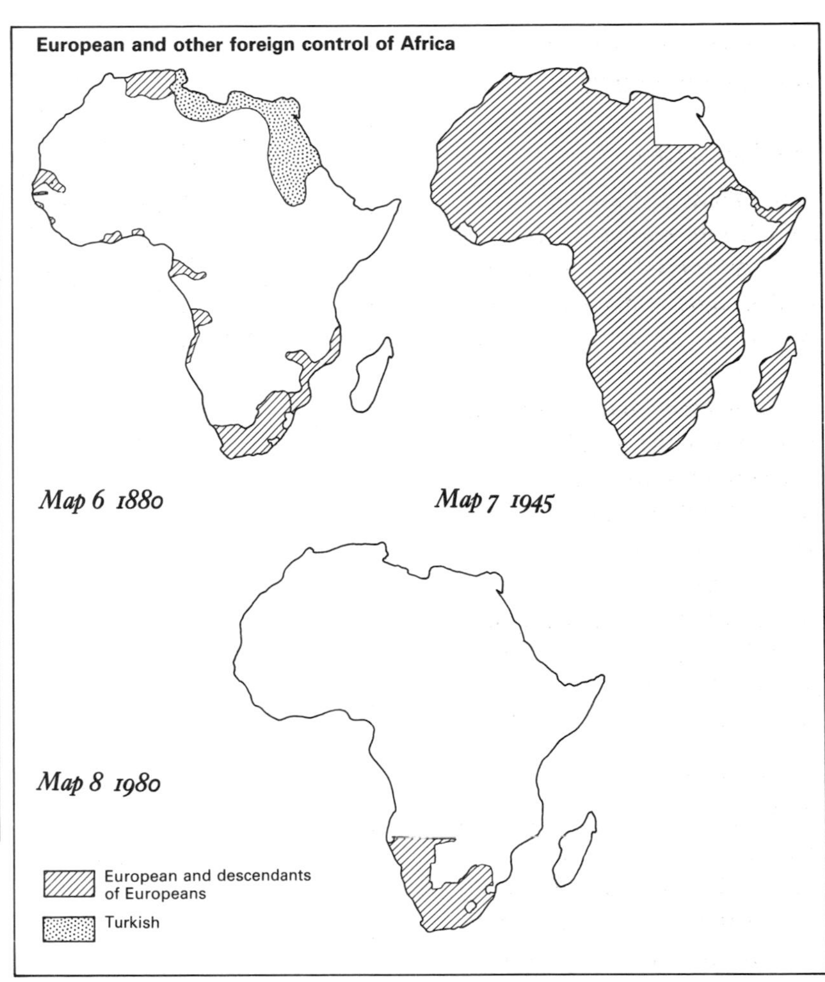

European and other foreign control of Africa

The speed of change

Freedom—colonisation—freedom

We saw at the beginning of this chapter how Harold Macmillan spoke of 'the wind of change'. He was referring to the events in Africa in the late 1950s and what he could foresee for the 1960s. The changes in these years did happen very quickly; indeed, the Ghanaian leader, Dr Nkrumah, said that it was 'no ordinary wind, but a raging hurricane.' In fact, on more than one occasion during the whole century from about 1880 to 1980 events had moved with remarkable speed. Maps 6, 7 and 8 show you how the continent moved from a fringe of European control to almost complete European control to almost complete freedom all within a hundred years.

Political maps of Africa

The 1880s and 1890s were the years known as 'the scramble for Africa'. As you can see from Map 5, by 1914 seven European countries had helped themselves to the continent. Now compare Map 5 with Map 8. This will show you some of the changes that had taken place by 1980. The dates are the years in which the various colonies became independent. As you can see, 1960 was indeed the year of the wind of change.

Africa is, of course, a whole continent and there are many different countries. It is impossible to tell the story of them all. We have therefore selected some of the more important and interesting for discussion here.

North and West Africa

The Maghreb

The Arabic name for the north-west bulge of the continent of Africa is 'Maghreb'. The countries are Morocco, Algeria and Tunisia. Most of the people of these countries are Arab or Berber, though for many years they were French colonies. Morocco and Tunisia became independent in 1956. In Algeria there was a bitter war from 1954 to 1962 (see p. 148).

Since 1975, when the Spanish left Western Sahara, Morocco has tried to take over this land. A resistance movement called Polisario has been supported by Algeria.

The struggle for freedom in Africa

Map 9 Africa in 1985, with dates of independence (and new names)

Ghana

The great Sahara desert divides the northern, Arab part of the continent from the largest portion, often called 'Black Africa'. Ghana was the first black African colony to be given independence by its imperial masters.

Before it became independent, Ghana was the British colony of the Gold Coast. By African standards of the time it was quite wealthy and the people well educated. The leader of the independence movement was a teacher named Kwame Nkrumah. He was imprisoned for his part in demonstrations for independence. In 1951 the first elections for an African government for the Gold Coast were held. Nkrumah's party won most of the seats, so he had to be released from prison in order to become prime minister!

But the Gold Coast was not yet fully independent. In 1953 Nkrumah made a famous speech demanding full independence. He completely rejected the idea that some colonies might not be ready for independence. He said:

> According to the motto of the valiant *Accra Evening News*—'We prefer self-government with danger to servitude in tranquillity'.... As long as we are ruled by others we shall lay our mistakes at their door, and our sense of responsibility will remain dulled. Freedom brings responsibilities and our experience can be enriched only by the acceptance of those responsibilities.

How far do you think that the motto of the *Accra Evening News* sums up the attitude of all the countries we are studying in this chapter? In 1957 the Gold Coast was given this full independence and took the African name of Ghana.

Nkrumah realised how important it was to help other colonies gain their independence and for the small and weak African countries to band together for greater strength. In 1958 he therefore acted as host at the first conference of independent African states in his capital, Accra.

But by the early 1960s Nkrumah's autocratic ways were making him unpopular in his own country. He allowed no other parties but his own Convention People's Party: Ghana became a one-party state. He imprisoned his opponents and took the title 'Osagyefo', the Redeemer. The economy of the country also suffered. He introduced expensive prestige projects such as grandiose buildings and road schemes. The only useful project was the great Volta River dam which became a major source of hydro-electric power. He was forced to flee the country in 1966. Since then Ghana has had mainly military governments.

Kwame Nkrumah of Ghana (1909–72)

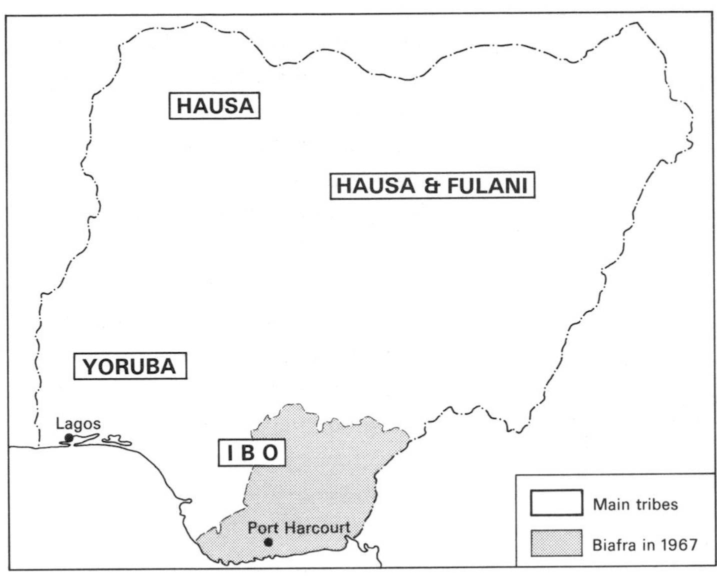

Map 10 Nigeria during the Biafran war, 1967–70

Colonel Ojukwu, the Biafran leader

Nigeria

Having launched Ghana as an independent state, the British then turned their attention to Nigeria. The problem of Nigeria was more complicated. It is a much larger country and has a number of different, tribal peoples, as you can see from Map 10. The question was, Could these people live in co-operation once the British had left?

Nigeria was given independence in 1960. For seven years the three main tribes, the Hausa, Yoruba and Ibo shared power in the government uneasily. But in 1967 suspicions and quarrels betwen the Ibo people of the Eastern Region and the Hausa politicians in the capital, Lagos, came to a head. The Ibo leader, Colonel Ojukwu, declared the Eastern Region independent with the name of Biafra. There followed three years of horrible civil war. The central government forces invaded Biafra. They gradually reduced the amount of land held by the Ibos and reduced the Ibo people to starvation. From 1960 to 1985 there were five military coups and Nigeria was governed by the army for two-thirds of that period.

East and Central Africa

The Belgian Congo/Zaïre

By and large the British made reasonable preparations for the independence of their colonies. The Belgians did not. And their one main colony was the vast area of the Congo. In 1960 the Belgians gave the Congo its independence. But there were no African army officers or senior civil servants—no Africans, in fact, to take over and keep control. The Belgians left. The army mutinied. The country fell into chaos. Tribes fought against each other. Dreadful tales of atrocities were told, of men tortured to death, women raped, nuns crucified. A man named Patrice Lumumba became prime minister, but he was murdered. Western countries wanted to keep control of the south-east province of Katanga because of its great mineral wealth.

The U.N. was called in to bring

United Nations troops in the Congo (later Zaïre)

peace to this torn, unhappy country. But even this operation had its own tragedy. The problem was so serious that the U.N. Secretary-General, Dag Hammarskjöld, visited the country himself. His aeroplane crashed and he was killed.

Eventually, in 1965 General Mobutu took control and since then the country has suffered increasingly from his corrupt dictatorship. In 1971 the name of the country was changed to Zaïre.

Uganda

Uganda has suffered considerably since its independence in 1962. Starvation and violent death have been the result of:

1 Drought.
2 Inter-tribal rivalries.
3 Violent rule. In 1971 Idi Amin overthrew the President, Dr Milton Obote. He killed many people and the country fell into chaos. In 1979 the Tanzanian army invaded Uganda and Amin fled. Obote returned to power, but proved equally bloodthirsty. He was overthrown by the army, 1985.

Idi Amin, President of Uganda, 1971–79

Kenya

The highlands of Kenya have a cool climate and rich farmlands. For this reason it was a popular colony for British settlers. Arrangements for independence were therefore complicated by the need to protect the white people. Some Africans became impatient with the delay. A secret society called Mau Mau was organised. They tried by brutal methods to force the white people out and to force other Africans to join them in this campaign of terror. Civil war raged from 1952 to 1955.

The leading Kenyan politician was Jomo Kenyatta. But he was imprisoned for suspected involvement with the Mau Mau. When it was clear that his party was the most popular, he was released (like Nkrumah - see p.182) to become prime minister. Kenya became independent in 1963 and the various peoples have lived quite happily together since. Kenyatta was the first president, from 1964 until his death in 1978.

Jomo Kenyatta. His close supporter, Tom Mboya (left), was murdered, 1969

Ethiopia

From 1930 to 1936 and again from 1941 to 1974 the Christian empire of Ethiopia (or Abyssinia) was ruled by Haile Selassie (see p.63). He was then deposed and a military government set up. Throughout the 1970s the Ethiopian army was involved in much fighting.

1 Eritrea is a province along the Red Sea coast. In 1952 it became part of Ethiopia. The people of Eritrea disliked this arrangement. They fought fierce guerrilla wars to gain their independence.
2 The eastern province of Ethiopia is called the Ogaden. The people who live there are Somalis. The Republic of Somalia has tried unsuccessfully to capture this area. The fighting has made the dreadful famines, 1975 and 1985, even worse.

The struggle for freedom in Africa

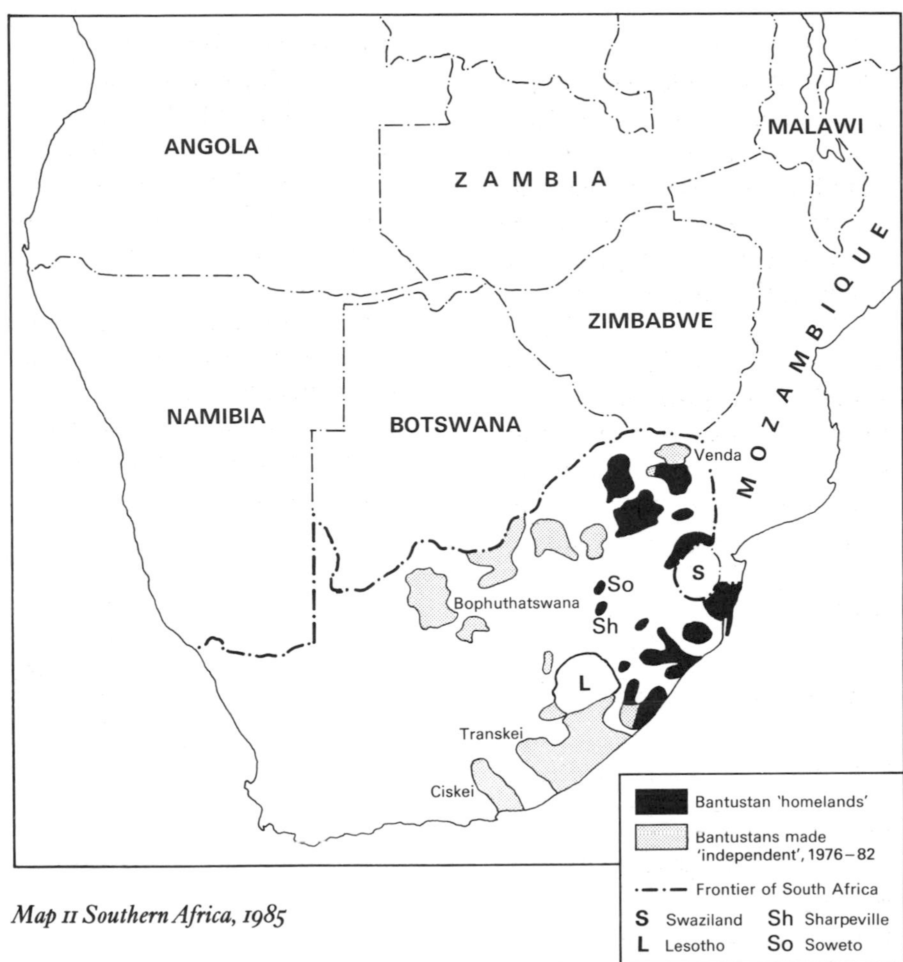

Map 11 Southern Africa, 1985

Southern Africa

White control

By about 1970 the only countries in Africa still under white control were: Angola, Mozambique, Rhodesia, South-West Africa (or Namibia) and South Africa (see Map 11). This is a large and rich area and many white people hoped and thought that they could keep control for a long time. In fact, only Namibia and South Africa remained in white control by 1980. Much of this section of the chapter explains this dramatic change.

Portuguese colonies

The Portuguese started to settle on the coasts of Africa as early as the sixteenth century. By the twentieth century, as you can see from Map 5, they had two very large colonies in southern Africa—Angola and Mozambique. The Portuguese looked upon these lands not so much as colonies but as part of the 'Portuguese Union'. They did not expect them to become independent. But these African people wanted their freedom like the other colonies. So they started to fight hard guerrilla wars against the Portuguese army. The guerrillas in Angola were given help by Cuba. Suddenly, the situation changed. In 1974 there was a revolution in Portugal and the new government gave independence to their African colonies the next year.

A young Angolan guerrilla

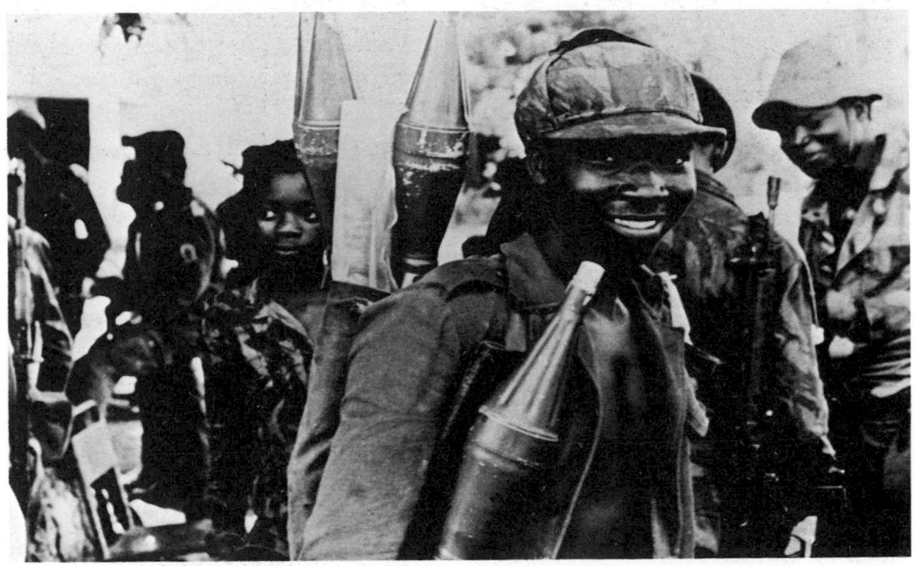

Rhodesia/Zimbabwe

In 1953 the British government created the Central African Federation. This consisted of the colonies of Northern Rhodesia, Southern Rhodesia and Nyasaland. This was not, however, a popular arrangement. In 1964 Northern Rhodesia became independent with the new name of Zambia, and Nyasaland became independent as Malawi. Kenneth Kaunda became President of Zambia and Hastings Banda became prime minister, later President, of Malawi.

Southern Rhodesia was a much more difficult problem because so many white people had settled there. The British government refused to give the country independence until arrangements were made for a democratically elected government. But the white people refused to give up their privileges. And so in 1965 the government of Rhodesia (as Southern Rhodesia was now called) made a Unilateral Declaration of Independence (U.D.I.). In other words, they declared that Rhodesia was independent whether Britain liked it or not. The leader of the white Rhodesians was Mr Ian Smith. He was prime minister from 1964 to 1978.

Robert Mugabe during the talks which established open elections and majority rule in Zimbabwe. On the right is Joshua Nkomo, with whom he quarrelled after independence

Ian Smith, a photograph taken when he declared independence for Rhodesia

British governments tried to force or persuade Mr Smith to agree to a solution on the basis of NIBMAR (No Independence Before Majority African Rule). Britain and other countries imposed economic sanctions. That is, they refused to trade with Rhodesia. But Rhodesian firms and the government found many ways round these restrictions. Because these efforts failed, the black Rhodesian people organised guerrilla armies to fight for their independence. The granting of independence to Angola and Mozambique was important for them. As you can see from Map 11, Rhodesia was now almost completely surrounded by black-governed countries. Mozambique and Zambia gave great help to the Rhodesian guerrillas.

The guerrillas were so successful that in 1980 white Rhodesians agreed to the holding of elections in order to bring the war to an end. Robert Mugabe's party won the great majority of the seats and he became prime minister. The handing over of power by the whites to the blacks was quite peaceful. The country was renamed with the African name of Zimbabwe.

South Africa in the first half of the century

South Africa is a country of very varied racial ingredients. Approximately seven out of every ten people belong to one of the several black Bantu-speaking tribes. The white people are either of British descent or Dutch (called Boers or Afrikaners). There is also a large community of mixed race (Coloured people) and a smaller one of people of Asian origin.

At the turn of the century the most severe quarrel was between the Boers and their rulers, the British. This quarrel led to the Boer War (1899–1902). In 1910 the Union of South Africa was created. In practice South Africa was now independent. South Africa fought against Germany in the First World War. Field Marshal Smuts became a famous world leader. He was prime minister from 1919 to 1924. He worked for co-operation between Boers and British. His rival was Hertzog who was prime minister from 1924 to 1939. Hertzog wanted the Boers to control South Africa.

The struggle for freedom in Africa

Apartheid

The Afrikaners were very anxious to keep the white and black people apart. In 1948 the National Party, led by Dr Malan, won the election. They set about organising the system of apartheid. This is an Afrikaans word meaning 'separateness'. Under prime ministers Verwoerd (1958–66) and Vorster (1966–78), the policy was put into practice very thoroughly.

B.J. Vorster

The idea has been that black and white people want to lead different lives and so they should be kept apart. Therefore, land was set aside for 'Bantustans' for the black people. As you can see from Map 11, these occupy about thirteen per cent of the land, whereas the Bantus are about seventy per cent of the population. Also, until the black people can return from the towns to the Bantustans they have had to keep apart from white people—using different buses, park benches, restaurants. And the white police have enforced these laws very rigorously.

The Afrikaners have argued that the black people benefit because they have a higher standard of living than they would enjoy in black-ruled countries. The black people have argued that the apartheid system is unjust and, in practical terms, white South Africa would collapse without them. One of the most famous books attacking apartheid is *Cry, The Beloved Country*. It was written in 1948 by the white novelist, Alan Paton. Here is one passage describing the conditions. The speaker is an angry black inhabitant of Johannesburg.

'We live in the compounds, we must leave our wives and families behind. And when the new gold is found, it is not we who will get more for our labour. It is the white man's shares that will rise, you will read it in all the newspapers. They go mad when new gold is found. They bring more of us to live in the compounds, to dig under ground for three shillings a day. They do not think, here is a chance to pay more for our labour. They think only, here is a chance to build a bigger house and buy a bigger car. It is important to find gold, they say, for all South Africa is built on the mines.'

He growled, and his voice grew deep, it was like thunder that was rolling. 'But it is not on the mines,' he said, 'it is built on our backs, on our sweat, on our labour. Every factory, every theatre, every beautiful house, they are all built by us.'

P W Botha, State President, South Africa until 1989

Problems of the 1980s

In 1978 P. W. Botha became prime minister and, in 1984, president. He faced greater difficulties than his predecessors for three reasons:

1 From 1974 to 1980 Angola, Mozambique and Zimbabwe came under black control. As a result, those governments became unfriendly and even allowed opponents of the South African government to set up bases in their countries.

2 International opposition to apartheid became more intense (see p. 188).

3 Demonstrations by the black people became more intense (see p. 188).

Botha's policies

To ease these problems Botha tried four policies:

1 He relaxed the petty apartheid laws which had made it unlawful for Blacks and Whites to mix socially.

2 He tried to persuade western governments that his plans for reform were sincere.

3 By both force and negotiation he reduced the support given by Angola and Mozambique to his opponents planning to fight for black majority governments in Namibia and South Africa.

4 He introduced constitutional reforms in 1984 so that the Coloureds (of mixed race) and Asians could have their own parliaments. But these total only just over 3 million people compared with just over 22 million Blacks, still without their own parliament.

Protests against apartheid

1 The main organisation in South Africa opposing apartheid has been the African National Congress. This was made illegal in 1961. A year later its leader, Nelson Mandela, was arrested and sentenced to life

The struggle for freedom in Africa

Bishop Desmond Tutu (Archbishop of Cape Town from 1986)

Nelson Mandela, leader of the African National Congress, imprisoned 1962–90

imprisonment. Other black leaders have included Albert Luthuli and Bishop Desmond Tutu, both of whom received the Nobel Peace Prize.

2 Many demonstrations have taken place. But even when these have been peaceful the security forces have used brutal methods to disperse the crowds. Besides many thousands who have been wounded, the major incidents involving the deaths of Blacks have been at Sharpeville (1960; 67); Soweto and nearby towns (1976: official figure, 236; unofficial estimate, 600); throughout South Africa, started largely in protest against the constitutional reforms of 1984 (e.g. September 1984–December 1985: 1000).

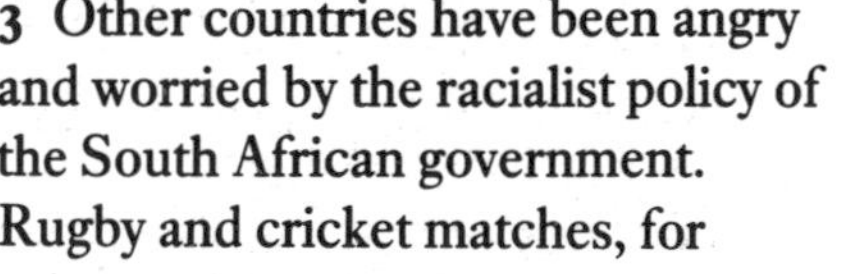

3 Other countries have been angry and worried by the racialist policy of the South African government. Rugby and cricket matches, for example, have been cancelled in protest about how the teams have been selected. By 1985 people in many countries came to believe that trade with South Africa should be reduced: this is a policy called 'sanctions'. Also many countries have argued that South Africa should give independence to South West Africa (or Namibia to give it its African name). This had been a German colony and South Africa obtained it as a mandate after the First World War.

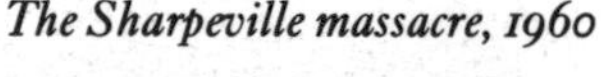

The Sharpeville massacre, 1960

Problems and achievements in Africa

The ruins of Zimbabwe. The city flourished between the 9th–14th centuries A.D.

Aspects of African nationalism

Traditions

Many nationalists like to try to restore the past glories of their people. We saw in Chapter 4, for instance, how Mussolini tried to revive the ancient Roman Empire. African nationalists too have been very keen to emphasise the history of their continent. The names of countries have been changed for this reason. The French colony of Soudan became Mali. The British colony of the Gold Coast became Ghana. Both of these names belonged to strong kingdoms in West Africa in the Middle Ages. The name of Zimbabwe was taken for Rhodesia because of the famous ruins in that country that show what a high level of civilisation existed there hundreds of years ago.

There are attempts also to preserve the best traditions in the African way of life. President Nyerere of Tanzania has written the following:

> Those of us who talk about the African way of life, and, quite rightly, take a pride in maintaining the tradition of hospitality which is so great a part of it, might do well to remember the Swahili saying: ... 'Treat your guest as a guest for two days; on the third day give him a hoe!' In actual fact, the guest was likely to ask for the hoe even before the host had to give him one—for he knew what was expected of him, and would have been ashamed to remain idle any longer.

President Sekou-Touré of Guinea making a speech at the closing session of the O.A.U. in Freetown, Sierra Leone, 4 July 1980. Which languages are on the banner and why?

Pan-Africanism

Look again at Map 9. You see that the continent is divided into many different countries. Some people think that large parts or even the whole of the continent should be united. What advantages do you think this would bring? The African leaders give several:

1 The boundaries are quite artificial, in most cases arranged by the colonial countries at the time of the Scramble for Africa. They do not match the areas where different tribes live.
2 All African countries have had and continue to have similar needs; to gain independence and to develop economically.
3 Individual African countries are weak; by joining together they can be stronger.

In 1963 the Organisation of African Unity (O.A.U.) was set up. Through this organisation the countries of Africa have been able sometimes to collaborate.

Problems and achievements in Africa

Problems

Borders and tribes

One of the first decisions made by the O.A.U. was that the borders of the countries should not be changed. Many countries contain many different tribes. And several tribes live on land stretching across several different countries. We have seen how tribal quarrels led to bloodshed in the Congo and Nigeria (p.183).

Changes in government

In a number of African countries, nationalist leaders stayed in control of the governments for many years after independence had been gained. But in many others there were serious quarrels and the army took control of the government to keep law and order. This taking control by force is called a *coup d'état* (pronounced coo-day-ta). There were many coups in Africa in the 1960s and 1970s.

East Africa is a region where many different tribes live. There is a strong physical difference between some of these tribes. Both men above are from Tanzania, a Masai (top) and a Hene (below)

Poverty

Generally speaking, Africa is a very poor continent. The majority of the population are peasant-farmers. You can gain some idea of the poverty of Africa by the following figures. The U.N. named the twenty five poorest countries or 'least developed countries' of the world. Seventeen of these are in Africa. Several suffered severe famines in the 1970s and 1980s.

Achievements

Since 1945 the news stories from Africa that have hit the headlines have been the problems, especially the violence. But has the history of Europe in this century been any less bloody? The African countries need time to settle down and develop their economies and devise the best forms of government for themselves. Already, a number of countries have made very good progress in these ways. Also the O.A.U. has been set up as an important body for discussing and sometimes settling disagreements among the African leaders.

Balance sheet

Do you think that the colonies in Asia and Africa benefited or suffered more from being under the control of Europeans? Compare the following quotations about the British Empire to help you think about this. The first is from an American philosopher; the second, from an Indian historian; the third, from an Irish playwright.

Never since the days of heroic Greece has the world had such a sweet, just, boyish master. It will be a black day for the human race when scientific blackguards, churls and fanatics manage to supplant him.

Ruled by highly industrialised Britain, the overwhelming majority of Indians lived in . . . unbelievable filth and squalor, reminiscent of the early Middle Ages . . . ill-housed, ill-clothed and undernourished.

. . . every Englishman is born with a certain miraculous power that makes him master of the world. When he wants a thing, he never tells himself that he wants it. He waits patiently until there comes into his mind, no one knows how, a burning conviction that it is his moral and religious duty to conquer those who have got the things he wants. Then he becomes irrestible. . . . As the great champion of freedom and national independence, he conquers and annexes the world, and calls it Colonisation.

Time chart

Freedom for the colonies

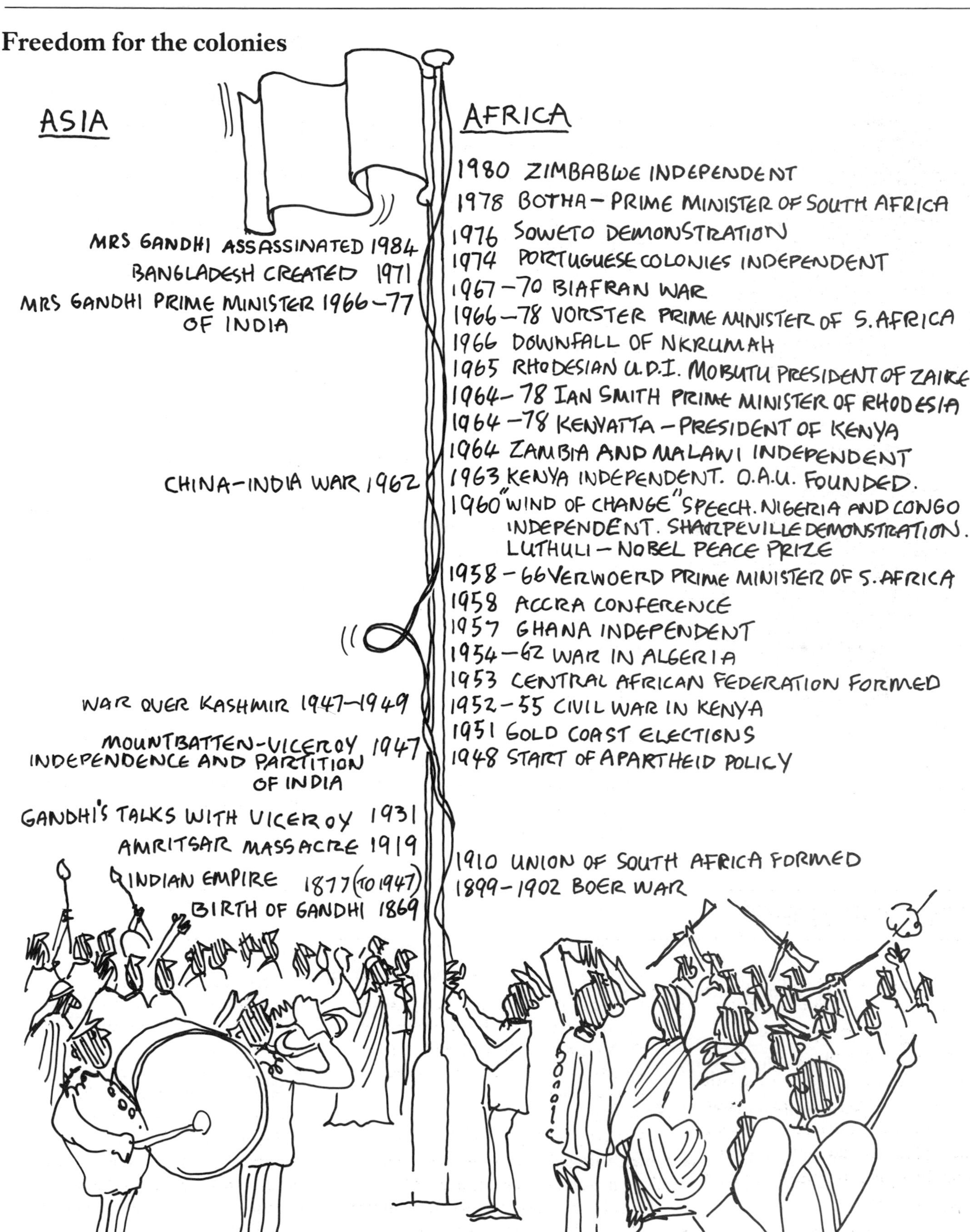

ASIA
MRS GANDHI ASSASSINATED 1984
BANGLADESH CREATED 1971
MRS GANDHI PRIME MINISTER 1966–77 OF INDIA
CHINA–INDIA WAR 1962
WAR OVER KASHMIR 1947–1949
MOUNTBATTEN–VICEROY 1947
INDEPENDENCE AND PARTITION OF INDIA
GANDHI'S TALKS WITH VICEROY 1931
AMRITSAR MASSACRE 1919
INDIAN EMPIRE 1877 (TO 1947)
BIRTH OF GANDHI 1869
AFRICA
1980 ZIMBABWE INDEPENDENT
1978 BOTHA – PRIME MINISTER OF SOUTH AFRICA
1976 SOWETO DEMONSTRATION
1974 PORTUGUESE COLONIES INDEPENDENT
1967–70 BIAFRAN WAR
1966–78 VORSTER PRIME MINISTER OF S. AFRICA
1966 DOWNFALL OF NKRUMAH
1965 RHODESIAN U.D.I. MOBUTU PRESIDENT OF ZAIRE
1964–78 IAN SMITH PRIME MINISTER OF RHODESIA
1964–78 KENYATTA – PRESIDENT OF KENYA
1964 ZAMBIA AND MALAWI INDEPENDENT
1963 KENYA INDEPENDENT. O.A.U. FOUNDED.
1960 "WIND OF CHANGE" SPEECH. NIGERIA AND CONGO INDEPENDENT. SHARPEVILLE DEMONSTRATION. LUTHULI – NOBEL PEACE PRIZE
1958–66 VERWOERD PRIME MINISTER OF S. AFRICA
1958 ACCRA CONFERENCE
1957 GHANA INDEPENDENT
1954–62 WAR IN ALGERIA
1953 CENTRAL AFRICAN FEDERATION FORMED
1952–55 CIVIL WAR IN KENYA
1951 GOLD COAST ELECTIONS
1948 START OF APARTHEID POLICY
1910 UNION OF SOUTH AFRICA FORMED
1899–1902 BOER WAR

Questions

1 Read the following paragraph and then answer the questions below.

European control of Africa has gradually been reduced since 1945. The French, for example, gave Algeria independence in 1962. The British surrendered most of their colonies to the native Africans in a peaceful way, although there was a long struggle with the Mau Mau in Kenya before independence was given. In other parts of Africa the control of the Europeans remained strong even in the late 1960s. The Republic of South Africa continued its policy of apartheid in spite of Harold Macmillan's warning about 'the wind of change' sweeping through Africa. Rhodesia, led by Ian Smith, ignored such warnings when it declared U.D.I. in November 1965 rather than face black majority rule.

- **a** Who was President of France when Algeria was granted independence?
- **b** What was the Mau Mau?
- **c** Who was the leader of Kenya when it became independent?
- **d** Of which country was Macmillan Prime Minister?
- **e** What did Macmillan mean when he spoke of 'the wind of change' sweeping through Africa?
- **f** What is the meaning of apartheid? Describe its effects.
- **g** Write a paragraph about the problems which faced Rhodesia after U.D.I.

2 Describe the development of India from Raj to Independence. Include in your answer:

- **a** Congress Party and reforms
- **b** Gandhi
- **c** Pre-independence unrest.

3 Describe the problems that have been faced by Pakistan since 1949. You may find it useful to include in your answer:

- **a** partition and independence—the problems facing Pakistan,
- **b** disputes with India,
- **c** Ayub Khan's military rule, 1958–69,
- **d** the Bangladesh war,
- **e** Bhutto, Zia and continuing unrest in Pakistan.

4 Write an essay about the history of South Africa from 1902 to 1966. You may find it useful to include in your answer:

- **a** divisions between the Boers and the British,
- **b** South Africa becoming a Dominion in 1910—and its role in The First World War,
- **c** Smuts and Hertzog,
- **d** the Nationalist Party—its ideas and its rise to power,
- **e** apartheid and Verwoerd.

5 **a** What is the meaning of 'African Nationalism' and when and why did it gain momentum?

b Choose **two** of the following countries and show how their paths to independence reflected the differing attitudes of their former European rulers.

(i) Nigeria. (iii) Algeria.
(ii) Angola. (iv) The Congo.

6 Write an essay on the British colonies in Africa. Include in your answer the following points:

- **a** The names of six of the most important colonies in 1900.
- **b** Choose **two** of these and describe how they became independent.

7 In a paragraph (10–20 lines) explain why Rhodesia unilaterally declared independence in 1965 and the problems she has faced since that time.

8 Describe in a paragraph (10–20 lines) the main problems faced by the Congo (Zaire) since independence. How have they been dealt with?

9 In 1945, only four independent states existed in Africa, but by 1966 most of the continent had freed itself from colonial rule.

- **a** Name **two** of the four independent states of Africa in 1945.
- **b** Explain the meaning of 'colonial rule'.
- **c** Describe the way in which **two** African countries achieved and maintained independence in the period after 1945.

10 Read the following extracts and answer the questions below.

Source A The recollections of a Kenyan nationalist leader.

'I moved to Nairobi in 1939. Nairobi was full of annoying pinpricks in those days: the Railway Station lavatories marked EUROPEANS, ASIANS, NATIVES: hotels we could not enter except as servants, and even certain kinds of beer we could not drink.

Questions

'Late in 1941 I decided to go into the army. In 1944 we returned from the battlefront. Among the shells and bullets there had been no air of superiority from our European comrades-in-arms. We drank the same tea, used the same water and lavatories, shared the same jokes. There were no racial insults, no references to "niggers", "baboons" and so on. The white heat of battle had blistered all that away and left only the common humanity and our common fate. I had learnt much, too, about military organisation.' (From *Nations and Empires* by R. C. Bridges,)

Source B The recollections of a Mau Mau leader, Karari Njama.

'It was July 26, 1952 and I sat in the Nyeri Show grounds packed with a crowd of 30,000 people. The Kenya African Union was holding a rally and it was presided over by Jomo Kenyatta. He talked first of land. This forced me to turn my eyes towards the Aberdare Forest. I could clearly see Karari's Hill, the hill that bears my grandfather's name and whom I am named after. Surely that is my land by inheritance.

'When Kenyatta returned to the platform he explained the flag. He said, "Black is to show that this is for black people. Red is to show that the blood of an African is the same colour as the blood of a European, and green is to show that when we were given this country by God it was green, fertile and good, but you see that the green is below red and is suppressed."

'What he said must mean that the black was separated from the green by red: the African could only get to his land through blood.' (From *The Mau Mau from Within*, by D. Barnett and Karari Njama.)

Source C Harold Macmillan speaks to the South African Parliament, 3 February 1960.

'The wind of change is blowing through this continent and whether we like it or not this growth of political consciousness is a political fact and our national policies must take account of it.'

a Look at Source C.
  i) What position was held by Harold Macmillan?
  ii) Why was it important that his speech was made to the South African Parliament?

b i) Look at Source A. Why would the writer be especially annoyed by the use of the word natives?
  ii) Look at Source B. Explain why Kenyatta did not state clearly the meaning of the flag, but left his audience to work it out for themselves.

c Look at Sources A and B. Show: (i) the differences; and (ii) the similarities in the attitudes of the two nationalist leaders.

Postscript

We have traced the story of our century to the end of 1985. The following notes will help to bring you up-to-date to May 1993. (Entries in the Postscript do not appear in the Index.)

Chapter 3

The Chernobyl disaster

Chernobyl is a town in the Ukraine. In April 1986 an accident occurred at the nuclear power plant there. As a result, huge areas of the surrounding countryside have suffered from radioactive contamination, a number of people were killed and injured, and many people had to be evacuated. Also, as the radioactive cloud drifted over many European countries, they were affected by radioactive particles in the rain. It was by far the most serious nuclear power-plant accident to have happened so far.

Reforms

From 1987 Gorbachev introduced many changes, mainly because the Russian economy was in such a bad state. These changes were based on two principles:

1 *Glasnost* This means 'openness'. Criticism of the government and suggestions for improvement were now allowed. People who had been imprisoned for political opposition were released. Protest meetings were, generally, not dealt with brutally by the police or army.

2 *Perestroika* This means reconstruction. The control of the economy by the government and Communist Party officials was relaxed.

In addition, political reforms were introduced.

1 A new position of State President (similar to the position of the US President) was established. Gorbachev took this post himself.

2 A new parliament was elected. Some candidates were elected because of their known wish to force the pace of reform.

One of the most famous campaigners for reform, the scientist, Andrei Sakharov, died in 1989.

Nationalities problem

The Union of Soviet Socialist Republics was a federation of states composed of different nationalities. Gorbachev's relaxation of control encouraged several of these to express their grievances.

1 Azerbaijan and Armenia fought with each other.

2 Nationalist movements demanding less control from Moscow grew up in the western republics, especially the Baltics (see also p.37).

3 In 1990 a leading advocate of reform, Boris Yeltsin, became President of the Russian Republic, the biggest member of the USSR. He also resigned from the Community Party.

Boris Yeltsin

Collapse of the U.S.S.R.

During the second half of 1991, important events happened with great speed.

1 Opponents of Gorbachev tried to remove him from power, but the plot failed.

2 Dislike of the Communist Party became very strong. It was disbanded.

3 Gorbachev resigned.

4 All the republics declared their independence so that the U.S.S.R. came to an end. It was replaced by a very loose Commonwealth of Independent States (C.I.S.) Eleven republics joined: Armenia, Azerbaijan, Belarus, Kazakhstan, Kyrgystan, Moldova, Russia, Tajikstan, Turkmenistan, Ukraine, Uzbekistan.
Four did not:
Estonia, Georgia, Latvia, Lithuania.

Three serious problems faced the former Soviet republics:

1 Most have mixed population: would they be able to live together in harmony?

2 How were the former Soviet armed forces to be allocated? In particular, there was the danger that strict control over nuclear weapons might be relaxed.

3 The main reason for the fall of Gorbachev and Communism was the poor state of the economy. But the change to a free, capitalist economy was very difficult.

Chapter 7

George Bush

Bush, who had been Reagan's Vice-President, became President in 1989. He faced two big problems.

1 Reagan had borrowed huge sums of money to pay for his spending, especially on weapons. By 1989 the

Postscript

George Bush

national debt was equivalent to $11,000 for every American.
2 Drug addiction and crimes related to it, including murder, had become an epidemic.

Bush organised campaigns with the governments of some Latin American countries where the cocaine is produced, Colombia particularly. At the end of 1989 he ordered American troops to invade Panama to overthrow its President, General Noriega, partly because he had been involved in the drugs trade.
3 Poverty, especially among Blacks and Hispanics, caused discontent. The most serious riot in the U.S.A. this century broke out in Los Angeles in 1991.

Bill Clinton

The Democrat, Bill Clinton, became President in 1993.

Chapter 8

Demands for democracy

Deng's policy of economic reforms (see p. 122) led people to hope for changes towards democracy. But demonstrations in 1978, 1986 and 1989 showed the government unsympathetic. In 1989, encouraged by the changes happening in Russia, crowds gathered in Tiananmen Square in Peking (sometimes spelt Beijing). Troops were used to disperse them. Many were killed and many of those arrested were executed.

Chapter 9

Changes in Eastern Europe

In 1989 Communist governments collapsed or were overthrown throughout eastern Europe. There was little bloodshed, except in Romania. In that country, a violent uprising overthrew the hated dictator Ceausescu. In East Germany many people started to flee to West Germany. The Berlin Wall was demolished and the Communist government resigned. In 1990 East and West Germany were united.

In Yugoslavia the collapse of Communism brought to the surface the national hatreds among the different republics of the federation. By 1992 they became independent. However, bitter fighting took place, especially brutal in Bosnia in 1993. (See the map on page 196).

End of the Cold War

By the mid-1980s, Reagan accepted that Gorbachev wished for friendlier relations. They held several meetings, most importantly at Reykjavik in Iceland in 1986.

The next year they signed a treaty to destroy land-based I.N.F. weapons (see p. 140). In 1990, the Conventional Forces in Europe (C.F.E.) treaty was signed to reduce the numbers of non-nuclear forces. In 1992 the START (see p. 140) treaties were signed to reduce the U.S. and Russian long-range nuclear warheads from a total of 23,000 to under 8,000.

European Security

Even after the end of the Cold War, the peace of Europe could still be

Germans on the Berlin Wall

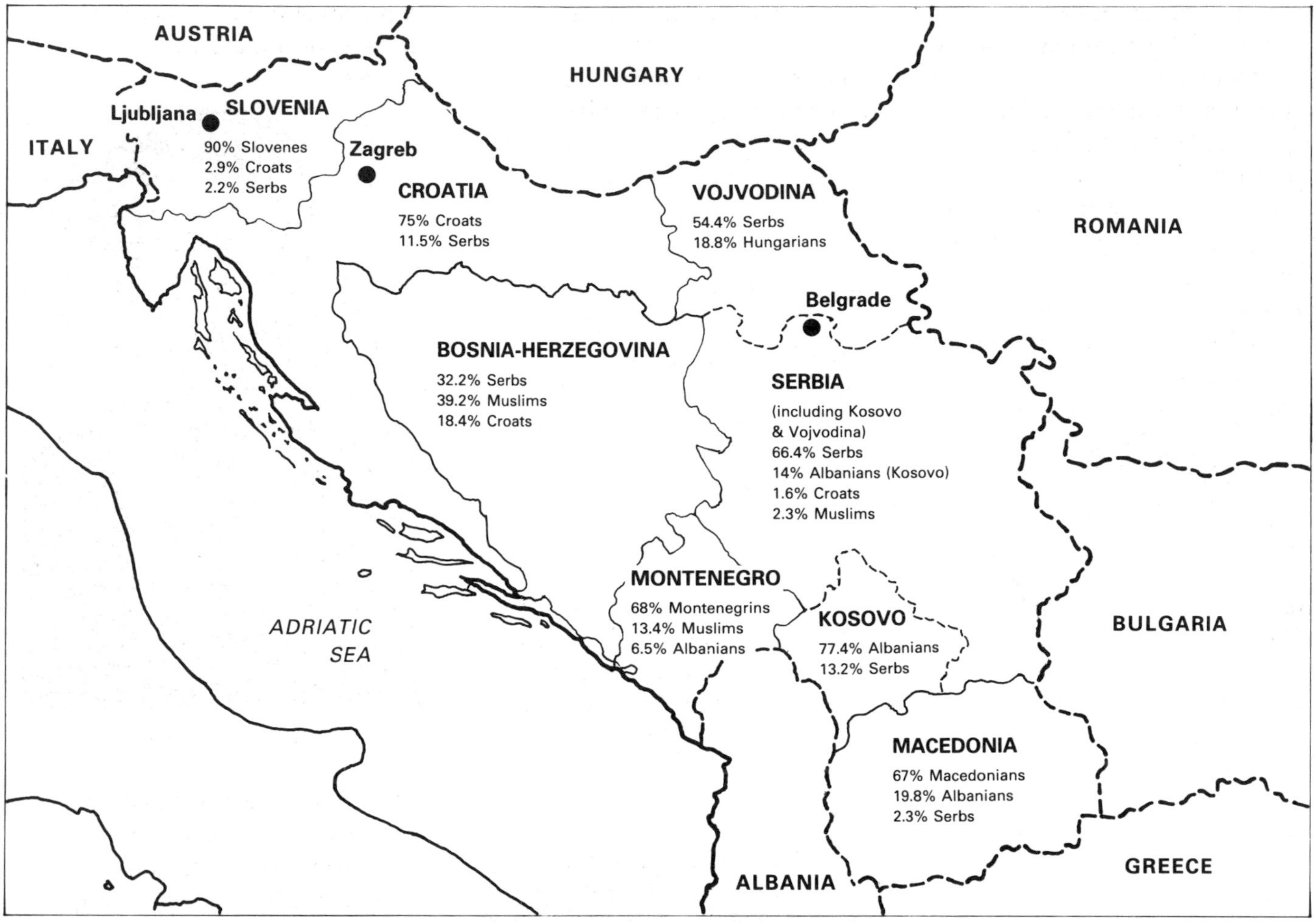

Postscript

AUSTRIA
HUNGARY
Ljubljana
SLOVENIA
ITALY
90% Slovenes
2.9% Croats
2.2% Serbs
Zagreb
CROATIA
75% Croats
11.5% Serbs
VOJVODINA
54.4% Serbs
18.8% Hungarians
ROMANIA
Belgrade
BOSNIA-HERZEGOVINA
32.2% Serbs
39.2% Muslims
18.4% Croats
SERBIA
(including Kosovo
& Vojvodina)
66.4% Serbs
14% Albanians (Kosovo)
1.6% Croats
2.3% Muslims
MONTENEGRO
68% Montenegrins
13.4% Muslims
6.5% Albanians
KOSOVO
77.4% Albanians
13.2% Serbs
BULGARIA
ADRIATIC
SEA
MACEDONIA
67% Macedonians
19.8% Albanians
2.3% Serbs
ALBANIA
GREECE

Yugoslavia's internal boundaries and ethnic distribution before the civil wars, 1991–93

threatened – by terrorists, wars between states or civil wars.

In 1993 a Conference on Security and Co-operation in Europe (C.S.C.E.) met in Helsinki. 35 states attended. Especially since 1990, arrangements have been made to strengthen this organisation. By 1992 the membership had increased to 51.

Chapter 10

Britain

Mrs Thatcher remained Prime Minister during the 1980s. The Labour Party was weak and attempts to organise a strong centre party failed. Many changes were introduced, including the privatisation of nationalised industries. But the basic weaknesses of the economy (see p. 151) remained. The balance of payments deficit of £20 billion for 1989 was the worst ever.

John Major

In 1991 Mrs Thatcher became very unpopular. She was replaced as Prime Minister by John Major.

Ireland (p. 151)

During 1986 slow progress was made to put into effect the Hillsborough Agreement, signed in 1985. This was an arrangement for improving co-operation between the British and Irish governments on the problems of Ulster, especially security.

Postscript

European Community
By the late 1980s many new changes were under way:
1 Improvements in the CAP (see p.155) had reduced the food 'mountains'.
2 Several other countries started to apply for membership. By 1992 the following had made formal application: Austria, Cyprus, Finland, Malta, Norway, Sweden, Switzerland, Turkey.
3 The member-states agreed to bring about a Single European Market by the end of 1992. This involved reducing the right of the member countries to regulate their own economic systems in many ways.
4 The President of the Commission, Jacques Delors, produced plans for:
a A Social Charter to protect people's rights;
b A European Bank;
c European Monetary Union (e.g. one currency, one policy on exchange rates).

Jacques Delors

In 1991 the twelve leaders of the EC states signed the Maastricht Treaty. This made arrangements for even closer economic and political unions among the members. By 1993 all twelve countries had agreed to this.

Chapter 11

Libya (see p.170–1)
The U.S. President, Reagan, believed that Colonel Qaddafy was responsible for much of the terrorism in Europe and the Middle East. In April 1986 U.S. aircraft were sent from Britain to bomb supposed terrorist headquarters in Libya.

Palestinians (see p.167)
Arafat changed from terror tactics to diplomacy. But the Palestinian people in the occupied territories of Gaza and the West Bank became impatient and in 1987 started rioting *(intifada)*.

A Palestinian protester

Iran (see p.171)
In 1988 the war between Iran and Iraq came to an end. In 1989 Khomeini died.

Iraq (see maps, pp.159 and 160)
In 1979 Saddam Hussein became President of Iraq. His dictatorship has been bloodthirsty and aggressive.

A mural of Saddam Hussein

1 People who have opposed him have been tortured and executed.
2 Large numbers of Kurdish people living in the north of Iraq have been killed. Poison gas has been used against them.
3 Iran was attacked. The war which resulted, lasted from 1980 to 1988.
4 Iraq seized control of Kuwait in August 1990.

Saddam's blatant capture of Kuwait led to protests throughout the world. The United Nations approved sanctions against Iraq (i.e. no one was allowed to trade with Iraq). Large military forces (mainly American) were assembled in Saudi Arabia to protect it and force Iraq to surrender control of Kuwait.

In 1991 the allied forces attacked Iraq. Kuwait was liberated though it had suffered massive damage. Hussein remained in power and continued to persecute many of his own people, especially the Kurds.

Postscript

Benazir Bhutto

Chapter 12

India (see p.180)
During the late 1980s relations between India and Pakistan became more friendly. Mr Gandhi was assassinated in 1991.

Pakistan (see p.180)
Pakistan was very much involved in the civil war in Afghanistan (see p.142). Millions of refugees sought sanctuary there. In 1988 General Zia was killed. Democratic elections were held and Benazir Bhutto became Prime Minister, but was dismissed in 1990 because of alleged corruption. (She is the daughter of Z.A. Bhutto – see p.180). Pakistan left the Commonwealth in 1972 but became a member again in 1988.

Southern African states
1 Angola and Mozambique (see p.185). Dreadful civil wars continued to rage throughout the 1980s, with many deaths, especially in Mozambique.
2 Namibia (see p.188) became independent in 1989.

South Africa (see pp.185, 187–88)
The troubles in South Africa continued into the late 1980s and became so serious that the government imposed a state of emergency in order to be able legally to arrest people without charge and to censor the news. In addition to the continuing violence, two other matters became important.
1 The black people became increasingly divided among themselves. Fighting even broke out in some townships between the young 'comrades' (wanting change) and the older 'vigilantes' (supporting the government). Also Chief Buthelezi of the Zulus showed his belief in slow negotiation with the government and opposed the A.N.C.

F.W. de Klerk and Nelson Mandela

2 The rest of the world became seriously concerned. Almost every country came to believe that pressure should now be put upon the South African government to abolish apartheid. Most believed that economic sanctions would be the only effective way. But the countries with the biggest economic interests in South Africa – namely Britain, the U.S.A. and West Germany – disagreed. Their governments argued that sanctions would not work.
In 1989 President Botha resigned. He was replaced by F.W. de Klerk. De Klerk started talks to try to speed up reforms in favour of the black people. Several black leaders were released from imprisonment, including, in April 1990, Nelson Mandela (see pp.187–8).

By 1993 there were plans for elections and the writing of a new constitution in 1994.

Poverty in Africa

Poverty and international debt increased during the 1980s in sub-Saharan Africa. Interest on loans was so high that these countries spent more on repaying loans than they received in aid. Conditions were made worse in some countries like Somalia and Mozambique in the 1980s and early 1990s because of civil wars.

Index

NOTES

1 Because the following countries are mentioned so many times in the book, they are not listed in the index: China, France, Germany, Great Britain, Italy, Russia, the U.S.A.
2 Battles, Conferences, Operations (code-named during the Second World War), Revolutions, Ships' names and Treaties are listed under those entries.
3 When countries have changed their names, they are listed under the names most often used in this book. Their other names are placed in brackets after.
4 No references are made to either the Questions or the Postscript.

Index

Index

Acknowledgements

The publishers would like to thank the following for permission to reproduce photographs:

Aerofilms p.2; Anglo-Chinese Educational Institute p.120 (*bottom*); Associated Press pp.189, 196 (*bottom*); Auckland Collection p.55 (*top*); BBC Hulton Picture Library pp.10, 18, 22, 36 (*bottom*), 44 (*top*), 59 (*left*), 60, 63, 67 (*bottom*), 68 (*bottom*), 74 (*top*), 89 (*bottom*), 90, 98, 116 (*top and centre*), 149 (*centre*), 162, 164, 165 (*bottom*), 178; Bettmann Archive p.97; Camera Press pp.14, 25, 39 (*centre right*), 104 (*both*), 106, 108 (*both*), 118, 119, 121, 122 (*top and centre*), 127, 168 (*both*), 169, 170, 171, 180, 186 (*left*), 188 (*top left and right*); Central Office of Information p.151; Central Press p.182; Commonwealth Secretariat p.194 (*bottom*); Fotomas Index p.35 (*top*); Group W Productions p.36; G. D. Hackett pp.74 (*bottom*), 78, 81, 88 (*centre*); John Hillelson/Robert Capa pp.63 (*bottom*); Alan Hutchison p.190 (*top*); Imperial War Museum pp.75, 76, (*top left and bottom right*), 83 (*top left*), 88 (*top*); Keystone Press pp.30, 33, 38 (*top*), 39 (*top*), 44 (*centre and bottom*), 47, 49, 51, 52 (*bottom*), 83 (*top right and centre bottom*), 84, 89 (*top*), 110, 117, 124, 133 (*top*), 135 (*bottom*), 137, 138, 142, 148 (*bottom*), 149 (*right*), 153, 163, 165, 183 (*top*), 184 (*left*), 185; London Express News and Feature Service pp.68 (*top*), 155; Mansell Collection pp.17, 19, 31 (*bottom*), 53 (*top*), 82, 83 (*bottom*), 103, 177; Museum of Modern Art, New York, p.64 (*top*); Novosti pp.27 (*top*), 29 (*right*), 34; Österreichische National Bibliothek p.66; Popperfoto pp.7, 16 (*centre left*), 29 (*left*), 39 (*centre*), 45 (*bottom*), 55 (*bottom*), 83 (*centre top*), 86, 91 (*bottom*), 105 (*bottom right*), 107 (*bottom*), 110, 120 (*top*), 136 (*bottom*), 146, 150, 161, 165 (*centre*), 166, 171, 176, 184 (*right*), 186 (*top*), 187 (*top*); Preussischer Kulturbesitz pp.6 (*bottom*), 61, 67 (*top*), 69, 77, 88 (*bottom*), 114, 147 (*top*), 194, 195, 196 (*top*), 197; Punch, pp.6 (*top*), 59 (*right*), School of Slavonic Studies p.145; SCR USSR p.31 (*top*); Snark International/Dumage p.149 (*bottom*); Süddeutscher Verlag pp.15, 16 (*top right, centre right, and bottom right*), 39 (*bottom*), 46, 48, 50, 54, 56, 76 (*top right and both centre*), 79, 80, 85, 87, 91 (*top*), 101, 107, 115 (*top*), 129, 130, 133 (*bottom*), 134, 135 (*top*), 136 (*top*), 141, 147 (*bottom*), 148 (*top*), 149 (*top*), 171 (*bottom left*), 179, 183 (*bottom*), 188 (*bottom*); Jeff Tabberner p.122 (*bottom*); Thames and Hudson p.35 (*bottom*); John Topham p.190 (*bottom*); Ullstein Bilderdienst pp.16 (*top left and bottom left*), 27 (*bottom*), 45 (*top*), 53 (*bottom*), 65, 115 (*bottom*), 123, 154; US International Communications Agency pp.99, 105 (*except top right*), 112; Western Americana p.102 (*left*); Weiner Library p.52 (*top*); ZEFA p.92; Die Zeit/Flora p.153.

Every effort has been made to trace copyright holders but in one or two cases without success. If anyone claiming copyright of material published but not acknowledged will contact the publishers corrections will be made in future editions.

The publishers would also like to thank the following Examinations Boards for kind permission to reproduce questions from their history examination papers:

Associated Lancashire Schools Examining Board. Alternative B; Section I Questions 2, 5, Section II Questions 2, 4, 7, 9, 10, 11, 12.

East Anglian Examinations Board. 1979 Mode I South (Syllabus B) Paper II; Questions 1, 2, 3, 5, 6, 8, 9, 15, 18.

East Midland Regional Examinations Board. 1979 Syllabus 3; Part Two, Question 17.

Midland Examining Group. 1987. Specimen Questions for Joint GCE/CSE Examination. Reproduced by permission of the University of Cambridge Local Examinations Syndicate.

South-East Regional Examinations Board. 1976 Paper E; Questions 31, 33, 37B, 38B, 39, 43; 1977 Paper E; Questions 31B, 38B, 40B, 42, 44, 45, 46, 48; 1978 Paper E; Questions 31B, 37B, 38B, 44, 46; Paper E; Questions 46B, 56, 57, 58, 59, 60, 63, 64.

Southern Regional Examinations Board. 1979 Syllabus R, Section E; Paper 1 Question 5, Paper 2 Question 2 (first choice), 5, 9 (first choice), 11, 12 (first choice).

West Midland Examinations Board. 1979, Syllabus C Paper 1; Questions 13A, 13C, 14B, 14C, 15A, 16A, 17A, 19C, 21A.

Yorkshire Regional Examination Board. 1979 (Modern World); Questions A3, A4, B7, B15.